Brazil

Michael Reid

Brazil
The Troubled Rise
of a Global Power

YALE UNIVERSITY PRESS
NEW HAVEN AND LONDON

For information about this and other Yale University Press publications, please contact:
U.S. Office: sales.press@yale.edu   www.yalebooks.com
Europe Office: sales@yaleup.co.uk   www.yalebooks.co.uk

Set in Minion Pro by IDSUK (DataConnection) Ltd
Printed in Great Britain by TJ International Ltd, Padstow, Cornwall

Library of Congress Control Number: 2014934350

ISBN 978-0-300-16560-9

A catalogue record for this book is available from the British Library.

10 9 8 7 6 5 4 3 2 1

MIX
Paper from
responsible sources
FSC
www.fsc.org   FSC® C013056

For Emma

Contents

Illustrations

Plates

1. Engraving of a Tupi family, in Jean de Léry, *History of a Voyage to the Land of Brazil* of 1578. Courtesy of the John Carter Brown Library at Brown University.
2. Frans Post, painting of a seventeenth-century sugar mill in Pernambuco. The Art Archive/Musée du Louvre, Paris/Gianni Dagli Orti.
3. Print of slaves washing precious stones in Minas Gerais. Mary vans/BeBa/Iberfoto.
4. Arnold van Westerhout, engraving of Antonio Vieira. Private collection/The Bridgeman Art Library.
5. Portrait of Dom Pedro II. The Art Archive/Miramare Museum Trieste/Collection Dagli Orti.
6. *La Récolte du café dans une fazenda du Brésil*, 1911. Bibliotheque des Arts Decoratifs, Paris, France/Archives Charmet/The Bridgeman Art Library.
7. Tarsila do Amaral, *Abaporu*, in MALBA, Buenos Aires. Reproduced by kind permission of Tarsilinha do Amaral.
8. Getúlio Vargas. © 2000 Topham Picturepoint.
9. Copacabana, 1950s. © TopFoto.
10. Juscelino Kubitschek inaugurates a residential block in Brasília, 1960. Globo/Getty Images.
11. Tanks in the streets of Rio de Janeiro, 1964. Mondadori/Getty Images.
12. General Ernesto Geisel. © TopFoto/UPP.
13. Luiz Inacio Lula da Silva as strike leader. Folha Imagems.
14. 500,000 cruzeiro note.
15. Fernando Henrique Cardoso with one-real note, 1994. Reuters/STR New.
16. Luiz Inacio Lula da Silva's Inauguration, 2003. Joedson Alves/Agencia Estado/AE (Agencia Estado via AP Images).
17. Dilma Rousseff's inauguration, 2011. AP Photo/Silvia Izquierdo.
18. The sertão, the drylands in the interior of north-east. AP Photo/Eraldo Peres.

Maps   *page*

Charts

Acknowledgements

My first debt of gratitude is to *The Economist*, for sending me to Brazil in the first place, and allowing me to spend so much time there over subsequent years. I am especially grateful to John Micklethwait and Edward Carr for having let me take time off from my day job to complete the writing of this book. I have benefited from the reporting of those who succeeded me as the newspaper's Brazil correspondent – Peter Collins, Brooke Unger, John Prideaux and Helen Joyce. I am particularly indebted to Helen Joyce, a wonderful colleague and friend who encouraged my frequent research visits to Brazil, let me tag along on some of her own reporting trips and was eagle-eyed in spotting mistakes in the manuscript. Nathália Sardelli in *The Economist*'s Brazil office helped with tracking down data, as did David Camier Wright. Thanks to Adam Meara for the maps, and particularly to Celina Dunlop for helping me obtain photos.

I should stress that this is not an '*Economist* book'. On the two or three occasions where I have reproduced almost verbatim material from *The Economist*, it has been of stories that I reported and wrote myself. The analysis and judgements are my own.

I have been fortunate to be able to talk to many of Brazil's political and business leaders over the past seventeen years, and to have benefited from the time and insights of countless academics, journalists, leaders of civil society and ordinary Brazilians. Many are named in the book. Special thanks go to a number of people. When I set out to write this book, Eduardo Giannetti da Fonseca gave me valuable advice on what to read (and as importantly, what not to read). He also offered searching comments on the manuscript. Leslie Bethell not only gave me the benefit, in conversations over the years, of his encyclopaedic knowledge and wisdom about Brazil, but also saved me from numerous mistakes in the manuscript. Freddy Bilyk in São Paulo has been exceptionally generous in plying me with books and magazine and newspaper clippings. As well as putting out what is perhaps Brazil's best newspaper, Celso Pinto, Célia de Gouvea Franco and Vera Brandimarte of *Valor Econômico* have offered me their friendship and much help over the years in trying to understand their country. I am similarly grateful for the friendship and insights over many years of Sérgio Amaral. Roberto Jaguaribe, the Brazilian ambassador in London in recent years, has been generous not just in his hospitality but in discussing all things Brazilian with me. Thanks, too, for many useful conversations to Norman Gall, Richard Lapper and Mac Margolis; and to Nilson Viera Oliveira for trips to the São Paulo "periphery". Peter Hakim and Tim Power were kind enough to share unpublished articles. Charlie Forman and John Prideaux made helpful suggestions on the early chapters. Needless to say, none of those named bear any responsibility for the judgements in the book, which are purely my own.

Thanks are also due to Arthur Goodhart, my agent; to Robert Baldock at Yale, not least for his patience in waiting for a book that took longer than hoped; and to Rachael Lonsdale, Candida Brazil, Tami Halliday and the rest of the Yale team, for their swift and efficient production work. Once again my greatest debts of gratitude lie at home. Roxani, my daughter, and Torsten Wilberg, her partner, were exceptionally understanding of my non-availability for long periods. Emma, my wife, not only helped me with some of the research and made valuable suggestions on the text, but was endlessly supportive of the project, despite the inroads it made on her life. It is to her that the book is dedicated.

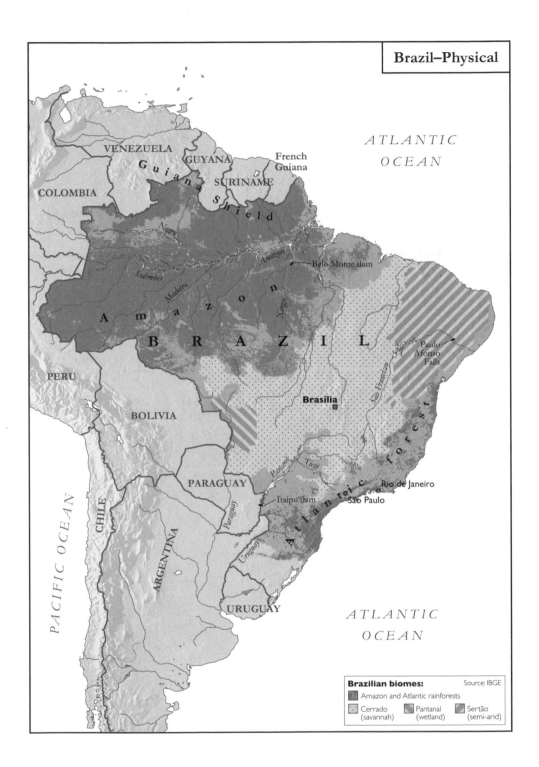

ATLANTIC
OCEAN

VENEZUELA
GUYANA
French
Guiana
Guiana
SURINAME
COLOMBIA
Shield

Negro

Amazon
Belo Monte dam

Solimões

Madeira

A m a z o n
B R A Z I L

Xingu

PERU

Paulo
Afonso
Falls

São Francisco

BOLIVIA

Brasília

Atlantic forest

Paraná

Tietê

PARAGUAY
Rio de Janeiro

Itaipu dam
São Paulo

Paraguay

PACIFIC OCEAN
ARGENTINA

Uruguay

CHILE

URUGUAY
ATLANTIC
OCEAN

Brazilian biomes: Source: IBGE

Amazon and Atlantic rainforests

Cerrado   Pantanal   Sertão
(savannah)   (wetland)   (semi-arid)

Brazil–Political

ATLANTIC OCEAN

1. RIO GRANDE DO NORTE
2. PARAÍBA
3. PERNAMBUCO
4. ALAGOAS
5. ESPÍRITO SANTO
6. RIO DE JANEIRO
7. SANTA CATARINA

VENEZUELA
GUYANA
French Guiana
SURINAME
COLOMBIA
RORAIMA
AMAPÁ
Manaus
Santarém
Belém
São Luís
Paragominas
AMAZONAS
PARÁ
MARANHÃO
Fortaleza
Natal
CEARÁ
B R A Z I L
Crato
Olinda
PIAUÍ
Timbaúba
Porto Velho
Petrolina
Recife
ACRE
TOCANTINS
Maceió
RONDÔNIA
Canudos
SERGIPE
PERU
MATO GROSSO
Salvador
DISTRITO FEDERAL
BAHIA
Cuiabá
Brasília
MINAS GERAIS
BOLIVIA
Goiânia
Diamantina
Rondonópolis
GOIÁS
MATO GROSSO DO SUL
Belo Horizonte
São José dos Campos
Ouro Preto
SÃO PAULO
Campinas
Juiz de Fora
PARAGUAY
Piracicaba
Macaé
PARANÁ
São Paulo
Rio de Janeiro
Asunción
Curitiba
Santos
Jaraguá do Sul
ATLANTIC OCEAN
Blumenau
São Borja
RIO GRANDE DO SUL
Novo Hamburgo
Porto Alegre
PACIFIC OCEAN
ARGENTINA
CHILE
URUGUAY
Montevideo
Buenos Aires
Colonia del Sacramento

NORTH
NORTH-EAST
CENTRE-WEST
SOUTH-EAST
SOUTH

INTRODUCTION
A New Power

CHAPTER ONE

Brazil's Troubled Rise

On a crisp November morning in 2009, the conference hall at the Marriott Hotel in London's Mayfair was packed with several hundred business people from across Europe as Luiz Inácio Lula da Silva went to the rostrum to speak. A former trade union leader, founder of the Workers' Party and the dominant leader of the Brazilian left for a generation, since becoming his country's president in 2003 Lula had become a master at seducing business audiences. In his gravelly bass voice, he began by urging that such gatherings should be more frequent: 'we need to meet more to understand each other . . . there's so much happening in Brazil we sometimes don't realize it.' He then launched into an account of his government's rural electrification programme (*Luz para Todos*, or 'Light for All'), which had hooked up some 2.2 million families to the grid. 'The cable we used is enough to go round the world twenty-one times – if the numbers they give me are right,' he said. The businessmen laughed. It cost the government 9 billion reais (around US$5 billion). But, he added, as a result of the programme, an extra million television sets and fridges were sold – by private businesses.

Lula had first stood for president back in 1989, preaching socialism and calling for Brazil to default on its foreign debt. He lost only narrowly. In the 1990s he ran and lost twice more, by bigger margins, to Fernando Henrique Cardoso, a sociologist with whom Lula had once been allied against Brazil's military dictatorship. Ahead of the 2002 election, Lula abandoned radical left-wing policies, moved towards the centre and reconciled himself to Cardoso's market-friendly reforms, which had tamed Brazil's chronic inflation and laid a platform for growth. Lula took to wearing Italian suits. His beard evolved along with his politics: now with more white hairs than grey, it was neatly trimmed, unrecognizable from the unruly jet-black affair of his union days. But Lula still enjoyed teasing the bourgeoisie. 'Capitalists in our country didn't realize that to have capitalism you need to have capital circulating,' he told the businessmen at the Marriott. A bit later he quipped: 'When they tell me the banks are making lots of money, I say thank God, because when they go bust it costs us a fortune.'

Lula's main purpose that day was to publicize what he called 'a silent revolution in Brazil, the recovery of a country's self-esteem'. Having begun his first term by adopting and tightening Cardoso's orthodox fiscal and monetary policies, Lula had presided over a quickening economy. His government managed to combine growth with income redistribution, through big rises in the minimum wage and ambitious social policies. Between 2002 and 2009, 30 million Brazilians had left poverty behind, he said. Endowed for the first time with disposable income, this burgeoning group – which some analysts hailed as a 'new middle class' – began to buy consumer goods, from cars to clothes. Thanks to its new-found strengths, Brazil had quickly shaken off the world financial crash of 2008–9 triggered by the souring of sub-prime mortgages in the United States. Having so often missed opportunities in the past, today 'Brazil is enjoying an excellent and exceptional moment,' Lula concluded. 'I'm convinced that the twenty-first century is Brazil's century.' He had spoken for almost an hour without notes or an autocue. As he returned to his seat among the audience, he was mobbed with the kind of fervour normally reserved for Brazilian footballers.

I had listened to Lula several times in the past, both in Brazil and abroad. Just three years before, I had watched him enjoy the pomp of a state banquet at Buckingham Palace. In September 2010, shortly before Brazilians elected his chosen candidate, Dilma Rousseff, to succeed him, I sat down with Lula for an hour and a half in his spacious office in the Planalto Palace in Brasília for an interview in which we reviewed the achievements and frustrations of his presidency. But I don't think I have ever seen him quite as ebullient as at that London conference in November 2009. It came as the world seemed to have woken up, in a myriad of different ways, to Brazil. At *The Economist* we tried to capture the mood with a cover that month which showed the iconic statue of Christ on Rio de Janeiro's Corcovado mountain rising into the air as if jet-propelled, under the headline 'Brazil takes off'.

Lula himself had suddenly become the man of the moment. In April of that year, at the London summit of the G20 countries called to discuss the international financial crisis, Barack Obama had gushed of Lula: 'he's my man'. A few weeks later Lula travelled to Ekatarinburg, in the Urals, for the first-ever presidential summit of the BRIC countries, a term bracketing Brazil with Russia, India and China. Disparate in many other ways, this quartet were yoked together by Jim O'Neill, an economist at Goldman Sachs, in 2001 to dramatize a fundamental shift in economic power in the world, away from the

United States and Europe; a shift to which the formation of the G20 gave belated recognition. Another symbolic hint that nothing much could be achieved in global diplomacy without Brazil and its new friends came at the United Nations meeting on Climate Change in Copenhagen in December 2009. When Obama turned up for last-ditch talks with the Chinese premier, Wen Jiabao, he found him seated round a table with Lula, India's Manmohan Singh and South Africa's Jacob Zuma. Obama took a seat beside 'my friend Lula'.[1] The European Union, to the chagrin of its leaders, was not present.

In the same city, just weeks before, Lula had been the beneficiary of a public snub to Obama. The International Olympic Committee awarded the 2016 Games to Rio de Janeiro. Chicago, Obama's political home town, was eliminated on the first round of voting despite the American president's last-minute dash to Copenhagen to try to rally votes. The decision seemed to meet with genuine goodwill around the world. It came on top of the award of the 2014 football World Cup to Brazil. A tearful Lula claimed that it showed that Brazil was at last recognized as a 'first-class country'.

Certainly Brazil is a country of superlatives, partly because of its sheer size. Its 8.5 million square kilometres comprise the world's fifth-largest country by area, equal to the continental United States and occupying almost half of the land mass of South America. All twenty-eight countries of the European Union would comfortably fit inside Brazil's territory. Its 200 million people make it the world's fourth most populous democracy. With a GDP of US$2.4 trillion in 2012, it was the seventh-largest economy, neck-and-neck with Britain, according to the IMF's calculations.* It is the third-largest food exporter; it will displace the United States to become the biggest by 2025, according to a forecast by the United Nations Food and Agriculture Organization (FAO). Already self-sufficient in oil, deep below the South Atlantic Ocean Brazil made some of the largest oil strikes of the twenty-first century, which should turn it into a big exporter by 2020. But it is also the world leader in plant-based fuels: half its cars run on ethanol derived from sugar cane. It is richer in fresh water per head than any other country in the world, according to a study by the FAO. It posseses some 70 per cent of the Amazon rainforest, and so it is a key player in the international debates about how to slow carbon emissions and mitigate climate change. But Brazil is not just a commodity producer: it was ranked as the world's sixth-biggest manufacturing power in 2010.

---

* Behind the United States, China, Japan, Germany, France and the United Kingdom at market-exchange rates. Brazil was also seventh on the IMF's list of economies measured according to purchasing power, but in this case India and Russia displace France and the United Kingdom.

When Goldman Sachs coined the BRICs label in 2001, there was some initial commentary that Brazil did not belong in such company. Its economy was growing much more slowly than the other three, and there were even worries that it might default on its debt in 2002. China was clearly in a class of its own: because of its size and rapid growth it was on course to become the only rival to the United States as a superpower. India was poorer than the other three, but it was growing fast (at least until 2012) and was the world's most populous democracy. As for Russia, it was the richest of the four, with an income per head of $15,800; it possessed nuclear weapons, a permanent seat at the UN Security Council and the geopolitical reflexes of a former superpower, with involvements in the Balkans and the Middle East.

In fact, Brazil enjoyed some advantages in relation to the other BRICs: its income per head of around $12,000 in 2012 in purchasing-power party terms was about a third higher than China's (although China was closing the gap fast) and almost three times as much as that of India. Almost half of Brazilians used the internet in 2012, a similar percentage to that of Russia, and more than that in China or India. Brazilians are the second most avid users of Facebook, after Americans.[2] More generally, Brazil was in many ways the most open and 'western' of the four (although in some ways that appearance can be misleading). And not only was it a democracy, but it was free of the religious or ethnic tensions and terrorist violence that plague the other three. It has no border disputes nor does it face any obvious strategic threats. China's rise to super-powerdom looks to be inevitable – in the end. But it would be surprising if its breakneck economic growth did not at some stage suffer a hiccup, and that in turn could unleash unrest and political tensions with unpredictable, but poten-tially momentous, consequences. As for India, it suffered widespread rural poverty and was riven by caste, religious and ethnic cleavages, so that its recent rise indeed looks 'strange' and 'in spite of the gods', to borrow the title of one account.[3] And Russia was arguably declining rather than rising. Russia's economy was even more dependent than Brazil's on commodity production (oil and gas in its case), and its political system was thuggish and corrupt.

Despite those initial doubts, thanks in large part to the economic reforms implemented by Cardoso and which Lula opted to maintain, Brazil seemed to have achieved the combination of faster economic growth and low inflation that had eluded it for so long. It was increasingly mentioned by business people and politicians in the same breath as China and India. 'Brazil is the place where everyone wants to be,' declared Paul Volker, the former chairman of the US Federal Reserve and an adviser to Obama, on a visit to the country in 2010.[4] When asked what his greatest regret was during his tenure as Britain's foreign secretary from 2007 to 2010, David Miliband replied, 'Not having visited

Brazil'.[5] Private equity firms tumbled over themselves to launch Brazil funds, while other companies, from advertising agencies to telecoms giants, paid seemingly crazy prices to gain a foothold in the country by buying local rivals.

At the same time, Brazilian companies started to make their mark in the world. As well as Petrobras, the national oil company, the growing cohort of Brazilian multinational giants included Vale, the world's second-biggest mining company; Embraer, its third-biggest maker of civilian jet aircraft; two big private banks, Itaú and Bradesco, and BTG-Pactual, Latin America's leading investment bank. JBS-Friboi, a family concern, had grown in less than sixty years from a small butchery business in Goiás state, deep in Brazil's centre-west, to become the world's biggest meat company. In addition to these, the lengthening list of budding multinationals included 'Brazilian firms you've never heard of', as Roger Agnelli, Vale's then boss, told the London conference, citing the likes of Brazil Foods, Gerdau (a steelmaker) and two engineering firms, Weg and Embraco. Minutes later, Emilio Botín, whose Banco Santander had just sold 16 per cent of its Brazilian operation to investors for $8 billion in the biggest initial public offering anywhere in 2009, stepped up to proclaim that São Paulo would soon be 'a financial centre of world importance'.

Hope followed by disappointment

All this boosterism naturally provoked the sceptical thought that it might be overdone. 'Hope followed by disappointment' is a characteristic Brazilian pattern, as Cardoso has pointed out.[6] The country's potential has long been obvious, to Brazilians and outsiders alike. In 1940, Stephan Zweig, an Austrian writer who moved to Rio de Janeiro to escape the Nazis, wrote a glowing book called in its English translation *Brazil: A Land of the Future.*[*7] But popular humour in Brazil quickly added the rider: 'and always will be', a joke which turned into a resented cliché. The country was a byword for promise bewilderingly unfulfilled.

Sure enough, after economic growth peaked at a blistering 7.5 per cent in 2010, an election year in which Lula oversaw the triumph of his chosen successor, Dilma Rousseff, Brazil began to suffer disappointments and something of a reputational backlash. As we wrote in our cover leader of November

---

[*] The original edition in German was called simply *Brasilien*, but its frontispiece quoted a letter of 1868 by an Austrian diplomat, Count Prokesch-Osten, in which he praised the country as 'A new place, a magnificent port, distant from shabby Europe, a new political horizon, a land of the future . . .'

2009, 'just as it would be a mistake to underestimate the new Brazil, so it would be to gloss over its weaknesses'.[8] Many Brazilian manufacturers were uncompetitive, while its service businesses were hobbled by low productivity. That was partly because of Brazil's weak educational performance; it was also because of a burdensome tax system and senseless red tape. In a country that was still young demographically, pension spending was rising alarmingly. Meanwhile, public investment in infrastructure remained derisory: Brazil's ports, airports and roads were clogged, and its ability to generate enough electricity to power economic growth was questioned by some. Inequalities of income and power were starting to be reduced but remained glaring. While a rich minority luxuriated in vast landholdings or in the opulent apartments of Rio de Janeiro's southern beachside suburbs and São Paulo's leafy neighbourhoods of Jardims, Vila Nova Conceição and Morumbi, a mass of poor migrants from the countryside were crowded into often squalid *favelas* (shanty towns). Violent crime, and sometimes violent policing, remained a blight on the lives of many, especially the young, the black and those who dwell in favelas. Political life was marked by an exaggerated proliferation of parties, the shameless pursuit of patronage and pork, and the veto power exercised by entrenched interests. The judiciary was cumbersome. The state struggled to enforce the rule of law. Corruption remained widespread. For all these reasons, oil wealth could as easily prove to be an economic bane as a benefit.

Temporarily overshadowed during the boom of the Lula years, these deep-seated problems loomed larger during the presidency of his successor, Dilma Rousseff. Although she owed her victory to Lula's extraordinary popularity and energetic sponsorship, it marked another milestone for Brazil in that she was the first woman to govern the country. Her first task on becoming president was to deal with the consequences of the expansionary economic policies that had helped to get her elected. Dilma, as Brazilians call her, faced an awkward balancing act, trying to sustain growth while restraining inflation and grappling with the consequences of a wildly overvalued currency (partly the result of the desperate efforts of central banks in the United States and Europe to pump money into their economies, but also a consequence of Brazil's savings shortage and high interest rates). Her government did not handle this challenge well: it zigzagged from one policy to another, and its constant meddling generated uncertainty. The economy ground more or less to a halt in mid-2011, and stagnated for eighteen months before a lukewarm recovery. Inflation edged up to over 6 per cent a year, and the pace of growth in real incomes slowed. Several leading Brazilian economists warned that the broad consensus about economic policy that underlay the country's progress over the previous two decades had begun to fray, and that the government was returning to some of the interventionist habits of the past.[9] They argued that without a new round of liberal reform, Brazil could not grow by more than 2–3 per cent a year without triggering inflation. Outside commentators, too, began to focus once again on Brazil's weaknesses.[*]

Nevertheless, the widely held assumption in Brazil was that Rousseff was cruising towards a second term in 2014. Then, suddenly, in June 2013 the country was convulsed by street protests on a scale not seen for a generation. In essence, they were a cry of frustration at what many Brazilians saw as a corrupt, unrepresentative and self-serving political class and at the poor quality of public services – hospitals and health care, education and public transport. Though they soon died away, the protests were a profound shock to the political system. Taken together with the economic slowdown, they suggested that the heady cycle of progress over the previous two decades has at least paused.

The country has flattered to deceive in the past. From 1930 to 1980 Brazil's economy was amongst the fastest growing anywhere in the world. In the 1950s Juscelino Kubitschek, an elected president, breezily promised 'fifty years of development in five', and set out to turn Brazil into an industrial power. As a statement of the country's modernity and a symbol of its ambition, he built a new capital, Brasília, deep in the *planalto*, the high plateau of the interior. Similarly, in the 1970s, the generals who were by then ruling the country proclaimed an economic 'miracle' as growth reached double-digit rates, and launched a propaganda campaign entitled 'Brazil – a Great Power'. On both these occasions outsiders were caught up by the wave of optimism, only for Brazil to lose its way again. It was only on the football pitch that it became a superpower, winning five World Cups between 1958 and 2002, more than any other country has done. But no Brazilian has yet won a Nobel Prize.

When I lived in Brazil from 1996 to 1999 as *The Economist*'s first resident staff correspondent, I became convinced that the country had great strengths, some hidden, as well as its more obvious weaknesses. I believed that a far-reaching process of reform was under way that would see the country advance

---

[*] The renewed scepticism was summed up in an article in *Foreign Affairs* magazine ('Bearish on Brazil: The Commodity Slowdown and the End of the Magic Moment', May/June 2012) by Ruchir Sharma, an economist at Morgan Stanley, a Wall Street investment bank. He attributed Brazil's faster growth entirely to the boom in world commodity prices prompted by China's industrialization and to the global liquidity glut. With China slowing and the imminent end of cheap money in the rich world, he argued that Brazil would be punished for its addiction to high interest rates and an expensive welfare state, the consequences of an obsessive search for stability rather than growth. Sharma's article contained some mistakes (e.g. the Bolsa Família cash-transfer programme is not in fact an expensive budget item). But it also conveyed a large grain of truth.

over the coming years. I have visited Brazil frequently since, spending long periods in the country. I still believe that its recent progress is based on far more solid economic and socio-political foundations than it was during the Kubitschek era or the generals' economic 'miracle'. This progress is dissected in Part II, which forms the bulk of the book. Brazil's strengths in energy, agriculture and, increasingly, science and research, are real and will not disappear. Brazilian society is vibrant and creative (though it is still unjust). But while I do not think the country risks another economic collapse, like many Brazilians I worry that without the right political leadership and policies and without political and other reforms, its pace of advance may disappoint Brazilians and outsiders alike. To try to encapsulate those doubts, at *The Economist* we reprised our 2009 cover in September 2013, showing the Corcovado statue heading down to earth again and asking 'Has Brazil blown it?' In Part III I attempt to answer that question, and also to explore what Brazil's impact in the wider world will be in the years ahead.

As hundreds of thousands of sports fans from around the world prepare to visit Brazil, first for the World Cup and then for the Olympics, they will encounter a country that is more complicated than meets the casual eye. Although tourism has picked up in recent years, Brazil is still surprisingly unknown to the outside world, at least beyond the clichés, and relatively understudied. That may be partly because Portuguese is spoken by relatively few non-Brazilians around the world. Even most 'Latin Americanists' speak only Spanish.

The main purpose of this book is to try to provide an interpretation and an explanation of Brazil today. To do that, I have dug back into the past. Unlike India or China, with their unbroken histories of civilization and culture stretching back millennia, Brazil is a relatively 'new' country. But in other ways, Brazil is not so new. It has retained broadly the same borders since colonial times (unlike the United States). It is an older-established nation-state than Germany or Italy. Brazil's history has marked it in fundamental ways which help to explain its contemporary problems and its *modus operandi*. That history is the subject of Part I of the book, which focuses in particular on several themes that continue to cast their shadow over today's Brazil. One is the difficulty that Portugal, a relatively weak colonial power, faced in settling and maintaining control of its huge colony; another concerns the unique circumstances in which the country gained its independence in 1822. Brazil's experience as a colony and then an independent monarchy affected the country's habits of government, although these then evolved dramatically in the twentieth century, as the country strove to catch up economically. The third overriding theme is the way in which the large-scale practice of slavery and the forcible import of millions of African slaves marked Brazil's society and its politics indelibly, and is the single most important explanation for its continuing social inequalities. Although Brazil never practised the racial segregation that marred the United States or South Africa, many of the poor in today's Brazil are of darker skin than the better-off.

This history distinguishes Portuguese-speaking Brazil from its Spanish-speaking neighbours, too. Most obviously, on achieving political independence, Spanish America fractured into more than a dozen separate republics, while Brazil remained united. In several respects, Brazil bears comparison with the United States: both are vast continental land masses with sharp regional variations in climate, topography and people; both were marked by an open internal frontier, and the restless energy that stemmed from it; and both are racial melting pots, though the details differ importantly. As in the US, many things in Brazil tend to be big: distances, truck stops, restaurants and portion sizes, for example. Like Americans, Brazilians think nothing of driving for several days to get somewhere. The result is that the two largest countries in the Americas resemble each other, though often as if seen through a distorted mirror. That may be the reason why each is often frustrated and disappointed by the behaviour of the other.

In sum, Brazil is a world of its own, and Brazilians, like people from the United States, have a strong sense of exceptionalism. They have long been aware of their country's potential, and frustrated and unnerved by its failure to realize it. By way of a *petisco* (canapé) before the main menu of the book, the next chapter offers a brief portrait of this exceptional land and its people.

CHAPTER TWO

The Brazilian Way of Life

'Brazil is an immense country, a continent of great human, ecological and social complexity,' as Lula declared in his inaugural address as president on 1 January 2003. Geographically, most of Brazil lies within the tropics. The country contains many of the planet's various environments, but it lacks alpine conditions: the highest mountain, Pico da Neblina, is just under 3,000 metres and rises on the Venezuelan border in the Guiana Shield, the geologically ancient heart of South America. Three great river basins divide the country: the Amazon, the Paraná in the south-west, and the São Francisco, which rises in Minas Gerais and runs northwards in parallel to the coast before meeting the sea between Recife and Salvador. Even in its somewhat diminished condition, the Amazon rainforest still covers almost half of the country. Much of the rest is *cerrado*, the great rolling savannah that stretches in a huge crescent from Mato Grosso to Piauí and Maranhão. The relatively narrow coastal strip and its immediate hinterland remain the most heavily populated part of the country.

Brazilians themselves divide the country into five regions (see map on page x). The south is a temperate zone which attracted much European migration (from Germany, Italy and Eastern Europe) in the past two centuries. It is the home of family farming and of many blond Brazilians, who confound outsiders' stereotypes of the country, and of place names such as Novo Hamburgo and Blumenau (which holds a well-attended Oktoberfest). With 26 million people, the south makes up only 7 per cent of the national territory; it is the second-richest area in income per head, after the south-east, but has the highest levels of human development. Paraná and Santa Catarina have many modern industrial plants. Rio Grande do Sul, whose inhabitants are known as *gaúchos*, is a frontier state which played an important role in Brazilian history. Some of its traditional industries, such as shoemaking, metal-bashing and wine production, have struggled to compete in recent decades.

The south-east is Brazil's heartland and economic powerhouse, with 77 million people, and includes the two biggest cities. Rio de Janeiro is a largely Portuguese and African city, but as the capital from 1763 until 1960 and the main port until the late nineteenth century, it is a naturally cosmopolitan place. It is blessed with one of the most beautiful and dramatic urban settings on the planet, with its nippled mountain stumps and residual forests rising above the Atlantic, the constant interplay between land and water in coastal lagoons and the island-studded Bay of Guanabara. The city embodies the characteristic Brazilian mix of the breathtaking, the picturesque and the squalid. As well as many favelas, Rio possesses two of the world's more famous urban neighbourhoods in Copacabana and Ipanema, developed in the 1890s only after tunnels were blasted through the granite mountain separating them from the city centre. *Cariocas*, as Rio's inhabitants are called, are seen by other Brazilians as better at partying than working. That is partly because in Rio, one of the biggest seaside cities in the world, the beach is a prominent social space. It is a place to meet and make friends, play football and sometimes talk business, as the city's biographer, Ruy Castro, writes: 'In Rio people just go to the beach like going to the cinema, the shops or the bank, because it's there, 24 hours a day, all year round.'[1] After the federal government moved to Brasília, Rio suffered decades of economic decline, corrupt misgovernment and narcissistic introversion. But in the past few years it has enjoyed a renaissance, thanks to the growth of the oil industry, which is headquartered in the city; important industrial investments in the surrounding state; and the rise of electronic trading, which has allowed much of the asset-management branch of finance to move back from São Paulo to the smart beachside district of Leblon. *Cariocas* hope the Olympics will set the seal on this revival.

Originally a provincial outpost, coffee and then industrialization turned São Paulo into one of the world's fastest-growing cities throughout much of the twentieth century: its population rose from just 65,000 in 1890 to 570,000 by 1920, becoming a metropolis of 12 million by the 1970s and around 18 million today. It became Brazil's economic and business capital and, by the 1970s, the largest industrial city in the southern hemisphere. Claude Lévi-Strauss, the French anthropologist who taught at the newly founded University of São Paulo in the 1930s, wrote of the city at that time: 'Cow pastures lay at the foot of concrete blocks, a whole area could suddenly spring into being like a mirage.' He noted that in its vertiginous growth it was often compared to Chicago; today the comparator would be Chinese cities such as Chongqing or Chengdu. Like Brazil's south, São Paulo drew in immigrants from Italy and Germany but also many Syrians and Lebanese as well as Japanese and Koreans. If Rio depended on government, São Paulo was all about business. The difference between the two was expressed by Victor Civita, an Italian immigrant who founded Grupo Abril, Brazil's biggest publishing group. When he arrived in Brazil in 1949, people in Rio told him that São Paulo was provincial, lacking the creative people required by a media company. But Civita liked São Paulo, seeing it as full of entrepreneurs. It reminded him of his native Milan, while he saw *cariocas* as Romans, good at playing but not at working.[2] São Paulo went through a harsh transition with the opening of the economy in the 1990s. It shed much of its industry and emerged as Brazil's business, financial and cultural capital, a world city. Its image went through a similar metamorphosis. It was often portrayed as an urban dystopia. The super-rich flit above it by helicopter, while down below in the ugly, traffic-snarled streets flocks of *moto-boys* (motorbike dispatch-riders) dice with death and *paulistanos* scurry between work and their homes in the countless tower-blocks, fortified with guards and high iron fencing. In recent years, São Paulo has also come to be seen as the acme of Brazilian cool, with its modernist buildings and extraordinary creative energy, its thriving contemporary art market and gourmet restaurants. Yet away from the old centre and a few other business districts, it has an oddly suburban feel, reflecting a city that was thrown up quickly rather than one that has evolved organically.

The city's economy is powered by a vast upstate hinterland, the centre of Brazilian agribusiness and home to a string of smaller cities with modern high-tech industries, such as Campinas and São José dos Campos. Many of the fastest-growing and most liveable cities in Brazil are now mid-sized ones, in São Paulo state and elsewhere across the country. In all, São Paulo state, with a population of around 40 million, accounts for a third of Brazil's GDP; its economy of more than $800 billion is bigger than those of Argentina, Uruguay and Paraguay (Brazil's founding partners in the Mercosul trade area) combined.

Minas Gerais, the second most populous state with 20 million people, is extremely diverse. Rolling hills planted with coffee and studded with towns of light manufacturing predominate in the south-west; the formerly forested zone in the south-east is in many ways an extension of Rio de Janeiro; the centre of the state features mountains, mining and heavy industry; the north-eastern corner is poor and rural; while in the west, the area known as the Triângulo Mineiro possesses thriving modern agriculture and logistics businesses. João Guimarães Rosa, a writer sometimes called 'Brazil's James Joyce', described his home state as 'a mountain, mountains, erect space, constant emergence, hidden verticality, static force' but he added: 'Minas is many.

There are, at least, several Minas.' It was, he wrote, 'Brazil in interior point, Brazil contained, the heart of the matter.'[3] Minas has a powerful political tradition, mixing liberal rebellion and agrarian conservatism. *Mineiros* are seen by other Brazilians as reserved, wily and astute.

The north-east has long been Brazil's poorest area. Its coastal belt grows sugar and cotton; inland lies the arid *sertão*, home to extensive cattle-raising and subsistence farming. The north-east's 53 million people have an income per head of only around two-thirds of the national average. Of the region's nine states, the three most important are Bahia, Pernambuco and Ceará, with their respective capital cities of Salvador, Recife and Fortaleza. Their relative fortunes have oscillated. Pernambuco, a state with a strong liberal and rebellious tradition, declined for much of the twentieth century but has grown strongly under vigorous political leadership in this century. Bahia benefited from investment in heavy industry by the military governments of 1964–85. Its vast western plateauland has recently developed modern farming, and resembles the centre-west. Salvador, the capital of colonial Brazil until 1763, is the country's most African city and is a centre of black Brazilian culture and music. Ceará, once one of the poorest states, implemented pioneering reforms from the late 1980s, investing in community health and education; with lower labour costs than Rio Grande do Sul, it has become a centre of shoe-manufacturing. Piauí and Maranhão now vie for the ignominious distinction of being Brazil's poorest state. Maranhão has been run since the 1980s by José Sarney, a former president, and his family.

The centre-west is a fast-growing region, both economically and in terms of population. It is Brazil's agricultural frontier, occupying much of the *cerrado*, given an initial impulse by the creation of Brasília as the federal capital, and turned from a vast wilderness into farmland by Brazil's 'green revolution' of the 1970s. It is the source of much of the soyabean crop, as well as of sugar and cotton. It has recently attracted industry, such as food processors, sugar and ethanol mills and even car plants. Seen from the air, much of the centre-west is a seemingly empty landscape of vast fields, great rectangles and circles of brown and green, Brazil's prairies.

The north comprises six states and accounts for two-fifths of Brazil's total area. It rivals the north-east in the poverty of its people, and the centre-west in the speed of its population growth. Throw in Mato Grosso, Tocantins and the western half of Maranhão, as the Brazilian government does, and you have 'the legal Amazon', the territorial unit to which various development, and more recently conservation, policies apply. This vast area amounts to 60 per cent of the country. It contains not just the world's greatest rainforest, but is also home to 24 million people, most of them living in cities. The two biggest,

Manaus and Belém, each have a population of around 2 million. Belém is a great port near the mouth of the Amazon. Manaus, in the heart of the forest at the confluence of the Solimões (Amazon) and Negro rivers, is the site of a celebrated opera house built at the height of the late nineteenth-century rubber boom but is better known to Brazilians as the place where most of the country's output of consumer electronic goods are assembled, the bizarre result of a tax-free zone instituted by a military government in the 1960s.

Football, the family and other religions

If Brazil is indeed 'the world's most exciting nation', as the *Financial Times* recently claimed, it is not just because of its geography but also because of its people, their culture and their increasingly vibrant democracy. What defines Brazilians? In the caricature, the answers would start with football, carnival and sex, and a tropical exuberance summed up by Carmen Miranda, a Brazilian singer who found fame in Hollywood partly by wearing fruit bowls as hats. Brazilians naturally resent being reduced to such stereotypes, though these indeed provide some clues to the national psyche and culture.

Start with football. It arrived in 1894, introduced by Charles Miller, the son of a Scottish railway engineer who is unknown in Britain but is a household name in Brazil, commemorated in statues and street names. Brazilians swiftly took to the sport, and became better than anybody else in the world at it. At their best – the national teams of the 1950s to 1980s – they played football as an art form, as *o jogo bonito* ('the beautiful game'). Gilberto Freyre, an anthropologist and writer, thought that Brazilians played 'as if it were a dance', a quality he attributed to the African influence in Brazil.[4] In fact, Brazilian football has often mixed magical creativity with a dour physical side (embodied in the team that won the World Cup in 1994). Football is perhaps the best example of Brazilians' prowess at teamwork, noted by management theorists.[5] But it has also become a powerful factor in Brazilian national identity. Success on the field has provided 'a confidence in ourselves that no other institution has given Brazil to the same extent', as Roberto DaMatta, an anthropologist, has written.[6] And loyalty to a particular football club is a way of establishing a social identity. 'Which club do you support?' is one of the first questions strangers will ask of each other. Of all Brazil's many religions, football is one of the strongest. The country shuts down completely on days when Brazil is playing in the World Cup, the streets of São Paulo and other cities falling eerily silent. Before the 2010 tournament, the workers at Embraer, the plane-maker, chose to work seven minutes more each day for several weeks in order to have time off to watch Brazil's matches.[7] It is the only country in the world whose national team is expected to win the World Cup as a right and an obligation – which will put the *selecāo* under enormous pressure when the tournament is played in Brazil in 2014. Home advantage should help: no fans in the world are noisier or more passionate than Brazilians, both men and women. Though a minority of Brazilians have no interest in the sport, they are a silent one.

Carnival is another expression of Brazilians' flair for teamwork, as well as for cultural fusion. Its origins go back to the Italian-style carnival brought by the Portuguese court during its brief sojourn in Brazil during the Napoleonic wars, but by the late nineteenth century this had merged with a black Brazilian carnival, of neighbourhood celebration. Samba, the music of carnival, also dates back to the nineteenth century. The spontaneous local character of carnival as a giant street party survives in some places today. In Salvador, it features deafening sound systems mounted on trucks. In Rio, it has been over-shadowed by the organized competition between samba 'schools'. These have become influential social institutions, running community projects and spending months preparing for the festivities. Carnival is a gorgeous, elabo-rately choreographed multimedia spectacle of music, singing and costumed dance, 'an opera in the open air', as Ruy Castro has written.[8] It is a fabulously democratic opera. For carnival also represents the world turned upside-down for a few days. Carnival costume, tellingly called *uma fantasia* (the Iberian term for fancy-dress), 'allows the free movement of people in a social space that the everyday world makes impossible with hierarchical repression and prejudices', as DaMatta puts it.[9] Like football – and in sharp contrast to much of daily life and politics – carnival follows strict rules which apply to all participants alike. And like football teams, samba schools are largely drawn from the poorer sectors of society. Both are arenas in which rich and poor, black and white, mingle on equal terms.

Carnival's orgiastic character owes much to climate – nobody wants to dance with many clothes on in heat of well above 30 degrees centigrade – and to Brazilians' generally relaxed attitude to nudity and sex. This has been noted by many observers over the centuries. Its origins seem to lie in the cultures of the three founding peoples of Brazil, Amerindians, Portuguese and Africans (see chapter three). As early as the sixteenth century, a popular saying held that 'sin doesn't exist south of the equator', to the horror of the Catholic Church.[*] José Bonifácio de Andrade e Silva, a statesman of Brazilian inde-pendence, remarked of his people that they were 'passionate about sex because

---

[*] This saying was first recorded by Caspar van Baerle, a Dutch historian attached to Prince Maurits of Nassau's expedition to Pernambuco in the seventeenth century; more recently it was the name of a popular song by Chico Buarque.

of the climate, lifestyle and education'. Brazilians are generally sexually tolerant. The world's largest Gay Pride parade takes place in São Paulo though there has been a worrying recent rise in homophobic killings in the country.

The climate also means that the beach plays a central role in Brazilian culture; it was not by chance that Brazil invented the tanga or the skimpy, tight-fitting trunks worn by men. And perhaps that is why Brazilians are so concerned with their personal appearance. They devote more of their disposable income to beauty and personal care products than anyone else in the world, according to Euromonitor, a market research firm. In 2013 they were expected to spend some $29 billion on their bodies, overtaking Japan to become the world's second-biggest market, after the United States.[10] Brazil can also claim more or less to have invented plastic surgery as an industry. As income has risen over the past decade, so has the number of operations, to over 900,000 a year in 2012, second only to the United States, according to Richard Lapper, the editor of *Brazil Confidential*, a newsletter. It is not confined to the rich. Ivo Pitanguy, the country's best-known plastic surgeon, has set up a charity ward at a public hospital in Rio, arguing that 'aesthetic surgery is not a luxury . . . it should be available to everyone'.[11]

But outsiders who assume that Brazilians are libertines are wrong, as Larry Rohter, an American journalist who knows Brazilian culture well, points out. Sexual freedom goes hand in hand with a strong streak of moralism in what is in some ways a conservative society.[12] Nelson Rodrigues, a journalist and dramatist who almost single-handedly invented Brazilian theatre in the 1940s and 1950s, found his plays frequently blocked by government censors because they dealt with themes such as adultery, abortion and incest.[13] This conservatism surfaces from time to time today, for example in 2009 when a young woman was briefly expelled from a private university in São Paulo for wearing a mini-dress held to expose too much thigh (she was reinstated after protests).[14]

Such moralism is a reminder that Brazil is a deeply religious country. Not for nothing is its best-known symbol the giant statue of Christ the Redeemer atop Rio's Corcovado mountain, erected in 1931. Brazil was the world's largest producer of bibles until China recently overtook it. Gospel music of various kinds is hugely popular. Ordinary Brazilians often end a conversation by saying *Vá com Deus* ('Go with God'). But which God? Catholicism has long coexisted with Brazilian versions of African religions, such as *candomblé* and *macumba*. Many Brazilians will pray to both a Catholic saint and an African *orixá* (deity). Another element in this cocktail of faith is spiritism, a cult founded by Alain Kardec, a Frenchman, who believed in the possibility of communication with the dead through mediums and whose ideas were blended with *macumba* in *umbanda*, another home-grown Brazilian sect.[15]

Over the past few decades evangelical Protestantism has made big inroads. While in 1960 93 per cent of Brazilians said they were Catholic, only 65 per cent do today, according to the 2010 census. Even so, that makes Brazil the world's biggest Roman Catholic country. But 22 per cent of Brazilians now describe themselves as evangelicals, belonging to a myriad of churches, some based in the United States but most (and most of the biggest) home-grown. With their message of teetotalism, hard work and advancement by personal effort, the evangelicals have been especially successful at recruiting poorer and black Brazilians.[16] They offer a structure to people who often suffer multiple problems, including family breakdown. Some of their pastors have become rich and controversial businessmen. The business empire of Edir Macedo, the founder of the Universal Church, includes TV Record, which he has built into Brazil's second-biggest television network. *Forbes* magazine estimated his personal wealth at $1.1 billion in 2012; perhaps because of that, his church has begun to lose members to rivals.[17] The evangelical churches have collaborated among themselves to elect members of Congress, and some have begun to espouse American-style social conservatism. The main response of the Catholic Church has been the charismatic movement, which uses similar methods to the evangelicals. Its priests use television, rock music and social media to appeal to the faithful. The best known of them, Father Marcelo Rossi, has topped both the pop charts and the bestseller lists.[18]

Along with football and carnival, another institution that unifies Brazilians and contributes to the national conversation is the *telenovela*, the television soap opera. Thanks in large part to its prowess at the genre, Globo TV, the biggest network with 122 local stations, retains an audience share of around 50 per cent, a figure that US networks can only dream of. Largely because of the popularity of *telenovelas*, television still took 64 per cent of the total advertising spend in Brazil in 2010, the highest share in the world. Owned by the Marinho family, Globo has 10,000 employees and a further 20,000 contract staff; it invests serious money in its soaps, especially those in the prime-time slot. Often criticized for showing an idealized, white and plutocratic Brazil, in fact the soaps take on socio-political issues. Nowadays the *novelas* have gay couples, although they don't kiss on screen. Globo's research shows that 70 per cent of the audience live outside the big cities, are socially conservative and often watch as a family. While women are happy that the soaps deal with female orgasm or male impotence, they don't want to be embarrassed in front of their children, according to Octavio Florisbal, Globo's managing director. 'We reflect social behaviour rather than trying to be in the vanguard,' he told *Valor Econômico*, a Brazilian newspaper.[19] Nevertheless, the soaps may have contributed to forging social trends: researchers have found that Globo's expansion across the country, and its portrayal of small, happy families in its soaps, seem to have contributed to the decline in the fertility rate and even to have had a slight impact on rising divorce rates as women become more independent.[20] Globo is certainly a sharp observer of social trends. *Avenida Brasil*, one of its most-watched and discussed recent soaps which commanded a nightly audience of up to 80 million for six months, portrayed the 'emerging' lower-middle class of the suburbs and was seen by many critics as a landmark in Brazil's acceptance of itself (see chapter nine).[21]

In many other ways, too, the family is the central institution of Brazilian society. If national identity in the United States is rooted in its founding revolution against authority and in Anglo-Protestant values of individualism, a wide scholarly consensus holds that Brazilian national identity is founded on loyalty to the family. Because of the relative weakness of Portugal as a colonial power, and the lack of a tradition of social organization, the family 'furnished the norm of power, of respectability, of obedience and of cohesion', according to Sérgio Buarque de Holanda in 'Raízes do Brasil', an influential essay published in 1936. The result was 'an invasion of the public by the private, of the state by the family'.[22] In a country of few public heroes, neither independence nor democracy came about through a national revolution. There is no Brazilian Bolívar or Zapata.

A society based on ties of family and friendship was the main obstacle to the rule of law, Buarque argued. A desire to personalize all relationships was one means of managing the conflict inherent in slavery. Brazilians liked to see themselves as 'cordial, hospitable and generous'. Indeed, for Buarque the 'most specific Brazilian trait is a horror of social distance'. And also of physical distance: Brazilians are uniquely tactile. Foreigners are often taken aback (literally) by the Brazilian habit of standing much closer to their interlocutor than others feel comfortable with. Brazilians are extraordinarily friendly, and quick to get on apparently intimate terms. Someone you have never met will end an email with *Abraços* ('Hugs'), commonly abbreviated to *Abs*. Yet behind this cordiality lurks a lack of personal trust (at least according to opinion polls) and cynicism.[23]

The horror of social distance applies, too, to the issue of names, which bemuse foreigners. Brazilians have some of the longest names in the world, but they tend to use only one. Thus a nineteenth-century politician called Eusébio de Queirós Coutinho Matoso da Câmara was known simply as Eusébio. Tom Jobim, who wrote the music of 'A Garota de Ipanema' ('The Girl from Ipanema'), was really Antonio Carlos Brasileiro de Alameida Jobim. Brazilians will adopt one name, often the Christian name or a nickname, for their presidents, whether or not they like them much. Thus Lula, Dilma and

Fernando Henrique, rather than Da Silva, Rousseff or Cardoso. As a general rule, they will use their father's surname, which is placed after their mother's surname (in Spanish the order is reversed). But some, such as Fernando Collor de Melo, a former president, choose to use their mother's surname. Rather than their full names, politicians and footballers are often referred to by diminutives, nicknames or their place of origin: Paulo Pereira da Silva, a trade union leader and federal deputy, calls himself Paulinho da Força (after his union, Força Sindical); José Orcírio Miranda dos Santos pursued a political career under the name of Zeca do PT. Ronaldo de Assis Moreira was known as 'Ronaldinho Gaúcho' when he burst upon the football scene, because he was born in Rio Grande do Sul and to distinguish him from Ronaldo Luís Nazário de Lima, a slightly older footballer, known in Brazil as 'Ronaldinho' before he became just 'Ronaldo'. Brazilians also like making up new names. Maílson da Nobrega, a former finance minister whose father was a village tailor in rural Paraíba, wrote that parents in the north-east 'mix together names, inspired by films, football players and musicians, so that the names of their children might be different, original'. His own name was a mixture of Mae (mother) and Wilson, his father's name. All his siblings had names beginning with M: Milton, Marisa, Marilene, Marizete, Marcos, María Madalena, Mauricio and Milson.[24] On the other hand, Silva is an extraordinarily common surname, apparently because it was often bestowed on slaves who lost their names as well as their freedom on the South Atlantic crossing.

The pervasive influence of personal and family relations manifests itself in many ways in contemporary Brazil. For example, a peculiarity of the job market is that recruitment agencies are contacted only by foreign companies looking for senior managers. 'The rest of the recruiting is done by recommendation, and therefore depends on personal networking,' according to Luiz Antonio Concistré, a headhunter.[25] Nepotism rivals the siphoning-off of public funds as *the* Brazilian political vice, with legislators frequently found to employ relatives and retainers on their staff. But Brazilians also have a refreshingly flexible notion of the family, which is not confined to biological relations. In a widely reported case, a judge in Santa Catarina ruled that a stepfather should pay maintenance to his sixteen-year-old stepdaughter, whom he brought up for ten years. The biological father gave the child the sum of one minimum wage each month, but the stepfather, an engineer, was better off. The court said he should hand over 20 per cent of his income. This expressed a new view of family law, that the father is whoever brings up the child.[26] In a similar spirit, when Dilma Rousseff took her first holiday break as president, she went to a beach in Natal not just with her daughter, son-in-law and grandson as well as her mother and aunt, but also with her former

husband, his new partner and their two children.[27] This flexible approach to
the family may be deep-rooted. It was traditional in colonial Brazil for women
to accept the children of their husband's mistresses in the home.[28] Lévi-
Strauss found that some Brazilian Indians replenished their numbers by
forced adoption of children secured in raids on other villages.[29]

DaMatta draws a distinction, which he sees as fundamental in Brazilian life,
between *casa* (home) and *rua* (street).[30] The home is a harmonious world, where
a conservative discourse and traditional moral values hold sway. The street is a
place of struggle, of modern economic life and of confrontation: though
Brazilians like to see themselves as a peaceable lot, there is a persistent undercurrent of violence in the society. Nevertheless, inter-personal confrontation is less
of a cultural norm in business in Brazil than in the United States, according to
David Neeleman, a Brazilian–American entrepreneur who has founded low-cost
airlines in both countries.[31] And while home is the realm of family and friendship, the street is the place where Brazilians must grapple with the demands of a
theoretically impersonal law, demands they find impossible. To reconcile the
two, Brazilians resort to what they call *o jeito*, an almost untranslatable word
meaning, roughly, a fix or solution. At its coarsest, this means a bribe. More
benignly it can mean establishing some point of connection with an official so
that a way around a bureaucratic brick wall can be found. At its worst, it can
mean a refusal by the powerful or well-connected to follow rules, summed up in
the admonitory phrase '*Você sabe com quem esta falando?*' ('Do you realize who
you are talking to?').

A powerful interpretation of the *jeito* is that it is the product of a hierarchical
society, and that it is inimical to the rule of law. One of the themes of the chapters
that follow is how long and difficult Brazil's search for a society of equal citizens
has been. But the *jeito* is also one of many examples, albeit an unhappy one, of
Brazilians' great flexibility and pragmatism. It has led them to eschew political
extremes and political violence. In this they differ from many other Latin
Americans. It is a characteristic of Brazilian policymakers, as of the French,
whom in some ways they resemble, to approach any problem by first developing
an abstract conceptual analysis and drawing up a theoretically perfect law to deal
with it, only then to adopt a practical solution. The country's apparent candour
is thus sometimes misleading; as Tom Jobim once remarked, 'Brazil is not for
beginners'. Brazil is full of unexpected complexities and surprises. To take a
trivial example, its most popular music as measured by sales is not samba or the
works of internationally known singers such as Caetano Veloso, Gilberto Gil or
Chico Buarque, but *sertanejo*, or Brazilian country music, followed by gospel.

Perhaps the most obvious and attractive characteristic of Brazilians is their
alegria, or *joie de vivre*, a positive expression of a culture that places great value

on friendship and on the family and that finds consolation in religion, in carnival and football, and of a people who enjoy a country of great beauty and a warm climate. Caetano Veloso, a Bahian musician, put it thus in a song called 'Alegria, Alegria'

> Sem lenço, sem documento, Nada no bolso ou nas mãos, Eu quero seguir vivendo, amor, Eu vou, Por que não, por que não . . .
> (Without a handkerchief or a document, nothing in my pocket or in my hands, I want to carry on living, my love, I'm going to, why not, why not . . .?)

Why not, indeed? But *alegria* has its counterpart in *saudade*, a Portuguese word that is often translated as nostalgia but which, as Lévi-Strauss has written, is more accurately the sense of loss engendered by a consciousness of the fleeting intensity of the present.[32] Certainly, Brazilians have a tendency to live in the present and to give little thought to the long term – as evidenced by the country's secular incapacity to invest enough in capital, infrastructure and education and by its indefensibly generous pension system. Historically, this went hand in hand with a certain disdain for work, and especially for manual work, a consequence of slavery. These traits are encapsulated in 'O Empréstimo' ('The Loan'), a short story by Machado de Assis, a writer of the late nineteenth century whom many consider to be Brazil's greatest novelist. This tells the story of Custodio, a penniless man who combined 'the air of a beggar and of a general' and who seeks a large loan for an ill-defined business venture from a notary whom he barely knows. The notary replies that he doesn't have such a large sum of money, but that if he had he would have been delighted to help: 'Custodio cheered up; he lived in the present; he didn't want to know about the past, no nostalgia, no fears, no remorse. The present was everything.' In the end, the notary lends Custodio a tiny fraction of the sum originally requested; his offer to help him obtain a job by talking to his friend the justice minister is turned down. 'This Custodio was born with the vocation for wealth without the vocation for work,' Machado writes.[33]

Of course, many Brazilians have always worked hard. Brazil today is a complex and sophisticated democracy. But alongside its many achievements lie difficulties that it must overcome if is indeed to become the 'first-class country' that Lula proclaimed. Exploring those achievements and difficulties, where they come from and where they might lead, is the subject of the rest of this book.

PART I

History from Geography

CHAPTER THREE

The Forging of a People

The recorded history of Brazil begins with a misleadingly idyllic encounter between Europeans and Amerindians, and with a doubt as to whether it happened by accident or design. The story begins on Monday, 9 March 1500, when King Manoel of Portugal and his court gathered at the anchorage of Restelo on the Tagus, 3 miles downriver from the centre of Lisbon, close to the spot where the ornate tower of Belém and the giant sculpted monument to the Portuguese navigators now stand. The king, his retinue and a large crowd of ordinary *lisboetas* were there to see off the most imposing fleet Portugal had ever dispatched into the Atlantic, consisting of thirteen ships and 1,500 men under the command of Pedro Álvares Cabral, a young nobleman.

Although Christopher Columbus, a Genoese in the service of Castile, had made three voyages to the Americas in the eight years before Cabral's expedition, it was the Portuguese who were Europe's premier seafaring nation in the fifteenth century. Portugal had forged the first nation-state in Europe: its Christian kings ended five centuries of Islamic rule by the mid-thirteenth century, completing their *reconquista* some 250 years before their counterparts in Spain. By the late fourteenth century Portugal had achieved political stability under the kings of the House of Aviz. Isolated behind the mountain chains that separated the new nation from Castile, the Portuguese looked to the sea. They had absorbed from the Arabs the most advanced seafaring technology of the time, including the fixed keel, the lateen sail, the compass and the astrolabe. The Portuguese were a nation of traders: since feudalism was never very strong in Portugal, the country lacked rigid social hierarchies; success as a merchant offered a route into the nobility.

The Portuguese first established colonies in the Atlantic Islands (Madeira, the Azores and the Cape Verde archipelago). They edged their way down the

African coast and into the Indian Ocean, planting a network of fortified trading posts known as *feitorias* (factories). Lisbon became a thriving port, home not just to Portuguese merchants but to significant numbers of Genoese, Flemish and Jewish traders. Both Portugal and Castile sought and obtained Papal blessing for overseas conquests, in bulls which gave both monarchies the right to possess the New World and to 'reduce' its inhabitants to Christianity. In the Treaty of Tordesillas of 1494, sponsored by the papacy, the two monarchies agreed to fix the boundary between their putative empires 270 leagues further west than the Pope had originally done – as it would turn out, incorporating much of Brazil, as well as Africa, in Portugal's assumptive domain. Three years later, the Portuguese Vasco da Gama led the first European seaborne expedition to make landfall in Asia, at Calicut in India, returning with cargoes of spices and precious stones.[1]

The crown was eager for more, and Cabral's intended destination was India. But whether by accident or more probably because of prior knowledge gleaned by French and Portuguese seamen – a matter still debated by historians – Cabral's fleet swung far to the west, making landfall in Brazil.[2] On Thursday, 23 April it anchored near the mouth of a river, at a place the Portuguese would call Porto Seguro, today a popular beach resort. Cabral sent one of his most experienced pilots, Nicolau Coelho, in a boat to investigate the shore. Pedro Vaz de Caminha, the expedition's scribe, described in a letter to King Manoel what happened next:

> As he drew near, men began to arrive on the beach, in twos and threes, so that when the boat reached the mouth of the river, there were 18 or 20 men. They were brown, entirely naked, with nothing covering their private parts. In their hands they held bows, with their arrows. They all crowded round the boat; and Nicolau Coelho gestured to them to put down their bows. And they put them down.

They exchanged gifts, Coelho offering a red bonnet, the linen cap he was wearing and a black hat, and receiving a headdress of red and brown parrot feathers from one and from another a long string of small white beads. Over the next nine days Cabral's fleet landed at several points along the forested coast, and made further contact with its inhabitants. The Portuguese were impressed, and perturbed, by the natives' physical beauty, naked innocence and simplicity. Caminha described the men as having 'fine bodies and good faces'. Their lower lips were pierced with a white bone; their hair was straight, cut above the ears in pudding-basin style. Many painted their bodies in red and black vegetable dyes. They impressed him as being 'stronger and better fed than we are'. As for the women, Caminha found it hard to restrain his enthusiasm:

> three or four girls went among them, good and young and tender, with long very black hair hanging down their backs. And their privy parts were so high and tightly closed and so free from pubic hair that, even when we examined them very closely they did not become embarrassed.

Watched by the Indians, the Portuguese held mass on a beach. Cabral ordered two ship's carpenters to cut down a tree and erect a large cross to mark their visit to the land he named the island of Vera Cruz ('True Cross'), later changed by King Manoel to Santa Cruz ('Holy Cross'). When Cabral had his men kneel and kiss the cross, the Indians imitated them, arousing in Caminha the hope that 'if we could understand their language and they ours, they would immediately become Christians'. But it seems more likely that the Indians were fascinated by the carpenters' metal tools. For them, the Stone Age had abruptly ended, and their world would never be the same again.[3]

The natives encountered by Cabral's expedition were from the myriad Tupi-speaking tribes that predominated on much of the Brazilian coast. Like the other native peoples who lived in Brazil in 1500, they were hunter-gatherers. Over the preceding thousand years or so the Tupi had spread out from their original homeland around the rivers Paraguay and Paraná in the southern-central part of South America (their language is related to Guaraní, which is still widely spoken in Paraguay). Having traversed the vast *cerrado* (savannah), severely depleting its resources of big game as they went, they had penetrated the tropical forest that stretched for more than 2,000 kilometres along the South Atlantic coast and inland for up to 500 kilometres, clothing the mountain ranges that gird the shore. The Tupi lived in villages of between 300 and 2,000 people, in long communal huts, sometimes surrounded by palisades. They were superb hunters and fishermen: deer, rodents and other game, as well as fish, crabs and crayfish, made up an important part of their diet. They knew and gathered a hundred or so different forest fruits. Tupi women grew *mandioca* (cassava, a starchy root), tobacco, cotton, peanuts and a few other plants in plots laboriously cleared from the forest. This slash-and-burn farming quickly exhausted the nutrients in the fragile forest soils – a problem familiar in the Amazon today. Unlike the Incas of Peru, or the Aztecs and Maya, the Brazilian Indians lacked not just metal tools but domesticated animals. All this condemned them to a semi-nomadic existence, and meant they never developed any political organization beyond the village. Far from living in a pre-lapsarian state of grace, among the villages there was constant feuding and war. Its purpose may have been to expand hunting territory, or at least to reduce the pressure on supplies of game and fish. It was the custom of the Tupi to kill, dismember, roast and eat some of their prisoners, in an elaborate ritual. The Tupi called other Indian groups that spoke different languages from themselves the Tapuia, a term the Portuguese adopted.[4]

Finding no immediate evidence of any precious metals to detain them, after just eight days Cabral's expedition sailed off south-eastwards for India (both Cabral himself and Caminha would die in battle in Calicut). But the following year the crown dispatched a fleet of three caravels to explore the Brazilian coast. This expedition is remembered mainly for its contribution to nomenclature. Its chief pilot, Amerigo Vespucci, a Florentine chancer turned navigator, whose own first name would come to be applied to the continent, mistook the large bay of Guanabara (as it was called by the Tupi) for a river mouth; since the fleet entered it on New Year's Day he dubbed the place 'river of January' or Rio de Janeiro.[5] Secondly, this fleet loaded up with the first of what would be many consignments of timber from a tree whose wood exuded a red dye much in demand in Europe. The Portuguese had called similar trees they had found in Asia *pau brasil* (probably from *brasa*, their word for glowing coal). The name quickly stuck to the country, displacing Santa Cruz. The switch was appropriate: commodity production and mercantilism would vanquish faith and the conversion of the natives as the Portuguese crown's priority in Brazil. But it would be another two centuries before *brasileiro* became a term of nationality rather than a designation for a woodcutter.[6]

Indians, *bandeirantes* and Jesuits

As Portuguese colonialism unfolded slowly over the next three centuries, Brazil would evolve in significantly different ways from both the British and Spanish colonies in the Americas.[7] At first relations between Indians and Portuguese continued on the friendly course set at Porto Seguro. Cabral left behind in Brazil two of the *degredados* (convicts) who made up a significant part of the early expeditions. It was the practice of the Tupi to forge alliances with strangers by offering them young women as concubines; from Europeans they expected metal tools, mirrors and other trinkets in return. Once the tie of kinship was established, the stranger could require labour from the community. For much of the colonial period the vast majority of migrants from Portugal to Brazil were men. The Portuguese never showed any prudery in forming sexual relationships with, or marrying, indigenous women (and later African women). Miscegenation (interbreeding between races) would be even more widespread in Brazil than in Spain's American empire. According to

Sérgio Buarque de Holanda, this may have been a result of the 'absence of racial pride' among the Portuguese, a consequence of their own mixture of European and North African blood.[8] Indeed, Portuguese men were officially encouraged, by both government and church, to marry their indigenous concubines (and to a lesser extent African women slaves). The crown was conscious of Portugal's small population (only around 1.5 million in the 1530s). All this marked a clear contrast with New England, where the Puritan colonists migrated as complete families and lived apart from the indigenous population. Seen from the viewpoint of the women, these sexual relationships doubtless ranged from genuinely voluntary companionship to coercive, traumatic rape and abuse. The *degredados*, and other early Portuguese settlers, literally 'went native'. The best-known case involves João Ramalho, an early arrival in São Vicente (adjacent to the present-day port of Santos). His embrace of Tupi life scandalized royal officials. Manoel da Nóbrega, who was one of the first among many Jesuit priests dispatched to Brazil, complained of Ramalho:

> He has many women. He and his sons go with sisters and have children with them, both the father and the sons. They go to war together with the Indians, and they celebrate Indian feasts and they go about naked like the Indians.[9]

Nóbrega's disdain for Indian ways would be a portent. The Indians soon became the object of a struggle between the settlers and the Jesuits and other missionary orders.

The Portuguese crown, enriched by the Asian trade, at first gave little importance to Brazil beyond encouraging a few modest trading posts. Two things would change that: the growing presence of the French along the Brazilian coast, and the rise of sugar production. After ships from Normandy began to engage in the brazilwood trade, King João III responded by sending a group of colonists to set up a permanent outpost at São Vicente. He then briefly turned to private enterprise to settle Brazil: he divided up the coast into fifteen captaincies, and leased them to twelve *donatários*, who were given administrative powers and lands following a regime used previously in the Atlantic islands. But only two of the captaincies flourished, those of Pernambuco, in the north-east, and São Vicente. So in 1549 the king opted to turn Brazil into a crown colony, sending the first royal governor, who was instructed to build a capital at Salvador, in the captaincy of Bahia. Six years later, a 600-strong French expedition arrived in Guanabara Bay to set up a colony called *La France Antarctique*. This was a serious threat to Portugal's control of Brazil. But the Portuguese governor, Mem de Sá, proved more effective than the French at recruiting Indian allies. In 1565 he expelled the French, who were weakened by internal religious rivalries between Catholics, Huguenots (the majority) and Calvinists.[10] Mem de Sá, one of the more formidable Portuguese governors of Brazil, founded a town on the site of the French colony – and the future city of Rio de Janeiro was thus born.

Permanent settlement presaged a deterioration in relations between the Indians and Europeans, from kinship to enslavement. Not coincidentally this went hand in hand with a change in the image of the Indians in Europe. The first chronicles, illustrated with engravings often owing as much to fantasy as to fact, portrayed Brazil as a tropical paradise, an Eden inhabited by noble savages. (Indeed, the protagonist of Sir Thomas More's *Utopia*, published in 1516, is a Portuguese described as having been left behind in Brazil by Vespucci's expedition.) However, from the 1550s onwards, such chronicles tended to focus on the Indians' practice of cannibalism: the noble savage had become the barbarian eater of human flesh. Publishers took to illustrating early European accounts of Brazil, many semi-fictional, with salacious woodcuts portraying barbecues tended by naked crones who devour human limbs dripping with fat. Their cannibalism, and their nakedness, made it all too easy for the first missionaries to dismiss the Brazilian Indians as devils – especially after the first bishop appointed to the country was captured, killed and eaten. In Brazil the Portuguese Jesuits rarely showed the same respectful curiosity towards Indian culture that some of their Spanish colleagues would display to the Inca and Aztec empires. But the Tupi and the other Brazilian Indians had nothing to compare with the sophisticated civilizations and splendid cities of highland Mexico and Peru.[11]

In theory the Portuguese crown distinguished between peaceful Indians who converted to Christianity, and were to be treated as protected minors, and those who resisted conversion, against whom 'just wars' could be, and were, waged. The policy of the Jesuits and other missionary orders over the next two centuries was to 'descend' the Indians into *aldeias* (villages), where they were dressed in simple cotton shifts and obliged to live in nuclear families and to go through the motions of Christian worship. The Jesuits became very powerful in Brazil. Although they owned sugar plantations on the coast, they were especially active on the frontiers of Portuguese settlement, where autonomous Indians lasted longest, in São Paulo and the southern borderlands and in the north, in Maranhão, Pará and the Amazon. The Jesuit policy of gathering together the Indians had the tragic unintended consequence of speeding their exposure to European diseases (and to enslavement by planters).

One thing was common to the Portuguese, British and Spanish presence in the New World: the biological catastrophe visited upon the indigenous population through contact with Eurasian/African diseases to which they had no immunity. It was disease, rather than enslavement or maltreatment (although both were common), that was primarily responsible for the genocide of the Amerindians. In Brazil, the epidemics began with smallpox in 1562 and 1563, which killed some 30,000 Indians in Jesuit *aldeias* in Bahia alone. Measles, tuberculosis, typhoid and influenza also took a heavy toll.[12]

The settlers were rarely happy with the Jesuits' muscular paternalism towards the Indians. In search of forced labourers, they pressed the crown to allow them access to the Jesuits' Indians, sometimes raiding the *aldeias*. In fact Indian men were extremely resistant to plantation labour, not least because in their culture farming was women's work. The partial exception was the Guaraní people in the south west, who were good farmers and responded positively to the Jesuits. The fact that Portuguese kings repeatedly issued laws against Indian enslavement was a sign of how difficult these were to enforce.

It was in São Paulo that the Jesuit regime had its greatest successes and came under the most pressure. São Paulo de Piratinanga, as it was originally called, was founded in 1554 by Nóbrega and his fellow Jesuit, José de Anchieta, as an *aldeia*. Close to the river Tietê, on the rolling plateau above the steep 900-metre scarp that rises behind São Vicente, São Paulo was the first inland Portuguese settlement of any significance, but it would long be much poorer than the sugar-growing *captaincies* on the coast – too poor for the settlers there to afford African slaves. The children of Portuguese men and Indian women in São Paulo, known as *mamelucos*, adopted Indians tools, food and farming methods. Tupi was spoken at all levels of *paulista* society until well into the eighteenth century.

From the 1580s, mobile columns led by Portuguese and *mamelucos*, but made up mainly of Indians, began to strike out westwards along the Tietê and other tributaries of the Paraná river. These expeditions were known as *bandeiras* (because they carried a flag at the head of the column, an Indian custom). Their purpose was to find autonomous Indians to bring back as slaves, and to prospect for gold and silver. The *bandeiras* became a way of life. They involved both wanton cruelty and extraordinary courage and tenacity. Unlike the horse-borne Spanish conquistadors, the *bandeirantes* travelled like Indians, barefoot along rough forest trails, or by canoe. In an anonymous report a Jesuit noted with grudging admiration: 'They go without God, without food, naked as the savages, and subject to all the persecutions and miseries in the world.'[13] The most resolute of all the *bandeirantes* was Antonio Raposo Tavares. He first went forth and expelled Spanish Jesuit missions from Guairá (close to Brazil's present-day border with Paraguay). In 1649 he again set off from São Paulo, leading some 2,000 followers on an epic 12,000-kilometre journey that took his *bandeira* across the Chaco, where he sacked a Spanish Jesuit mission and massacred its inhabitants, past the foothills of the Andes and down the rivers Marmoré and Madeira to the Amazon. Many in the column died in Spanish and Indian attacks. Raposo Tavares arrived in Belém almost three years later with just fifty-eight followers. In the course of the century some *paulistas* migrated north to the *sertão*, the arid backlands of the north-east, setting up as cattle ranchers. One of them, Domingos Jorge Velho, became notorious for his brutality in putting down an Indian rebellion by the Potiguar tribe in Rio Grande do Norte and Ceará. He was himself of partly Indian blood; his scathing view of the Jesuits was that 'those who work to make [the Indians] angels before making them men do so in vain'.[14]

Though they were bitter rivals, the *bandeirantes* and the Jesuits were together responsible for pushing the boundaries of Brazil a long way further west and south-west than the limit fixed by the Treaty of Tordesillas. Whatever one thinks of their actions, the *bandeirantes* were crucial to the formation of Brazil. 'When the first *bandeira* enters the forest, the history of Portugal ends and the history of Brazil begins,' declared Cassiano Ricardo, a nationalist writer of the mid-twentieth century.[15] For that reason they are celebrated in São Paulo today: the state governor resides in the Bandeirantes Palace; one of the state's motorways is named after Raposo Tavares, and another after the *bandeirantes* in general. Just outside the city's Ibirapuera park, a huge, 50-metre-long granite monument by Victor Brecheret, a modernist sculptor, portrays a *bandeira* in heroic vein, dragging a canoe and their wounded, 'curving the vertical of Tordesillas' in the words of the inscription from a poem by Guilherme de Almeida.

But there were also Brazilian critics of the *bandeirantes*. One was Antonio Vieira, the most indefatigable and impressive of the Jesuits, who, while Portuguese-born, was raised in Brazil. In the course of a long and remarkable life – he died in 1697 aged eighty-nine – Vieira, a tall and imposing figure with a full beard, was by turns a missionary; a preacher, chief political adviser and propagandist for the Duke of Braganza, who as King João IV restored an independent Portuguese monarchy after six decades of Spanish rule; a prolific writer of sermons (he published some 200 of them), replete with baroque rhetorical fireworks; a campaigner on behalf of Luso-Brazilian Jews and against the Inquisition; and an adviser to the Papacy in Rome.[16] When a missionary in Pará during the second of his three long stints in Brazil (totalling more than half a century), he interviewed the survivors of Raposo Tavares's *bandeira* when they reached Belém, and took grim satisfaction in what he saw as the divine retribution meted out against the column in the form of 'plague, hunger and war'. Another critic was Capistrano de Abreu, a historian of colonial Brazil who died in 1927, who asked: 'Are such horrors justified by the consideration that, thanks to the *bandeirantes*, the devastated lands now belong to Brazil?'[17] But it is also hard not to see in the *bandeirantes* and their Indian foot soldiers a continuation of the Tupi tradition of incessant war against neighbouring tribes, which similarly featured the enslavement of prisoners. The Indians respected fearsome warriors such as Domingos Jorge Velho and, once defeated, were prepared to follow him. The *paulistas* used the Tupi as soldiers or bowmen, hunters, canoeists and porters, all activities to which they were accustomed and which they were prepared to perform.[18]

The other main theatre of missionary activity was in the north, in the Amazon. When the French established a fort at São Luis in Maranhão, the Portuguese were able to raise an Indian army to expel them in 1614. The Portuguese went on to found a fort further to the west, which became Belém, close to the mouth of the Amazon. The governor sent an expedition upriver, placing a boundary marker close to the modern border between Brazil, Peru and Colombia. The Jesuits and other missionaries mounted expeditions in which they 'descended' some 200,000 Amazonian Indians into fifty-four *aldeias*, where many of them died of disease or were seized by settlers. Appalled by their enslavement of Amazonian Indians, Vieira damned the settlers as living in mortal sin. He persuaded the king to issue a new law against Indian enslavement in 1655. His actions prompted a settler rebellion that led to his arrest and banishment to Portugal.

A century later, Sebastião José de Carvalho e Melo, better known as the Marquis of Pombal, permanently expelled the Jesuits from Brazil. Pombal, the chief minister of King José I throughout his reign (1750–77), was a modernizing despot who sought to apply the ideas of the Enlightenment to Portugal and its empire. His motives were partly economic. By the mid-eighteenth century Brazil had become the chief source of the Portuguese crown's revenue. In Pombal's view, the Jesuits had become a state within the state in Portugal's most important colony: the order owned sixteen sugar mills, vast cattle ranches and schools, as well as seminaries and churches in every large town. It also angered Pombal that the Spanish Jesuits had defied the Treaty of Madrid of 1750, under which the present-day states of Paraná, Santa Catarina and Rio Grande do Sul were awarded to Portugal in return for ceding its forward settlement on the river Plate at Colonia del Sacramento to Spain. The Jesuits' refusal to move seven Guaraní missions to the west bank of the Uruguay river, as the treaty required, was met by a joint Spanish and Portuguese army. In a matter of minutes 'European artillery and cavalry slaughtered 1,400 Christian Indians who were pathetically holding aloft their banners, crucifixes and holy images', as John Hemming, a historian of the Brazilian Indians, puts it. It would not be the last time in Brazil's history that the forces of modernization slaughtered stubborn and humble upholders of conservative tradition. But if Pombal's practice towards some of the Brazilian Indians was despotic, his theory was enlightened: he decreed an end to all racial discrimination and declared the Indians to be free citizens.[19]

Estimates of the population of Brazil in 1500, when Cabral dropped anchor at Porto Seguro, vary between 2.4 million and 5 million. By 1800, the Indian peoples numbered just 600,000, according to Hemming. By then, those of them living within the Portuguese pale of settlement were in a wretched condition, having lost their tribal traditions and pride.[20] Without the contribution of the Indians, Brazil would not have its present dimensions or some of its defining cultural characteristics. Brazilians benefited from the Indians' knowledge of the land and especially of its forests. A pidgin version of Tupi, called the *lingua geral* ('general tongue'), was spoken across much of Brazil for centuries. It survived in villages on the Rio Negro until 1940, even though the Tupi never lived in the Amazon.[21] Outside the north-east, where Indians were quickly wiped out, the Tupi provided many place names, and those of trees and animals, that are in use to this day. Brazilians' everyday diet includes Indian food such as *farofa*, the roasted, powdered cassava flour that is sprinkled on food and is ubiquitous on restaurant and household dining tables. And Brazilians' fondness for washing, for personal cleanliness and adornment, and their sexual candour are all legacies of the Tupi as well.

Sugar and slavery

Almost from the beginning of their permanent settlement of Brazil, the Portuguese began to plant sugar cane. Sugar had been brought from Asia to southern Europe by the Muslims after they swept westward in the seventh and eighth centuries. The Muslims set up slave-worked sugar plantations in Sicily, then southern Spain and finally in the Algarve in Portugal, while Christian Crusaders and Venetians did the same in Cyprus. As the Portuguese colonized the Atlantic islands, they took sugar with them, first to Madeira, then the Canaries (soon seized by Spain) and finally to São Tomé, in the Gulf of Guinea, settled in the 1490s. In São Tomé, which would later be used as an offshore *entrepôt* for the slave trade, they set up extensive sugar plantations worked by thousands of slaves from the African mainland – a model they found easy to copy in Brazil. As Europe's population recovered from the Black Death of the fourteenth century, and Europeans slowly became more prosperous, their demand for sugar to sweeten an unexciting diet grew.

Sugar cane proved to thrive in the north-east, in the red soil of the cleared forests on the coastal plains of the captaincies of Pernambuco and Bahia.

Between the 1570s and 1670s Brazil was the world's biggest exporter of sugar (a status it enjoys again today). Its production was an agro-industrial operation of a complexity almost unparalleled anywhere at the time, combining intensive farming with a manufacturing process in the *engenho* (mill). The harvesting and crushing of cane, and the refining of sugar, involved back-breaking manual labour in tropical heat. At first the labourers were Indians. But from the mid-sixteenth century onwards, the Portuguese began to import African slaves in ever greater numbers to work on the sugar plantations. Sugar and the import of African slaves would mark Brazil even more profoundly than the Tupi and the *bandeirantes*.

The Portuguese did not invent slavery.[22] It was practised on a large scale by the ancient Greeks and the Romans, within Africa and among the indigenous peoples of the Americas. But the Atlantic slave trade of the sixteenth to the nineteenth centuries marked the first time that slavery became an international commercial system, in which large sums of capital were deployed. Its origins are intimately associated with sugar cane.

Brazil had a crucial geographical advantage when it came to sugar: on the one hand, sailing times to Lisbon, at around fifty days, were shorter than between any other point in the Americas and Europe; and on the other hand slave ships crossing from Africa to Brazil took only around a month, half the time to the Caribbean or North America.[23] Sugar quickly became the dominant economic activity in Brazil, with some 350 *engenhos* (sugar mills) by 1630.[24] The industry required large amounts of land, labour, fuel and capital. Although the crown's initial land grants (known as *sesmarias*) were fairly modest, they soon came to involve vast tracts, though boundaries and titles were normally vague. Cattle ranches in the *sertão* were even bigger than the *engenhos*, which tended to buy in some of their cane from independent farmers or sharecroppers as a way of reducing their need for capital. Those farmers formed part of a small middle class, along with some artisans and merchants. The average *engenho* was worked by sixty to 100 slaves, a big one by up to 200. It also required up to a score of skilled artisans, technicians and managers. These were sometimes immigrants from Portugal or the Atlantic islands, and sometimes slaves or free blacks.[25] Fuel for the *engenhos'* furnaces was provided by timber from the Atlantic rainforest. Presiding over the whole enterprise, the *senhores de engenho*, as the planters were known, exercised socio-political power as well as enjoying economic wealth. Unlike the landowners of Spanish America, they tended to live on their estates, though many also kept a house in the nearby town. Some planters invested in cattle estates and in shipping, acting as merchants as well. According to Gilberto Freyre, a social theorist who chronicled north-eastern sugar society in a classic but controversial book, *Casa-grande*

& senzala (translated as 'The Masters and the Slaves'), they formed a 'patriarchal and polygamous white and whitish minority, dominating from on high in their "big houses" of stone and lime'. The plantation formed a whole economic, social and political system: of production, work, transport, religion; family and sexual life; as well as serving as 'a fortress, bank, cemetery, guest house, school and asylum for the elderly, widows and orphans'.[26]

It was a system built on forced labour. As Luis Vahia Montero, the governor general, declared in 1729, 'the most solid properties in Brazil are slaves, and a man's wealth is measured by having more or fewer . . . for there are lands enough, but only he who has slaves can be master of them'.[27] Thanks to their network of trading forts on the African coast, such as São Jorge da Mina (today known as Elmina, a small town on the coast of Ghana), the Portuguese were the prime movers in the Atlantic slave trade, though their early monopoly was breached during the sixteenth and seventeenth centuries by the Dutch, English and French. Portugal established alliances with African rulers and merchants, many of whom were willing and active participants in the trade. Alone among the Europeans during this period, the Portuguese penetrated beyond the African coast, establishing a permanent presence inland from Luanda, in what is today Angola and what was then at the southern edge of the kingdom of the Kongo. By the start of the seventeenth century Brazil's sugar plantations were sufficiently profitable to furnish the capital required for the large-scale import of Africans. At first the main source of slaves reaching Brazil was West Africa, from the Yoruba, Wolof, Magindo and Hausa peoples among others. Some were Muslims; many were herdsmen, of independent temperament. By the eighteenth century most of the slaves reaching Brazil were Bantu from the Kongo, Angola and Mozambique, who were of shorter stature, animist religion and mainly farmers. Slave owners considered the West Africans to be better for field labour, while the Angolans were better as artisans. Roughly a third of all slaves reaching Brazil were women and children.

Brazil would import more slaves from Africa and over a longer period than any other country. According to calculations by Herbert Klein, a total of some 12.5 million Africans were acquired and embarked for the Americas between 1500 and 1866. Of these, more than 1.5 million are thought to have died of overcrowding, disease or hunger while tightly packed on ships during the notorious 'middle passage' across the Atlantic. An unknown number died before being embarked. Of the 10.7 million who disembarked in the Americas, almost 4.9 million were imported by Brazil, compared with fewer than 400,000 by the United States. The numbers of slaves landed in Brazil tended to rise over time: fewer than 600,000 arrived before 1700; arrivals then rose from around 15,000 a year in the early eighteenth century to twice that level a hundred years later.[28]

Why was the demand for slaves in Brazil so great? The first reason is that their import was much cheaper than it was in the Caribbean or North America. Brazil was closer to Africa, so sailing times were shorter. Klein also points out that the slave traders' single biggest cost was the purchase of the trade goods demanded by African merchants who supplied the slaves. Brazil was the only American territory to export goods itself to Africa. Many Portuguese slave traders were based in Salvador and Rio de Janeiro rather than in Lisbon. From the seventeenth century, they began a two-way trade across the South Atlantic, exporting Bahian tobacco, rum, gunpowder and firearms in return for slaves.[29] (The Portuguese also took cassava and peanuts from Brazil to Africa, where they would become staple foods.)

The second reason that Brazil imported so many slaves was because for long periods it proved almost impossible to attract free labour. The European settlement of Brazil was a slow business, both because of Portugal's small population and because its American colony offered few initial attractions. Vicente de Salvador, a Franciscan friar in Bahia who published the first history of Brazil in 1627, complained that the Portuguese, rather than settle the interior, 'are content to claw the seaboard like crabs'.[30] But the obstacles to broader settlement and the development of Iberian-style peasant farming were formidable. They started with the barrier of the coastal mountains and the Atlantic forest. Traversing the scarp stretching along the coast from Rio de Janeiro southwards was extraordinarily arduous, as accounts by travellers make clear. Fernão Cardim, a Jesuit, wrote in 1585 of the 72-kilometre journey from São Vicente to São Paulo, which took him four days, that 'the road is so steep that at times we were clinging on by our hands' amid mud and torrents.[31] (The motorways that today snake their way up the same route are a spectacular succession of breathtaking viaducts, tight bends and tunnels.) After spending a day near Bahia in 1832 Charles Darwin exclaimed that 'delight . . . is a weak term to express the feelings of a naturalist who, for the first time, has wandered by himself in a Brazilian forest'.[32] But that was not the feeling of most settlers. Unlike the British Puritans in New England, the Portuguese in Brazil found a world entirely strange to them, and because of the difficulty of conquering the tropical environment 'his dominant sentiment would be terror', argued Vianna Moog in an influential work on the differences between Brazil and the United States.[33] Those fears were of wild animals, insects and tropical diseases, as well as of the dark, damp labyrinth of the forest itself.

The most daunting obstacles to farming were the insects, pests and plagues, especially the dreaded *saúva* or leaf-cutting ants, as Warren Dean, an environmental historian, has written.[34] Within two or three years of a field being cleared of forest, the ants would appear. Their burrows were visible as mounds on the surface, up to eight metres across and half a metre high; below they formed vast chambers, up to 25 metres deep and filled with a gooey fungus that grew from the leaf mulch in which the ants bred. *Saúva* were capable of stripping a cassava field in a night or two. No counter-measures proved effective until the advent of chemical pesticides in the mid-twentieth century. Gabriel Soares de Souza, a chronicler, lamented in 1587:

> if it weren't for [the ants], many parts of Spain [he was writing during the union of Iberian crowns] would be emptied in order to populate Brazil, for everything that one might want will grow in it, but this damnation prevents it, so that men lose their taste for planting any more than they must in order to survive on the land.[35]

Were it not for the *saúva*, as Dean argues, cleared fields would have had much more value, which in turn would have encouraged the Portuguese to use the plough and other agricultural technology. It would also have helped if land titles had been more precise and secure. As it was, the settlers practised precarious slash-and-burn farming, moving on as the soil quickly became exhausted. And they relied on Africans to provide muscle power.

The shortage of food and poor diet were constant themes in Brazil from the sixteenth century right up until the past few decades. That was especially so in the north-east, where sugar monoculture and unequal landholding were often blamed. They certainly played a role. But poor, acidic soils (away from the coastal strip) and a hostile environment, including regular and often catastrophic droughts in the *sertão* associated with the El Niño weather pattern, were probably more to blame. When Lula launched a programme called Fome Zero ('Zero Hunger') on taking office in 2003, he was tapping into a deep-rooted collective memory.

But if slavery became so prevalent in Brazil, it was also because the Portuguese crown did not intervene to prevent it. In 1684 the crown did set rules for the provisioning of slave ships and for the maximum number of slaves per tonne; death rates on board fell, but never below one in twenty. The Spanish crown, fortified by a strong tax base at home, rarely recoiled from attempting to impose its will in the Americas, and it was more vigorous in restricting Amerindian slavery. But the Portuguese monarchs depended on the revenues from trade with their colonial outposts – at first Asia and then, from the seventeenth century onwards, Brazil. They hesitated to alienate the planters and merchants who were the dominant force in Brazilian colonial society.[36] For all these reasons, while in New England migrants were setting up family farms in the seventeenth century, Brazil remained a realm of coastal plantations and a slave labour force. Slavery became self-reinforcing, and abolishing it would prove extraordinarily hard.

Children of God's fire

In the first half of the seventeenth century, a landowner recovered the cost of a slave within thirteen to sixteen months; even after 1700, when the price of sugar fell and the price of slaves rose, the corresponding figure was around thirty months. So there was little incentive to improve working conditions. These were punishing: estimates of the useful life of a slave in mining in the eighteenth century ranged from seven to twelve years. The *engenho*, with its blazing furnaces and boiling cauldrons, was often described as a kind of hell by priestly observers.

In one of several powerful sermons imparted to mixed congregations of both slaves and masters at the Church of the Black Brotherhood of the Rosary in Salvador in the 1680s, Antonio Vieira said to the slaves that 'there is no work nor way of life in the world more similar to the crucifixion and passion of Christ than yours'.[37] But slavery was only of the body, not the soul, he insisted. In return for serving their masters 'with a good will' the slaves would find the tables turned in the afterlife. 'You are the brothers of God's preparation and the children of God's fire,' he told the slaves. Suffering had 'brought you the light of the Faith and the knowledge of Christ's mysteries [which would prepare you for] eternal freedom'. But Vieira also chastised the masters for working their slaves too hard and preventing them from marrying, for 'putting your lust for gold and your damned and always ill-acquired possessions ahead of their salvation'. Many of the masters would not go to Heaven, he preached:

> What theology could justify the inhumanity and brutality of the exorbitant punishments with which these same slaves are mistreated? ... Tyrannized, one might say, or martyred; because they injure these miserable people, drop hot fat or wax on them, slash them, cudgel them, and inflict many other kinds of excesses upon them ... Well, be certain that you should not fear such injustice less than the slave themselves: I say rather you should fear them more, because God feels them much more ... Know full well that God hears these cries for help which you do not hear; and though they do not touch your heart, you should know that they make your own punishment certain.[38]

Vieira's preaching was aimed at eliminating the ill-treatment of slaves, not the institution of slavery itself. Like all the Jesuits, he applied a double standard: the Indians were barbarians whose saving grace was that their souls were open to God; but for Africans it was captivity that was the road to evangelization.[39] The Jesuits, after all, owned African slaves on their own sugar plantations.

Vieira's baroque theological broadsides have echoed down the ages not just because of their eloquence, but also because they address a matter of intense historical debate. Was slavery less oppressive, less inhumane, less bad in Brazil than in the Caribbean or the United States – or even worse? The view that Brazilian slavery was more benign than its counterparts elsewhere was given powerful voice by Gilberto Freyre, who portrayed the sugar society of the north-east as paternalist. In his view 'the shortage of white women created areas of fraternization between conquerors and the defeated, between *senhores* and slaves' in which 'antagonistic extremes were in large part countered by the social effects of miscegenation'.[40] He argued that in some ways the slaves were worse off when left to fend for themselves after abolition. Freyre, an anthropologist, writer and journalist of striking originality who grew up in Recife shortly after abolition, is widely acknowledged today as the first thinker to have given due weight to the contribution of blacks and of Africa to Brazilian society and culture. And he was the first to apply Freudian psycho-sexual notions to Brazil. But his excessively rosy vision of slavery is now seen as myth. 'How pleasant would it be if it was the whole truth, on the condition that we were all *senhores*', as Fernando Henrique Cardoso, a sociologist as well as a politician, wrote.[41]

There are few accounts by slaves or former slaves themselves. Foreign visitors tend to paint a mixed picture, in which some owners treated their slaves well, and others abominably. Typical was a report by H. Augustus Cowper, the British Consul in Recife. After a visit to several estates in Pernambuco in the 1840s he wrote to Lord Aberdeen, then the British foreign secretary, who was pushing Brazil hard to abolish the slave trade and slavery. Cowper was favourably impressed by Colonel Gaspar de Menezes Vasconcellos Drummond, a former army officer who had become the local police chief and who used English steam engines and water power at his *engenhos*. His 400 slaves were protected by a code of conduct which barred overseers from punishing them; they worked from daybreak till 8.00 p.m. and were allowed not to work when ill; their rations of dried beef and *farinha* (manioc flour) were of similar quantity to those of a soldier of the line; and the colonel himself played affectionately with the slave children. On the other hand, his neighbour Colonel Francisco de Rego Barros was said to have worked his slaves twenty hours a day, 'to be in the constant habit of maiming them', and to have killed more than twenty of them. Cowper observed that 'the most barbarous crimes enjoy absolute legal impunity' and that some masters punished male slaves with castration. Less drastic, but still barbaric, forms of corporal punishment were common, such as the lash. The *engenhos* and some towns had a *pelourinho* (pillory), where the punishment of a slave was a public demonstration intended to inspire obedience in others. (The *pelourinho* in Salvador today gives its name to a restored colonial neighbourhood of steep cobbled street that is the centre of both the city's cultural life and its tourism.)[42]

Slave rebellions of various kinds were common. These ranged from individual acts of disobedience to occasional full-scale revolts. Afro-Brazilians had their own leaders, sometimes unknown to their masters; they were often those who had been kings or chiefs back home. Abusive masters ran the risk of being killed by their slaves (the knowledge of which may have served to limit the worst abuse). Escape was frequent. The Brazilian countryside was dotted with *quilombos* and *mocambos*, as settlements of escaped slaves were called. These could be just a few huts, often outside towns, but some were villages. Their inhabitants lived from farming, fishing and preying upon white society, sometimes amalgamating with unpacified Indian villages. In the seventeenth century a network of fortified *quilombo* villages, known as the Kingdom of Palmares and containing perhaps 10,000 people, came into being in what is today Alagaos state. Palmares survived for decades, partly because the Portuguese authorities were distracted by war against the Dutch. It resisted several military expeditions, with considerable losses on both sides. In 1678 the governor of Pernambuco entered into a peace treaty with the kingdom. But in 1695 the crown called upon Domingos Jorge Velho, the *paulista* backwoodsman and scourge of the Potiguar Indians, who finally defeated Palmares. Its last leader, Zumbi, was captured and beheaded on 20 November – a date that in recent years has come to be celebrated by some black Brazilians and by the government as Black Consciousness Day. Many *quilombos* still survive today across the country, either as place names or as communities of descendants of escaped slaves. The Lula government began to give them rights over the land they once claimed to have occupied, sparking a rash of property disputes.

But hard though life was for the slaves, there is no reason to believe that it was any worse in Brazil than in the Caribbean or the American Confederacy, as academics in the United States have taken to arguing. Their contention is based firstly on the fact that the slave population within the United States reproduced itself faster than that in Brazil. Because of the sexual imbalance among the Africans who were sent to Brazil, with two men for every woman, the slave population did not reproduce itself; instead, it was constantly replenished by new arrivals. But in fact that was generally true elsewhere in the Americas until the nineteenth century. If it remained the case in Brazil, it was largely because of the large number of free blacks combined with the prevalence of tropical diseases.[43] The second argument is that slaves in the Confederacy benefited from living in a more developed society: according to Robert Conrad, in Brazil in 1872 less than one in 1,000 slaves was registered as literate, while in 1860 'probably' one of every twenty slaves in the United States could read and write.[44] Certainly the fact that slavery was so widespread in Brazil was closely associated with the country's shameful neglect of education. And Protestantism, with its emphasis on Bible-reading, may have engendered wider literacy than Brazilian Catholicism. But in other ways these arguments are reductive: the life expectancy of whites was similarly lower in Brazil than in the United States because the physical conditions of life were harder for everyone. The life expectancy of a male slave born in the United States in 1859 was 35.5 years; in Brazil, the equivalent figure for a slave was around twenty years, but for the population as a whole it was only 27.4 years.[45]

What is true beyond dispute is that slavery as an institution had some strikingly different – and more flexible – characteristics in Brazil than in the United States. Many artisan jobs, and some supervisory ones, were filled by slaves, who also made up part of the crew on Brazilian slave ships. Manumission – the freeing of slaves – was much more common even than in Spanish America, and dramatically more so than in the British or French colonies. That meant that Brazil quickly developed a large population of free blacks. Among the black population, those who were free tended to have been born in Brazil rather than Africa, were more likely to be women than men and be of relatively lighter skin. The first official counts to report racial distinctions, taken shortly after the Portuguese court arrived in Rio de Janeiro in 1808, found that of a total population of slightly more than 2 million people, 28 per cent were whites, 38 per cent were slaves, but 28 per cent were free blacks or *mulatos* (some 6 per cent were Indians, almost certainly an underestimate). This contrasts strongly with the French and British Caribbean, where free blacks made up no more than 8 per cent of the population in the late eighteenth century.[46]

The second big difference was the prevalence in Brazil of miscegenation and racial mixing. The numbers of *mulatos* steadily grew. A consequence of these differences was that socio-economic status did not rigidly correspond to skin colour. The place of *mulatos* in the social scale varied mainly according to their occupations. If a *mulato* became a priest or was appointed as a magistrate, 'his papers might state him to be white, even if that is not visibly so', according to Henry Koster, a Briton who lived in Pernambuco from 1809 to

1820 as a slave-owning landowner. Koster asked one of his slaves whether a certain *capitão-mor* (militia captain) was not a *mulato* and received the answer: 'he was, but is not now . . . Can a *capitão-mor* be a *mulato*?'[47] João Antonio Andreoni, an Italian Jesuit who in 1711 published an account of the colony's economy, wrote that 'we find confirmed the proverb which states that Brazil is hell for blacks, purgatory for whites, and paradise for *mulatos* of both sexes'.[48] (Their alleged good fortune was attributed to what nowadays might be called their erotic capital.)

Some Brazilian *mulatos* and free blacks themselves owned slaves. Machado de Assis, Brazil's greatest novelist, was a *mulato*. So was André Rebouças, an economist and engineer who built new docks in Rio in the nineteenth century and was a leading campaigner for the abolition of slavery. He was a confidant of the emperor, Dom Pedro II, and a frequent visitor to the royal palace in Rio de Janeiro. But when he visited New York in 1873 he was refused a hotel room on grounds of colour. The Brazilian consul managed to get him accepted 'in a third-class hotel . . . under the condition that I eat in my room and never in the restaurant', Rebouças wrote. 'Colour prejudice prevented me from attending the performance in the Grand Opera House.'[49] And this was in New York after the Civil War, not the south.

While slavery in Brazil rarely gave rise to racial segregation, it did involve racial prejudice. But the differences from the United States or South Africa have big implications for the way in which racial issues have been addressed – and should be addressed – by government and society (see chapter nine). And while Catholicism may have militated against literacy, it was more accommodating of religious syncretism (the mixing of elements from different religions). African deities were enthusiastically worshipped in the *senzala*, sometimes masquerading as Catholic saints. This syncretism is a distinctive aspect of Brazilian culture to this day. It was celebrated in the stories of Jorge Amado, a popular Bahian novelist. Every year when tens of thousands of *cariocas* (inhabitants of Rio de Janeiro) swarm to Copacabana beach on New Year's Eve, they dress in white and throw flowers into the Atlantic as offerings to Yemanjá, the Yoruba goddess of water, who happily doubles as Our Lady of the Seafarers for Catholics. In other ways, too, African culture blended into the mainstream of Brazilian culture, in food, music, dance and language, for example.

Things might have turned out very differently had Brazil ended up in the hands of the French, or of Dutch Puritans, as it might so easily have done. The wealth of the sugar industry meant that Brazil became a theatre in Europe's Thirty Years War (1618–48), and Portugal's control over its vast American colony faced its most serious challenge. After the young Portuguese king

Sebastião perished without an heir in 1578 while attempting to capture northern Morocco, the throne passed to his uncle, Philip II of Spain. Portugal and its colonies retained their own system of governance. But the Protestant Dutch, engaged in a long struggle for independence against the Spanish Habsburgs, saw the Portuguese empire as a target of opportunity in their own expansion as a maritime power. The Dutch West India Company dispatched two huge military expeditions against Brazil, the first briefly capturing Salvador, and the second, of sixty-seven ships and 7,000 men, seizing Pernambuco in 1630. The Dutch also occupied São Jorge da Mina, São Tomé and Luanda, cutting Brazil off from its supply of slaves. Much of the north-east corner of Brazil would remain a Dutch colony for a quarter of a century. It was in some ways an enlightened enterprise. Prince Johan Maurits of Nassau, sent out in 1637 to lead the colony, built a planned, modern town and port at Recife (called Mauritstaad by the Dutch), down the hill from Olinda, the Portuguese provincial capital, with its jumble of lanes and convents. Mauritstaad's paved streets, four-storey houses, bridges and a dike to channel the Caparibe river, resembled a mini-Amsterdam in the tropics. Its infrastructure would not be matched by other Brazilian cities for at least a century and a half.[50] The phrase 'the work of a Dutchman' is still used in Pernambuco to denote something of quality.

Nassau brought with him a group of artists and scientists. Brazilians owe to him the first naturalistic visual record of their country, albeit a Eurocentric one. Frans Post, schooled in the great tradition of Dutch landscape painting, produced scores of canvases as a result of his sojourn in the new colony. Many feature detailed portrayals of the flora and fauna of Pernambuco. In Post's rendering, the sugar plantations of the north-east are a bucolic arcadia, peopled by black and Indian workers going about their business with the calm industry of Dutch peasants. Albert Eckhout was assigned to document the people: he painted large, statuesque figures of Indians and blacks that are of infinitely greater ethnographic value than the early woodcuts. However, some of the Indians are portrayed with the accoutrements of cannibalism even though this had largely died out in the area of European control.[51]

The Portuguese Brazilians fought back against the Dutch, who eventually withdrew in 1654, unable to match on land their domination of the sea. The Dutch assault on its empire prompted a nationalist reaction in Portugal, which led eventually to the restoration of its independence from Spain under a new royal house, the Braganzas. Brazilian historians have likewise seen in the guerrilla resistance to the Dutch an early assertion of a national spirit. The Portuguese enlisted hundreds of black and Indian soldiers, under their own commanders, to fight a guerrilla campaign against the Dutch. Much of the military effort was financed and organized locally. The recapture of Luanda and São Tomé by an expedition organized from Rio de Janeiro by Salvador de Sá, the governor general and grandson of Mem de Sá, showed a degree of colonial initiative that would have been almost unthinkable in Spanish America. But the decisive factor in Brazil remaining in Portuguese hands was that the war in Pernambuco imposed heavy economic losses on the Dutch West India Company, and its shareholders eventually forced an end to the venture.[52] Similarly, the rebellion of the planters against the Dutch was motivated more by a desire to escape their debts to the West India Company than by Luso-Brazilian patriotism.[53] The Braganzas, for their part, consolidated their hold on power and on Brazil by reinforcing Portugal's longstanding ties with Britain. This renewed alliance was sealed by the marriage of Catherine of Braganza to Charles II. If Portugal's control of Brazil was not seriously challenged for the next century and a half, this was in large part because it was implicitly guaranteed by the Royal Navy (in return for tariff and commercial concessions for British traders in Portugal).

It took Pernambuco a century to recover from the war against the Dutch, and the centre of Brazilian sugar production shifted to Bahia. At the instigation of Father Vieira, ever the man of affairs as well as the theologian, Portugal organized a trading company and convoy system for its sugar fleets. Sugar would remain the largest single industry and export in Brazil. But its dominance of the world market was over, eclipsed by new competitors in the Caribbean. The Dutch, who had become important participants in the slave trade, would take the technology of sugar production to their colonies in Suriname and the Antilles. Sugar was planted by the French in Saint-Domingue (Haiti) and the British in Barbados and Jamaica, where plantations were larger and more efficient than those in Bahia and Pernambuco. In the last third of the seventeenth century Brazil's economy stagnated.

The gold rush

Thrusting above the gentle green hills north of Lisbon, the giant monastery-palace of Mafra can be seen from the Oporto motorway, some 12 kilometres away. Its three storeys of severe baroque stonework cover an area of almost 4 hectares, and contain more than a thousand rooms. Its façade is 232 metres long; the sides over 200 metres; the library is 85 metres in length, containing 36,000 books from the sixteenth and eighteenth centuries. It is a cold and gloomy place. Its massive bulk is its purpose: seemingly what mattered was that it was even bigger than El Escorial, its no less gloomy inspiration and equivalent in Spain, built by Philip II, the usurper of the Portuguese throne. Building

Mafra occupied much of the long reign of João V (1706–50). It was the most grandiose manifestation of the sudden wealth that turned the Braganzas into the richest family in Europe.

The source of those riches lay deep in the interior of Brazil. In the 1680s the crown had appealed to the São Paulo *bandeirantes* to redouble their efforts to find the deposits of gold and diamonds that rumour had long held to exist. In the following decade, the *paulistas* were at last successful, finding gold in the alluvial streams that score the flanks of the rugged mountains of what would quickly be called Minas Gerais ('general mines'). Discoveries of diamonds and emeralds in the area soon followed, along with gold strikes in southern Bahia, at Cuiabá in Mato Grosso and in Goiás. The news triggered a gold rush, as people from all over Brazil and beyond flooded into the mining regions. For the first time, large numbers of Portuguese migrated to Brazil: some 600,000 arrived from the mainland and the Atlantic islands in the first sixty years of the eighteenth century. Miners used slaves to work the new discoveries. Townships grew up almost overnight. The Portuguese authorities struggled to keep control: they could not prevent violent clashes between the *paulistas* and later arrivals over mining rights, and the king was obliged to allow local officials more autonomy. The crown's main effort, never wholly successful, was to oversee and tax gold production. The officially registered output of gold increased tenfold in the first half of the eighteenth century, peaking at almost 3 tonnes a year in the early 1750s, before declining to barely more than a third of that level by the end of the century. Unofficial output may have been almost as large: the *garimpeiro*, or wildcat miner, has been part of Brazilian life – and environmental degradation – ever since. Even so, the crown extracted huge revenues from 'the royal fifth' (of output), from monopoly contracts for supplies and from miscellaneous taxes and duties. This revenue not only built Mafra but paid for the reconstruction of Lisbon after the catastrophic earthquake and tsunami of 1755. But the gold rush also transformed Brazil.[54]

At last large numbers of Portuguese began to settle in the interior, not just in the mining towns themselves but also because of the need to provide them with food and all manner of other supplies. Mining prompted a big expansion in cattle-raising, both in the *sertão* and in the southern grasslands. The *sertão* became a vast cattle range. Its people, known as *caboclos* or *pardos*, were of mixed Indian, African and white blood. They dressed in leather to protect themselves against the thorn scrub. The window and door flaps of their huts were similarly of leather, like those of Scottish peasants in the sixteenth century. Mule trains began to knit disparate areas of Brazil together, albeit with painstaking slowness: the journey from the gold towns of Minas to the coast at Santos or Paraty, today a pretty tourist town with a literary festival but then an important gold port, took around a month. Getting from São Paulo to Cuiabá, largely by canoe, took from five to seven months. The main towns began to grow: by the mid-1770s, Salvador's population was over 36,000, bigger than any city in British North America except Philadelphia (40,000) while Recife, the fourth city, may have been bigger than Boston.[55] In 1763 the crown recognized the southward shift in Brazil's economic centre of gravity by designating Rio de Janeiro as the capital in place of Salvador.

Unlike the patriarchal society of the *engenhos* in the north-east, mining areas were social melting pots. Most gold mining was carried out by blacks. At first this took the form of panning, at which men from the Gold Coast of West Africa were skilled and experienced. Later, more elaborate techniques, including dredging and sluicing, were used. The work involved standing for many hours knee-deep in the cold waters of the highland rivers. Miners found it expedient to free many of their slaves, either because of the high cost of feeding them, or to motivate them to work harder. In addition, many were able to buy their freedom through freelance gold panning. The governor of Minas Gerais wrote that:

The freedom which the blacks of this captaincy have [is] unlike that in other parts of America, certainly it is not true slavery the manner in which they live today as it more appropriately could be called licentious liberty.[56]

By the first decade of the nineteenth century free blacks outnumbered slaves in Minas Gerais and had become the biggest single group in the captaincy's population. While most blacks remained poor, a middle class of artisans and farmers arose.

Minas Gerais also experienced an extraordinary cultural flowering. The gold rush financed an orgy of baroque church-building in Brazil as well as in Portugal. The Franciscan church in Salvador, with its shimmering gold interior, is only the most lavish example. In Minas Gerais, and in Pernambuco, a distinctly Brazilian architectural style emerged. Villa Rica (known today as Ouro Preto), Mariana, Congonhas and the other mining towns are graced by a stunning collection of churches, many with rococo tubular towers, and imposing public buildings, including theatres where orchestras played and dramas were staged during their golden age. Xica da Silva, a *mulata* who married a diamond dealer and whose life story of successful social climbing has on several occasions been turned into a television soap opera, built a theatre at her country villa near the town of Arraial do Tijuco (now called Diamantina). It was symptomatic that the outstanding figure of *mineiro* baroque should have been another *mulato*, Antonio Francisco Lisboa, better known as Aleijadinho ('the little cripple'), whose carved wooden statues decorate the interior of many of the churches. The son of a Portuguese carpenter and an African slave woman, Aleijadinho became ill in his forties, losing his hands and feet (he probably suffered from syringomyelia or Lazarus's disease). He carried on working, tying boards to the stumps, and managed to oversee the completion of his greatest work, the Stations of the Cross, in which twelve larger than life-size statues of the apostles ascend the hill to the church in Congonhas. For want of marble, he worked in local soapstone. This emerging Brazilian cultural identity would be paralleled by incipient stirrings of political nationalism, again centred on Minas Gerais.

As gold production gradually declined after the 1750s, Pombal sought to increase the colony's other exports by establishing monopoly trading companies. He promoted new crops (such as cotton in Maranhão, and rice and coffee in Maranhão and Pará) and the planting of sugar and tobacco in the south. Except for the monopoly companies, these policies were broadly maintained by Rodrigo Souza de Coutinho, a disciple of Adam Smith who was the most able minister in the subsequent governments. By the turn of the century, they helped to bring about an economic revival. In addition, the sugar industry benefited from the withdrawal from the market of its chief rival, as a bloody slave rebellion transformed Saint-Domingue from France's richest colony into independent but devastated Haiti. Brazil's sugar exports doubled between 1790 and 1807.[57]

But before then, an official effort to collect alleged arrears in payment of the royal fifth by imposing a poll tax in Minas Gerais had sparked a conspiracy against the Portuguese authorities in 1788–9. By then the mining region was suffering economic decline: the population of Ouro Preto fell from around 20,000 in 1740 to 7,000 sixty years later. Influenced by the example of the newly independent United States, the conspirators planned to proclaim a constitutional republic in Minas Gerais, declare a moratorium on debts to the crown, and free the slaves with no compensation for their masters. The *Inconfidência mineira*, as it was called, involved a score of the richest, most cultured and powerful men in Minas Gerais, including crown judges, clerics, *fazendeiros*, merchants, priests and regular army officers. But the plot was discovered. Five of the conspirators were banished to Angola; another, Joaquim José da Silva Xavier, a dragoon officer and dentist known as Tiradentes ('the toothpuller'), was selected as a scapegoat and hanged. In a country with remarkably few official heroes, he eventually was adopted as one, celebrated in street names and by a public holiday on 21 April, the day of his execution. Salvador saw a more radical conspiracy in 1798, whose aim was an armed uprising of *mulatos*, free blacks and slaves. But it too was crushed. In the end, independence would come to Brazil in a unique manner – one that would not involve rebellion.[58]

Patriarchal society, patrimonial state

Portuguese colonialism was in some ways a looser and more entrepreneurial affair than its Spanish counterpart, although the crown did its utmost to tighten its control after the discovery of gold and especially when Pombal was in office. The difference was symbolized by the rigid grid pattern of the planned colonial towns of Spanish America, normally sited in valleys, compared with the anarchic sprawl of their Portuguese counterparts, often on hilltops like medieval villages in the Mediterranean countries. Rather than grand palaces or barracks, the most important buildings left by the colonial period are churches and convents.[59] Colonial Brazil had few institutions. Formal political power lay with the Portuguese governors. Then there were the municipal councils and the judges. The army rarely amounted to more than a few locally raised regiments, backed up by a militia. More influential was the Catholic Church. Blacks had their own churches, lay institutions and militia regiments. Portugal was even less effective than Spain in enforcing its proclaimed monopoly over trade with its American colonies; British merchants, directly or indirectly, did much business with Brazil.

Pombal required all provincial governors to report directly to Lisbon. In 1774 he integrated Grão Pará e Maranhão, a separate state in the north since 1621, into an enlarged Estado do Brasil, or state of Brazil, under a single governor in Rio (though well into the nineteenth century outsiders often referred to the country as 'the Brazils' in the plural). He strengthened the authority of crown judges at the expense of municipal councils. But this fell some way short of the ruthless recentralization of power imposed in Spanish America by the Bourbon reforms of the same period. The Bourbons evicted *criollos* (American-born whites) from bureaucratic office in Spain's colonies, sending out a cohort of professional administrators from Madrid charged with levying new taxes. By contrast, in Brazil most high colonial offices continued to be held by men (and they were men) born in the colony, rather than in Portugal, removing a big potential source of grievance. As Leslie Bethell, a British historian of Brazil, notes, Brazilians had much less cause for dissatisfaction than had the creoles of the Spanish American colonies with Spain: 'much more than Spain, Portugal governed through the local dominant class, which was directly involved in at least the implementation if not the formulation of policy'.[60]

Portuguese Brazil was more tolerant than Spanish America. When Ferdinand and Isabella celebrated the fall of Muslim Granada and the completion of the *reconquista* by expelling the Jews and *marranos* (Jews who had adopted Christianity, or feigned to do so) from Spain, King João III offered them asylum. Some 80,000 may have crossed the border to Portugal. However, they were soon required to convert. Many 'New Christians', as they were called, found their way to Portugal's Asian colonies and to Brazil, where they were prominent among the merchants in Salvador, Recife and Rio de Janeiro (as they were in the Low Countries, where they dominated the trade in Brazilian sugar). They were intermittently persecuted by the Portuguese branch of the Inquisition. Unlike in Spanish America, the Inquisition was never formally constituted in Brazil. New Christian merchants were on occasion sent to Lisbon to face charges, often as part of tussles for local power with landowners. But the Inquisition's sporadic efforts in Brazil, at their most intense during the period of Spanish rule of Portugal, came to be targeted mainly against sexual behaviour, such as sodomy, fornication and bigamy.[61]

Nevertheless, the Portuguese crown did not want Brazilians to have too many ideas of their own. The expulsion of the Jesuits left an educational vacuum. While Santo Domingo, Lima and Mexico all possessed universities by 1551, colonial Brazil had none, though a few Brazilians studied at Coímbra in Portugal. Requests for university status by the Jesuit college in Salvador were rejected. One of the proposals of the *inconfidentes* in Minas was to establish a university in Vila Rica. Brazil did not even have a printing press; one was briefly set up in Rio in 1747 but quickly shut down by royal order.

By the beginning of the nineteenth century, Brazil was home to between 2 and 3 million people.[62] A third or more were slaves; a further 30 per cent were *mulatos* or free blacks. It was already richer than Portugal, whose population was only slightly bigger, at somewhat over 3 million. Its boundaries had been established by the Treaty of Madrid, fairly close to where they lie today.* The gold rush and the associated dynamism of the internal economy meant that Brazilians were no longer just clustered on the coast, as they had been a century earlier. Brazil had become home to a distinct people, forged from the blending of African, Indian and Portuguese blood and culture. Some have seen in this the main achievement of the colonial period in Brazil.[63] Racial mixing would eventually be recognized as one of Brazil's great assets. Millions of migrants would later arrive as indentured or free labourers or to escape persecution – Italians, Germans, Eastern

---

* The treaty was soon repudiated, and Brazil would fight intermittent wars on its southern and south-western borders for more than a century, but the country's broad outline did not change much after 1750.

Europeans, Japanese, Syrians, Lebanese and Koreans – and they would give a distinctive character to parts of Brazil. But they inserted themselves into a cultural template, a Brazilianness laid down before they arrived. In many ways Brazil would become a more complete melting pot than the United States. Until very recently, there were no 'hyphenated Brazilians'. But nowadays there are powerful currents of opinion in universities and government that seek to resurrect the separate identities of Afro-Brazilians and Indians, on the grounds that the dominant national ideology sought to 'whiten' Brazil (see chapter nine). Certainly, the country's racial mixture is blacker, more *mulato*, than that of most of Spanish-speaking America (though not Cuba).

Slavery was perhaps colonial Brazil's most powerful institution, and that affected the whole society and the character of the masters, too. One of the many negative consequences was a disdain for manual work among Portuguese Brazilians, at least until the arrival of other European migrants in the nineteenth century. As Moog put it, Brazilian society as it emerged in the colonial period was characterized by the short-term pursuit of easy, extractivist wealth, rather than the rewards of patient labour; it was symbolized by the *bandeirante* rather than the pioneer of New England.[64] While not segregated by race, Brazil was highly stratified – an 'American Russia', as Freyre once called it, with slavery occupying an equivalent role to Tsarist serfdom.[65] Landholding was highly unequal and there was no free market in labour, though there was an intermediate stratum of traders, financiers, artisans and farmers with small and medium holdings. All but a small minority of Brazilians were illiterate and without any education.

There is much argument among scholars of Brazilian history as to the relative power of the socio-economic elite – the planters and the merchants, the miners, the churchmen and the lawyers – and the state. For Sérgio Buarque, who was influenced by the ideas of Max Weber, the great German sociologist, the colonial state was subverted from within by a rural, patriarchal society, in which ties of kinship, family solidarity and personal loyalties predominated. Raymundo Faoro, writing in the 1950s, applied Weber's concept of patrimonial domination to the Brazilian state. In this view, the monarchy's early centralization of power and the absence of a feudal aristocracy in Portugal allowed the crown to act as if Brazil was its personal patrimony. The crown's power was exercised through a bureaucratic machine, which co-opted merchants and landowners through the grant of posts, privileges and monopolies. Either way, private interest trumped the public good and the rule of law.[66] No wonder that Brazil would find economic development, political democracy and social justice a long and difficult business, as this distinct people turned to the task of forging a nation-state.

CHAPTER FOUR

From Monarchy to Coffee Republic

The landing stage at Praça XV, in the historic heart of Rio de Janeiro, is the terminal for the frequent ferries from Niteroi, across Guanabara Bay. Commuters, shoppers and sightseers are disgorged on to a concrete esplanade that covers a stretch of urban motorway, built on land reclaimed from the bay. Two centuries ago, passengers would have disembarked at the open square, facing what was then the modest palace of the governors of Brazil. It was here in March 1808 that the Portuguese royal family arrived to set up court in their largest possession, a move from metropolis to colony that has no parallel in European history.

Like Cabral three centuries before, the royal family had taken ship at the anchorage at Belém. But in contrast to Cabral's bold armada, their ramshackle fleet was engaged in ignominious flight. Portugal had found itself ineluctably dragged into the worldwide conflict unleashed by Napoleon Bonaparte. Lisbon was the conduit for British trade with Brazil and Iberia. It was a crucial chink in Napoleon's Continental System, his response to the British naval blockade of France and its vassals. Napoleon gave the Portuguese crown an ultimatum: close its ports to Britain and expel British merchants, or face invasion. The prince regent, who would become king as João VI in 1816, at first prevaricated. But as Marshal Junot crossed the border with a French army, the prince yielded to pressure from his own advisers, as well as from the British, and agreed to carry out a longstanding contingency plan, first dreamed up by Antonio Vieira: to save the monarchy, the court should move to Brazil. During three chaotic days, countless crateloads of royal treasures, state papers and the royal library were loaded at Belém. Along with João and his mother, the mad Queen María, more than 10,000 courtiers, nobles, priests, functionaries and hangers-on crowded on to the fleet, made up of three dozen ships of varying size and seaworthiness. Escorted by a British naval squadron, they crept out into the Atlantic only hours before Junot's exhausted troops arrived in Lisbon. After an uncomfortable voyage, in which water and food were scarce and lice and seasickness abundant, the ships carrying the royal party anchored at Salvador on 22 January 1808, before sailing on to Rio de Janeiro.[1]

Brazil immediately became the centre of the Portuguese empire. This would lead in short order to national independence, but in unusual circumstances. When João and his vast entourage arrived in Rio de Janeiro, what had been a busy but isolated colonial port of some 60,000 people was swiftly transformed into an imperial capital. João's advisers, led by Rodrigo Sousa Coutinho, who resumed the role of chief minister, set to work founding a state in Brazil. As Kenneth Maxwell, a British historian, points out, it was the crown which instituted all the country's founding institutions, 'usually the task of a post-colonial government'. It established a centralized bureaucracy; higher courts of law; a National Library; a school of medicine and law; a national press; a national bank and stock exchange; and a military academy. Dom João also set up a botanical garden in Rio de Janeiro (whose magnificent royal palms still enchant visitors today) and distributed new varieties of sugar, coffee and cotton to planters.[2] Once Napoleon had been defeated, João invited a French artistic mission to come to Brazil. It set up Rio de Janeiro's school of fine arts and introduced neo-classical architecture, which displaced the baroque in public buildings. This was the start of a persistent strand of French intellectual influence over a segment of Brazil's political and cultural elite. (Later in the nineteenth century, French scientists would found a school of mining in Ouro Preto, while in the 1930s a French mission including Fernand Braudel, the historian, and Claude Lévi-Strauss, the anthropologist, would help to found the University of São Paulo.) The monarchy also promoted visits by natural scientists from other European countries. Earlier royal decrees discouraging manufacturing in Brazil were revoked. João took other steps that weakened the ties with Portugal. His first act on arrival in Salvador was to open Brazil's ports to shipping from other countries – the pay-off demanded by Britain for Royal Navy protection. Tariffs on British imports were lowered to a maximum of 15 per cent.

When peace returned to Europe in 1815, João opted to stay in Brazil, which he decreed to be a kingdom of equal status to Portugal. It was the home country, devastated by war and foreign military occupation, which began to feel like the ignored colony. In 1820 a Liberal rising in Oporto installed a constituent assembly, purportedly for the empire as a whole, and demanded the return of the king. He complied, leaving his eldest son, Pedro, in charge in Brazil. The Portuguese Liberals then tried to turn the clock back, ordering the dismantling of the government in Rio and the return of Pedro too. That was too much for the merchants and planters of Rio de Janeiro, as Pedro's chief adviser, José Bonifácio de Andrada e Silva, realized. An Enlightenment scientist who had spent many years serving the crown in Portugal, José Bonifácio is widely regarded as the architect of Brazilian independence. On 9 January 1822 Pedro duly declared: 'Tell the people that I am staying.' This declaration of defiance became known as the *Dia do Fico* ('Day of the Staying'). On 7 September, while at the Ipiranga river near São Paulo, he received a letter from the Cortes reiterating the order to return. He is said to have crushed it under his heel, drawn his sword, and proclaimed: 'Independence or death! We have separated from Portugal!' The 'Cry of Ipiranga' is celebrated as Brazil's Independence Day. Pedro wrote to his father, with cutting realism: 'Portugal is today a fourth-class state and needful, therefore dependent; Brazil is of the first class and independent.' He proclaimed himself emperor (rather than mere king), in grandiloquent recognition of Brazil's size and diversity. He recruited Thomas Cochrane, a British admiral who had fought for the independence of Chile and Peru as a mercenary, to organize a Brazilian naval squadron. Cochrane saw off the limited resistance offered by the Portuguese fleet and garrisons in the north-east and north.[3]

Brazil was the only independent country in the Americas, apart from Canada, to adopt monarchy for any length of time. Partly as a result, in Brazil, even more than in Spanish America, independence represented the upholding of the colonial social order and therefore of slavery. It was Portugal, not Brazil, which experienced revolution in the 1820s. There was no violent break with the past, no equivalent of the civil wars and republican revolutions in Spain's colonies. And yet the monarchy, which lasted until 1889, could claim some significant achievements. Remarkably, Brazil would remain united while Spanish America splintered into many separate republics. And while much of Spanish America lapsed into the often chaotic rule of *caudillos* (strongmen), Brazil achieved political and economic stability and established at least the outward forms of constitutional, representative government. These achievements were neither inevitable nor easy. When the country became independent, 'there was no great sense of national identity in Brazil', as Bethell has argued. 'The centre-south, the north-east and the north were to a large extent different worlds, with their own integrated economies, separated by huge differences and poor communications, though no great geographical barriers.'[4]

Pedro and José Bonifácio, backed by the merchants and planters of Rio who benefited from their city's elevation to the status of imperial capital and from the rising coffee trade, were determined to keep Brazil united. But that outcome was the result of a struggle, not a general consensus, as Boris Fausto, a Brazilian historian, notes.[5] Rebellions for secession or local autonomy, or for the restoration of Portuguese rule, broke out, especially in the north-east and north. Pernambuco saw several secessionist revolts, perhaps because its struggle against the Dutch had cemented a strong provincial identity. There was no general agreement about how the new nation should be governed. What emerged, after two decades of almost constant political strife, was a centralized, hereditary constitutional monarchy, but one in which the emperor enjoyed certain absolute powers.

The constitution of 1824 was imposed by Dom Pedro after he had convoked and then dissolved a constituent assembly. It stipulated a fifty-member Senate chosen by the emperor from three-member lists elected in each province and a 100-member chamber of deputies indirectly elected on a franchise restricted to those with a certain income. The emperor appointed the presidents of the provinces (they would not become states until the proclamation of a federal republic in 1889), as well as ministers and judges. He could veto legislation. And he chose a ten-member Council of State whose job it was to advise him on his use of his 'moderating power' to dissolve parliament or to appoint a new Cabinet. The constitution guaranteed political and religious freedoms and, on paper, equal treatment before the law, though of course none of this applied to the third of Brazilians who were slaves. Pedro personally favoured the abolition of slavery. So did José Bonifácio, for whom it was 'the noblest and most sacred cause'. But they dared not antagonize the landowners.[6]

Despite his promise, in the end Pedro himself did not stay in Brazil. Amid mounting anti-Portuguese feeling, prompted partly by his failed war to seize the Banda Oriental of the river Plate (now Uruguay), in 1831 he abdicated in favour of his five-year-old Brazilian-born son (Pedro II), returning to Portugal on a Royal Navy ship. The abdication marked the completion of independence, the severing of the last links with Portugal – but not with monarchy.[7]

A Habsburg in the tropics

After several years of factional fights, in 1840 Pedro II was declared to have come of age and installed as monarch at the tender age of fifteen. He would go on to reign for half a century. 'Because of the longevity of his rule, and the transformations effected during it, no other head of state marked the country's history more deeply', José Murilo de Carvalho, his latest biographer, claims.[8] Dom Pedro II was in many ways an incongruous figure – a 'Habsburg lost in the tropics' in Carvalho's words. His mother, Leopoldina, was the daughter of the emperor of Austria. Pedro was tall (1.90 metres or almost 6 foot 3 inches), blond, blue-eyed and with a thick beard. He grew up an orphan (his mother died when he was one, his absent father when he was nine). He was shy, bookish, self-controlled and conscientious (the opposite of his coarse, womanizing father). He spoke six languages and could read half a dozen more (including Tupi–Guaraní); his idea of fun was to translate from Sanskrit, devour scientific journals, or correspond with European intellectuals, such as Victor Hugo or Louis Pasteur. Not until Cardoso would Brazil again have such a cultured ruler. He liked technology: he was the first head of state in the world to take photographs, and he was an enthusiast for the telephone. Pedro was publicly loyal to his wife, Teresa Cristina, the younger sister of the Bourbon king of the Two Sicilies, whom he found disappointingly plain but whom he came to respect. But Pedro's private passion was the Countess of Barral, the daughter and wife of sugar planters, with whom he corresponded through much of his life and for a shorter period held amorous encounters in Petropolis, his country retreat from the summer heat of Rio de Janeiro where the countess had a chalet (though they sometimes used a hotel). Pedro was a glutton for government paperwork: he was usually better informed than his ministers – a trait he shared with Dilma Rousseff. He made regular, lengthy trips around his vast country; he became an intransigent Brazilian patriot. He was personally austere, and hated ceremonial. He confided in his diary: 'I would prefer [to be] a president of the republic, or minister, than to be emperor.' Though he handed out grandiose titles of nobility, these were non-hereditary; the Brazilian empire did not have an aristocracy or even an organized court. Pedro despaired at the slowness of the bureaucracy, complaining 'anything that is not routine suffers a thousand setbacks', a sentiment identical to that expressed to the author by Lula in 2010. He was an unwavering supporter of a free press (although he was much lampooned in it) and of political liberties, and a campaigner for public education. Much of the little that was done in the way of the provision of schooling in the nineteenth century was due to him. Even so, the first census, taken in 1872, found that only 15 per cent of the population of 12 million could read, and fewer than 2,000 of the 1 million slaves.[9]

The main political argument during the monarchical period was one that Brazil has never definitively settled – perhaps because there is no definitive answer. It concerned the relative strengths of central and local authority in a vast and diverse country. Conservatives believed that only a strong central government could hold Brazil together, curb separatist tendencies and constrain the powers of local notables. Liberals favoured more autonomy for provinces and municipalities, and they wanted a locally commanded National Guard as a counterweight to the (small) imperial army. The Liberals, in power at the start of the regency in the 1830s, passed a law abolishing the Council of

State and creating powerful provincial assemblies. But these changes unleashed factional struggles for power among local oligarchs, which in turn triggered wider social conflicts. The regency saw the bloodiest regional rebellions in Brazil's history. In Pará, perhaps 30,000 died, and Belém, the capital, was all but destroyed in an inchoate explosion of rage by Indians and *caboclos*. At the other end of the country, the *farroupilha* ('ragamuffin') rebels turned Rio Grande do Sul into a quasi-independent republic for ten years until 1845. This rebellion, in which Giuseppe Garibaldi, the itinerant Italian revolutionary, gained his first experience of war, ended only when the imperial government granted many of the insurgents' demands, such as protection of their jerked-beef industry. Several foreign visitors to Brazil in this period predicted the country's imminent break-up. But the rebellions prompted a Conservative reaction which saw the restoration of the Council of State, of the monarch's 'moderating power', and of central control over the judiciary and police chiefs. Broadly speaking, these arrangements lasted until the end of Dom Pedro's reign, and were at least tacitly accepted by both Conservatives and Liberals, which proceeded to organize themselves as formal parties.[10]

The conventional wisdom in Brazilian historiography used to be that the empire's elaborate machinery of constitutional government was a piece of political theatre that cloaked the rule of a small landholding oligarchy. Certainly, what divided the two parties was not so much ideology as an argument about how power should be exercised: those who favoured local elites over national ones tended to be Liberals. Most of the progressive reforms under the monarchy were carried out by Conservative governments. Other scholars, such as Faoro, have argued that it was the patrimonial imperial state that created the nation. In this view, its civil servants, many of them schooled in the law faculties set up in São Paulo in 1827 and Olinda/Recife in 1828, constituted a mandarin caste, beholden to the state itself and not to the planters. Paulino José Soares de Sousa (later ennobled as the Viscount of Uruguay), who was one of the Conservative architects of the re-centralization of government, saw this as a means of imposing the voice of 'national reason' and the public good over the 'petty voices of the localities'.[11]

The reality was probably somewhere in between. Bolívar Lamounier, a Brazilian political scientist, argues that the concession of constitutional and representative government was the price demanded by local elites for sharing the burden of maintaining order and political control.[12] The resulting arrangement involved a relatively high degree of political participation for the time: 10.8 per cent of the total population of about 10 million voted in 1872, for example, which translated into about half of the non-slave adult male population. Elections were indirect, for an electoral college which then chose the deputies. A law of 1881 introduced direct elections for Congress, but added a literacy requirement, which curtailed suffrage much more than the income requirement, and meant that it would not be until 1945 that the percentage voting exceeded its level of 1872. The combination of a top-down state – whose leaders saw themselves as a modernizing force – with the careful maintenance of elections as mechanisms of consultation and consent has been the dominant strand in Brazilian political life ever since. Unlike many of its neighbours in Latin America, Brazil has only briefly seen unalloyed personal rule.

Some writers have compared imperial Brazil to Victorian Britain (Pedro himself resembled the British monarch in his dedication to duty and self-discipline). But electoral fraud was systematic, and the governing party always won; alternation in power was achieved by Dom Pedro's periodic exercise of the 'moderating power' to dismiss a Cabinet and to invite the opposition to form one. And the backbone of the system was patronage – the basic currency of Brazilian politics to this day. Politicians were benefactors as much as representatives, their power depending on their capacity to distribute favours. This bred, and reflected, abiding social relations based on paternalism, deference and clientelism, summed up in the saying 'quem tem padrinho não morre pagão' ('s/he who has a patron will not die a pagan').[13] Thus, the main job of provincial presidents was to provide electoral victories for the government by dispensing public jobs to reward and guarantee past and future loyalty.[14] Away from the coastal cities, power in much of rural Brazil lay with local potentates, who came to be called *coroneis* ('colonels') because they held that rank in the National Guard. And that was the central contradiction of Imperial Brazil: slavery and the power of the landholders limited the reach of the constitution, of liberalism and of a 'hollow' state, whose writ did not reach behind the gates of the *fazenda*, a large agricultural estate.[15] As José Bonifácio asked: 'How can there exist a liberal and lasting Constitution in a country constantly inhabited by a huge multitude of brutalized and hostile slaves?'[16] In the end, the monarchy would win the battle against the slavocrats, but it would be exhausted in the process.

The weakness of the economy also served to limit the strength of the state; conversely, a stronger state might have helped to launch economic development. According to one calculation, economic growth between 1822 and 1914 merely kept pace with Brazil's rapid population growth of 1.8 per cent a year. In other words, the country got no richer, in contrast to the United States, where income per head increased by 1.5 per cent a year in the nineteenth century. Historians and writers of the left-wing dependency school argued that the cause of this stagnation was that Brazil merely swapped submission to Portugal for dependence on Britain. Certainly the commercial treaty of 1827 that codified João's tariff cut on British imports was unfair, as *The Economist* pointed out in the lead article in its first edition, in 1843: Britain maintained tariffs of 300 per cent on Brazilian sugar and 200 per cent on coffee.[17] While it lasted, the low tariff on British goods may have hindered manufacturing. But when the treaty lapsed that year, with Britain offering no concessions, Brazil refused to renew it (and would not do so for half a century), raising its average tariffs to around 25 per cent. By 1913, duties collected amounted to 40 per cent of the total value of imports.[18] So, contrary to myth, Brazil rarely enjoyed anything close to free trade. And anyway, there is no evidence that trade impoverished the country, nor that it was the main factor in holding back industrialization. Most of the labour force was engaged in producing food for the domestic market.

The overall stagnation of Brazil's economy in the nineteenth century conceals sharp variations. In the second half of the period, growth picked up. And the locus of economic dynamism shifted to the south-east. The sugar industry stagnated; it was too backward to compete with Cuba's steam-powered sugar mills (though British tariffs may not have helped). Largely as a result, the north-east entered upon a long-term decline that only began to be reversed in the twenty-first century. But coffee cultivation grew steadily, at first in the Paraíba valley in the hinterland of Rio de Janeiro, and then in São Paulo and Minas Gerais. In 1822 sugar and cotton made up 49 per cent of total exports and coffee 19 per cent; by 1913, coffee accounted for 60 per cent, while the share of sugar and cotton was just 3 per cent. This geographical shift in the economy helps explain the persistent rebellions in the north-east: as Nathaniel Leff argues, the region would have benefited from having its own, weaker, currency (its position was analogous to that of southern Europe in the eurozone).

The biggest constraint on Brazil's economic development remained the enormous difficulty and cost of transporting goods around the country. Before railways were built, transport costs absorbed a third of the value of coffee shipments, and half the price of cotton shipped from the São Francisco valley to Salvador. The cost of transport also inhibited the growth of the domestic market. That meant that there was little incentive for farmers to increase food production.[19] Although railways were urgently needed, Brazil was slow to build them. The first proper line, the Dom Pedro II, which connected Rio to the Paraíba valley, was completed in the early 1860s. By 1875, less than 470 miles (750 kilometres) of track had been laid in Brazil, less than in other big Latin American countries. By 1914, the network extended to over 16,000 miles (26,000 kilometres) – the biggest in Latin America, but a figure that the United States had surpassed in the 1850s.

Why was Brazil so slow to build railways? Many Brazilians were well aware of the need. 'I compare Brazil to a child crawling on all-fours; it'll only begin to walk when it's got lots of railways,' though this 'won't happen [even] in fifty years,' says a character in a story by Machado de Assis which satirizes both plagiarism by politicians and the almost religious belief at the time that only with railways would Brazil evolve.[20] Government reports stated that railways would promote industrialization and help agriculture and commerce as well as being a force for national unity and greatness.[21] But difficult topography made construction an expensive and risky business. At first, British investors put up most of the capital. But to be profitable, railways had to charge high freight rates; although the government offered profit guarantees, the consequent uncertainty deterred foreign investors. Brazilian entrepreneurs, such as Irineu Evangelista de Sousa (ennobled as the Viscount of Mauá), complained that the government was hostile to them. Though Mauá, who set up an iron foundry and shipyard and invested in railways, had benefited from government support before he went bankrupt by overextending himself, the charge was partly true. A pro-business commercial code approved in 1850 was soon reversed. Companies could henceforth be formed only with the imperial government's permission. Dom Pedro did set up a school of mining in Ouro Preto, inviting French professors to staff it. The state stepped in to provide finance for railway-building on a limited scale – it put up half the cost of the Dom Pedro II line, for example – but was held back by its lack of revenues. As Steven Topik notes, the imperial government found it easier to obtain foreign loans than internal tax revenue. Independence was financed by a loan arranged by the Rothschilds on the London market. The imperial government borrowed more in London than any other Latin American country at the time. Unlike its neighbours, it repaid its loans, maintained a stable exchange rate, and as a result enjoyed better credit than many European countries.[22] The government relied on customs revenues for around 70 per cent of its income. Raising other taxes was both costly and politically difficult in an economy based on extensive grants of public land and on low wages.

Abolition, immigration and capitalism

In April 2010, as part of an ambitious scheme to beautify the run-down port area of Rio de Janeiro for the 2016 Olympic Games, municipal workers were replacing the drainage system in a shabby square when they came across some old cans. The mayor's office called in archaeologists. Their excavations at the Praça do Jornal do Comercio unearthed the remains of Valongo, the main slave market in nineteenth-century Brazil. Until 1808, slaves were landed, along with everybody else, at what is now called Praça XV.* But once the monarchy was installed in the modest palace on Praça XV, the slave trade was diverted to a new landing stage at Valongo, hidden from the monarch's sight around the corner to the north-west. Between 1811 and 1843 around 500,000 slaves were landed there, transferring via small boats from the slave ships anchored in Guanabara Bay, according to Tânia Andrade Lima, the archaeologist in charge. Valongo was not just a dock; it was a large commercial complex. Slaves were displayed in shops on Rua do Comercio, which curves uphill from the square towards the city centre just as it did when it was called Rua do Valongo. Next door there was a cemetery. The archaeologists have recovered personal objects lost or hidden by the slaves, or taken from them. They include delicate bracelets and rings woven from vegetable fibre; lumps of amethyst and stones used in African worship; and cowrie shells, a common currency in Africa. They are poignant reminders of a history that until recently Brazil preferred to ignore. Valongo ceased to operate in 1843, when it was paved over by a grander dock built to welcome Dom Pedro II's bride, Teresa Cristina. The stone column that rises in the centre of the square commemorates the empress, not the slaves.[23]

In William Wilberforce's view, Brazil was 'the very child and champion of the slave trade, nay the slave trade personified'.[24] Britain predicated its recognition of Brazil's independence on a promise that the new state would abolish the trade by 1830. A law to do so was passed, but, as is still not uncommon with Brazilian laws, *não pegou* ('it didn't stick'). The trade went underground, but continued on a large scale. Many Brazilian politicians saw this as an assertion of national sovereignty in the face of British bullying. The law was *para inglês ver* ('for the English to see'), as one of its authors put it: a phrase that entered the language, meaning to pay lip service. In an early example of a superpower asserting what today would be called a responsibility to protect the vulnerable, the British parliament responded to this defiance in 1845 by approving the Slave Trade (Brazil) Act (better known as the Aberdeen Act after the foreign secretary, Lord Aberdeen). It authorized the Royal Navy to treat Brazilian slave ships as pirate vessels, to be seized and tried in British admiralty courts. The British Navy then began to raid Brazilian ports.[25]

By then a strong Conservative government was in power in Brazil. With Argentine meddling in Uruguay a constant worry for Brazil, Dom Pedro and his capable foreign minister, Paulino José Soares de Sousa, wanted to secure British neutrality in the event of any conflict. The government pushed through

---

* It is named for 15 November, the date in 1889 when the monarchy was overthrown.

a law setting up special maritime courts to try slave traders. This time the law stuck: the trade quickly came to a halt, the last landing taking place in 1855. This government approved other reforms, in a determined, but frustrated, effort to inject dynamism into the economy. As well as the short-lived commercial code, these included a law requiring that public lands be sold, rather than granted in *sesmarias*, and that stipulated that landowners who wanted their title confirmed should pay for a survey to fix boundaries. Even though the government dropped a proposed land tax, the land law was one that didn't stick. To this day, many land titles in Brazil are confused and vague.[26]

The abolition of the slave trade meant that the end of slavery itself was only a matter of time. Capital released by the end of the trade was redeployed to found banks and to invest in railways and coffee plantations. Brazil was responsible for three-quarters of the growth in world production of coffee in the nineteenth century. The planters believed that coffee grew best in newly cleared virgin forest soils. So 'the coffee frontier swept forward like a brush fire' across the hillsides of the south-east, obliterating thousands of square kilometres of the Atlantic forest, according to Warren Dean. In Colombia, coffee cultivation took place on family farms, and created a rural middle class. Not in Brazil: slavery and the lack of clarity over land titles favoured the concentration of land ownership in few hands. Local notables seized public lands. By 1920, less than 3 per cent of the rural population held title to land, and 10 per cent of these people controlled three-quarters of those lands.[27] After 1850, an internal trade in slaves developed, with between 100,000 and 200,000 being sold by masters in the north-east to the coffee planters in the south-east. Nevertheless, coffee and railways would eventually reinforce each other in a triumphant, if belated, march of capitalist development centred in São Paulo. These forces unleashed a massive demand for labour and reshaped Brazilian society over the coming decades, their repercussions being felt long after the fall of the monarchy in 1889, to which they contributed.

A British company finally laid a railway line up the scarp from Santos to Jundiaí, which began operating in 1868; in the same year, local investors floated the Paulista railway company, one of several which built lines further into coffee country on the vast, undulating plateau of São Paulo and the hills of south-western Minas Gerais. The railway's freight rates were only about a third of those charged by the muleteers. This triggered an economic take-off in São Paulo. Santos displaced Rio de Janeiro as the main coffee port. Coffee output soared, but so did that of foodstuffs. Contrary to the claims of the dependency school, the railways provided a powerful boost to the domestic economy: government regulations required the companies to transport foodstuffs for a lower rate than coffee.[28] The city of São Paulo enjoyed vertiginous growth: in just ten years between 1890 and 1900, its population increased from 64,000 to 239,000.

The coffee *fazendeiros* invested in railways in part because they saw them as a way of overcoming the looming labour shortage triggered by the imminent end of slavery. Not only did the railways allow muleteers to be redeployed to plantation work, but they were also seen as necessary to attract European settlers. And this, many among the Brazilian elites had concluded, was urgent. In 1866 Dom Pedro came out publicly in favour of abolition. After a long parliamentary battle, in 1871 a law was approved declaring that the children of slave women would be born free. This was followed by the formation in São Paulo of companies promoting the import of European immigrants. The monarchy had earlier encouraged immigration to the south to populate what it saw as a vulnerable frontier region. About 39,000 Germans arrived between 1846 and 1875, followed by Italians and Eastern Europeans. Most became family farmers, and they would give a different socio-economic, as well as ethnic, character to Santa Catarina, Paraná and parts of Rio Grande do Sul.

The rising flow of immigrants would become a flood after the fall of the monarchy.[29] Between 1887 and 1914, some 2.7 million arrived in Brazil. More than half went to São Paulo, where the state government paid their passage and initial accommodation. Most of the rest went elsewhere within the south and south-east. Of the total, around a third were Italians, nearly all of whom went to São Paulo. Most of them came from northern Italy, especially the Veneto and Lombardy, though later arrivals included many from Naples and Calabria. At first many Italian labourers on the coffee plantations found themselves treated little better than slaves; in 1902 the Italian government outlawed subsidized immigration to Brazil. Even so, many managed to establish themselves as family farmers, or eventually in industry and commerce. The second-largest immigrant group were the Portuguese, more than a million of whom went to Brazil in the century after independence. Most went to the cities, especially to Rio de Janeiro and São Paulo. The Portuguese typically set up as small traders or shopkeepers: the Portuguese *padaria* (bakery cum delicatessen and café) is still the social and commercial hub of neighbourhoods across Brazil. In the first two decades of the twentieth century, Spaniards became the largest new immigrant group, establishing themselves as farmers producing for the local market in São Paulo. So did the Japanese who arrived in significant numbers in the 1920s under an agreement between the São Paulo government and Japanese emigration companies. Syrians and Lebanese, fleeing the chaos surrounding the breakup of the Ottoman Empire after the First World War, settled in the cities, along with Jews. The streets of the city of São Paulo resounded with 'a polyphonic clamour' of languages, including Hebrew and German, Spanish and Arabic.[30]

This wave of European immigrants 'whitened' Brazil's racial mixture. That was part of its purpose. The country's elites subscribed to the 'scientific racism' – in fact, unscientific prejudice – propagated by some European and North American writers in the late nineteenth century. This held that miscegenation bred 'degeneration', a physically weak and morally corrupt non-white race.[31] Nevertheless, the demonstration that Brazil could attract immigrants also gave force to the arguments for the final abolition of slavery. In the 1880s this became the first popular campaign in Brazilian history, backed by an incipient urban middle class. Its most eloquent leader was Joaquim Nabuco, a Liberal legislator and writer from Pernambuco. He argued that slavery's pervasive influence over Brazil's institutions, and its corollary of large landholdings, was incompatible with the formation of a modern urban economy. As increasing numbers of slaves began to abandon the plantations in 1888, with Dom Pedro away on a European trip, his daughter and heir, Princess Isabel, signed the 'Golden Law', as it was called. It was one of the shortest documents in Brazilian history. It simply said: 'Slavery in Brazil is declared extinct from this date. All contrary dispositions are revoked.'

War and the end of monarchy

Apart from the campaign for abolition, the second and bigger shock to the monarchy was triggered from a more distant quarter. Brazil's far southern border had been a source of problems since colonial times. The legacy of a previously fluid border was that some 40,000 Brazilians lived in Uruguay, where they made up around a fifth of the population and owned a third of the national territory and about 1 million cattle. In 1864, a Uruguayan government of the Blanco party imposed a tax on cattle exports to Rio Grande do Sul. Brazil invaded, overthrowing the Blancos, and installing a government of the pro-Brazilian Colorado party. The Blancos had struck up an alliance with Paraguay, a poor and landlocked state but a militarized one, whose dictators had built a powerful army. Francisco Solano López, Paraguay's president, responded to Brazil's actions in Uruguay by invading Rio Grande do Sul (crossing Argentine territory to do so) and Mato Grosso.

Solano López miscalculated: he would be opposed by a Triple Alliance of Argentina, Brazil and Uruguay. The war that followed was by far the longest and bloodiest of any waged by Brazil, which would do most of the Alliance's fighting. Solano López mobilized around 100,000 troops; at the outset of the war, Brazil had 16,000, Argentina 8,000 and Uruguay 2,000. Around 135,000 Brazilians would eventually fight in the war. The Brazilian Navy defeated Paraguay's fleet of armed river steamers at Riachuelo on the river Paraguay.

By the end of 1865, the Triple Alliance had pushed the Paraguayans back from Rio Grande do Sul and from the Argentine province of Corrientes. But Dom Pedro refused any suggestion of a negotiated peace, even after Argentina dropped out of the war. He insisted on the overthrow of Solano López. That took until 1870, as the Paraguayans fought tenaciously to defend their territory. Paraguay was devastated; according to wildly varying estimates by historians, between 15 and 60 per cent of its population perished. Some 50,000 Brazilian troops died too; as with the Paraguayans, most of the deaths came from cholera and other diseases, and insufficient food.[32]

The long-drawn-out war weakened the monarchy. It exposed the frailties of the Brazilian nation and of the imperial state. It also increased the power of the army, and gave it a corporate identity for the first time in a country that previously had had no military heroes. Defying his Liberal chief minister, in 1868 Dom Pedro had imposed as military commander the Duke of Caxias, a Conservative army officer who had taken part in the suppression of the Pará rebellion during the regency. As Carvalho argues, this was the first time in Brazil's independent history that the military had triumphed over the civilian power. It would be a portent. Mid-ranking officers came to resent civilian politicians. The military academy began to be pervaded by positivism, the 'religion of humanity' propounded by Auguste Comte, a French philosopher and sociologist who died in 1857. Positivism is a footnote in European history. But in the late nineteenth century it became hugely influential in Latin America, especially in Brazil and Mexico. Comte believed that a secular elite of scientists and professionals could lead a transformation to a modern industrial society without either violence or class struggle. Orderly progress was Comte's aim. His view of industrial society was managerial, according to Raymond Aron. It went against the liberal contention that progress would come from the combination of economic and political freedom. All this struck a chord with sections of Brazil's incipient middle class, especially among the army officers, teachers, engineers and doctors to whom positivism offered a role as self-appointed apostles of national development. Positivism was not militarist. But it reached the army through the teachings of Major Benjamin Constant, who had fought in the Paraguayan war. Constant and his fellow positivists saw an enlightened but dictatorial republic as a superior evolutionary stage of civilization to monarchy.[33] Positivism represented the first of several ideologies, or currents of opinion, over the next century whose proponents sought to turn Brazil into a modern country by republican, but not necessarily democratic, means, using a strong state as the central instrument of modernization.

The war also gave a boost to more liberal republican ideas. A Republican Club was founded in 1870. Like the campaign for abolition, republicanism

took hold among the growing urban middle classes of professionals and
artisans, who for the first time began to play an influential role in political life.
But their liberalism was not without ambivalence: 'they continued to judge
patronage from the point of view of liberalism and judge liberalism from the
point of view of patronage', according to Emília Viotti da Costa.[34]
Republicanism also appealed to the coffee *fazendeiros* of São Paulo, many of
whom lacked slaves. Their province was under-represented in the imperial
parliament. They came to believe that their prosperity was jeopardized by the
highly centralized government of the empire, which limited their ability to
control immigration and railway policy or to influence economic policy. The
central government received 80 per cent of all tax revenues in 1868, with the
provinces getting only 16.7 per cent and municipalities just 2.5 per cent.[35]

The rigours of war had aged Dom Pedro, and he became ill with diabetes.
Most republicans were content to wait for his death, confident that the
monarchy would expire with him. But a faction of young positivist army
officers was more impatient. They persuaded Deodoro da Fonseca, an elderly
martial who considered himself a friend of Dom Pedro and who was not a
republican, to lead a bloodless coup on 15 November 1889. Pedro greeted it
with resignation. When later asked why he did not resist, he replied: 'Resist,
why? Brazil has to know how to govern itself; it doesn't need a tutor.' His main
irritation was that he was driven to the docks, and to exile, in the dead of
night; the conspirators feared there might be popular demonstrations in his
favour. He died of pneumonia in Paris in 1891. In Brazil, shops closed, flags
were lowered to half-mast and many in the cities wore black armbands. The
New York Times pronounced him 'the most enlightened monarch of the
century'.[36]

The monarchy had secured the unity of Brazil, which by 1870 had a
population of almost 10 million, and established the principle of representative and constitutional government. It gave the country political stability, and,
eventually, a sense of nationhood, even if this was forged in part in a largely
pointless war. It had abolished slavery without bloodshed and without
compensating the slave owners – something neither the United States nor
Cuba managed. Dom Pedro was a tolerant ruler, and one who was not
personally racist. Several of the leading cultural figures of the late empire were
black or *mulato*. They included Luis Gama, a *mulato* former slave, a satirical
poet who was an active abolitionist and a founder of the Republican Party in
São Paulo. Machado de Assis, also a *mulato*, was the founding president of the
Brazilian Academy of Letters; he was politically discreet, but deployed a
delicate irony to deadly effect in exposing social hypocrisy in his novels and
short stories.

But for all of the evolutionary changes that it had managed to achieve, Dom Pedro's reign had failed to disrupt the patriarchal society that formed the bedrock of much of rural Brazil, or bridge the chasm of inequality that this entrenched. Abolition had taken too long. And two big opportunities to create a more egalitarian society had been missed. The first was the failure to implement the 1850 land law, which might have encouraged more equal landholding and a bigger rural middle class. The second was the collective decision to opt for European immigration: this brought new talent and new ideas, but it also meant that wages did not increase, and that there was less incentive for Brazil to invest in turning the freed slaves into citizens through the robust provision of public education, as Nabuco had urged.[37] There were only 700 primary schools in the whole country.[38] That was in sharp contrast with Argentina, which under the presidency of Domingo Faustino Sarmiento (1868–74) established a publicly subsidized national school system, setting up some 800 primary schools in those six years alone.

But these were not the reasons for the overthrow of Dom Pedro. Nor was abolition, as has often been argued: by the end, only the coffee *fazendeiros* of the Paraíba valley still defended slavery, and they had lost economic clout and political influence.[39] Rather, two other things doomed the monarchy. One was its succession problem: Princess Isabel was distrusted by the politicians because of her intense Catholicism and her unpopular French husband. Second, a sentiment had spread among better-off Brazilians that the centralized government embodied in the monarchy was holding them and the country back.

An oligarchical republic

Brazil had become a republic almost by accident. In an election less than three months before the coup, just two of the 125 victorious parliamentarians were Republicans. There was no great popular mobilization against the monarchy, or for the republic. The only time the emperor had faced a hostile crowd was in 1880 when an increase of 20 réis (known as a *vintém*) in the fare charged by trams in Rio de Janeiro prompted three days of rioting before the army opened fire on protesters (the fare rise was swiftly cancelled). Those who had supported the coup against Dom Pedro were themselves divided into three camps. First, a group of army officers around Deodoro da Fonseca, many of whom had fought in the Paraguayan war, wanted to protect and promote the army's corporate interests, which they felt were threatened by the monarchy's civilian politicians. A second, younger group of positivist army officers gravitated to the leadership of another general, Floriano Peixoto. Positivists also dominated the local Republican Party in Rio Grande do Sul.

Neither of these two groups believed in liberal democracy. A third group were liberals (in the British sense of the word, rather than that now current in the US): best organized among them was the Paulista Republican Party and a smaller group in Minas Gerais. Their interest in local autonomy clashed with the first two groups' desire for a stronger state that would bind the nation together.

These three factions were soon locked in strife. Deodoro, who styled himself *generalíssimo*, ruled as a provisional military dictator, by decree. He sent troops to shut down monarchist publications. But partly because the republic had been coldly received in Europe and by Brazil's creditors, Deodoro felt compelled to set up a Constituent Congress, and this was dominated by the liberals. The constitution they drew up, ratified in 1891, was influenced both by the positivists and by the constitution of the United States. By Latin American standards, it was creditably short: just ninety-one articles, the fewest of any Brazilian constitution. The country became a federal republic, officially called, until this changed in 1967, Os Estados Unidos do Brasil (The United States of Brazil). In Brazil it was thus the centre that created the states, not vice versa as in the United States. Nevertheless, the states were given wide-ranging powers, not least to draw up their own constitutions: state governments were allowed to tax exports, to raise foreign loans and to create their own armed forces. States and municipalities were made responsible for education, thus dropping the 1824 constitution's stipulation that the national government should provide four years of free primary education. The central government retained the power to create banks and money, and to intervene in states in certain circumstances. The constitution called for a directly elected two-chamber legislature and president. There was no income requirement for voting, but illiterates were excluded. The result was that electoral participation was lower than during the monarchy. There were few mechanisms to guarantee personal freedoms. Positivist influence was reflected in the constitution's separation of church and state. And a positivist was given the job of designing the new national flag: to the imperial background of green and yellow was added a blue globe with the stars of the Southern Cross and the positivist slogan *Ordem e Progresso* ('Order and Progress'). The army and navy were declared to be responsible for the maintenance of internal order as well as external defence – a portent of things to come. Notwithstanding the constitution, Deodoro and his allies sent troops to close down the congress and decreed a state of siege. That was too much for the local political elites in the states. Ill and elderly, Deodoro turned over power to Floriano Peixoto, his vice-president, who proceeded to rule in a similarly authoritarian manner. But his attempt to stay in power failed. Prudente de Morais, a modest liberal lawyer from upstate São Paulo who had presided over the constituent congress, was chosen as president in 1894.[40]

As during the regency in the 1830s, power battles at the top contributed to local conflicts. In Rio Grande do Sul the state's positivist political boss Júlio de Castilhos – 'a *gaúcho* Robespierre' in the words of Fausto – put down with great severity a rebellion by his liberal opponents, but only after a war lasting more than two years in which perhaps 10,000 died (many had their throats slit after surrendering) and lasting political hatreds were created.[41] In the drought-stricken *sertão* of Bahia, Antonio Conselheiro, an itinerant millenarian preacher who dedicated himself to repairing neglected churches, attracted thousands of followers among impoverished tenant farmers, sharecroppers, cowherds and fugitive slaves. Conselheiro was a monarchist who refused to recognize the authority of the republic. In 1893 the governor of Bahia sent police to arrest him, but they were driven off. Thereupon Conselheiro led his followers to Canudos, in a rugged recess of the *sertão*, where they founded a settlement which grew to have some 5,000 huts and a population of perhaps 25,000, making it temporarily the second-biggest town in Bahia state. The government, and especially the Jacobins, as the military radicals around Floriano called themselves, chose to see Conselheiro's community as an existential threat to the republic. As the *Gazeta de Noticias*, a Rio newspaper put it: 'Revolutionary monarchism is out to destroy the Republic, and, with it, Brazilian unity.'[42] The authorities would send four successive military expeditions to crush Canudos, each bigger than the last. The first three were humiliatingly defeated, by the rigours of the parched environment, their own failings of logistics, leadership and tactics, and by the tenacious resistance of the backlanders, who augmented their armoury of knives, swords, clubs and muskets with the captured rifles and cannon of their opponents. Thanks to newly installed telegraph lines, the Canudos conflict was the first to receive daily coverage in the newspapers of Rio de Janeiro and São Paulo, adding to the pressure on the government. Eventually an expeditionary force of 10,000 troops with heavy artillery crushed Canudos in 1897, but only after a four-month siege and weeks of house-to-house fighting. The army set up a camp on Monte Favela, a hill overlooking the settlement. As a result, the word favela entered the language to mean a shantytown. Perhaps 15,000 backlanders died at Canudos; so did about 5,000 government troops, including 200 officers. Many on both sides died of dysentery, hunger, thirst or wounds, but some of the defenders were executed after they had surrendered.[43]

So the republic of high-minded positivists and liberals began with what might nowadays be called a crime against humanity. The Canudos campaign was the subject of an epic book, *Os Sertões* (translated as 'Rebellion in the

Backlands') by Euclides da Cunha, a disillusioned former army officer and positivist who covered the later stages of the fighting as a reporter for *O Estado de São Paulo*, a liberal newspaper. Da Cunha was a *mestizo* of partly Bahian ancestry. Although he sometimes spouts the conventional racist wisdom of the day, his own account gives the lie to this. While presenting the *sertanejos* of Canudos as religious fanatics and half-crazed degenerates, he simultaneously admires their courage, resilience and adaptation to their adverse environment, asserting that they are 'the very core of our nationality, the bedrock of our race'.[44] He chides the Brazil of the southern cities for its neglect of the interior: 'caught up in the sweep of modern ideas, we abruptly mounted the ladder leaving behind us in their centuries-old semi-darkness a third of our people in the heart of the country.'[45] He concludes:

> This entire campaign would be a crime, a futile and barbarous one, if we were not to take advantage of the paths opened by our artillery, by following up our cannon with a constant, stubborn and persistent campaign of education, with the object of drawing these rude and backward fellow-countrymen of ours into the current of our times and our own national life.[46]*

In the aftermath of the Canudos campaign, a Jacobin soldier tried to assassinate President Prudente de Morais, killing his war minister instead. The resulting wave of revulsion fatally discredited the Jacobins. The civilian liberals consolidated their control of the republic. Prudente de Morais was followed in the presidency by two other *paulista* civilian statesmen. But the liberals proved unable to create a broad-based and durable democratic polity. Nor did the First Republic heed da Cunha's warnings of the urgent need for popular education and social inclusion.

There were two main reasons why this didn't happen. First, the corollary of a devolved federation was that local political elites gained power at the expense of the centre. In each state, the same oligarchs who had formed the monarchical parties simply relabelled themselves as the local Republican Party. São Paulo, the coffee colossus, and Minas, where cattle-raising was important, provided all but two of the First Republic's presidents under an informal power-sharing arrangement that became known as *café com leite* ('coffee with milk'). Minas Gerais had

---

* Mario Vargas Llosa, the Peruvian novelist, drew heavily on da Cunha's book in his novel *War of the End of the World*. On the border between Santa Catarina and Paraná, several thousand rural workers staged another millenarian insurgency (known as the Contestado) between 1912 and 1915, in protest at the intrusion of a railway company and a logging enterprise.

the biggest congressional delegation and tended to dominate the federal cabinets. São Paulo's state government used its new devolved powers to the full. Its ability to levy export taxes and to borrow abroad made it financially stronger than the federal government. It set up a state militia of 14,000 men, equipped with artillery and aircraft and trained by a French military mission; a civil police force; and a professionalized judiciary. But the two dominant states still needed allies: that became clear when Ruy Barbosa, a lawyer backed by the São Paulo liberals, was defeated in the 1910 election by Hermes de Fonseca, a conservative army officer. And so presidents resorted to 'the politics of the governors', a mutual back-scratching under which the central government supported the dominant political groups in the states in return for their backing. In rural areas, the power of the *coronéis* increased, especially in the north-east. They gave electoral support to the state governor in return for being able to nominate the local police chief, the judge, the tax collector and the primary school teacher. Along either side of the São Francisco river, *coronéis* ran quasi-independent fiefs. After the National Guard was dissolved in 1918, some raised private armies of *cangaçeiros* (hired gunmen), interlocking with banditry (alas, rarely Robin Hood-style 'social banditry' of the kind romanticized by Eric Hobsbawm). The *coronéis* were both a cause and a consequence of the poverty of the backlands.[47]

Second, the liberals were in some ways less liberal than they purported to be. The republic saw a continuation of the economic growth that had started in the later years of the empire. But it began with a wild speculative bubble, unleashed by the deregulation of banks and a credit boom. When coffee prices fell, largely because of overproduction, the republic found itself on the brink of bankruptcy. Manoel de Campos Salles, who succeeded Prudente de Morais, negotiated a new loan from the London branch of the Rothschilds, Brazil's bankers ever since the 1820s, in return for a commitment to deflation, abandoned a few years later. The republic cast aside Dom Pedro's austerity: it ran a fiscal deficit in thirty-two of its forty-one years, in thirteen of them of more than 25 per cent of government income. Inflation became the norm.[48]

At the behest of coffee interests, São Paulo's state government began a scheme known as 'valorization', in which it put a floor under the coffee price, buying up and storing the crop when the world price fell below this level for later resale. As well as being a kind of socialism for the rich, valorization reinforced the economy's dependence on coffee. A rubber boom began in the 1880s in the Amazon, which saw more than 100,000 north-easterners migrate there; it was curtailed during the First World War when plantations were set up in British and Dutch colonies in Asia. Brazil's share of the world market in sugar and cotton continued to decline. According to Warren Dean, 'Brazil's overseas trade appears to have been limited to commodities in which overwhelming comparative advantage

offset high costs of production and commercialization and high internal taxes.'
Both government and the private sector saw the problem as one of export price
maintenance and 'little attention was displayed to competitiveness'.[49] These
attitudes would prove remarkably durable.

Seeking a modern identity

In February 1922 in the municipal theatre in São Paulo a group of mainly
young writers, artists and musicians marked the centenary year of independence by staging a Modern Art Week. They rejected the derivative European
classicism which constituted a suffocating cultural orthodoxy in Brazil at the
time, summed up in the theatre itself, a splendid but eclectic *belle-époque*
wedding cake modelled on European opera houses and opened in 1911. Many
of the participants in the week – in fact, three nights – would become leading
figures in the modernist movement that dominated Brazilian culture for the
next half-century. They included painters such as Anita Malfati, an expres-
sionist portraitist, and Emiliano Di Cavalcanti, whose subjects were mainly
mulata nudes; the sculptor Victor Brecheret, dubbed 'the Brazilian Rodin';
Heitor Villa-Lobos, a composer; and poets such as Mário de Andrade and
Oswald de Andrade (who were not related). In a lecture on modern art delivered from the stage, Menotti del Picchia, a writer, explained that

> to our eyes, scored by the speed of electric trams and of aircraft, it is the
> vision of the unchanging mummies of the art of the embalmers that is a
> shock . . . we want light, air, fans, aeroplanes, workers' demands, idealisms,
> motors, factory chimneys, blood, speed, dreams, in our art.

This self-conscious embrace of the modern industrial world and rejection of
the academicism of 'the embalmers' was reminiscent of Italian Futurism. Over
the next few years the modernist movement spearheaded the creation of a
Brazilian intelligentsia, which in turn crystallized a new, nationalist vision of
Brazilian identity and of the country's problems, which like that of the Futurists
would prove to be not incompatible with political authoritarianism.[50]
    In its cultural aspect, this vision would be summed up in two manifestos
published by Oswald de Andrade. In the *Manifesto da Poesia Pau-Brasil* ('Brazilwood Poetry Manifesto') of 1924, he called on artists 'to see with unfettered eyes'
and 'to be regional and true to our time'. He took these themes further in the
Manifesto Antropófago ('Cannibalist manifesto') of 1928 ('the 374th year of
the Devouring of Bishop Sardinha' – see chapter two). This sought to resolve the
dilemma of how to be an authentically Brazilian modern artist, given that

modernism itself was derived from European vanguards. The answer: 'Absorption of the sacred enemy. To transform him into a totem.' In other words, Brazilians would draw freely from universal art and regurgitate it as something uniquely national – a nationalism free of xenophobia. The manifesto was illustrated with a sketch by Tarsila do Amaral of her new painting, *Abaporu* ('Man-eater' in Tupi), a strange and distorted figure, of massive foot and hand but pin-head, against a background of a giant cactus and sun, all painted in bold, pure colours. Tarsila, who had grown up on a *paulista* coffee *fazenda*, was the most strikingly original of Brazil's modernist painters. Influenced by Cubism (she had studied in Paris with Fernand Léger) and Surrealism, her work is impregnated with Brazilian subjects, colours and the naïf tradition. In a letter from Paris in 1923, she had written to her family: 'I feel ever more Brazilian: I want to be the painter of my land.'[51] (In 1995, after Brazil had been impoverished by fifteen years of economic stagnation, *Abaporu* was sold at auction in New York for $1.25 million to Eduardo Costantini, an Argentine financier and collector; it forms the centre-piece of his pioneering Museum of Latin American Art in Buenos Aires. Many Brazilian plutocrats would now like to have the chance to buy it back.)

Modernism also revolutionized other branches of culture. It would be expressed in the architecture of Oscar Niemeyer, who took the straight-line functionalism of Le Corbusier and added curves, found in 'the mountains of my country, in the sinuousness of its rivers, in the waves of the ocean and on the body of the beloved woman'.[52] Other modernist architects would build concrete apartment blocks clad in cool white mosaics and steel shutters in São Paulo suburbs such as Higenópolis, or adopt art-deco in the Rio beach districts of Copacabana and Flamengo. Villa-Lobos, the composer, took part in jam sessions with black musicians and incorporated popular music into his work. Mario de Andrade's writings gave new value to folk art, of which he was a collector. The São Paulo 'gang of five' (the two de Andrades, Tarsila, Malfatti and Menotti) travelled to the baroque towns of Minas Gerais, and 'rediscovered' the neglected work of Aleijadinho. Another regional group around Gilberto Freyre in Recife spawned novelists who began to write about the harsh social realities of the north-east.

Above all, the modernist intelligentsia revolutionized Brazilian thinking about the racial question. They argued that racial interbreeding was a positive Brazilian asset. Mario de Andrade's novel *Macunaíma* featured an Indian 'black as night' who becomes white.* The works of Gilberto Freyre and Sérgio

---

* In a neat, perhaps too neat, postmodernist conceit, John Updike adapts this in his novel *Brazil* (1994), in which a black youth from the Rio slums meets an upper-class white girl and both proceed to change colour.

Buarque, in different ways, urged Brazilians to lose their inferiority complex in relation to Europe and embrace their racial mixture as the core of their national identity. But modernism was yet another top-down movement: the São Paulo group were in the main the children of rich families; they cruised around the city in the 1920s in Oswald de Andrade's green Cadillac. The Modern Art Week's most recent chronicler, Marcos Augusto Gonçalves, notes that it was sponsored by a group of São Paulo millionaires, headed by Paulo Prado, a leading coffee planter and investor. It was in part an exercise in one-upmanship by the rising bourgeoisie of São Paulo, a challenge to Rio's officially sponsored cultural predominance. The audience at the events, held at the height of summer, were men in three-piece suits and women in high heels. Modernism was 'aristocratic in spirit', Mario de Andrade admitted in a critique in 1942. It had little to say about democracy. But in manner, more than substance, it was strikingly modern: the organizers hired a claque of students to cause a stir by disrupting the opening night. 'In the end we got we wanted: celebrity,' Mario de Andrade wrote afterwards to Menotti.[53]

Modernism was itself a product of a changing country. Between 1872 and 1920, the population tripled to 30.6 million. By 1920, the city of Rio de Janeiro had a population of 1,150,000 and São Paulo 570,000. The coffee *fazendeiros* built lavish *belle-époque* mansions along the Avenida Paulista, a 3-mile boulevard built on a ridge looking down on the old city centre of São Paulo. Agriculture still dominated the economy, but coffee created the conditions for industrial development. By 1920, industry employed 14 per cent of the labour force, many in small workshops but also in factories making textiles and food and drink. Immigrants were important in industry, both as entrepreneurs and workers. Foreign companies, from Britain and increasingly the United States, were prominent in public utilities and banks, and handled much of Brazil's foreign trade.

Compared with Argentina or Chile in the same period, Brazil during the First Republic saw less economic growth and less social and political progress. The 1920 Census found that less than 25 per cent of the population was literate. Life expectancy had risen a little, but it remained pitifully short, at just 31.4 years. In Argentina, by contrast, in 1914 life expectancy had reached forty-eight and 65 per cent of the population of almost 8 million was literate.[54] There was no move to broaden the franchise, or introduce the secret vote. Electoral fraud remained routine, and often egregious. Instead, the oligarchical order began to come under social and political challenge in extra-parliamentary ways. Inflation prompted strikes, mainly organized by anarcho-syndicalists among the immigrant workforce, many of whom worked in factories where conditions were exploitative and dangerous. This agitation led to some minimal workers' rights, such as compensation for workplace accidents, two weeks of paid holidays and the restriction of child labour. Former anarchists were prominent in the formation of the small Brazilian Communist Party in 1922.

In addition, the army reappeared as a political actor, most visibly in the shape of a movement of *tenentes* (lieutenants, though some were captains or majors). The *tenentes* staged an initial rebellion at the Copacabana fort in Rio de Janeiro in 1922. They had some military grievances, over the difficulty of promotion and the army's eclipse by the state militias. They lacked a clear political programme, but they saw the First Republic as corrupt and vitiated by electoral fraud. They believed that only a strong army and a strong central state could develop Brazil and implement agrarian and other social reforms. Not coincidentally, perhaps, many army officers came from impoverished branches of once-rich families in the north-east, or from Rio Grande do Sul, still a positivist redoubt. In 1924, the *tenentes* staged further rebellions in São Paulo – which they held for a fortnight, being dislodged only by government artillery bombardment which killed scores of civilians – and in Rio Grande do Sul. These two groups joined up in Paraná, under the leadership of Captain Luis Carlos Prestes, who had grown up in a positivist household in Rio Grande do Sul, and Major Miguel Costa of the São Paulo militia. They set off on an epic march of 24,000 kilometres across thirteen states which lasted almost two years, before retreating into Paraguay having largely avoided combat. Never more than 1,500 strong, the Prestes Column, as it became known, lacked popular support but was a powerful symbolic act of armed propaganda for the *tenente* cause.[55] The emergence of the *tenentes* coincided with moves to professionalize the army. In 1919 a French military mission arrived – and would stay for two decades – to advise on the army's organization and training. The army came to think of itself as the embodiment of the idea of the state, and, following Canudos, as responsible for national integration and internal security. An editorial in the first issue of *A Defesa Nacional*, a specialist journal, in 1913 stated that the army 'should be prepared to correct the internal disturbances that are so frequent in the tumultuous life of developing countries'.[56]

As Boris Fausto notes, the federal government was not simply a coffee planters' club. It still received 60 per cent of total tax revenues, and it did continue to try to promote national integration as well as industry. A steel company, Belgo-Mineira, was set up in 1921, in part by a group of professors and students from the Ouro Preto School of Mines.[57] But decentralization under the First Republic exacerbated the gaps between the expanding economy of the south-east, the declining north-east and the still largely unconnected interior. São Paulo's demand for federal support for coffee valorization had helped to unleash inflation. Other states, especially Rio Grande do Sul, began to resent São Paulo's pursuit of sectional interest. When the alliance between São Paulo and Minas Gerais then broke down, so did the First Republic. The trigger was the decision by Washington Luís Pereira de Sousa, the president from 1926 to 1930, to break the unwritten rule of *café com leite* and choose a fellow *paulista*, Julio Prestes, as presidential candidate. His aim was to continue his policy of financial stabilization, at a time when the economy was feeling the effect of the Wall Street Crash of 1929. He secured the support of seventeen states. But Rio Grande do Sul and Minas Gerais demurred. They backed the candidacy of Getúlio Vargas, a *gaúcho* (as the inhabitants of Rio Grande do Sul are called). Vargas had briefly served as Washington Luís's finance minister before becoming governor of his state. He campaigned under the banner of a Liberal Alliance. Its programme opposed coffee valorization, supported monetary stabilization, and in a bid to attract middle-class support favoured some social reforms, such as pensions and paid holidays.

Both sides resorted to fraud (in Rio Grande do Sul, for example, Vargas was declared to have won almost 300,000 votes to just 982 for Prestes). Prestes was declared the winner by 1.1 million votes to 737,000 (and in fact had probably won). But younger politicians in Rio Grande do Sul and Minas Gerais opted to organize a rebellion against the result. They reached an agreement with many of the *tenentes*, although several of Vargas's closest aides, such as Osvaldo Aranha and Lieutenant Colonel Pedro Aurélio de Góes Monteiro, had helped to crush *tenente* risings. In October 1930 – six months after the election – the rebellion began, commanded by Góes Monteiro and backed by state militias in the south, with support in Belo Horizonte and the north-east. The armed forces' high command stepped in and deposed Washington Luís, claiming to exercise a 'moderating power' in the manner of Dom Pedro. An attempt to form a military junta proved short-lived. Getúlio Vargas, dressed in military uniform and wearing a *gaúcho* cowboy hat, arrived in Rio de Janeiro with 3,000 of his troops. On 3 November he took office as head of a provisional government. The First Republic had ended, just as it had begun, with a military coup.

CHAPTER FIVE

Getúlio Vargas and 'National Developmentalism'

Getúlio Vargas governed Brazil for more than eighteen years (1930–45 and 1951–4), longer than anyone except Dom Pedro II. For seven of those years (1937–45) he ruled as a civilian dictator, enjoying unequalled personal power. More than anyone else, he could claim to have created a modern nation-state in Brazil. He was a figure of many paradoxes – a status he revelled in. 'I prefer to be interpreted than to explain myself,' he wrote in his diary. He was at once an authoritarian and a conciliator. He was a conservative who went on to create a Labour Party, court the masses and come to be seen in some ways as a symbol of the left. Of *fazendeiro* origins, he promoted industrialization. He did little to reduce Brazil's searing inequalities and liked to smoke cigars, yet his acolytes dubbed him 'the father of the poor'. He was not a democrat by nature, but he would be forced by circumstances to try to rule as one in his final government. He crushed regional autonomy, but cultivated his *gaúcho* identity: on visits to his home state he would don *bombachas* (the baggy knee-breeches worn by cowboys) and get out his *chimarrão*, a bulbous, long-stemmed pipe used to imbibe *mate*, a bitter herb tea. He was the founder of modern Brazilian nationalism, yet he was not hostile to foreign capital, and preferred golf and whisky to football and *cachaça*. He flirted with fascism yet sent Brazilian troops to fight alongside the Allies in the Second World War. He was a short, physically unimposing man, a wooden orator, and of cold and calculating personality – a charismatic leader devoid of charisma. He was a dictator uninterested in pomp: he would sometimes walk to his office in the Catete Palace, a former coffee-planter's mansion, being greeted with respect by passers-by. In sum, he was a pragmatic authoritarian, for whom ideology was always subordinate to his own continued exercise of power. 'Getúlio was a man who believed in power almost as one believes in a divinity,' according to Tancredo Neves, who was justice minister in Vargas's final government (and who would be chosen as the first president in Brazil's current democratic period). To his foes, that belief made him a *gaúcho* caudillo, a dissembler who could not be trusted.[1]

Getúlio was born in 1882 at Fazenda Triunfo, his father's ranch 30 kilometres from São Borja, a small farming town. Originally the site of a Jesuit mission, São Borja lies 600 kilometres across the endless pampas from Porto Alegre, but just across the river Uruguay from the Argentine province of Corrientes. Its peaceful aspect belies a history of 'wars, massacres and throat-slitting', according to one Brazilian historian.[2] Getúlio's father fought in the Paraguayan war, rising from corporal to lieutenant-colonel; as the local political boss for Júlio de Castilhos, he became the mayor of São Borja. Getúlio's mother's family were also from São Borja, but had backed the opposite side in Rio Grande's civil war of 1893. Some think this family divide accounts for Getúlio's conciliatory streak. It did not extend to others in his family: two of his brothers were accused of murders. Getúlio spent a short spell in the army and toyed with a military career before opting to study law and to enter politics in his home state.

Perhaps it was not coincidental that the man who was Brazil's authoritarian nation-builder should be born into this positivist, frontier milieu. More than anywhere else in Brazil, Rio Grande do Sul had a martial tradition; much of Brazil's army was traditionally stationed there. Its inhabitants considered themselves to be Brazilians by choice; its politicians considered their state to be better governed and less corrupt than others, and thought it their mission to save Brazil. Getúlio's pragmatic, managerial authoritarianism was a faithful updating of *gaúcho* positivism.[3]

The Vargas era

In power, Vargas's overriding goal was to establish a strong, centralized state; part of the price of that was a strong federal army. His first move as head of the provisional government was to abolish by decree the 1889 constitution and its state counterparts. He dissolved Congress and the state and municipal assemblies, and replaced the elected provincial presidents with federal appointees called *interventores*, many of them former *tenentes*. The federal government took over coffee policy from the states, which were barred from contracting foreign loans without federal approval and from spending more than 10 per cent of their revenue on their military police forces, or equipping them with heavy weapons. Vargas created two new ministries, one of labour, industry and commerce, and the other of education and public health.

If the Vargas government was also more interventionist in economic policy, at first that was largely because it took power just as the Wall Street

Crash of October 1929 had pitched the world economy into depression and Brazil's economy into chaos. (Brazil was one of seven Latin American countries to experience a military coup in the two years following the crash, marking the end of oligarchical constitutionalism in the region.) Coffee prices plunged, by 1931 amounting to barely a third of their level of the late 1920s. Foreign trade collapsed: between 1928 and 1932, imports fell by three-quarters and exports by more than three-fifths. Brazil suffered what economists would nowadays call a 'sudden stop' in capital inflows. It ran out of foreign exchange, and halted capital repayments on its foreign debt for the third time since 1889, raising a funding loan to cover interest payments. The government devalued the mil-réis by more than 60 per cent in the aftermath of the crash and introduced foreign exchange controls. In a desperate effort to push up the price of Brazil's main export, between 1931 and 1944 it bought up and destroyed 78 million bags of coffee, equal to three years of world consumption. It also wrote off part of the coffee farmers' debts. All these measures combined to produce a swift economic recovery. In particular, the devaluation provided an incentive for import-substitution, especially in textile manufacturing and food-processing. As much from necessity as by design, the government had engineered a deficit-financed economic stimulus. By 1933, GDP was already 7.7 per cent above its 1929 peak. Industrial production grew at an annual average rate of 11 per cent for the rest of the decade. But the foreign debt remained a problem, and Brazil again defaulted in 1937.[4]

Vargas's centralization of power prompted resistance, especially in São Paulo. He eventually prepared to convoke a Constituent Assembly to legitimize his rule. In February 1932 the government issued a new electoral code, which maintained the literacy qualification for voting but extended suffrage to literate women. It introduced the secret vote and an electoral tribunal, measures which reduced electoral fraud. But the *paulistas* distrusted Vargas (despite his attempt to mollify them with his coffee policy). In July 1932 the São Paulo state military forces, and the federal army units based there, rebelled in the name of constitutionalism. In all, they numbered between 40,000 and 50,000. The rising enjoyed popular backing in São Paulo. But the state forces in Minas Gerais and Rio Grande do Sul remained loyal to the federal government. São Paulo faced 60,000 better-armed and -equipped government troops under General Góes Monteiro. The civil war that followed was on a larger scale than any other in Brazilian history: it lasted almost three months, and involved the use of heavy artillery, infantry advances against entrenched positions and aerial bombardment. The death toll is uncertain, but at least 600 *paulistas* were killed before São Paulo accepted defeat.[5]

Vargas was magnanimous in victory, and went ahead with the Constituent Assembly. The *interventores* created new parties in the states loyal to the government. Nevertheless, the 1934 constitution was surprisingly liberal. It was a partial restoration of the 1891 document, guaranteeing civil and political freedoms, the autonomy of labour unions and some states' rights. It introduced national ownership of mineral rights, a minimum wage, and free and compulsory primary schooling. The assembly elected Vargas for a four-year term, with no re-election allowed. But in his diary, Getúlio described the new constitution as 'monstrous' and 'an obstruction'. He had no intention of being bound by it.[6]

In Brazil, as in Europe, the 1930s saw the emergence of mass movements of both right and left. They were the first national political organizations that were created from below, rather than by the ruling political elite, but both rejected liberal democracy. Ação Integralista Brasileira (AIB), a fascist party founded by Plínio Salgado, a *paulista* journalist, gained more than 100,000 members, mainly from the urban middle class, and the sympathy of General Góes Monteiro and others in the regime. It was opposed by the Aliança Nacional Libertadora (ANL), a broad front of Communists, *tenentes* and other leftists, which similarly drew support from the urban middle class, and quickly grew to over 70,000 members. After it called for a national uprising to install a revolutionary government, the ANL was outlawed and driven underground. Drawing on the example of the *tenentes*, the Communist Party mistakenly believed a revolutionary situation was at hand. Luis Carlos Prestes, the party's leader, returned clandestinely from Moscow, accompanied by Comintern agents. In November 1935 poorly co-ordinated military risings by army non-commissioned officers, some organized by the communists, took place in Natal, Recife and Rio de Janeiro. They were easily crushed, but gave Vargas the excuse to crack down. Thousands of leftists, including Prestes, were arrested, and many tortured. Prestes would spend nine years in jail. His companion, Olga Benario, a German Jewish Communist who was seven months pregnant, was handed over to the Gestapo, to die in a concentration camp in Germany. Such left-wing *tenentes* as remained in the government were purged. So was Pedro Ernesto Baptista, a surgeon often described as Brazil's first populist politician: as mayor of Rio since 1931 he had built a political base in the favelas by founding hospitals and schools and by using regular radio broadcasts, techniques that Vargas would soon copy.[7]

Two years later, army commanders claimed to have discovered another Communist plot to overthrow the government. In fact, the 'Cohen Plan' was a forgery written by Captain Olímpio Mourão Filho, an integralist intelligence officer. It provided the pretext for a military coup to keep Vargas in power. On

10 November 1937 General Eurico Gaspar Dutra, the war minister, sent the police to shut down Congress. The government issued a decree cancelling the election due in 1938, at which Vargas could not be a candidate, setting aside the 1934 constitution and proclaiming in its place an unashamedly authoritarian Estado Novo ('New State'). The coup was greeted quietly, with no resistance. That evening Vargas fulfilled a dinner engagement to bid goodbye to the Argentine ambassador.[8]

The Estado Novo was the only unbridled personal dictatorship in Brazilian history. It drew inspiration from the authoritarian regimes of Antonio Salazar in Portugal (similarly called the Estado Novo) and of Mussolini in Italy, as well as that of Marshal Pilsudski in Poland. Though dubbed fascist by its enemies, it wasn't quite. Vargas did not create a mass party: much to Salgado's disappointment, the government dissolved the AIB, imprisoning 200 of its leaders. For their part, the tenentes had failed to establish a national revolutionary party (some had joined the AIB or the ANL). The Estado Novo was certainly anti-Communist, anti-liberal and anti-democratic. It was repressive, but not especially so by Latin American standards.

To justify his dictatorship, Vargas resorted to a longstanding obsession among Brazilian conservative leaders: the fear of national disintegration. In a letter to Osvaldo Aranha, his ambassador in Washington and the most liberal among his original allies from Rio Grande, he denounced constitutionalism as involving

> the arrogant imposition of regional interest superimposed on the legitimate interests of the nation. It was against this state of affairs, undoubtedly threatening to national unity, that we reacted, it was this that was crushed with a revolution from the top downwards, without struggle, without upset, and which received general acceptance.[9]

To ram the point home, the following month the flags of the states – including even the farroupilha of Rio Grande do Sul – were burned in a ceremony behind the presidential palace in Rio de Janeiro. It was the federal government that was going to create state and nation.

The Estado Novo had two essential features. First, as Bethell puts it, it was 'the personal dictatorship of a civilian politician . . . maintained in power by the military'. Ever since 1930, Vargas and his military leaders, especially Góes and Dutra, had enjoyed a close alliance of mutual convenience. The generals were happy to leave Vargas to govern; he was happy to let them get on with forging a powerful national army that both he and they saw as a tool to modernize Brazil. The army grew from 38,000 officers and men in 1927 to

95,000 in 1940 – or double the total headcount of the state police forces. The share of the federal budget going to the armed forces – which included a newly formed air force, as well as the army and navy – reached 36.5 per cent in 1942, up from 20 per cent in 1930.[10] But Vargas was not a mere pawn of the army. As the Second World War unfolded, he overrode the Axis sympathies of Góes and Dutra. Vargas was an Anglophobe, but liked Americans and got on well with Franklin Roosevelt. He forged an alliance with the United States, which involved trading military bases and minerals (including rare earths) and other raw materials at fixed prices, for cheap loans, notably to build Brazil's first large-scale steelworks at Volta Redonda. Natal, in the north-east, became a large and strategically important US air base, controlling the mid-Atlantic. Brazil became the first Latin American country to declare war on the Axis powers, and the only one to commit troops. A Brazilian Expeditionary Force (FEB) of 25,000 troops was dispatched to Italy, where it entered combat during the final months of the war. Less successful was a wartime 'battle for rubber' in which the government sent some 60,000 workers from the north-east to Amazonia, of whom perhaps half died from disease and poor living conditions.

The second defining feature of the Estado Novo was corporatism. As formulated by mainly Catholic thinkers in Europe in the late nineteenth century, corporatism was, like positivism before it, a response to an emerging industrial society and a reaction against both liberal individualism and Marxism. Corporatism held that the state should organize society as a community and on functional lines, arbitrating between the interests of capital and labour as organized groups and thus transcending class struggle.[11] Vargas's early enthusiasm for corporatism had expressed itself in the inclusion in the 1933 Constituent Assembly of forty indirectly elected members, representing business, labour and the professions, and above all in the provisional government's labour legislation. His first labour minister, Lindolfo Collor, a *gaúcho* positivist, had decreed the eight-hour day, paid holidays and equal pay for women; made contracts obligatory (in the form of the *carteira de trabalho* or work card); and begun to deprive labour unions of their autonomy. Corporatism became more explicit under the Estado Novo. In 1943, even as it was preparing to send troops to fight fascism in Italy, the regime decreed a labour code, the Consolidação das Leis do Trabalho (CLT), based in part on Mussolini's Carta del Lavoro – and still largely in force today. The government established a minimum wage. Unions became a branch of the state, financed by a compulsory deduction of one day's pay from workers who were obliged to be members. Their leaders had to be approved by the Labour Ministry. (They became known as *pelegos*, after the lambswool blanket horsemen place over a saddle to smooth the ride, in reference to their role as shock-absorbers.) Strikes were made illegal; instead, the government set up labour courts to settle disputes. An incipient social security system, providing retirement pensions and medical help, was extended to all urban workers (or at least those with a *carteira de trabalho*).

The Estado Novo promoted economic development through technocratic government. Vargas founded the rudiments of a civil service. The Administrative Department for the Public Service (DASP), set up in 1938, introduced recruitment by competitive examination and a career structure for public servants. But many appointments remained discretionary. A host of state agencies and technical councils were set up for economic policy, industrial development and foreign trade, drawing on the private sector and the labour unions. Most private business people, even *paulistas*, had concluded that Vargas was not a threat to their interests. Many industrialists supported the regime's nationalist campaigns aimed at creating a steel and oil industry in Brazil. Several important state-owned companies were set up, including Vale do Rio Doce (which took over, by agreement, an iron ore mine and railway developed by a British investor), CSN (which operated the Volta Redonda steel works) and CHESF, which built a big hydroelectric dam on the São Francisco river (the first of many such hydroelectric projects in Brazil).[12]

In a speech in São Paulo in 1938, Vargas expounded his corporatist doctrine:

The Estado Novo doesn't recognize individual rights against the community. Individuals don't have rights, they have duties. Rights belong to the community! The State, placing itself above the struggle of [vested] interests, guarantees the rights of the community, and ensures that duties to it are carried out.[13]

In other words, Vargas sought to detach the idea of progress from that of individual freedom. It was a twentieth-century re-formulation of the old patrimonial state. This New State smacked of Orwell's omniscient 'Big Brother', or the 'philanthropic ogre' of Octavio Paz, a Mexican liberal writer. Nevertheless, it showed a degree of Brazilian flexibility. It equipped itself with an official propaganda department which censored the press and even carnival songs, and created a personality cult around Vargas, who began to make weekly radio broadcasts in which he promoted the values of nationalism and work. But in sharp contrast to European fascism, official ideology – for the first time – held up racial mixing and *mestiçagem* as the essence of Brazilian nationality. *Feijoada*, the stew of pork and beans invented in the slave-quarters, was proclaimed to be the national dish. The regime embraced samba schools, and such Afro-Brazilian practices as *capoeira*, a dance-like version of kick-boxing, and *candomblé*, the worship of African deities. All of this, together with the labour legislation, helped to create an emotional bond between Vargas and the urban masses. The Estado Novo – and especially Gustavo Capanema, the education and health minister from 1934 to 1945 – recruited many of the leading lights of modernism with government jobs or contracts. Oscar Niemeyer's first significant building was for the education ministry itself; Villa-Lobos, the composer, ran a government office for musical education.[14]

An experiment in democracy

In joining a war for democracy in Europe, Vargas signed the Estado Novo's death warrant. The regime began to splinter, with the middle class, sections of the political establishment and some military chiefs pushing for elections (which the US also quietly encouraged). Vargas decreed that presidential and congressional elections would be held in 1945. Recognizing that at last he must create a political vehicle for his rule, it was a sign of the complex ambiguity of *getulismo* that he opted to launch two parties, rather than one. The Partido Social Democrático (PSD) brought together the official political machines of the *interventores* and professional politicians in the states, and was backed by industrialists and some big landowners. The smaller Partido Trabalhista Brasileiro (PTB), inspired in part by the British Labour Party, was based on the official unions and the political apparatus of the labour ministry. Faced with the need to compete electorally, Vargas reinvented himself as a populist.[15] He expressed his personal sympathy for the PTB; his propagandists came up with *trabalhismo* ('labourism') as a new political doctrine.

In response, the opposition formed the União Democrática Nacional (UDN), which brought together a disparate assortment of liberals, conservatives and (initially) some leftists, united only by their hostility to the dictator. It was symptomatic of the political role that the armed forces had acquired that both the main parties picked military officers as their presidential candidates, General Dutra for the PDS and Brigadier Eduardo Gomes, an air-force officer and former *tenente,* for the UDN. The Communist Party (PCB) emerged from hibernation, and Prestes staged big rallies. But Vargas had not resigned himself to losing power: amid a strike wave prompted by a wartime increase in inflation, his labour supporters launched a movement aimed at keeping him in office, either by proclaiming him as the presidential candidate of the PTB (an aspiration he repeatedly denied) or perhaps through a coup. Vargas's ambiguity concerning his intentions and his increasingly populist stance prompted the army to demand – and get – his resignation as president in October 1945. In colluding with the generals' ambitions for so long, Vargas had begotten a power he ultimately could not control. General Dutra won the election, with 55 per cent of the vote.[16]

Brazil thus embarked on what Thomas Skidmore, an American historian, called 'an experiment in democracy'. It was a limited democracy, but much less so than the First Republic. Illiterates – and thus most of the poor – were still denied the vote. A new constitution maintained the suffrage provisions of the 1934 document: urbanization and a concomitant modest increase in literacy saw the numbers voting expand: registered voters rose from 7.5 million in 1945, or less than a third of the adult population,* to 18.5 million, or more than half the adult population, in 1962.[17] The Communist Party was briefly legalized, winning almost 10 per cent of the vote in 1945. But the democratic experiment was dogged by several difficulties that would ultimately doom it to failure. The basic one was that the political institutions, still dominated by supporters of the conservative order in the countryside, proved unable to adapt sufficiently quickly to rapid economic growth and accelerating social change. Second, political tensions were exacerbated by a background of ideological confrontation engendered by the Cold War (which saw the Communists banned again in 1948). And thirdly, the army had arrogated to itself the 'moderating power' to regulate political life exercised by Dom Pedro during the monarchy.[18]

Vargas would once again find himself the victim of this power. He had finally given lukewarm backing to Dutra and retired to his ranch in São Borja. But he had not been politically extinguished: the PTB had inscribed him as a candidate for senator or deputy in seven different states, and he won 1.3 million votes (almost 40 per cent of Dutra's total). He stuck to his new-found populist discourse. He blamed his fall on 'the agents of international finance, who want to keep our country in the situation of a simple colony, exporting raw materials and buying manufactured goods abroad'. In 1949 he told a journalist: 'I will return, not as a party leader but as a leader of the masses.' The following year he duly campaigned for and won the presidency on a platform of nationalism and social reform, and in coalition with Ademar de Barros, a landowner and industrialist who as Vargas's appointed *interventor* of São Paulo and then as its elected governor built a populist political machine based on appealing to the middle class with public works. Ademar had no compunction in accepting

---

* Or 13.4 per cent of the total population of around 46 million in 1945, at last exceeding the 1872 percentage.

the epithet *rouba mas faz* ('he steals, but gets thing done'). In office, Vargas again pushed state-led industrialization. He founded two institutions that would play a central role in Brazil's economy to this day. The first was a national development bank – the Banco Nacional do Desenvolvimento Econômico or BNDE, to whose name would later be added an 'S' for 'Social'. In response to a broad-based national campaign, backed by the armed forces, Congress also approved the establishment of a national oil company, Petrobras. It was granted a monopoly over exploration and development.

Vargas appointed as his labour minister João 'Jango' Goulart, the thirty-five-year-old son of a family friend and fellow rancher from São Borja, who became a protégé of Getúlio's during his self-imposed exile. Goulart had made his fortune as a cattle dealer (as a young man he had bought a Cessna light aircraft and a fleet of cars), but he had a social conscience and, at Vargas's urging, had joined the PTB. As minister, he proposed to double the minimum wage. That alarmed the opposition and part of the armed forces. They worried both about inflation and fiscal irresponsibility, but also feared that Vargas planned to ape Juan Perón, who in Argentina had installed an authoritarian populist regime. Those fears were exaggerated, but Vargas himself stoked them. On 1 May 1954 he harangued the workers, declaring: 'You are the majority. Today you are with the government. Tomorrow you will be the government.' As in 1945, by tilting so far to the unions, Vargas had upset the army and the industrialists, the other legs of the tripod that had sustained him in power for so long.[19]

The denouement came with a bungled assassination attempt against Carlos Lacerda, a UDN politician and journalist who was Vargas's most intemperate foe. Lacerda escaped with a minor injury to the foot, but a major from the air force – a hotbed of anti-Vargas and *golpista* (pro-coup) sentiment – guarding him was killed. The assassin turned out to have been sent by Gregorio Fortunato, the head of the president's personal bodyguard. Vargas almost certainly had no knowledge of the plot, but the army once again pressed him to resign, as in 1945. Faced with humiliating political defeat, Vargas took a far more radical step. After a sleepless night, at 8.30 a.m. on 24 August, he retired to his room on the top floor of the Catete Palace, reached for his revolver and shot himself through the heart. His suicide note was a political testament of pure populist nationalism. He had returned to power 'in the arms of the people', he declared, only to be brought down by a campaign by powerful foreign and national interests because of his defence of the workers. 'If the birds of prey want someone's blood, if they want to continue bleeding dry the Brazilian people, I offer my life in holocaust,' he said. He concluded: 'I gave you my life. Now I offer my death. I fear nothing. Serenely I take the first steps on the road to eternity and I leave life to enter history.'[20]

Vargas's suicide was greeted with a massive outpouring of popular grief. Hundreds of thousands of Brazilians took to the streets across the country. A vast throng accompanied his coffin to Rio de Janeiro's Santos Dumont airport, where it was flown to São Borja for burial. By granting some basic benefits to the urban masses, including retirement pensions, he assured himself of their lasting loyalty: a study of older residents in Rio de Janeiro's favelas conducted in 2001 found that when asked 'Which politician has most helped people like yourself?' the most frequent answer was Vargas.[21] The Catete Palace is now a museum: the presidential bedroom has been faithfully recreated as it was when Gétulio shot himself, a memorial to Brazil's most influential ruler of the twentieth century.

While modernization came about in some Latin American countries through popular revolution – as in Mexico (1910–17) or Bolivia (1952) – or social democracy (in Uruguay and to an extent Chile), Brazil had Vargas. He gave the state a central and lasting role in economic development. He also implanted the notion that citizenship, benefits and social inclusion flowed from the top down, granted by a beneficent state rather than being won through democracy and civic mobilization. Liberal democracy, he had preached, was a mere front for rule by reactionary regional oligarchies. And yet he had left the political power of the landowners largely intact, and eschewed land reform. All this helps to explain why Brazil remained a deeply unequal country, and why at the same time a genuine social-democratic party took so long to emerge. Even in death, Vargas would remain a dominant and polarizing figure in Brazilian politics for a further decade. That polarization culminated in the overthrow of democracy by a military dictatorship dedicated to expunging his political legacy – even as it eventually adopted much of it.

The immediate effect of Vargas's suicide was to turn the tables on his opponents. The 1955 presidential election was won by Juscelino Kubitschek of the PSD – though he gained only 35.7 per cent of the vote – with Goulart of the PTB as his vice-president.[22] In contrasting ways, they were both heirs of Vargas. In the army, constitutionalists, led by General Henrique Lott, the war minister, now had the upper hand. Lott scotched several coup attempts aimed at preventing Kubitschek from taking office, the most quixotic of which saw Lacerda and his military friends embark on the *Tamandaré*, a naval cruiser, in Rio de Janeiro and steam along the coast in a bid to start a rising in Santos.

Kubitschek and the building of Brasília

Juscelino Kubitschek was a dashing and attractive figure. He was born in Diamantina, the remote former diamond-mining town in Minas Gerais, which after its brief eighteenth-century refulgence had long sunk back into sleepy poverty. Like many towns of the interior at the turn of the last century, it lacked a sewage system, clean drinking water and electricity. Juscelino's father was a muleteer who died when he was two. His mother was a school-teacher whose grandfather was a Czech immigrant and whose surname Juscelino chose to use. Having qualified as a doctor, he served in that capacity in the Minas military police. He then rose through the *mineiro* political hier-archy, serving as a federal deputy and mayor of Belo Horizonte, before being elected as state governor in 1950. He brought to all these jobs whirlwind energy and the boldness of a political entrepreneur. As mayor, he built Pampulha, a middle-class suburb in Belo Horizonte, hiring Niemeyer to design it and Candido Portinari, a modernist painter, and Roberto Burle Marx, an extraordinarily original landscape gardener, to adorn it. As governor, he focused on building roads and hydroelectric dams, as if determined to banish from the state the lightless isolation of his Diamantina childhood.

Kubitschek managed to make it seem as if Brazil's experiment with democ-racy might work. His presidency represented 'a magic moment of economic growth, political democracy and cultural flowering', in the words of his latest biographer, Claudio Bojunga.[23] Despite his *getulista* background, the new president was a democrat by conviction. He was a natural conciliator, possessed of great charm. He was adept at obtaining political support through the deployment of small bureaucratic favours, such as public works or nomi-nations for public-sector jobs. This kind of politics was the hallmark of the PSD. As Tancredo Neves later put it, 'between the Bible and Das Kapital, the PSD preferred the official gazette'.[24] Kubitschek used these political skills to strengthen his initially weak mandate, co-opting the more progressive wing of the UDN, and achieving political stability.

The president also projected that most precious of political assets, bound-less optimism. On taking office in January 1956, he announced a Plano de Metas (Plan of Targets), in essence a crash programme of industrialization. As well as Kubitschek's gubernatorial obsessions of roads and electricity generation, the plan involved moving beyond light manufacturing by creating a car industry and expanding steel and shipbuilding. Most of the spending on infrastructure would come from the state. The government invited foreign car and truck manufacturers to set up plants in Brazil, but on the undertaking that the vehicles produced would eventually be wholly made in the country, thus bringing into being a local car parts industry.

Kubitschek's economic policies came to be called 'national developmen-talism', a term that continues to resonate in Brazil today. The government's slogan was 'fifty years' progress in five', and official propaganda emphasized national greatness as Brazil's destiny. But the president's nationalism and statism were pragmatic. 'What Juscelino cared about was "where was the factory and not where the shareholder lived'", according to Roberto Campos, an economist who advised him. Lucas Lopes, who headed the BNDE and was in charge of implementing the *Plano de Metas*, saw the role of the state as a 'manipulator of incentives and not a controller of decisions' and as 'a pioneering and supplementary investor, and not an all-absorbing Leviathan'. Foreign firms were given incentives to import machinery, provided they associated with Brazilian counterparts in joint ventures. In this way, Brazil quickly built a car industry from scratch, with production of 100,000 vehicles a year by 1961, though to the chagrin of nationalists no durable Brazilian-owned car firm would emerge.[25]

Kubitschek's boldest stroke was to build a new capital, Brasília, in the Planalto Central (central plateau), more than 1,100 kilometres from Rio de Janeiro, in what was then trackless *cerrado* (savannah and scrub). The idea of creating a capital in the interior dated from Pombal. It was adopted by José Bonifácio in his instructions to the *paulista* deputies in the Lisbon cortes of 1821; he suggested it be called either Brasília or Petropole. The 1891 constitution had required the government to set aside an area of land in the Planalto for the new capital; Deodoro da Fonseca set up a commission which chose a site more or less where the city now stands. But nothing more had happened. Kubitschek had a *mineiro* grasp of the importance of developing the interior (and many *mineiros*, though not the president himself, made fortunes building the new city). He argued that Brasília would give new impetus to national integration, in the manner of the *bandeirantes*, ending the Brazilian habit of clinging to the seaboard; that it would give politicians 'a broader vision of Brazil as a whole' and that it would act as a crossroads, with highways stretching from the new capital to Belém and Acre. Above all, he saw it as a declaration of national ambition. Launching the building of the new capital in October 1956, he said, in words that are today carved on a massive oblong marble block raised in the Praça dos Três Poderes (Square of the Three Powers), the windswept open space that forms the ceremonial heart of the city:

> From this central plateau, from this solitude that will soon be transformed into the nerve-centre of the highest national decisions, I cast my eyes once again on my country's tomorrow, and I foresee its dawning with unshakeable faith and boundless confidence in its great destiny.[26]

Kubitschek set up a special government agency to build the city, bypassing the bureaucracy. He persuaded the Congress to approve an insanely ambitious timetable of less than four years for its completion. An international jury chose a modernist plan drawn up by Lucio Costa, full of sweeping highways,

functionally segregated districts and uniform housing blocks, with a somewhat Orwellian feel to which Oscar Niemeyer's minimalist palaces and cathe-
dral added grace. Kubitschek was able to inaugurate Brasília in April 1960.
From the start, the city had mixed reviews. It 'represents the triumph of
modern man over nature,' said Arnold Toynbee, a British historian. 'The city
of tomorrow became yesterday's science-fiction,' wrote Robert Hughes in
Time magazine in 1976.[27] It would take another couple of generations before
Brasília developed the lived-in feel of a large city, complete with the inevitable
favelas just outside the borders of the Federal District. It was unfortunate that
Costa's modernist infatuation with the motor car, and consequent neglect of
mass-transit systems, would soon seem dated. Half a century later, Kubitschek's
boldness has in some ways been vindicated: without Brasília, it is hard to
imagine that the development of the centre-west and the agricultural miracle
of the *cerrado* would have happened as quickly. But many Brazilians believe
that the corralling of the country's politicians into a town where government
is the only industry helped to breed a mentality in which shameless robbery of
the public purse came to be seen as acceptable, even normal. Consciously or
not, Brasília was a positivist project to remove the people from the seat of
power, according to Raymundo Faoro.[28]

In the short term, building Brasília came at a massive price. It was not
properly budgeted for, and the opposition claimed the project was stained by
monumental corruption. Lopes, who became finance minister in 1958, argued
that it should have been built gradually over fifteen years, but he was disre-
garded. Kubitschek oversaw an economic boom, but he took even less heed of
economic stability than his predecessors. Inflation shot up and the balance of
payments' deficit ballooned. The government began talks for an IMF loan.
The Fund pressed for tighter policies to stabilize the economy. In 1959
Kubitschek broke off negotiations, wrapping himself in the flag of nationalism. His main aim was to prepare the ground for a return to the presidency
in 1965. He had presided over a growth spurt that saw an annual average
increase in GDP of 8.1 per cent during his term. But critics jibed that Brazil
suffered 'fifty years' inflation in five'. Brasília was only one of several reasons
that the government resorted to deficit financing on a massive scale. The inflation rate of nearly 40 per cent in 1959 was 'probably a record since the early
1890s', according to Marcelo Paiva de Abreu, an economic historian.[29]

The breakdown of democracy

Kubitschek certainly generated a feel-good factor. He was helped when
Brazil's football team in 1958 won the World Cup for the first time: Edson

Arantes do Nascimento, known by his nickname of Pelé, an eighteen-year-old black in a team that had once been white-dominated, and Mané Garrincha, a bow-legged winger born in poverty, became national heroes. A fresh burst of cultural creativity included the advent of *bossa nova*, a cool, whispery fusion of jazz and samba. As Caetano Veloso, one of Brazil's most talented popular musicians of the past half century, noted, *bossa nova* was 'a form of high modernist art that somehow became one of the most popular musics on earth ... it took the samba and added harmonic sophistication, extended chords and so on – and it added a degree of lyrical complexity'.[30] The *cinema novo* of Glauber Rocha and others adapted the techniques of Italian neo-realism to cast a harsh light on Brazil's socio-political backwardness. The concretists, a loose movement of conceptual poets and visual artists, formed a more original vanguard than their predecessors of the 1920s. These new movements were championed in the Sunday cultural supplement of *Jornal do Brasil*, a Rio daily newspaper (though when the cost of paper rose steeply, its managers decided they could no longer afford to publish concrete poetry, with its reams of white space).[31] The concretists spawned a distinctively Brazilian avant-garde, which in the 1960s deployed the techniques of abstraction, visual semantics, spectator participation and performance art, personified in the work of Lygia Clark, Hélio Oiticica and Mira Schendel.[32]

But Kubitschek also bequeathed a difficult legacy of mounting economic problems and unresolved social conflicts to successors who lacked his political skills. The 1960 presidential election was narrowly won by Jânio Quadros, a maverick populist of unstable temperament. A former schoolteacher who had risen meteorically from city councilman to governor of São Paulo, Quadros had been adopted by the UDN, which was desperate to find a vote-winner. His campaign symbol was a broom, with which he promised to sweep away corruption and immorality. On handing the presidential sash to Quadros, Kubitschek said that 'democracy is consolidated among us, and peace established that we all hope will be lasting'. It was not to be.[33]

Quadros arrived in Brasília with no previous national political experience, no clear programme and no majority in Congress. Even his vice-president was an opponent, João Goulart, Vargas's populist labour minister, of the PTB; under the 1946 constitution, voters chose the president and vice-president separately. But Quadros made a difficult situation far worse by his high-handed manner and refusal to negotiate with Congressional leaders. He took some measures to stabilize the economy, but irritated his UDN backers by adopting a left-wing foreign policy, embracing the Cuban revolution and decorating Ernesto Che Guevara when the Argentine revolutionary visited Brazil. Quadros began to mutter that Brazil was ungovernable as a democracy.

In August 1961, after less than seven months in office, he suddenly resigned. He apparently expected this histrionic gesture to prompt a wave of popular support that would allow him to assume dictatorial powers. Instead it was met with disbelief. 'The people, where are the people?' he muttered when he landed at Guarulhos airport in São Paulo and found no crowds to welcome him.[34] Congress swiftly accepted his resignation, with no dissenters.

His departure triggered a political crisis that brought Brazil to the brink of civil war. The constitutional position was clear: Goulart, who was out of the country, having just visited Communist China, should take over as president. But he was anathema to the conservatives in the armed forces and the Lacerda wing of the UDN; they saw in him the revival of the nationalist labourism of Vargas that they had overthrown in 1954. The military ministers issued a statement saying that Goulart would be arrested if he returned. Leonel Brizola, the PTB governor of Rio Grande do Sul who was also Goulart's brother-in-law, launched a 'campaign for legality'. Clutching an automatic rifle, he harangued the crowds in Porto Alegre. The commander of the Third Army, based in the south, backed Goulart's claims, and prepared to march troops northwards. With the army divided, a compromise – albeit an unconstitutional one – was struck: Goulart would be allowed to become president, but he would have to accept a parliamentary system, with a prime minister heading the government.[35]

Brazil was increasingly polarized. New groups emerged on the left, inspired in part by the Cuban Revolution of 1959. Agitation spread to the countryside. In Pernambuco, Francisco Julião, a lawyer, organized peasant leagues, which resisted evictions of small-scale farmers. 'Agrarian reform will be done, by law or by force, with flowers or with blood,' he declared. Julião visited Cuba, and received help and military training from Fidel Castro to start a rural guerrilla movement in the north-east, though his plans were soon thwarted by the security forces. Hundreds of unions of rural workers were formed, variously backed by the PCB, the Labour Ministry and the Church. Left-wingers secured many leadership posts in the labour unions, with the support of the Labour Ministry. They organized a national confederation, the CGT, which was illegal but accepted by Goulart. A movement of sergeants and other NCOs emerged; when their initial, justified, grievances over working conditions were settled, they took up left-wing political demands. After the supreme court ruled that a serving NCO was ineligible for election to Congress, several hundred sergeants staged a rebellion in Brasília, taking public buildings and holding a court justice and the president of the chamber of deputies for several hours. Students and some Catholics also swung to the left. The most prominent leader of the radical left was Brizola who built many schools in Rio Grande do

Sul and expropriated an American-owned telephone company operating in his state as well as two *fazendas*.[36]

Goulart was not the radical leftist, let alone Communist, that some of his opponents, in Brazil and in Washington, would claim. Rather he was a moderate would-be reformer. But he was a weak and indecisive politician, whose zig-zags ended up depriving him of support in the centre and turning him into a hostage of an increasingly extremist extra-parliamentary left. Goulart spent his first eighteen months in the presidency battling to restore his full powers, which he achieved in a plebiscite in January 1963, winning 9.5 million of 12.3 million votes cast. Thus fortified, he appointed an economic team from the moderate (or 'positive') left. San Tiago Dantas, the finance minister, and Celso Furtado, the planning minister, drew up a three-year plan to stabilize the economy, a prerequisite for maintaining political stability. The plan involved a mixture of spending cuts, wage restraint, tax rises on the better-off and a commitment to enact the 'basic reforms' that both Goulart and the left supported. These included granting labour rights to rural workers; the extension of the franchise to illiterates and members of the armed forces; the legalization of the Communist Party; and agrarian reform, involving the redistribution of 'unproductive' land, with compensation in government bonds, rather than cash as the constitution required. Most of these measures were modest enough. But the right was implacably opposed to some of them. Three attempts to pass a constitutional amendment to facilitate a moderate land reform failed in 1963. But the government did enact a statute extending the labour laws to rural workers.[37]

Brizola and the far left irresponsibly attacked the three-year plan. Goulart decided that stabilization carried too high a political price, and withdrew his backing for Dantas. The economy began to spin out of control. Inflation rose, from 55 per cent in 1962, to 81 per cent in 1963. Economic growth came to a halt for the first time in two decades. The alliance between the centrist PSD and the centre-left PTB that had sustained Brazilian democracy since 1945 was fraying. With his base in the PTB under threat from the extremists, Goulart veered left. Brizola, whose family relationship with Goulart disqualified him from being a presidential candidate in 1965, preached that Congress's failure to enact the reforms had rendered it illegitimate. He began to form cells of armed activists.* He called on Goulart to take dictatorial powers. In early 1964 Goulart began a series of rallies, seemingly convinced that he could arouse what he believed to be

---

* Brizola was another product of the violent world of rural Rio Grande do Sul. His father was a poor farmer and pedlar who was murdered after being captured by the troops of Borges de Medeiros, Castilho's successor, in a civil war in 1922. He worked his way through law school.

overwhelming, but latent, mass support for reforms. On 13 March, in the square in front of Rio de Janeiro's main railway station, he spoke before a crowd of around 150,000, many bused in, the scene a sea of red flags. He signed two decrees there and then, one declaring subject to expropriation 'under-used' farms of over 500 hectares within 6 miles of federal highways, railways or dams, and the other nationalizing private (Brazilian-owned) oil refineries. In an improvised speech of over an hour, he called for constitutional changes and a long list of other reforms.[38]

The problem was that the opposition of the right, and the extremism of the left, meant that the reforms had become a revolutionary demand. And the forces of counter-revolution were stronger. The rally had the effect of pushing the centre into the arms of the right. The PSD as well as the UDN and the most important state governors now believed that Goulart would seek to supress constitutional restraints on his power – and indeed the evidence suggests that this was so.[39] As a result, a small clutch of right-wing conspirators morphed into a broad coalition in favour of military intervention to overthrow the government. Some 400,000 people, many of them middle-class women, took part in a march in São Paulo of 'the family, with God and for liberty'. Goulart's final, fatal misstep was to flirt with the subversion of military discipline by supporting moves to unionize the lower ranks. On 25 March he condoned a sailors' mutiny in Rio, sacking the navy minister who tried to repress it. The mutinous sailors met in a labour union headquarters, invoking the spectre of a Soviet-style soldier–worker alliance, a kind of Smolny Institute in Guanabara, with Rio de Janeiro as Petrograd. Five days later, Goulart met the rebellious NCOs – a move which caused many wavering military officers to support a coup against the government.[40]

This began early on 1 April when General Olímpio Mourão Filho, who as a captain in 1937 had forged the Cohen Plan which served as the pretext for the Estado Novo, ordered his troops to march from Juiz de Fora to Rio de Janeiro. His extemporaneous move triggered more organized plans by a group of officers around Marshal Humberto Castelo Branco, the armed forces chief of staff who had been one of the commanders of the Brazilian Expeditionary Force of 1944–5. Although some in the army hesitated, within twenty-four hours the coup was successful. 'The army went to sleep *janguista* on the 31st and woke up revolutionary on the 1st,' as General Oswaldo Cordeiro Farias, one of the conspirators, put it. Goulart flew to Porto Alegre, where Brizola and the local army commander urged resistance. The president preferred to seek exile in Uruguay.[41]

As in 1889, 1930, 1937 and 1945, the military coup met little public resistance and involved almost no bloodshed. The CGT's call for a general strike was ignored. The left had overplayed its hand, and wildly overestimated its public support. The coup was backed by the governors of the three main states: Ademar de Barros in São Paulo; Carlos Lacerda in Guanabara (i.e. the city of Rio de Janeiro) and José de Magalhaes Pinto in Minas Gerais. It commanded widespread support among the middle class, fed up with inflation and strikes. It was backed by most of the press, the Bar Association, the Catholic bishops, nearly all of the UDN and about half of the PSD. The *golpistas* claimed it was they, not Goulart, who stood for constitutional legitimacy; they claimed to be leading a popular revolution, rather than a counter-revolutionary coup. A strongly Catholic population was responsive to the banner of anti-Communism waved by the armed forces.[42]

The coup was also backed by the United States. The Kennedy administration was determined to prevent any repeat of the Cuban Revolution in Latin America. It saw Goulart as anti-American, and as heading a government penetrated by Communists. It was irritated by Brizola's nationalization of a subsidiary of IT&T, and by Goulart's backing for a law limiting profit remittances and his refusal to break ties with Cuba. The US channelled aid to opposition state governors, while the CIA also funnelled money to the opposition. The administration dispatched Colonel Vernon Walters to Brasília as military attaché. He had served as liaison officer and interpreter between the American Fifth Army and the FEB in Italy, and was a friend of Castelo Branco and of Golbery do Couto e Silva, a retired general who founded IPES, an anti-Goulart think-tank linked to the private sector. The US was thus kept informed of Castelo Branco's conspiracy. By mid-1963, the American ambassador, Lincoln Gordon, was convinced, as he put it in a telegram shortly before the coup, that 'Goulart is now definitely engaged on [a] campaign to seize dictatorial power' and that if successful, Brazil would either fall under Communist control or suffer an elected populist dictatorship akin to Perón's in Argentina in 1945–55. On 20 March Lyndon Johnson, who had replaced the assassinated Kennedy, approved a contingency plan to send an aircraft carrier, with support vessels and supplies of fuel (but no troops) to Brazil, to support the anti-Goulart forces in the event of the civil war that some American officials saw as possible. But the coup succeeded before the US fleet had left the Caribbean. In a message to Dean Rusk, the secretary of state, on 2 April, Gordon called the fall of Goulart a 'great victory for the free world', adding that 'the West could have lost all the South American republics'. The evidence shows that the US looked favourably on the coup and was prepared to provide arms to the rebels. But the US did not create the coup or participate in it, contrary to the myth nurtured by the Brazilian left ever since.[43]

Was the 'democratic experiment' doomed to fail? A stronger and more skilful president than Goulart might have been able to forge congressional support for at least some reforms. On being chosen as the PSD's presidential candidate for 1965, just days before the coup, Kubitschek said that agrarian reform was 'inevitable', but that he would do it by consensus. 'A reformist government' did not have to be 'a threatening and subversive government', he argued. Most of the electorate was centrist. But no democratic government since 1945 had shown itself willing to take unpopular measures to stabilize the economy. The underlying problem was that many political leaders on both right and left had ceased to be committed to democracy. The UDN felt cheated of power by Quadros's resignation. Men like Lacerda had long knocked on the barracks' door, seeking power by non-democratic means. As Afonso Arinos, one of the UDN's wisest leaders, said of his party's betrayal of liberalism and embrace of conservatism: 'we were against dictatorship when this represented a form of social progress, and we went on to accept dictatorship when this became a way to contain social progress.'[44] Many on the left, for their part, thought that Cuba or Peronism offered a more attractive route to radical social change than democratic reformism. Just like Lacerda, Brizola was a sectarian demagogue, entirely uninterested in consensus-building. From Vargas to Quadros to Goulart, the view had grown that Brazil was ungovernable as a democracy.

The Long Dictatorship

On the evening of 7 April 1964, Francisco Campos, a conservative lawyer who in 1937 as Vargas's justice minister had drawn up the decree imposing the Estado Novo, sat down to type out another death certificate for Brazilian democracy. His Institutional Act No. 1 (AI-1), drafted at the request of the rebel generals, stated that 'the victorious Revolution invests in itself the exercise of Constitutional Power'.[1] The civilian politicians who backed the coup were swift to bless this contradiction; many of them thought that the army was once again exercising its 'moderating power', that it would install a provisional government until the 1965 election and then return swiftly to barracks. That was indeed the intention of Castelo Branco, who was chosen by his peers to serve the rest of Goulart's term as president. But the civilians would have far more time than they expected in which to repent of their error: the armed forces would govern Brazil for twenty-one years.

The military commanders opted to exercise power themselves because they had become convinced that this was necessary to purge the country – and the armed forces themselves – of Communism and the political system of corruption on the one hand, and to take the unpopular actions required to sustain economic development on the other. Many, though not all, of the victorious generals had, as young *tenentes*, supported Vargas's 1930 revolution; they similarly referred to the 1964 coup as the 'revolution'. According to Alain Rouquié, a scholar of Latin American armies, 'the dream of the *tenentes* of a conservative modernization carried out by a "depoliticized state" was finally realized after 1964.' Ever since the 1935 putsch, and long before the Cold War, the army had seen Communism as the biggest threat to internal security.[2]

That the armed forces remained in power for so long was partly because of their own divisions: the years of military rule were marked by constant factionalism, backbiting and mistrust. The bitter split of the 1950s between military conservatives and nationalists evolved after 1964. The group around Castelo Branco became known as the 'moderates'. Many of them had served in the FEB in Italy, where they had come to know the American army. They went on to found the Superior War School (dubbed 'the Sorbonne') in 1949, where they developed a doctrine of national security. They were anti-Communist, but believed in constitutional order, at least in theory, and wanted to purify democracy rather than abolish it. Some of them were relatively liberal in economics. A second group, the 'hardliners', gravitated initially around General Arthur da Costa e Silva, the war minister under Castelo Branco. They favoured greater repression and wanted to remain in power indefinitely. Many of them were also more nationalist on economic questions. Indeed, the overriding doctrine of the 1964–85 dictatorship, to which many moderates would eventually subscribe, was neither fascism nor liberalism, but a 'nationalistic statism', as Fernando Henrique Cardoso put it. Of course many officers behaved opportunistically, backing whichever current seemed to be in the ascendant.[3]

In important ways, Brazil's military dictatorship differed from the many others in Latin America in the 1960s and 1970s. It maintained a façade of constitutional rule throughout its two decades. It manipulated elections but did not abolish them, seeking a popular mandate, though this often proved elusive. For all except one period of almost two years in 1969 and 1970, Congress remained open, although it was heavily purged. In this way the armed forces sought to maintain the consent of regional elites and share the burden of government – just as the monarchy had done. The generals relied on the support of some civilian politicians and technocrats, especially UDN lawyers and economists, although their role was ultimately a subordinate one. Although the dictatorship was more repressive than the Estado Novo, it was less so than its counterparts in Argentina and Chile. It also institutionalized itself. The Brazilian army had long disdained the military caudillos of Spanish America. There would be no Brazilian Pinochet.

Castelo Branco, who had always been a legalist and was close to the UDN, had a particular horror of caudillos. Nevertheless, he was pressed by the hardliners, both military and civilian, to cancel the 1965 election and extend his term by fourteen months until 1967. He was succeeded by Costa e Silva, who suffered a severe stroke two years later. The following three presidents were senior generals who each served a single term of five or six years, their elevation being rubber-stamped by the purged Congress. In 1968 Costa e Silva would launch the dictatorship's most repressive phase. The ascendancy of the hardliners continued throughout the term of his successor, Emilio Garrastazu

Médici, until 1974, a period which Brazilians call *os anos do chumbo* ('the leaden years'). The moderates regained power with Ernesto Geisel, the third *gaúcho* president in a row and, as a Lutheran, Brazil's first non-Catholic head of state. Geisel became the most personally powerful and respected of the military presidents. He announced a gradual political opening, which was completed under the final military president, João Batista Figueiredo.

The dictatorship deepened its control of the country by means of a series of decrees, or Institutional Acts, which modified the constitution and the laws. Campos's AI-1 gave the president greater powers, including that of purging Congress. Thousands of leftist activists were arrested. The regime revoked the mandates of fifty-five members of Congress and six state governors. Goulart and Kubitschek, then a senator, were stripped of their political rights for ten years. After protégés of Kubitschek defeated the UDN for the governorships of Guanabara and Minas Gerais in 1965, Castelo Branco issued AI-2. This abolished existing political parties and created two new ones: the pro-government ARENA (Aliança Nacional Renovadora), made up of legislators from the UDN and the PSD, and the opposition MDB (Movimento Democrático Brasileiro), drawn from the PSD and PTB. AI-2 also made elections for president, vice-president and state governors indirect, and allowed the president to pack the supreme court and carry out a new round of political purges. A further act decreed the appointment, rather than election, of mayors in important cities. All this was codified in a new constitution in 1967, which also granted the executive tighter control over public spending and sweeping security powers. A new National Intelligence Service (SNI) under General Golbery became a state within the state, setting itself up in every ministry.[4]

Castelo Branco handed economic policy to two civilian technocrats, giving them broad powers. Otávio Bulhões, the finance minister, was a liberal from the private sector; Roberto Campos, who had advised Kubitschek and whom his critics dubbed 'Bobby Fields' because of his anglophilia, was planning minister. The two proceeded to stabilize the economy, slashing the fiscal deficit, curbing wages, devaluing the cruzeiro and rescheduling much of the foreign debt. This laid the foundations for a new spurt of growth: the economy grew by 5.1 per cent in 1966, while inflation fell to 25 per cent the following year. Bulhões and Campos also made some institutional reforms: they set up a Central Bank, which Brazil had lacked, and prohibited states from issuing bonds without federal approval (just as Vargas had done in 1931). While abolishing automatic job stability, they created an unemployment insurance scheme, the Fundo de Garantia por Tempo de Serviço (FGTS), financed by a payroll tax.

The leaden years

In 1968 the government faced an upsurge in opposition. Strikes broke out in Belo Horizonte and São Paulo, while students, like their counterparts in many other parts of the world that year, staged protests. Márcio Moreira Alves, a journalist and opposition congressman, used Congress to denounce police brutality and torture. The government wanted to expel him, but the Congress voted against, with ninety-four ARENA deputies defying the regime. These events prompted a severe crackdown. The regime issued the fifth Institutional Act (AI-5), which suspended Congress indefinitely, as well as many state legislatures; imposed censorship of the media and of popular music; and put the army in charge of state police forces. The government packed the supreme court again and expelled a further eighty-eight congressmen. Two young popular musicians, Caetano Veloso and Gilberto Gil, were arrested and exiled; they were leading figures in the Tropicália movement, the Brazilian expression of the worldwide current of rebellious youth culture.[5] In all, between 1964 and 1973, 4,841 Brazilians were deprived of their political rights, of whom 513 were stripped of elected office; 536 unions were taken over and their leaders kicked out; 133 university professors or researchers were stripped of their posts; and 1,313 military officers, including forty-three generals, were expelled from the armed forces.[6]

The muzzling of legal opposition gave impetus to several small urban guerrilla groups formed by Communist dissidents, Trotskyists and radical Catholics. Most of their recruits were middle-class students, plus a few leftist army officers. They robbed banks to raise funds, and some were trained in Cuba and North Korea. In 1969 guerrillas kidnapped the American ambassador, releasing him after the government complied with their demands to broadcast a manifesto and release fifteen prisoners, who flew into exile. Further kidnaps of diplomats followed, as did isolated bomb attacks on army facilities as well as acts of terrorism, such as the murder of an American army captain studying Portuguese in São Paulo. On each occasion, the security services arrested hundreds of people, subjecting them to systematic torture. The torturers extracted information that allowed them to ambush and kill Carlos Marighella, a former PCB leader who was the most substantial political figure among the guerrillas.

By early 1973 the urban guerrillas had been crushed; most were dead, the others in jail or exile. The only attempt to set up a rural guerrilla front, in Araguaia, in southern Pará, also failed after it was discovered and wiped out by the army. Why did the guerrillas fail, while they would succeed a few years later in parts of Central America? With 93 million people in 1970, Brazil was much larger, the state was more sophisticated, and the guerrillas lacked a deep knowledge of Brazilian society. But in addition, the country was enjoying another burst of rapid economic growth, which averaged 11 per cent a year between 1968 and 1974 (while inflation averaged 17 per cent). Hundreds of thousands of north-easterners found jobs in the factories (and kitchens) of São Paulo. The dictatorship continued Vargas's policy of granting social benefits: in 1971 it extended the right to retirement, pensions and medical assistance to rural workers, which helped give it lasting electoral support in rural areas. The Médici government (1969–74) set up a sophisticated propaganda operation to capitalize on 'the economic miracle', as it was dubbed, and on Brazil's victory at the football World Cup in 1970. The president, a football fanatic, had intervened in the selection of the squad, installing Mário Zagallo as the manager, despite his Communist sympathies. Médici received the victorious players at the Planalto Palace for a photo op. The government licensed many more television repeater-stations, facilitating the growth of TV Globo, which became the dominant – and generally loyal – private broadcaster. A manipulated election for Congress gave ARENA a resounding victory. The dictatorship was in triumphalist mood. João Paulo dos Reis Velloso, the planning minister, claimed that Brazil would enter the developed world by the start of the twenty-first century. Government slogans proclaimed 'Nobody can stop this country now' and 'Brazil, love it or leave it'.

The regime's anti-Communism was at its most sweeping and obsessive under Médici. The chief of the general staff, General Breno Borges Forte, declared that the 'internal enemy' was:

undefined, he adapts to any environment and uses any means, both licit and illicit, to achieve his goals. He disguises himself as a priest, a student or a peasant, as a defender of democracy or a progressive intellectual.[7]

But even during the *anos do chumbo* there were one or two small chinks of light. The military justice system, to which political cases were referred, offered a vestige of due process and a record of at least some acts of repression: one study found that of 6,196 defendants tried under security laws from 1965 to 1977, 68 per cent were acquitted. Some newspapers drew their readers' attention to censorship by publishing obvious fillers, such as inedible recipes or poems. According to Skidmore, these lapses by the dictators 'seemed to signal a lack of total confidence in their ideology and a lack of total commitment in applying it'.[8]

The regime's controlled retreat

When it came to choosing Médici's successor the military moderates managed to outmanoeuvre the hardliners, securing the top job for Ernesto Geisel, who had been head of Petrobras. He announced a policy of *descompressão* (détente) and *abertura* (opening), aimed at achieving a gradual and controlled return to democracy. What motivated this? The moderates had never intended the armed forces to stay in power for long. OPEC's action in forcing up the world oil price fourfold in 1974 was a blow to the economy, which was highly dependent on imported oil. The moderates were conscious, too, of growing criticism in the United States of Brazil's abuse of human rights. But perhaps the biggest factor in the calculations of Geisel and General Golbery, his closest aide and the architect of *abertura*, was the desire to reassert military discipline and hierarchy. This was threatened both by the complexity of the military's bureaucratic empire, with thousands of officers, serving and retired, in well-paid jobs in government and state companies and, above all, by the growing autonomy of the proliferating repressive networks the regime had engendered. As well as the SNI, these included separate intelligence services in each branch of the armed forces and joint army-police counter-subversive units called DOI-CODI,* with hundreds of agents, where torture was routinely practised. In addition, private business financed an army counter-subversive outfit in São Paulo. Inevitably the DOI-CODI attracted a number of psychopaths. They carried on operating even after the guerrilla threat had been extinguished. In 1975 Vladimir Herzog, a journalist, was murdered (by strangulation) within twenty-four hours of voluntarily attending the São Paulo DOI-CODI, which became particularly notorious. When a union leader was killed in similar circumstances a few months later, Geisel acted, firing the São Paulo army commander, a prominent hardliner.

Geisel wrested power away from the armed forces commanders when, in a carefully planned operation in 1977, he sacked his hardline army minister, General Sylvio Frota, who had ambitions to succeed him and to reverse *abertura*.[10] He went on to revoke AI-5, restore *habeas corpus* and lift prior censorship of radio and television. His successor, General Figueiredo, issued an amnesty law in 1979, allowing the remaining exiles to return, restoring political rights, and granting immunity from prosecution to those guilty of both 'political crimes' and the 'connected crimes' of repression. In response to all this, some DOI-CODI thugs turned to terrorism: a letter-bomb sent to the Bar Association killed a secretary; an attempt to bomb a left-wing concert at the Riocentro in Rio de Janeiro failed when the bomb exploded in the car park, killing a sergeant and wounding a captain who were carrying it in their car.

---

* The initials stood for Destacamento de Operações de Informações–Centro de Operações de Defesa Interna (Intelligence Operations Squad–Centre for Internal Defence Operations).

The hardliners could not derail *abertura* because Geisel had convinced the senior generals that a controlled withdrawal from the exercise of power was in the army's interests. The economy was deteriorating fast. When the price of oil surged in the 1970s, the Geisel government had borrowed abroad to finance the balance-of-payments deficit. It also tried to reduce Brazil's dependence on imported oil: Petrobras stepped up offshore exploration; the government built Itaipú, a giant hydroelectric dam on the Paraná river; it poured subsidies into Pró-Álcool, a scheme to produce ethanol as a fuel for cars; and it invested in nuclear power stations. None of this was enough when the Iranian Revolution caused the oil price to leap again: the bill for Brazil's oil imports more than doubled between 1978 and 1980. Geisel's finance minister, Mario Henrique Simonsen, was forced out when he argued that the country had to apply the brakes. Figueiredo recalled Delfim Netto, who had run the economy under Costa e Silva and Médici, and who resorted to increasingly desperate quick fixes. Even so, the economy contracted in 1981 by 4.5 per cent, the first recession since the 1930s.

Against that background, in November 1982, 45 million Brazilians turned out to vote for Congress and, for the first time in twenty years, for state governors. To try to fragment the opposition, Golbery had dreamed up a new law of political parties. This dissolved ARENA and the MDB, which reformed as the Partido Democratico Social (PDS) and the Partido do Movimento Democratico Brasileiro (PMDB) respectively. It also allowed new parties to register. Those that did included the Partido dos Trabalhadores (PT), the Workers' Party, linked to a new group of trade union leaders and the PTB, though this label was denied to Brizola, who formed the Partido Democratico Trabalhista (PDT). Golbery's strategy of divide and rule helped the PDS to retain a narrow majority in Congress, and in the electoral college which was to choose the next president (where the PDS had 356 seats to the opposition's combined total of 330). But the opposition won nine governorships, including São Paulo, Minas Gerais (where Tancredo Neves was elected for the PMDB) and Rio de Janeiro, where Brizola won.[*]

The regime's problems steadily worsened. A steep rise in interest rates in the United States jacked up the cost of servicing Brazil's debt. Mexico's debt default in 1982, followed by that of other Latin American countries, prompted a sudden stop in new loans. The economy subsided into a downward spiral of stagnation, inflation and devaluation. Within a fortnight of the election, Delfim turned to

---

[*] The electoral college consisted of the membership of both houses of Congress, plus six representatives of the majority party in each state.

the IMF, a step regarded as a humiliation in Brazil ever since Kubitschek's break with the Fund. Days later, the government asked its bankers to reschedule its $80 billion foreign debt; in July 1983 it defaulted on interest payments.

Abertura and economic difficulties prompted civil society to stir. The most dramatic manifestation of this was labour unrest. In 1978 some 500,000 workers in São Paulo's industrial suburbs, many of them in the car plants, went on strike for higher wages. Further strikes followed in 1979, when over 3 million took part, and in 1980. The strikes were organized by a new cohort of grassroots union leaders who demanded union autonomy, the right to strike and free collective bargaining. The strikes turned their most prominent leader, Luiz Inácio Lula da Silva, into a national figure. The Catholic Church also moved into opposition, partly because the bishops were shocked by the severity of the repression in the 1960s and 1970s, and partly under the influence of tens of thousands of grassroots base communities (Comunidades Eclesiasticas de Base or CEBs), many of which were influenced by liberation theology. Under the leadership of Raymundo Faoro, who was a lawyer as well as a writer, the Bar Association, too, joined the chorus of criticism of the regime, campaigning to restore *habeas corpus*. Private business began to be irritated by Delfim Netto's maze of controls and the relentless expansion of state companies. Some prominent São Paulo businessmen issued a public call for a return to democracy.

The regime, further weakened when Figueiredo was debilitated by a heart attack, clung grimly to its strategy of a controlled return to civilian rule. But the opposition pushed for a direct presidential election in 1985. The campaign for *Diretas Já* ('Direct Elections Now!'), launched by Franco Montoro, the newly elected PMDB governor of São Paulo, mobilized millions of Brazilians. It was notable for the participation of popular musicians, such as Chico Buarque (who had spent the *anos do chumbo* in voluntary exile in Italy). Sócrates, a football star, promised to turn down a transfer from São Paulo's Corinthians to Italy if a direct election was approved. TV Globo initially ignored the campaign; Roberto Marinho, its owner, feared losing his licences. But after several hundred thousand people gathered for a rally in São Paulo's central Praça da Sé, Marinho was persuaded that Globo's failure to cover the campaign was damaging its credibility. It broadcast part of the subsequent demonstration in Rio de Janeiro, despite a military helicopter buzzing the window of the television centre.[10]

In the event, a constitutional amendment to allow a direct election failed by only twenty-two votes to achieve the required two-thirds majority (of 320 votes), with fifty-five PDS deputies defying the party line to support it. But the dictatorship was fatally damaged, and had lost control of events. It lined up as its presidential candidate Paulo Maluf, a *paulista* businessman of Syrian descent and horse-riding friend of Costa e Silva who had served as the appointed mayor of São Paulo and then as state governor. But Maluf, a corrupt and authoritarian figure, was rejected by an important segment of the PDS, who broke away to form the Liberal Front Party (PFL). The opposition united around the candidacy of Tancredo Neves, a conciliatory figure. As vice-presidential candidate, he picked José Sarney of the PFL. Neves won discreet support from Geisel and TV Globo. One opinion poll found that he would defeat Maluf in a direct election by 70 per cent to 19 per cent. In January 1985 the electoral college chose Neves by 480 votes to 180. At last Brazil had a civilian president again. It also had an economic crisis.

The dictatorship scarred a generation. According to the most authoritative estimates, 379 people were killed or 'disappeared' as a result of government repressive operations during the dictatorship; far-left armed groups were responsible for seventy-three deaths in assaults, fire fights or 'executions'.[11] That was a far lower death toll than under the dictatorships in Argentina (where more than 9,000 were killed or 'disappeared') or Chile (over 3,000), let alone Central America. But torture was widespread: the Catholic Church published a report, drawn entirely from military justice records, which both documented in harrowing detail the brutalities and named 444 police and military officers who had perpetrated them. Many lives were disrupted, stunted by fear, or worse; others benefited, embarking on political careers that would continue after democracy returned. Those who paid a price included the three people who have governed the country since 1994, who each opposed the dictatorship in a different way. Fernando Henrique Cardoso, a rising left-wing academic in 1964 (and son of a retired general who supported Goulart), immediately went into exile. He returned in 1968, but shortly afterwards was stripped of his post as a professor at the University of São Paulo. Thereupon he joined other expelled academics in setting up a think-tank, CEBRAP, to promote peaceful political opposition to the dictatorship, and which survived despite a degree of harassment. Lula organized strikes in defiance of the regime's labour law. He was twice removed from his union post and detained for a month. One of those who suffered torture was Dilma Rousseff, who as a student joined a small urban guerrilla group. She was arrested in São Paulo, and repeatedly subjected to electric shocks on various parts of her body as well as to the *pau de arara* ('parrot's perch'), which involved being suspended upside down and naked from a stick, with wrists and ankles bound. She was jailed for three years.[12] Democratic governments did not try to unpick the 1979 amnesty, as happened in Argentina, partly because the repression was more limited but also because of the typically Brazilian consensual nature of the transition. But Cardoso's government awarded compensation to the victims of repression. Lula's administration floated the idea of a Truth Commission. This was finally established in 2012 under Dilma Rousseff. The courts recently began to accept civil actions against torturers.

Economic miracles and mirages

Throughout the half-century of political turbulence from 1930 to 1980, Brazil's economy grew strongly, expanding at an annual average rate of 6.5 per cent (see chart 1, p. 290). Though there were one or two slowdowns – in the late 1930s and especially in the early to mid-1960s – there were also spurts: growth averaged 7.5 per cent a year between 1942 and 1962 and 10.7 per cent between 1968 and 1974. Overall, Brazil's rate of economic growth in the five decades to 1980 was probably the fastest in the world, according to Angus Maddison, an econometrician. It was similar to those registered by several Asian economies in more recent years. So Brazil had its 'China phase'.[13]

The fast growth stemmed in part from a rapidly expanding population, and thus labour supply. The population increased at 2.8 per cent a year between 1930 and 1980 (when it reached 119 million), though the rate of expansion dropped sharply from the 1960s onwards. But income per person grew rapidly too. Measured in 2003 dollars, it rose from around $1,050 in 1929 to $6,000 in 1980; by then it was around 85 per cent of the equivalent figure in Argentina, compared with between a quarter and a third in 1929. Brazil moved from being a desperately poor country to a middle-income one. Above all, economic growth stemmed from industrialization. Industrial concerns began operating in the late nineteenth century, and multiplied rapidly in the first three decades of the twentieth century, substituting imported products with local manufactures. From the 1930s onwards, industry replaced coffee as the motor of economic growth, though not of foreign-exchange earnings.

Industrialization and economic growth became the overriding goals of government economic policy; conversely, the state became the organizer and protector of economic activity. Commitment to *laissez-faire* liberalism, and particularly to a low tariff, was 'virtually non-existent' in Brazil, according to one account. The coffee planters, who had long benefited from government interventions, were 'not credible liberals'.[14] The memory of the British-inspired low tariff before 1845 may have hurt the cause of liberalism. The urban middle and working classes would have benefited from an open economy and price stability as consumers, but not necessarily in their condition of industrial workers or government bureaucrats. So would businesses in the north-east, but they placed a higher value on the decision by Vargas and his successors to leave the rural social order intact.

Brazil's dirigiste tradition may have owed something to French intellectual influence, though it would also find justification in the 'inward-looking development' propounded by the UN Economic Commission for Latin America. Brazilians called it national developmentalism, and it had three main elements: the creation of a national capitalism; import-substitution industrialization; and an active state role in promoting economic development.[15] Dirigisme owed as much to market failure as to ideology: Brazilian entrepreneurs lacked the resources, and in many cases the ambition, to create on their own initiative capital-intensive industries, such as steel, car and petrochemical plants. Brazil was dogged by a lack of domestic savings. Until the 1970s, it was hard for private companies to tap foreign sources of financing. So the state stepped in. Geisel summed up the prevailing attitude:

One is not statist because one likes to be, one is statist because it's the only way to do things ... How are we going to develop the country, a poor country, without [creating] an adequate transport system, without cheap energy, without the production of raw materials like steel?

He argued that 'the nation doesn't develop spontaneously'. That may have been so, but the state crowded out private initiative in many industries.[16]

Only under Bulhões and Campos from 1964 to 1967 were more liberal economic policies applied. They devalued, cut import tariffs, introduced incentives for exports and issued laws to stimulate capital markets. They also created a modern tax system, introducing VAT and income tax. They placed rare importance on reducing inflation. But in 1967 the military regime turned back to national developmentalism under Delfim Netto, who remained finance minister until 1974. It set up a growing number of state-owned enterprises (SOEs), especially in heavy industry. In 1969, the state accounted for 60 per cent of total investment. The total number of SOEs rose from thirty-five to 646 in the three decades to 1980, when they employed over a million workers.

Contrary to conservative economic doctrine, dirigisme did not impede either fast growth or a reasonable degree of efficiency: total-factor productivity, a standard measure of the efficiency with which capital and labour are used, rose by 2.2 per cent a year between 1950 and 1980, though its rate of growth slowed in the 1960s and 1970s. This was mainly because – notwithstanding their nationalist rhetoric – governments were in practice fairly pragmatic in the implementation of policy. Vargas, Kubitschek and the military governments were all keen to attract foreign investment, though not in all industries, since they saw it as the only means of obtaining the technology and capital that Brazil lacked. (As soon as they had set up a plant in Brazil, multi-nationals tended to become enthusiasts for protection.)

Brazilian dirigisme had succeeded in creating by 1980 what was the largest and most sophisticated industrial base in the developing world. Some of the seeds planted by the military governments – and Geisel in particular – would germinate later: Petrobras and offshore oil; a petrochemical industry; Embraer (the aircraft manufacturer); huge hydroelectric dams; and ethanol. At last, farming began to expand rapidly, thanks to the opening up of the interior by new roads and Geisel's establishment of Embrapa, a state agricultural research service. Land under crops expanded from 19.1 million hectares in 1950 to 49.2 million in 1980. Delfim tried to help exporters with regular mini-devaluations. Exports grew (though less than imports). Brazil ceased to be dependent on coffee, as a host of non-traditional exports including cars, aircraft, arms and soyabeans came into being.

But the state's dirigisme became self-reinforcing and helped to generate distortions which eventually became unmanageable. Three sets of distortions were especially costly. The first was inflation (see chart 2, p. 291). This stemmed primarily from the persistent disregard of the need for macroeconomic balance and a political allergy to fiscal austerity. 'Developmentalist' economists tended to see inflation as being the result of a shortage of goods rather than of monetary and fiscal excess. The impact of deficits was aggravated because they were hard to finance without simply printing money. Inflation became an insidiously easy way for the government to finance itself. To reduce reliance on deficit financing, Campos and Bulhões began to issue treasury bills indexed to inflation. This would prove to be a fateful decision: it prompted generalized price indexation, entrenching inflation as a permanent feature of the economy, stimulating investment in government bonds rather than productive enterprise, and hurting the poor, whose incomes were often un-indexed.

The second big set of distortions concerned the currency and Brazil's persistent balance of payments problem. Asian countries that have industrialized recently have tended to maintain an undervalued currency and other incentives for exports. Brazil did things differently. From the late 1940s to the early 1980s the cruzeiro was persistently overvalued, sometimes hugely so. That was partly a result of the fear that devaluation would further stoke inflation. But the origins of overvaluation lay in the power of the coffee growers (many of whom also became industrialists). Because the country enjoyed a dominant share of the world coffee market until the 1960s, the cost of producing coffee in Brazil tended to determine the world price. As Marcelo Paiva de Abreu, an economic historian, points out, since coffee was priced in dollars, devaluation would have given coffee growers more cruzeiros per bag in the short term, but that in turn would encourage the release of stocks held in Brazil, which would drive down the world price. So the coffee *fazendeiros* were happy to have an overvalued exchange rate.

That led to persistent trade deficits, and a dollar shortage. The government responded to this in two ways. The first was exchange controls, which remained in force under various guises almost continuously from 1930 until the 1990s. Foreign exchange was rationed, and sold at differential rates according to use: the government subsidized the import of wheat and oil, seen as essential, and other favoured uses, such as the import of capital goods for industry that Brazil did not itself produce. The subsidies on wheat and oil were one reason for persistent fiscal deficits. The second response was high and rising protective tariffs to discourage imports of consumer goods. These gave a further boost to industrialization, but at a rising cost in coddling inefficiencies: a law applied aggressively from the 1950s allowed any Brazilian business to register its manufactured products for protection from 'similar' imported goods.[17] Protectionism reached its apogee with an Informatics Law of 1984 which tried and failed to stimulate a Brazilian IT industry by barring the import of computers, an extraordinary own goal against productivity.

The third set of distortions concerned the state's interventions in the economy. As well as imposing price, wage and exchange controls, the state handed out huge subsidies, in various guises. For example, industrial exports were subsidized at rate that averaged 20.8 per cent of their value in 1980, according to an estimate by the World Bank. Loans by the BNDES were only partially indexed; one study found that in 1974–87 the development bank's loans embodied a subsidy of $3.2 billion, with the fortunate recipients having to repay only 26 per cent of their real value.[18] Farmers enjoyed subsidies mainly through the Banco do Brasil (BB), which was both a commercial bank, responsible for rural credit, and the government's financial agent. When some of its functions were vested in the newly established Central Bank in 1964, the *fazendeiros* achieved an amendment in Congress that created a National Monetary Council, which was charged with supplying the BB with all the resources it needed through a 'movement account', financed from public debt. Credit to farmers was not indexed to inflation (and so was almost a gift). The National Monetary Council and its 'monetary budget' thus became a rival source of money creation to the Central Bank and operated a parallel budget unsupervised by Congress.[19]

Decades of state-led development bred the habit of mind among officials that the government could create growth through ever-more complicated manipulation of the economy. For their part, private businesses learned that the way to profit lay through lobbying for advantage in Brasília. As Miriam Leitão, an economic journalist, has written, family companies were assigned slices of the national market in the same way as *donatários* were granted their captaincy's in the sixteenth century. 'There are no modern capitalists in Brazil,' argued Raymundo Faoro. 'There are capitalists tied to the state' who execute 'projects dictated from the top down'.[20] This system was inflationary, highly unfair, and entrenched inequalities and privileges. It would come to haunt the country when the economic 'miracle' proved to be a mirage.

From countryside to city

In 1952 Dona Lindu sold her small plot of land near Caetés, a small town in Pernambuco, 250 kilometres inland from Recife. She sold her watch, her donkey, her figurines of saints, the family photos, everything she had, and went to the village shop to wait for the ramshackle lorry that would take her and seven of her children to Santos. They made the bone-shaking thirteen-day journey along with thirty or so others packed into the back of the open lorry, known (like the instrument of torture) as a *pau de arara* or 'parrot's perch' because the only seating was a plank wedged between the coachwork. At night they tried to sleep under the truck, or under its tarpaulin when it rained. Dona Lindu's youngest son, aged seven, was Lula. They arrived to find that Dona Lindu's husband, who had left Caetés for Santos shortly after Lula was born, had taken up with another woman, with whom he had two children. (In all, his father had twenty-three children with the two women.) After many vicissitudes, which included selling oranges on the street as a child, and just five years of formal schooling – he was the only one of his brothers to complete primary education – Lula managed to win an apprenticeship to train as a lathe-operator. That would take him into employment in a metal-bashing factory in the suburbs of São Paulo. Had he stayed in Caetés, he later mused, he would be 'a good drinker of *cachaça*', as Brazilian rum is called, or 'I would already have died of cirrhosis'. He might also have been illiterate, like his mother.[21]

Lula was just one of tens of millions of Brazilians who made the journey from countryside to city after 1940. The urban population rose precipitately from 12.8 million in 1940 to 111 million in 1991, while the rural population grew from just 28.3 million to 35.8 million over the same period. The urban population is over 85 per cent of the total today, according to official statistics. In fact, these slightly overstate the reality: if urbanites are defined as those living in towns of more than 50,000 people, the figure falls to 63 per cent.[22] The migrants were attracted by jobs in the booming manufacturing industries, or associated services. But they were also fleeing rural backwardness and poverty. Since the politicians had failed for generations to bring progress, opportunity or more equitable land ownership to the countryside, the more enterprising among the rural population voted with their feet. The move to the city in itself generally represented a step up the social scale, but not necessarily immediately. For most, their new home would be in the swelling favelas, and they would face years of urban poverty. Between 1940 and 1970 the population of greater São Paulo grew at an annual rate of over 5 per cent; in 1970 more than half its 7.8 million people were migrants. Public services could not keep up: according to a study by CEBRAP, in 1968 only one dwelling in two in Brazil's richest conurbation had piped water. Workers crammed on to impossibly crowded trains to get to work, some hanging from the carriage doorways.[23] Much the same went for other rapidly growing cities across the country, especially in the south-east.

In 1980 Brazil's indicators of social wellbeing were still unusually poor, both in relation to its level of income per head and in comparison with the rest of Latin America. There had been some catch-up, especially in the 1970s, thanks to economic growth, urbanization, falling poverty and a slow improvement in public health and in educational enrolment. Life expectancy had climbed to sixty-two years by 1980, and three-quarters of Brazilians were formally literate. But the average concealed deep inequalities. A third of Brazilian children were not at school in 1980. Since the government was spending so much public money to subsidize production, it was not coincidental that Brazil's economic success went hand in hand with continuing social backwardness.

Income inequality, already extreme, rose under the dictatorship: between 1960 and 1980 the share in national income of the poorest 20 per cent fell from 3.9 per cent to 2.8 per cent, while that of the richest 20 per cent rose from 39.6 per cent to 50.9 per cent.[24] Some blamed the wage restraint imposed by the regime. But the crucial factor was rapid economic growth amid a woeful education system, which pushed up the salaries that the minority of educated workers could command, as Carlos Langoni, an economist at the Getúlio Vargas Foundation, showed in a paper published in 1973. Stigmatized at the time as an apology for the dictatorship, Langoni's argument is now widely accepted. In 1980, the average worker had only 3.9 years of education, though the figure had risen from 1.8 years in 1950. This deficiency was only partially mitigated by an excellent apprentice training system, of which Lula was a graduate.[25] As industry clustered in the south-east and above all in São Paulo, regional inequalities widened too. Regional disparities were the greatest of any country in the world: the variation in income per head among Brazil's states was 8.6 to one in 1980, compared to 6.3 to one in Mexico and two to one in the United States. The north-east fell ever further behind.

No government since 1930 had managed to combine growth, price stability, greater equity and democracy. In a term coined by Edmar Bacha, an economist, Brazil had become *Belíndia* – a small rich Belgium, coexisting with an impoverished mass, as in India.[26] Brazil was 'no longer an underdeveloped country; it's an unjust country,' as Cardoso would later put it.[27] So there was much for the country's civilian leaders to do as they prepared once again to take charge.

PART II

The Making of Democratic Brazil

CHAPTER SEVEN

From Disorder to Progress under Cardoso

Brazilians normally see themselves, and are seen by others, as a happy, optimistic people. And they normally are. But in 1991 they were the most pessimistic people in the world, according to a Gallup poll. When Ayrton Senna, a Brazilian who had three times won the Formula One championship, was killed in a crash at Imola on 1 May 1994, the country was gripped by a paroxysm of grief that seemed to express a sadness deeper even than the loss of its great racing driver. 'Brazilian people are in need of food, education and health and a little bit of *alegria* – the *alegria* has just gone,' said one woman among the hundreds of thousands of people who lined the rainy streets between Guarulhos airport and the state assembly building at Ibirapuera Park to watch his hearse go by.[1] 'Brazil is going through a very bad time. No one feels like helping anyone any more. People just live for themselves,' said Viviane Senna, Ayrton's sister, in her funeral oration, explaining that in these circumstances her brother's dedication and success had made him so loved. Observers of Brazil despaired, too. 'Clumsy Giant' was the title of a Special Report on the country in *The Economist* in 1987. 'Drunk, not sick' (a description of Brazil by the economist Rudiger Dornbusch) was the verdict of the next such report in 1991. For years afterwards, academic studies of Brazil's new democracy pronounced it a failure, influenced by fieldwork carried out in the chaotic period from 1985 to 1993. In a gloomy travelogue called *A Death in Brazil*, Peter Robb paints a portrait of a country doomed by crime, corruption and inequality. In fact, even as some of those epitaphs were being penned, the country had found a way to conquer inflation at last, and with it bring order and stability to government, opening the door to two decades of socio-economic progress.[2]

The New Republic, as the politicians called the restored democracy, faced three main tasks: to dismantle the remains of the dictatorship, entrench liberties and provide effective democratic government; to conquer inflation and secure a return to economic growth; and to address the country's deep-rooted social problems. It seemed to struggle with all three. Begun amid such hope, the New Republic delivered only disappointments. Its first president died before he could take office; its second was impeached; vice-presidents governed for seven of the first ten years. All the while, inflation mounted, reaching 2,708 per cent in 1993, and the economy foundered. The chaos revealed deep-seated problems – some of which remain today – but also concealed a few achievements. Because the broad opposition coalition that had backed the *Diretas Já* campaign fractured, for better or for worse a potential opportunity for a radical rupture with the socio-economic patterns bequeathed by the dictatorship was lost. As so often, Brazil moved forward cautiously, gradually, with one step back for every step and a half forward.

The first big setback came while Figueiredo was still in the Planalto. On the night of 14 March, less than twelve hours before he was due to don the presidential sash, Tancredo Neves was rushed to a Brasília hospital with abdominal pains. After thirty-eight days and seven operations, he died on 21 April, Tiradentes Day. He would be mourned, on a similar scale to Senna, as a martyr for democracy. His death left the new government orphaned. José Sarney, sworn in as president in Tancredo's stead, was widely seen as an opportunist possessing no democratic legitimacy. A leader of the UDN's progressive wing in the 1960s, he then became a loyal supporter of the dictatorship. Only months before teaming up with Neves, as president of the PSD he had played an important role in defeating the *Diretas* amendment. Though he duly joined the PMDB, Sarney only episodically overcame his political weakness of origin. For several years, the politicians remained worried about the possibility of a renewed military intervention (Neves had tried to conceal his illness for that reason). Unlike in Argentina, the Brazilian armed forces had not fallen into general disrepute by their exercise of power.

Sarney was constrained in his selection of ministers: at first he inherited the Cabinet drawn up by Neves. Globo's Roberto Marinho boasted that he had chosen the army minister and the communications minister, whose job it was to regulate television. The president told Mailson da Nóbrega, who became finance minister in 1988, that he (Sarney) had to talk to Marinho before announcing the appointment (and it would in fact be revealed by Globo's evening news programme, *Jornal Nacional*). Sarney would also have ministers imposed on him by Ulysses Guimarães, the leader of the PMDB in Congress who considered himself to be the real power in the land. Sarney's efforts to seek personal popularity would see him launch four anti-inflationary plans, all of which failed, and in 1987 declare a unilateral default on the foreign debt. When he left office in March 1990, inflation in that *month* alone was 84 per cent.[3]

'A constitution too big for the GDP'

Sarney's main achievement was to oversee full democratization and a new constitution. Congress swiftly approved an amendment to the 1967 constitution granting the vote to illiterates (who formed up to a quarter of the population) and legalizing all political parties, including the Communists. Elections for Congress and governors in 1986 were thus based on universal suffrage, for the first time in Brazilian history. Thanks to the ephemeral success of the Plano Cruzado, one of Sarney's anti-inflation plans, the PMDB won an absolute majority in both houses of Congress and all but one of the state governorships. But some of its legislators were opportunistic recent converts: David Fleischer, a political scientist at the University of Brasília, calculated that the Congress contained slightly more former ARENA people than those who had been in the old MDB, the pre-1982 opposition.

Neves had agreed with the military commanders that the new constitution would be drawn up by the Congress, sitting in separate session, not by a specially elected Constituent Assembly. That was deplored by Guimarães and the PMDB left. They were the main authors of a preliminary draft which was 'a constitution that wouldn't fit inside the GDP', quipped Ives Gandra Martins, a prominent tax lawyer. Although this draft was heavily amended by a centre-right bloc (led by Delfim and Roberto Campos), as finally approved the 1988 constitution would be a progressive, and in many ways populist, document. It confused constitutional principles with policy choices, and sometimes involved an absurd level of detail. With 250 articles and seventy transitional measures, it was long compared with the US constitution (just seven articles) or that of Germany (146 articles), though shorter than some more recent Latin American ones.[4]

On the one hand, the constitution guaranteed individual rights and freedoms, and included some enlightened provisions. It abolished the literacy qualification for voting (though not that for being a candidate) and lowered the voting age to sixteen. It expanded the welfare state and over time would be seen to have paved the way for a reduction in inequality: for example, it instituted a minimum pension equal to the minimum wage, extended to the disabled and all over-sixty-fives, including rural workers, irrespective of contributions. It recognized the rights of Indians (as it calls them) to the lands they traditionally occupy and gave the federal government the power to demarcate these as protected reserves. It gave increased power and autonomy to public prosecutors, some of whom would prove energetic in investigating corruption and malfeasance.

On the other hand, the constitution was flawed and retrograde in many other respects. In reaction to the dictatorship's shackles on political parties, its drafters rejected any rules that might impose party discipline on legislators. With regard to the electoral system, it retained the proportional representation system of the 1946 constitution (since each state is a single, vast constituency this generates little sense of accountability of legislators to constituents), and kept, too, its skewing of the system, with each state having a minimum of eight deputies in the lower house of Congress, irrespective of population. The issue which exercised Sarney most was the length of the presidential term. The PMDB wanted four years. He secured a five-year term for himself, but only by handing out jobs, broadcasting licences and promises of spending in return for political support. The constitution reflected the weakness of Sarney's federal government. The state governors and mayors secured a greater degree of devolution of power and money than at any time since 1930. The Congress gained the power to remake the budget (though this proved to be partly theoretical). But the executive was granted the power to issue decrees (called *medidas provisórias*) for later ratification by Congress.

The constitution's biggest fault was that it entrenched the failing economic model of national developmentalism and corporatist privilege just when statist protectionism was going out of fashion across the world. It even included a cap on interest rates, at 12 per cent – a throwback to the anti-usury laws of the colonial period which was inevitably honoured in the breach until it was abolished by an amendment in 2003. Article 219 defined the domestic market as part of the 'national patrimony' and thus by implication to be protected. All three levels of government were granted the power to create new taxes.

The charter also carried the imprint of powerful lobbies. The Estado Novo's labour laws were preserved. Judges got higher salaries and resisted external control; delays in the judicial system were entrenched by a provision, reminiscent of Italy, that nobody can be sentenced until all appeals are exhausted. Pensioners, a relatively well-off group in Brazil, did especially well: all pensions were linked to the minimum wage; retired civil servants were to receive any wage increase granted to those in work. The retirement age of rural workers was lowered from sixty-five to sixty for men and from sixty to fifty-five for women. Teachers won the right to retire early; over-sixty-fives the right to free public transport. All those who had worked in the public sector for five years received absolute job tenure and full pension rights even if they had not sat competitive exams. As a result of all this, federal government spending on personnel (excluding pensions) increased from 2.5 per cent of GDP in 1986 to 4.5 per cent in 1989.[5] Once the veil of inflation was lifted to reveal the real state of the public finances, it would become clear that the constitution required a massive increase in taxation.

Few were satisfied with the final document. On the left, the PT called it 'conservative, anti-democratic and anti-popular'. Sarney complained it would make Brazil 'ungovernable'. As if the drafters were aware of the imperma-nence of their work, Congress was given the power to revise the constitution five years after it came into effect, by simple majority rather than the normal 60 per cent vote. But when it came, in 1993, that opportunity was not taken, because Congress was reeling from a scandal in which members of the budget committee were found to have taken bribes from construction companies. Of 30,000 proposed amendments, only five were adopted.[6] One of these further weakened the executive by cutting the president's term from five to four years. At the PMDB's insistence, a transitional measure allowed a referendum on creating a parliamentary system, which many of its leaders supported. When this was held in 1993 (with restoring the monarchy another option on the ballot) an overwhelming majority voted for presidentialism (as they had in 1963). But Brazil would soon find that bringing sanity to the economy required bruising battles to amend the constitution. By 2011 it had suffered sixty-seven amendments (compared with just twenty-seven since 1787 in the US, of which ten incorporated the Bill of Rights in 1791).

Collor: the Republic of Alagoas

Wedged between Pernambuco and the mouth of the São Francisco river, the small north-eastern state of Alagoas is blighted by a long-declining sugar industry and a tradition of clientelism, social neglect and political violence. It is almost a byword for the Brazil that remains a backward country. In 1986 42 per cent of Alagoans were unemployed, 65 per cent were illiterate and the infant mortality rate was roughly double the national average, at 125 per 100,000 live births. The state had been governed for decades by the Góes Montero clan (of which Getúlio Vargas's favourite general was a member). In 1950 Arnon de Mello, a largely self-made businessman and journalist, won an election for state governor, standing for the UDN, against Silvestre Péricles de Góes Monteiro. In his masterful account of the rise and fall of Fernando Collor (and the role of the media in both), Mario Sérgio Conti, a journalist, records that the defeated governor's last act was to visit the prison and offer to free any prisoner who managed to produce a kilo of shit. He ordered their faeces to be smeared around the walls, floor and furniture of the governor's palace as a greeting to his victorious opponent. Despite his campaign promises, political banditry continued under Arnon de Mello. By 1963 his feud with Silvestre reached Brazil's Senate, to which both had been elected. As Arnon made his maiden speech, Silvestre, hand on pistol, insulted him; Arnon fired his own pistol in Silvestre's direction, hitting a senator from Acre, who died from the wound. Both the parliamentary bandits were absolved by a jury. Arnon resumed his political career as an ARENA senator and built a television empire in Alagoas.[7]

Fernando Collor de Mello, Arnon's second son, was elected as governor of Alagoas in 1986 by promising to combat the privileges of public officials whom he dubbed *marajás* (maharajas, a term he overheard at a public meeting and seized upon). No matter that his last act as the appointed ARENA mayor of Maceió, the capital of Alagoas, had been to hire 5,000 extra functionaries. He used the family media empire to get his populist message across. Collor, who on his mother's side was the grandson of Lindolfo Collor, Vargas's first labour minister, had an acute 'sense of politics as a spectacle' and was adept at using the media to get himself nationally known, as Conti notes. He would send Hermès ties and boxes of Alagoan prawns to journalists from the national media whom he wished to cultivate.

In 1989 Brazilians at last had a chance to choose their president, something they had not done since the far-off day in 1960 when Jânio Quadros was elected. Of the electorate of 82 million (up from 15 million in 1960), 70 per cent would be voting for a president for the first time. Though Ulysses Guimarães had expected to win, Brazilians were unimpressed with the PMDB's dismal record in office (he got just 4.7 per cent of the vote). Two years earlier, a group of progressive PMDB politicians and intellectuals from São Paulo, including Fernando Henrique Cardoso, Franco Montoro, Mario Covas and José Serra, broke away to form the Party of Brazilian Social Democracy (PSDB). This espoused a modern, efficient state, democracy, social reform and an up-to-date view of development, according to Cardoso.[8] Covas, the new party's presidential candidate, delivered a stinging critique of the corporate state in a Senate speech:

> Enough of spending without having the money. Enough of so many subsidies, so many tax breaks, so many unjustified privileges. Enough of jobs for the boys. Enough of notaries ... Brazil doesn't just need a fiscal shock. It needs, as well, a capitalist shock, a shock of free-initiative subjected to risk and not only rewards.[9]

But Covas's campaign was slow to take off.

The Brazilian business and political establishment was scared at the prospect of 'Brizula' – that victory would go either to Brizola, the old warhorse of the populist left, or to Lula, who stood on a platform of full-blooded socialism. Collor sensed an opportunity. He took over a small party and allied it with two others, entitling him to three one-hour party-political broadcasts. Aged forty in 1989, he was telegenic: tall, with matinee-idol looks, Italian double-breasted suits and a young blonde wife. In public meetings and television interviews and commercials he railed against the Sarney administration (though he had been elected governor for the PMDB), and against privilege and corruption, promising to champion the *descamisados* (shirtless ones, a term copied from Argentina's Juan Perón). Soon Collor was the object of hysterical adoration at campaign rallies. He gained the influential support of Globo's Roberto Marinho. Very much in the mould of Quadros in 1960 (but with much more money), he projected himself as a national saviour, champion of a 'new Brazil'. He won 30.5 per cent of the valid votes, pitching him into a run-off with Lula (17 per cent), who had pipped Brizola (16.5 per cent). The run-off was a polarized and dirty fight between right and left: the Collor campaign bribed a former girlfriend of Lula, with whom he had a daughter, to claim that he had tried to force her to have an abortion. Collor claimed that Lula would confiscate the assets of the middle class and even savings-book accounts, which had been honoured by all governments since they were introduced by Dom Pedro. Collor won, by 35 million votes to 31 million.[10]

In the first direct presidential election in forty years, Brazilians had thus rejected the politicians who had fought to restore democracy, and all of the main parties that had dominated political life for the previous decade. They had entrusted the country to a little-known figure replete with paradox: a scion of the north-eastern oligarchy posing as a progressive reformer, a quintessential conservative populist who promised to modernize Brazil and would indeed begin the dismantling of the corporate state. Collor's exercise of power was cynical: the campaigner against corruption proved to be corrupt, and the candidate who accused his rival of plotting to confiscate savings would do exactly that himself. Like Quadros, he would arrogantly disdain Congress – and that would be his undoing. An obsessive practitioner of karate, Collor promised that he would kill inflation with an *ippon* – a single blow. The *ippon* he administered killed the wellbeing of many Brazilians, but not inflation.

As part of his plan to trim the federal government, Collor cut his Cabinet down to just fifteen ministers, twelve of them non-party technocrats. The finance minister was Zélia Cardoso de Mello, a little-known São Paulo economist.* Her

---

* No relation to either Fernando Collor or Fernando Henrique Cardoso.

first act was to freeze Brazilians' savings for eighteen months, as well as wages and prices. The savings freeze – in reality a partial confiscation, since inflation had eroded their value by 30 per cent when they were returned – prompted 'heart attacks, suicides, depression' as well as cancelled weddings; some people found themselves caught out between selling and buying flats, in the account of Miriam Leitão. In the early weeks, the plan saw 'a police state that committed innumerable arbitrary acts'. The manager of a São Paulo hypermarket was imprisoned because the police found a deodorant in the stockroom with two price labels on it.[11] The police raided *Folha de São Paulo*, a daily newspaper which had published several critical articles on Collor. The plan was initially popular, because Brazilians were fed up with inflation and most lacked savings accounts. But opinion turned when the economy plunged into recession (GDP contracted by 4 per cent in 1991) while inflation came roaring back. When the press reported that Zélia Cardoso was having an affair with the (married) justice minister, it seemed that Brazil's public life had turned into a *telenovela*.

Collor's government did take two important steps to reform the economy. The first was a decisive opening up of foreign trade: import bans and licences were abolished, including those on computers, and a timetable set to cut import tariffs to a maxim of 20 per cent and an average of 12 per cent within four years. When Collor complained that 'the Brazilian car is an old crock', this statement was 'worth innumerable seminars' on the evils of protectionism, according to Maílson da Nóbrega. The second was an effort to cut the fiscal deficit (of 8 per cent of GDP) and to start slimming the obese national-developmental state through privatization. Collor would sell off thirty-four state companies and thirty-two minority stakes, including part of the steel industry.

Collor made little effort to forge a stable coalition in Congress, and his approach to the media was to try to buy some proprietors and threaten others. That didn't help him when reports surfaced about the activities of Paulo César Farias, his campaign treasurer. Farias had raised $160 million from banks, construction companies and other donors for the presidential campaign, of which some $60 million was left over. It would transpire that he used this to pay Collor's personal expenses. These included buying a $3 million flat in Paris and a $2.5 million makeover of the garden at the president's private mansion in Brasília, involving the installation of eight electronic waterfalls, an artificial lake stocked with 100 Japanese carp and an extended swimming pool, all lit with 200 lamps and fifty floodlights. In addition, Farias invested in business ventures of his own, tried to pressure officials into favours and carried on extorting 'donations' in return for promises of public contracts. In another development worthy of a soap opera, Pedro Collor, Fernando's estranged younger brother who ran the family media business in Alagoas, blew the whistle on Farias's activities and his links to the president. As the media dug deeper, the politicians abandoned Collor. A Congressional investigation concluded that the president had profited from Farias's crimes and had facilitated influence-trafficking. The lower house voted (by 441 to thirty-eight) to impeach the president. On 29 December 1992 Collor resigned, after just thirty-three months in office. The next day the Senate condemned him by seventy-six votes to three, barring him from public office until 2000.

Farias fled to Thailand but was arrested, jailed and paroled after two years. In 1996 Farias's bullet-spattered body was found sprawled across a bed in his opulent beach house outside Maceió, together with that of Suzana Marcolini, his twenty-eight-year-old lover. Though conspiracy theorists had a field day, the overwhelming evidence is that she shot him and then herself after he told her over a drunken dinner that he planned to end their affair.* The soap opera had a happier ending for Collor himself. In 1994 the supreme court absolved him of corruption, citing flaws in the prosecution case. In 2006 he was elected as a senator for Alagoas. He became chair of the Senate infrastructure committee; he was a government ally under both Lula and Dilma Rousseff.[12]

Brazil could draw some consolation from the Collor saga. The media played an important role in exposing his misdeeds, and the Congress in punishing them. The institutions worked. For the first time in Brazilian history a president was removed from office by legal, constitutional means without the involvement of the army.[13] When Collor had called for manifestations of public support, he was answered by demonstrations of young people, faces painted black, calling for his impeachment, inspired partly by *Anos Rebeldes*, a Globo drama about the student movement of the 1960s. It was the biggest popular mobilization since the *Diretas Já* campaign. Yet it was somehow characteristic of Brazil's problems that the man who proclaimed it his mission to modernize his country (and in part did so) practised the old patrimonial vice of blurring the public interest with private ones.

The vice-president, Itamar Franco, a seemingly bumbling senator whose only administrative experience had been as a two-term mayor of Juiz de Fora, a city in Minas Gerais, took over as president. Like Sarney, he would have been few voters' first choice. But he did much better than Sarney. He formed a broad-based coalition government. Its most powerful figure would be Fernando Henrique Cardoso, initially the foreign minister and from May 1993 the finance minister.

---

* Prosecutors later re-opened the case, charging four Alagoan policemen detailed to guard the house with double murder. They were acquitted in May 2013.

The Real Plan conquers inflation

Inflation was an endemic disease in Latin America. It was often associated with populism. It was a way of softening conflicts over the distribution of wealth and income: governments could promise everything to everyone and the bill would magically be paid without people realizing it, because the real value of those spending promises quickly fell. After the region went bankrupt in 1982 several countries – Bolivia, Argentina and Peru, for example – suffered hyperinflation (usually defined as inflation of more than 50 per cent a month); their peoples would abandon the currency, trusting only in the dollar. These episodes were so disruptive of economic life that they rarely lasted long. By 1993, most of Latin America had overcome inflation through liberal economic reform: cutting the fiscal deficit by slimming a bloated state, and opening up to imports and foreign investment – the recipe that came to be called the Washington Consensus.

Why did Brazil take so long to reform? The roots of Brazilian inflation were uniquely deep and tangled. Indexation had become a way to make inflation tolerable to many sections of society. It also meant that the country never lost control of the currency; dollarization never happened in Brazil. But indexation also had a ratchet effect on inflation: any temporary increase in prices in one part of the economy (from a bad harvest, say, or a devaluation) would automatically result in a permanent increase in all prices. And inflation constituted a tax on the poor, who were obliged to hold cash. The stubbornness of Brazilian inflation prompted a debate among economists. Many concluded that the orthodox remedy, of cutting demand, didn't work in Brazil: the squeeze administered by Delfim under the IMF programme in 1981 prompted a deep recession, but annual inflation fell only from 110 per cent to 95 per cent. For one school, called 'neo-structuralists', the problem was that Brazil's economy was highly monopolized: when demand fell, firms were able to raise prices to preserve their profit margins. They argued for price and wage controls. Another group of economists, who gathered at the Catholic University in Rio (known as PUC-Rio) stressed the crucial role of inertia – or the self-fulfilling expectation that inflation would continue.[14]

The New Republic's first effort to tackle inflation, the Cruzado Plan (named for a new currency) of February 1986, reflected some of the new thinking. It involved a price freeze but, thanks to Sarney's hunger for popularity, bigger wage increases than his economic team had proposed. At first it seemed to be a spectacular success. Inflation quickly fell to zero. Consumption boomed. Then shortages appeared. The police were even sent out to arrest cattle, allegedly being held back from slaughter by *fazendeiros* rebelling against the price freeze. The plan fell apart and by January 1987 the monthly rate of inflation was back to 16 per cent. A further five anti-inflation plans would follow over the next six years. All contained variants of price and wage controls. They all failed. After the Cruzado Plan Brazil's high, but relatively stable, inflation accelerated into hyperinflation, even if at times this was temporarily repressed by price freezes.

No wonder that Cardoso felt he had accepted a poisoned chalice: Itamar Franco had burned through three finance ministers in less than eight months. But Cardoso also saw an opportunity. Brazilians were fed up with inflation. Congress and the traditional political leaders had been weakened by the Collor affair and the budget committee scandal. Cardoso had the president's trust. And in fact several of the necessary preconditions for taming inflation had quietly been put in place over the previous eight years. The public finances were still a mess, but somewhat less so. In the course of the Sarney administration, the 'movement account' allowing the Banco do Brasil to create money had been abolished, and a national treasury department set up. The 1988 constitution had imposed a single, unified budget, though the government still overspent wildly. Second, Collor's tariff cuts and trade opening meant that local oligopolies had to compete with imports and couldn't just raise their prices regardless. Access to imports also reduced the threat of shortages if demand surged. And third, through long negotiations begun in the late-1980s Brazil was close to an agreement with its foreign creditors, which would culminate in a partial debt write-off under the Brady Plan. This would allow the country to rejoin the international financial system.*

Cardoso recruited a team of brilliant economists from PUC-Rio, and demanded that they produce a politically coherent plan. This would have three main elements. The first was a new currency, called the *real* (pronounced 'ray-ahl'; *reais* in the plural), a word which means both 'real' and 'royal' in Portuguese and which gave its name to the plan. It would be the eighth new currency since 1942, so 'we knew it would have to be exceptionally strong' in order to gain credibility, Cardoso would say later. The second element was to cut a fiscal deficit of around 8 per cent of GDP. Edmar Bacha, an adviser to Cardoso, came up with a scheme whereby Congress agreed to un-earmark 15 per cent of the budget, giving the federal government complete discretion

---

* Named after Nicholas Brady, the US treasury secretary. The final obstacle to an agreement was that the US Treasury said it could not issue the bonds used as a guarantee in the Brady deals, which had already been struck with several other Latin American countries, unless Brazil had an agreement with the IMF. But the IMF demurred, because it didn't like the Real Plan. In the end Brazil bought the necessary US Treasury bonds itself.

over how and whether to spend it. (This scheme is still in place today.) Cardoso had earlier made emergency cuts totalling 9 per cent of federal spending (or 2.5 per cent of total public spending). In return for extending loan guarantees, state governments were required to clear the $2 billion they owed to the federal government and to devote 9 per cent of their revenues to debt payments. The third, and most innovative, aspect of the plan was the adoption of an idea conceived by Pérsio Arida and André Lara Resende, two young economists at PUC-Rio. This involved a virtual currency – called the Unidade Real de Valor or URV – which would allow a gradual de-indexing of the economy without contaminating the real in the process. In economists' terms, the URV was a unit of account, but not a means of payment. The idea was that Brazilians would convert prices from *cruzeiros reais*, the existing currency, into URVs, at a rate which would be adjusted for inflation every day (it began on 1 March 1994 worth 647.50 *cruzeiros reais*). The URV, which was itself fixed at par to the dollar, would eventually mutate into the real.[15]

The 1994 presidential election was another problem that Cardoso turned into an opportunity. He has said that he decided to stand for president because he failed to persuade Lula, the leader in the opinion polls, to support the Real Plan. He also clearly sensed that if the plan – at first dubbed in the media the FHC plan, after his initials – succeeded it would provide a springboard to the presidency. But to stand, he had to resign as minister in March, before the real itself existed. He took the gamble. The real was launched on 1 July, earlier than the economists wanted. By then it was worth 2,750 *cruzeiros reais*, and so involved mind-bending conversions. Fortunately Brazilians had become seasoned experts in currency matters and in mental arithmetic, and most grasped the intricacies of the URV. The important thing was that the real itself was seen as a strong currency; it was to float against the dollar within a narrow band, and immediately began to appreciate. The URV had sucked indexation out of the economy at last. In the year to June 1994, inflation was around 5,000 per cent. By September, the monthly rate was 1.4 per cent; in 1995 inflation was just 14.8 per cent, the lowest annual rate since 1958 (and by 1998 it would be 1.7 per cent), all without the need for a price and wage freeze.[16]

It is almost impossible to overstate the significance of the Real Plan's conquest of inflation. For Brazilians, everyday life had turned into an exhausting and anguished search for defences against the destruction of all monetary value. Those defences were easier for the rich. The middle class and workers would rush out on payday to supermarkets to buy everything they could. Inflation encouraged businesses to seek to derive profits from financial engineering rather than from making decent products cheaply. Retailers had to re-price and re-label their stock constantly, at times twice a day – and all this without up-to-date computers, until the Lei de Informática was scrapped. Long-term financial or household planning became impossible. Mortgages and other kinds of credit dried up.

Inflation also risked triggering a breakdown of trust in the restored democracy. Between 1985 and 1994, the currency changed its name five times and lost nine zeroes, before finally being divided by 2,750. As Miriam Leitão notes, between 1980 and July 1994, inflation had totalled over 13.3 trillion per cent, Brazil had thirteen different finance ministers – almost one a year – and three debt defaults. In the nineteen years after July 1994, accumulated inflation was little more than 200 per cent, and Brazil had just three finance ministers.[17] With inflation no longer eroding incomes, some 13 million Brazilians moved out of poverty between 1993 and 1995. Cheap imports, together with the boost to purchasing power from low inflation, prompted a consumer boom. Between 1994 and 1998, the retail price of a colour television in Brazilian shops fell from $700 to $400, and that of a bicycle from 300 reais to 90 reais. In those years, sales of products as diverse as yoghurt, shampoo, cars and colour televisions more than doubled.[18]

Cardoso felt the immediate impact of the Real Plan's success on the campaign trail. On 11 July, less than a fortnight after the real's launch, arriving in Santa Maria da Vitoria, a small town in the *sertão* of Bahia, 'I realized I would win the election,' he wrote in his memoirs. The townspeople held up one-real notes and asked him to autograph them. Lula was a symbol in himself; to beat him, Cardoso needed the symbol of the real. He won convincingly, with 34 million votes (54 per cent of the total) against 27 per cent for Lula. Brazil's slow, accident-prone transition to democracy finally seemed complete. While in several other Latin American countries liberal economic reforms were the work of authoritarian regimes, in Brazil inflation was vanquished by democracy.

Cardoso's battle to reform Brazil

As well as a politician, Fernando Henrique Cardoso was a sophisticated intellectual, one of Latin America's leading sociologists. In several meetings with him over the years, I found him to be a man of polished charm, extraordinarily articulate and an acute analyst of the problems of his country, its region and the world. As president, he had the academic sociologist's sense of the authority of his office, and the manner in which it should and shouldn't be used. Many Brazilians were relieved that at last their country was represented by someone of whom they could feel proud, able to discuss with world leaders fluently in English, French and Spanish. The same went for his wife, Ruth

Corrêa Leite Cardoso, a social anthropologist and feminist who had written much about social movements and who retained the respect of many on the left. His critics saw Cardoso as vain and lacking in the common touch, a representative of the elite rather than of the people.

Cardoso was born into a family of soldier-politicians. His paternal grandfather had been one of the republican army officers who ordered Dom Pedro to leave; his great uncle was Vargas's war minister during the São Paulo revolt; his father was a *tenente* who became a general and then a PTB congressman. Fernando Henrique became a Marxist academic. He was the co-author of an influential work on dependency theory.* After the 1964 coup, he went into exile in Chile and then France, and his views evolved. On returning to Brazil, he threw himself into politics, supporting the MDB, the democratic opposition. In 1978, he stood for the Senate from São Paulo; he came second. When Franco Montoro, who had come first, was elected state governor in 1982, Cardoso took up his Senate seat.

On taking office as president, Cardoso's task was to consolidate the early success of the real, to modernize the economy and restore rapid growth and to make Brazil a fairer country. 'Social justice', he said in his inaugural address, 'will be the number one objective of my administration.' All this required a radical reform of the Brazilian state, to transform the national developmental state into a regulatory one. 'Patronage, corporativism and corruption drain away the taxpayer's money before it reaches those who should be the legitimate beneficiaries of government activities, primarily in the social arena,' he added.[19]

The problem was that Cardoso had to deal with a Congress where such practices were ingrained. His centrist PSDB had forged an electoral alliance with two other parties. The conservative Party of the Liberal Front (PFL) represented the traditional political elite of the north-east. Its most prominent leader was Antonio Carlos Magalhães, a tough political boss from Bahia. The PTB was a small conservative party (bearing no resemblance to the party of Vargas and Goulart). A section of the PMDB later joined the governing coalition. On paper, the government commanded the support of 70 per cent of Congress, easily enough to secure constitutional changes. But in practice these required rounding up at least 60 per cent of the total membership of each house not just for formal votes on constitutional bills, in two consecutive

---

* Subscribed to by the Latin American left, dependency theory held that the region's 'subordinate' role in the world economy as an exporter of raw materials prevented it from achieving development and condemned it to political authoritarianism (though in Cardoso's version industrialization offered the hope of more autonomous development).

sessions of Congress, but also to knock down forests of line-by-line spoiling amendments by opponents. Cardoso admitted in his memoirs that he had to yield to party pressure – for patronage jobs and pork-barrel spending – more than he wanted to.[20]

Cardoso's biggest legislative success was in rolling back the state's domination of the economy. He began by getting Congress to approve constitutional amendments ending the state monopolies of oil, gas distribution, telecoms and merchant shipping, and granting the same treatment to foreign companies operating in Brazil as to local firms. He pushed ahead with privatization. All told, between 1991 and 2002 Brazil auctioned off control of 119 companies (and minority stakes in others), raising around $75 billion, plus $10 billion from selling new contracts for private provision of public services of various kinds. Among many other companies, Cardoso sold off Companhia Vale do Rio Doce (CVRD), the mining giant, and Telebras, the telecoms company, whose constituent parts fetched $30 billion in 1998 (then the world's biggest single privatization). Under private management, many of these companies were transformed, becoming much more efficient. The steel industry had needed 115,000 workers to produce 22.6 million tonnes of steel in 1990; six years later, its output was 25.2 million tonnes with just 65,000 workers. Vale (as CVRD renamed itself) went from being a sprawling national conglomerate into the world's second-biggest multinational mining company. Another big success was Petrobras. This was not privatized, but it lost its monopoly; the floating of 40 per cent of its shares on the stock market forced it to behave much more like a private company. Its output more than doubled as a result, from 700,000 barrels per day in 1995 to 1.5 million b/d in 2002. The transformation of telecoms was especially dramatic. In state hands, Brazil had just 20 million telephone lines. When I arrived in São Paulo in 1996 to set up *The Economist*'s Brazil bureau, the only ways to obtain a telephone line were to wait three years or to pay $4,000 in a thriving 'grey' market. Within four years of privatization, the number of landlines had doubled, while mobiles multiplied more than sixfold. Unlike in Mexico, where turning a state telecoms monopoly into a private one made Carlos Slim the world's richest man, Brazil managed to inject competition, at least in mobile telephony.[21] By 2010, there were 200 million mobile phone connections, but by then there were mounting customer complaints about poor service from what some believed had become an oligopoly.

Privatization in Brazil was not as far-reaching as in some other Latin American countries: Cardoso left the three big federal banks, as well as Petrobras, in public hands. Nevertheless, the policy became unpopular in Brazil (though less so than in many other Latin American countries). Geraldo Alckmin, the PSDB's hapless presidential candidate in 2006, refused to defend it. True, there were some failures. The most notable one was the electricity system: distribution companies were sold off, but four-fifths of generation remained in state hands; and the lack of an effective regulatory system contributed to widespread power cuts when drought reduced hydroelectric output in 2001. Vale, sold to a Brazilian consortium, was almost certainly undervalued. As with many Brazilian privatizations, public-sector pension funds played a key role in this consortium, giving the government continuing influence or even control. Often, the first thing private owners did was to lay off thousands of workers. But over time employment grew again in many privatized companies. Utility tariffs rose quite steeply after privatization, but that was inevitable given the previous subsidies, which were inequitable as well as inefficient.[22] Tellingly, neither Lula nor Dilma has attempted to reverse the privatizations directly.

The government was unwilling, or unable, to show the same energy in getting the public finances under control. This would prove costly. When I interviewed him in the Planalto in March 1999, Cardoso told me that in retrospect he should have been 'much more severe in controlling federal spending and in encouraging state governors to do the same.' Others agreed: Tasso Jereissati, a senior figure in the PSDB, said that 'one of the mistakes we made was not to do all the reforms together' at the start of the term, when presidential authority and popularity are normally at their greatest.

But this was politically difficult. Constitutional amendments – to reform pensions, the civil service and the tax system – languished in Congress. In his memoirs Cardoso states that outside the economic team there was no consciousness of the need for a fiscal squeeze, and that there was a legitimate demand for social spending.[23]

Instead of fiscal austerity, the government continued to rely on the exchange rate to curb inflation. But keeping the real strong in turn required high – and sometimes astronomic – interest rates. The policy combination of fiscal laxity, an overvalued real and high interest rates was costly – and would prove unsustainable. For many businesses the adjustment to an open market economy was rendered harder than it needed to be. For all its unquestionable benefits for the country at large, the Real Plan put tens of thousands of relatively well-paid industrial workers in São Paulo out of a job. Even so, Cardoso remained popular. As Eduardo Giannetti, an economist and philosopher then at São Paulo University (USP), put it to me in April 1996, shortly after I had arrived as *The Economist's* correspondent:

> Brazil has gone through a very powerful learning process. Without a stable currency there is no future for this country, and no self-respect. Ordinary people have learned that the fight against inflation is a matter of life and

death and has to be won. Cardoso was elected on this and has a mandate to finish the job.[24]

Cardoso's first term turned into a bruising battle to preserve economic stability in the face of repeated episodes of financial turbulence. The first test came in 1995 when in the aftermath of Mexico's chaotic devaluation capital flooded out of Latin America. The government responded with a small devaluation and the introduction of a 'crawling peg' (under which the real would move downwards within a narrow band), and raised interest rates. That brought two years of calm on the external front. The next test came at home. The end of inflation shone an unforgiving light on the banking system. Weaker banks had lived on lending their overnight cash float. In 1995–6 three of the top ten banks and more than fifty smaller ones went bust. The government's response was exemplary (far more skilful than the Bank of England's handling of the Northern Rock insolvency of 2007, for example). The Central Bank took over the stricken banks, sold off the viable bits and wound up the rest. Cardoso resisted heavy political pressure to bail out the bankers, rather than the banks. A new deposit-insurance scheme was set up, funded by the banks themselves. The bank clean-up programme, known as PROER, cost around 3 per cent of GDP. Though unpopular, it was money well spent: Brazil's banks today are solid and well capitalized. At the same time, as part of a broader restructuring and partial write-off of their debts the state governors were required to wind up or privatize their banks. This exercise cost the federal government around R/100 billion, half of it for São Paulo alone (the legacy of eight years of populist government in the state under the aegis of the PMDB's Orestes Quércia). The Banco do Brasil, too, needed an R/8 billion bail-out.

Clearing out these 'fiscal skeletons' as they were called, left behind by inflation, required years of dogged negotiation by Pedro Malan, the finance minister, a quietly forceful man, whose habit of smoking a pipe became more frequent in this period. The fiscal skeletons, and higher salaries and pension spending at the start of the government, had contributed to a deterioration in the public finances, which moved from a small surplus in 1994 to a deficit of 4.9 per cent of GDP in 1995. Malan insisted that the government was gradually getting on top of the public finances. The deficit indeed fell slightly in 1996. Revenues from privatization bought time. But from 1997 onwards, the high interest rates required to sustain the real pushed up the cost of servicing the public debt and the deficit, which reached 8.4 per cent of GDP in 1998.[25]

As well as a fiscal deficit, Brazil began to register a widening current account deficit. Only around 40 per cent of this was covered by foreign direct investment (the long-term kind in factories and the like). The rest was covered by short-term financial investment ('hot money') which – unlike the syndicated bank loans common in the 1970s – could leave as quickly as it came. Brazil found itself subjected to a roller-coaster ride in the financial markets.

Cardoso often warned about the dangers inherent in the extreme volatility of unregulated international capital markets. In a speech in 1995 he noted that the institutions set up at Bretton Woods in 1944 – the IMF and the World Bank – were no longer sufficient to deal with the challenges of the contemporary financial system:

> These institutions date from before the computer. Everything has changed now. Today a kind of massive speculation is possible, because there is so much more money that doesn't obey any authority, be it of a country or a Central Bank . . . So we have to face this problem.[26]

Globalization and computers had facilitated the 'virtualization' of money, he said on another occasion. Traditional finance capitalism was 'benign' compared with today's 'perverse' version:

> It perhaps makes explicit, in the most worked form, that the capitalist system contains an element of chance, of gambling, of pure speculation. And the most serious thing . . . is that the virtual has taken command of the real.

As president, Cardoso wrote repeated letters to the leaders of what was then the G7 of rich countries, alerting them to the risk that central banks would lose control over the financial system. The warnings were ignored but were premonitory: barely a decade later, these forces would trigger the world financial crash of 2007–8.[27]

The economic team was split about how to deal with Brazil's twin deficits. Pérsio Arida had resigned as head of the Central Bank in 1995 because he believed Brazil should have responded to Mexico's turmoil by floating the real. José Serra, the planning minister, agreed with him, and left the government the following year: he argued that 'stability' should not come at the price of 'development'. By early 1997 several other economists close to the government were pushing Cardoso to devalue. But Malan and Gustavo Franco, the Central Bank's international director (and its president from 1997), insisted that inflation had to be killed first. Franco defended the strong real as an instrument to modernize the economy, by forcing business to become more efficient and by lowering the cost of imported machinery and inputs.[28]

To make matters worse, as this debate raged Cardoso himself was preoccupied with a constitutional amendment to allow the re-election of the president, governors and mayors for two consecutive terms, which he secured in June 1997. This was something he had previously opposed; it was controversial, not least because it benefited an incumbent president. Cardoso argued that a single four-year term was too short.

The government thus lost the chance to devalue when financial markets were calm. When currency turmoil enveloped several Asian countries, Brazil's twin deficits made it vulnerable. To stave off a run on the real, in October 1997 the government doubled the Central Bank's short-term interest rate to 43 per cent, announced spending cuts and tax rises worth 2.5 per cent of GDP and began a fresh effort to get Congress to approve administrative and pension reform. But in a cruel twist of fate Cardoso lost his two most important political operators within three days of each other in April 1998: Sergio Motta, a PSDB stalwart and the communications minister, died of a lung infection, while a heart attack struck down Luís Eduardo Magalhaes, the forty-three-year-old son of Antonio Carlos, who was president of the lower house and with whom Cardoso had developed a close rapport. And turmoil soon returned to world financial markets in August 1998 when Russia devalued and defaulted on its debt. Once again investors dumped Brazilian assets and the real came under pressure. Once again the government responded by jacking up the interest rate, to almost 50 per cent. Just ten days before the October 1998 election at which Cardoso sought a second term, he announced harsh fiscal measures and said that Brazil would seek the help of the IMF. 'I will do everything, absolutely everything, to guarantee the stability of the real,' he declared. He won the election easily, winning 36 million votes (53.1 per cent); Lula, in his third successive defeat, managed 31.7 per cent.

Laying the foundations

In January 1999, less than a fortnight into his second term, Cardoso was forced into the devaluation he had fought so hard to avoid. In the previous five months, around $50 billion had left the country as investors became convinced that, despite the government's protestations, devaluation was inevitable. The credit squeeze had throttled economic growth. The Congress rejected a pension reform. The last straw came when Itamar Franco, who had been elected governor of Minas Gerais, announced a default on his state's debt – an apparent fit of jealousy over Cardoso's success. At the Central Bank, the president replaced Gustavo Franco, the chief intellectual defender of the strong real, with Francisco Lopes, whose attempt at a controlled devaluation swiftly failed. Cardoso then bowed to market pressure and let the real float: by early March it had sunk to 2.25 against the dollar (from 1.1 in early January), before stabilizing at around 1.7 by April.

The devaluation was a political defeat for Cardoso: he never regained the popularity of his first term. But it proved to be an economic victory for Brazil. To run the Central Bank, the president turned to Arminio Fraga, another economist from PUC-Rio who was working as a fund manager in New York for George Soros. At Fraga's instigation, the government adopted targets for inflation (to be not below 2.5 per cent and not above 6.5 per cent a year) and for the primary fiscal surplus (i.e. before interest payments) of 3.1 per cent of GDP. Fraga and Malan persuaded Larry Summers, the US Treasury secretary, of the wisdom of these policies; Summers in turn helped to convince the IMF that the $18.1 billion it had granted Brazil in November to prevent the devaluation, as part of a broader rescue package worth $41.6 billion, should be re-deployed to back the floating currency. The IMF wanted Brazil to adopt an Argentine-style currency board just when this arrangement was about to collapse in Argentina – the latest of many mistakes of judgement the Fund made with regard to Brazil. Financial turmoil shocked Congress into approving pension and administrative reforms at last, albeit in watered-down form. The government codified its reforms of the public finances in a Fiscal Responsibility Law. This fixed spending limits for all three levels of government, banned federal loans to states and municipalities, and limited payroll spending to 60 per cent of revenues. It threatened officials who broke these stipulations with criminal charges and prison (though this provision has never been applied).[29]

In the first couple of months of 1999, there was much commentary in Brazil and outside that the country had fallen back into the instability of the recent past. It was tribute to the depth of the changes Cardoso had wrought that it didn't. 'People said the government is about to collapse, but that's not true. We have been able to react,' the president told me in March 1999.[30] Inflation was quickly brought under control. The economy suffered a second year of stagnation in 1999, but not the deep recession which many had forecast. Malan's patient work of cleaning out the fiscal skeletons and of slimming the corporate state had finally paid off, allowing the government to achieve a primary fiscal surplus. The Central Bank was given operational independence to set monetary policy to meet the inflation target.

The new policy tripod of a floating currency, inflation targeting and a primary fiscal surplus allowed Brazil to achieve the elusive combination of economic stability and, eventually, faster growth. As it became more difficult to finance the current account deficit, the government took steps to stimulate exports, which had languished in the first term. But it would be Lula, not Cardoso and the PSDB, who reaped the fruits of these policies. After a promising recovery, with growth of 4.4 per cent in 2000, the economy was knocked back again, first by the power cuts of 2001 and then by the knock-on effect of the dotcom crash on Wall Street and, especially, Argentina's economic collapse at the end of that year.

While the economic dramas commanded most of the headlines, Cardoso also did much to reform and improve social policy. Previous presidents had treated the education and health ministries as political prizes; there were nine different education ministers between 1985 and 1994. Cardoso appointed Paulo Renato Souza, a capable university rector and educational reformer, to the job and kept him there for eight years. The government pushed through a constitutional amendment to create a fund, known as Fundef, to finance better salaries for teachers in the poorest states (where these were as low as US$20–US$30 per month). Between 1995 and 2002, primary school attendance increased from 88 per cent (75 per cent among black children) to 97 per cent (94 per cent among blacks). The number of secondary school pupils increased by 70 per cent in the same period.[31] José Serra, health minister in Cardoso's second term, implemented the constitutional mandate to unify federal, state and municipal health services, expanding provision and trimming waste. Serra told me that he was 'obsessed by cutting costs in health', and cited simple examples such as central ordering of vaccines which saved 60 million reais a year.[32] All told, the Cardoso governments increased health spending by 34 per cent in real terms.

The administration put in place a social safety net – 'with holes, but much better than nothing', as Vilmar Faria, an adviser to Cardoso put it in 1999.[33] This included a 1995 law which entitled the sick and disabled to a payment equal to the minimum wage. Much of the government's efforts went on trying to improve the management of social programmes, and to focus them on the poorest people and the poorest areas. In this effort much work was done by Ruth Cardoso, who set up a scheme called Comunidade Solidaria, to mobilize and co-ordinate 'third sector' (i.e. NGO and philanthropic activities) activities. This was a far cry from the traditional charitable work to which first ladies had dedicated themselves in the past. The safety net was reinforced in Cardoso's second term. A minimum-income scheme pioneered by PT local governments was turned into a federal programme called Bolsa Escola in 2001. Together with similar schemes from federal ministries, this provided a minimum income to around 5 million families.[34] The government also launched a massive land reform programme.

In his eight years in the Planalto, Cardoso could claim to have laid the foundations of a fairer, more democratic country and to have taken decisive steps to turn Brazil into a more modern and more competitive economy. Before him, only two elected presidents, Dutra and Kubitschek, had completed their terms since the far-off time of the First Republic. At last, Brazilian

democracy looked secure. Cardoso's proudest boast, oft-repeated to inter-
viewers, was that he had given Brazil *rumo* (a sense of direction).[35] Critics
thought that he made too many concessions to the backwoodsmen in his
congressional coalition. Depressingly, it took seven years for Congress to
approve a limited reform of the public administration. Promised reforms of
tax and the political system got nowhere. By 2001 the government had lost
control of its coalition, which became riven by in-fighting, especially between
the PFL of Antonio Carlos Magalhaes and the PMDB. Nevertheless, Cardoso's
administrations secured the approval of thirty-five constitutional amendments, most of them rolling back the corporate state.

Economically, the Cardoso era was bittersweet. Low inflation and economic
stability were historic conquests. But Brazil paid a price in economic growth
forgone for the government's over-reliance on the strong real and relative
fiscal laxity in the first term. Between 1995 and 2002 economic growth averaged just 2.3 per cent per year, though that disappointing performance was
partly due to a difficult external context of bouts of international financial
turbulence and low world prices for Brazil's commodity exports. The depreciation of the real meant the government missed its inflation target in 2001
and 2002. After rising in Cardoso's first term, average real incomes fell by
13 per cent between 1998 and 2003. The tax burden rose steadily throughout
the Cardoso years, and the public debt doubled. Unemployment rose too: by
March 1999, it had reached 7.8 per cent, the highest figure since 1982,
according to IBGE, the statistics agency. Dieese, a research centre linked to the
labour unions which used a different methodology, calculated unemployment
in greater São Paulo at 19.9 per cent in the same month, a near doubling in ten
years. Some of the job losses were the inevitable by-product of the transition
from an inward-looking industrial economy to one that had become part of a
globalized economy. The flip side was that productivity rose as businesses
invested in newer technology and in staff training: output per worker in
manufacturing industry in Brazil rose at an annual average rate of 8.4 per cent
in the 1990s, almost as rapidly as in South Korea and twice as fast as in the US,
according to a study by the Getúlio Vargas Foundation, a think-tank and
private university.[36]

The passage of time makes the Cardoso government look more exceptional both for the volume of reforms it achieved, and for its liberal outlook.
His critics, led by Lula and the PT, claimed that Cardoso's 'neo-liberal' policies constituted a 'cursed inheritance' that had destroyed Brazil's industrial
base. Cardoso himself has taken great pains to rebut the 'neo-liberal' tag: 'If we
did anything in the ten years I was minister or president, it was to rebuild the
administrative machinery, give greater consistency to public policies, in

summary to remake the state.'[37] Though the market turmoil and congressional delays meant that many observers failed to detect it at the time, Cardoso had indeed given Brazil *rumo*. Perhaps the greatest compliment he received was a back-handed one: Brazilians believed that they could now safely elect Lula to the presidency. And that was because Lula himself had made it clear he would continue and complement, but not dismantle, Cardoso's policies.

CHAPTER EIGHT

Lulismo and the Brazilian Dream

On 10 February 1980, some 1,200 people gathered at Colégio Sion, a Catholic school in Higienópolis, an affluent São Paulo neighbourhood of leafy avenues and airy apartment blocks, to found a new political party and approve its manifesto. The Partido dos Trabalhadores (PT) or Workers' Party arose from the political ferment unleashed by the decadence of the military regime and the great strikes of 1978–9 in the car factories of the industrial suburbs. The new party was the product of a lengthy debate, which took place mainly in greater São Paulo. In this debate, Cardoso was among those who argued that the left should work within the MDB, to turn it into the party of a broad, multi-class progressive movement. Lula had campaigned for Cardoso in his 1978 Senate race and in those days the two were friends. But others, especially the leaders of the 'new unionism', and eventually Lula himself, argued for a new socialist party based on the organized working class that would break the Brazilian mould of elitist political conciliation. Together with the union leaders, three other groups came together to form the PT. The biggest of them comprised Catholics drawn from the Christian base groups; influenced by liberation theology, many of them were active in social movements of urban squatters, landless rural workers and so on. Then there were the remnants of the guerrilla movements of the 1960s and 1970s and other small far-left currents, especially Trotskyists. The third group was leftist intellectuals and students. In other Latin American countries such broad coalitions of the left often fell apart amid sectarian squabbles. That the PT avoided that fate was partly because it allowed – but set rules for – organized internal factions, though this would cause other problems.[1]

The PT became Latin America's biggest, most original and most successful left-wing party. In its early years it was ambivalent about representative democracy, instead devoting itself to building a mass organization – it had about 230,000 active members by the end of the 1990s – and to extra-parliamentary action through social movements. Though PT candidates were elected as mayors in Porto Alegre (which became a PT bastion) and São Paulo in 1988, the party found electoral politics harder – until the 1989 presidential campaign established Lula as the undisputed leader of the left. The PT was able to grow, albeit slowly, despite the collapse of Communism in Europe. Although it contained Marxist factions these were never in the majority. It was not inspired by Moscow, Beijing or even Havana (though some of its leaders had sought refuge in Cuba during the dictatorship and many of its activists sympathized with Fidel Castro's regime). Instead, many of its intellectuals saw the PT as an expression of radical and egalitarian democracy. It could claim to be almost the only political party in Brazilian history organized from below, rather than from within the state. Its only rival in that regard was the Communist Party, which in its heyday in the late 1940s had around 300,000 members, but whose policies were in part dictated from abroad. The PT's original commitment to class struggle mellowed into a more modern and relevant crusade for 'citizenship' for all Brazilians. Raymundo Faoro, an intellectual sympathetic to it, accurately forecast in 1990 that the party would survive the fall of the Berlin Wall because, he said, it was 'the repository of the demand for social justice' in a country where the elite 'lacks all sense of social responsibility'.[2] Yet there was an unresolved tension in the PT's attitudes: its economic policy was thoroughly statist, and one of its core constituencies – current and retired public-sector workers – was a pillar of the corporate state. As Roberto DaMatta, the anthropologist, put it, 'part of the PT, like Vargas, doesn't see the individual' but instead only gives importance to collective categories and corporatist forms of organization.[3]

Many of the party's leaders drew the wrong conclusion from Lula's narrow defeat in 1989 in a polarized election against the backdrop of economic pain and the apparent failure of the New Republic. They believed it showed that the PT could win power on a far-left platform. Although Lula, who had never been a Marxist, became more moderate in the 1990s, the outdated state socialism to which his party clung doomed him to defeat in 1994 and 1998 against Cardoso. In Congress the PT delegation opposed all of Cardoso's constitutional amendments, even clearly progressive ones such as pension reform and Fundef, the fund to make education spending fairer. Because Lula was far more popular than the PT, and because he was its indispensable leader, each defeat strengthened his hand in relation to the party. But uniquely among Brazilian political parties, the PT's members elected the national leadership, which contained representatives from the competing internal factions. Lula and his key lieutenant, José Dirceu, who became the party's president in

1995, had to negotiate every move that the PT made towards the centre and towards becoming competitive in national elections.

'I changed, Brazil changed'

By 2002, these efforts reached fruition. On the one hand, the 1999 devaluation and the subsequent stop–go economy had deprived the Cardoso government of some of its popularity. Polls showed that unemployment had replaced inflation as Brazilians' biggest worry. On the other hand, Lula took more decisive steps towards the centre. His campaign team hired Duda Mendonça, then the country's top political marketing guru, who softened the candidate's image with the slogan *Lulinha, Paz e Amor* ('Lula [in friendly diminutive form], Peace and Love'). Lula had taken to highlighting his early life as a migrant from the north-east rather than his time as a strike leader. He portrayed himself both as a consensual negotiator and as the embodiment of the Brazilian dream of upward social mobility and of climbing out of poverty through his own efforts. He forced the PT to accept as campaign allies not just the usual clutch of small left-wing parties but also the Partido Liberal, a conservative outfit with strong ties to the evangelical churches, which provided his vice-presidential running mate, José Alencar, a textile manufacturer.

At its national meeting at the end of 2001, the PT approved a document which called for a 'necessary rupture' with 'the neo-liberal model' and the IMF, and the nationalization of the banks.[4] But Lula's campaign platform was much more moderate: it not only omitted any reference to socialism or to reversing privatization, but endorsed agribusiness as well as agrarian reform. 'I changed, Brazil changed,' he repeated during the campaign. Gone, too, was previous talk of renegotiating the public debt (which contrary to the left's rhetoric was mainly not 'foreign', but owned by Brazilian investors and pension funds). The final step in the march to the centre came in June 2002 when Lula issued a 'Letter to the Brazilian People' in which he made his peace with the Real Plan and the Cardoso reforms. 'Stability and control of the public accounts and of inflation are today the patrimony of all Brazilians,' he wrote. He has since said that he spent ten days hesitating before signing the letter 'because I had to change part of my history'.[5] Tellingly, the letter was issued in Lula's own name, not that of the PT.

Despite the Letter, as Lula climbed in the opinion polls, financial market investors fell prey to self-fulfilling panic. The real plunged to below three to the dollar, even though the Central Bank jacked up interest rates yet again. That raised fears that the public debt – which had climbed to around $350 billion or 62 per cent of GDP in July 2002 and most of which was linked to the dollar or to interest rates – would become unpayable. This in turn prompted what economists call a 'sudden stop' in capital inflows: nervous foreign banks yanked in their credit lines and investors dumped Brazilian assets. Some well-known economists in Washington forecast that the country would be forced into another debt default.[6] The markets were calmed, but only temporarily, when the government negotiated a fresh IMF loan, for $30 billion, aimed at warding off further speculative attacks on the real and to finance Brazil's big current account deficit.[7] The money was not due to be disbursed until after the election. Cardoso got Lula to declare his public support for the economic programme on which the loan was based, which involved raising the primary fiscal surplus to 3.75 per cent of GDP. Nevertheless, the financial markets plunged again when it became clear that Lula would win the election. He secured 46.4 per cent of the vote, well ahead of the PSDB's José Serra (23.2 per cent). Anthony Garotinho, the corrupt, populist former governor of Rio de Janeiro and an evangelical Christian, won 17.9 per cent and Ciro Gomes, a maverick former finance minister and governor of Ceará, obtained 12 per cent. In a run-off on 27 October 2002 Lula duly defeated Serra by 53 million votes (61.3 per cent) to 33 million (38.7 per cent).

'We can do much more'

Lula's election was the most significant achievement for the democratic left in Latin America since that of Salvador Allende in Chile in 1970 – and, despite the market turmoil, in far more propitious underlying circumstances. My view, as I wrote in a cover leader for *The Economist* on the eve of the election's first round, was that Lula's impending victory constituted

> a triumph for Brazilian democracy. In a region long ruled by generals or grandees, it would have been unthinkable not long ago ... [it] would do much to demolish the idea, more myth than fact, that Latin American democracy is still just a game rigged for the benefit of the better-off.[8]

On the night of his victory Lula told thousands of ecstatic supporters thronging São Paulo's broad Avenida Paulista that Brazil had 'rejected the current economic model, based on dependence, and in favour of a new model of development'. Lula would maintain that rhetoric in office, yet many of his actions belied it.

Lula has extraordinarily sharp political instincts and great empathy for ordinary Brazilians, whom he knew were not revolutionary or even left-wing. His own life had given him an abiding hatred of the injustice and humiliation suffered by the poor. But because of his trade union experience he was 'a man who knows the value of 3 per cent', as José Sarney put it in a widely quoted observation. He would often say that as the first manual worker to become president he 'could not afford to fail'.

Lula's inaugural speech in Brasília two months later was marked both by that caution and by his consciousness of the enormous symbolic significance of his election for Brazil's democracy:

> When I look back at my own life, at the refugee from the drought of the northeast, at the boy who sold peanuts and oranges on the wharves of Santos, who became a lathe operator and union leader, who went on to found the Workers' Party and who believed in what he was doing, who now becomes the head of state, I see and know, with clarity and conviction, that we can do much more.[9]

While declaring that 'change' was the emphatic message of the election, he said this was a 'gradual and continuous process' to be reached through 'dialogue and negotiation'. He added: 'we will have to control our many and legitimate social anxieties'; they would be dealt with 'at an adequate pace and at the right moment'.

It was this juggling act of gradual social change within the established order that Lula set out to achieve. It would make him enemies on both left and right. But it also brought him huge popularity both in Brazil and abroad. He portrayed himself as a man who could bridge two worlds, those of the haves and have-nots, symbolized respectively by the fat cats of the World Economic Forum in Davos and the leftist social movements who gathered in Porto Alegre in 2003 to launch a rival World Social Forum (WSF). Lula appeared at both that year: thereafter, he disappointed the utopians of the WSF rather more than the Davos crowd.

Installed in the Planalto, Lula called for six reforms – of pensions, tax, labour, the political system, land and the financial system – and set up various talking shops to discuss them. Most of these measures commanded a broad consensus, in theory if not in detail, though most were not favoured by many in the PT. But Lula's first task was to reassure investors. Days after the election, Antonio Palocci, a PT moderate who had been Lula's campaign co-ordinator and would become the finance minister, had announced that the new government would impose a further tightening of fiscal policy in order to stabilize the debt, raising the target for the primary fiscal surplus to 4.25 per cent of GDP. To head the Central Bank, Lula turned to Henrique Meirelles, a former chief executive of BankBoston, an American bank, who had been elected to Congress for the PSDB, not the PT. Meirelles proceeded to raise interest rates to defend the currency and to try to meet the inflation target. Over the next eight years, whenever Brazil's stubbornly high interest rates produced howls of protest, Lula always backed his Central Bank chief, who enjoyed operational independence (as his predecessors under Cardoso had). The president also included a couple of prominent businessmen in his Cabinet, in the agriculture and industry portfolios.

Palocci was a medical doctor, a former Trotskyist turned pragmatist. As mayor of Ribeirão Preto, a prosperous farming city in upstate São Paulo, he had established good relations with the local sugar barons and privatized some municipal services. Like Cardoso, he believed that globalization was inexorable, and not something that Brazil could choose to accept or reject.[10] He understood that the priority was to consolidate economic and financial stability in order to secure a return to growth. His first task as finance minister was to form a team with which to govern. The PT had many activists and intellectuals, but few technocrats except in public health, and little experience of governing beyond city level (of the bigger states, it had governed only Rio Grande do Sul). During the campaign, Arminio Fraga had briefed Palocci about the economic situation. He gave him a document drawn up by a broadly liberal team of social scientists containing policy suggestions to restore growth, reduce poverty and inequality and control violent crime. Called *A Agenda Perdida*, it had originally been commissioned by Ciro Gomes.[11] Palocci liked it. Marcos Lisboa, the report's main author, joined the economic team, along with Joaquim Levy, a former IMF official. Over the next couple of years the government proceeded to implement several of the report's recommendations. These included some important microeconomic reforms, such as a new bankruptcy law, a measure to allow credit providers to deduct loan repayments automatically from monthly salaries, and others to stimulate the moribund mortgage market. An innovation law allowed universities to keep some of the profits from joint-ventures with businesses.

In addition, the government pushed through a limited pension reform, raising the years of service required to retire and capping pensions for public-sector workers, but only for new recruits, at the maximum for workers in the national pension scheme for private-sector workers – the same measures the PT had denounced Cardoso for attempting.* This proved too much for some in the party's left wing: three of its deputies and a senator broke away to set up a far-left party, the Party of Socialism and Liberty (PSOL). 'Lula fell into the

---

* This reform was not implemented by Lula, but Dilma Rousseff put it into effect in 2012, when the ceiling was 3,912 reais a month.

trap of seeking power for its own sake. Maybe the PT has fallen into this trap,' said Luciana Genro, one of the dissidents.[12] While the PSOL gained the sympathy of a few prominent intellectuals, it did not pose a serious threat to Lula.

Since the run on the real and on other Brazilian assets had largely been prompted by scepticism about the last-minute nature of Lula's conversion to the market economy (and its incompleteness in the case of the PT), it quickly subsided once the government's commitment to economic stability and reform became clear. Meirelles's tight monetary policy strengthened the real and this, together with Palocci's fiscal squeeze, stabilized the public debt. The economic team faced pressure from the PT, state governors and public-sector workers to open the purse strings and abandon the Fiscal Responsibility Law. Palocci resisted. 'It is infantile to blame the IMF for these measures. We are taking them because they are in Brazil's interest,' he told a packed meeting of financiers at the Bank of England during a visit to London in 2003.[13] He was vindicated by the economy's swift recovery. It grew by 5 per cent in 2004, the real was back to 2.15 to the dollar by the end of 2006 and the risk premium – the spread over the interest rate on American Treasury bonds – demanded by investors for holding Brazilian bonds fell from around 25 percentage points in 2002 to just two. The debt bomb was defused: the government retired most of the dollar debt and replaced it with paper in reais, much of it at fixed interest rates. By 2005 the government was able to pay back its loans from the IMF early, and the Central Bank began cutting interest rates. The government's financial reforms unleashed a credit boom. The world economy, too, was moving decisively in Brazil's favour. As China and other Asian countries industrialized at a furious pace and their people grew richer, demand for commodities, including Brazilian iron ore and soyabeans, increased, prompting their prices to soar. Brazil's term of trade – the ratio of the price of its exports to the price of its imports – improved by more than a third between 2005 and 2011. Higher prices in turn encouraged Brazilian commodity producers and farmers to ramp up production. All this set the stage for a surge in economic growth.[14]

Oddly, Lula's government initially stumbled on social policy – an issue on which the PT had repeatedly criticized Cardoso for not doing enough. In his inaugural address, Lula had promised to make 'ending hunger a great national cause' and said that a food security programme called Fome Zero (Zero Hunger) would be his first priority. This turned out to be an old-fashioned and inefficient scheme for food stamps, drawn up by José Graziano da Silva, an agronomist from the University of Campinas, which reached only 800,000 families in its first year. At Palocci's instigation, Graziano da Silva was side-

1 Brazil as a tropical Eden: an early European portrayal of a Tupi family.

2 A sugar mill in Pernambuco during the Dutch occupation, painted by Frans Post.

3 The slaves' backbreaking labour: washing diamonds in Minas Gerais.

4 Antonio Vieira, the great Jesuit preacher and missionary.

5 Dom Pedro II, a Habsburg in the tropics.

LA RÉCOLTE DU CAFÉ DANS UNE FAZENDA DU BRÉSIL

La cueillette et le transport du café mesuré par «alqueiros» ou boisseaux. — Le lavage en bassin — Le séchage sur l'aire

6 The coffee boom, a belated march of capitalist development.

7 Abaporu by Tarsila do Amaral, the most original of Brazilian modernist painters.

8 Getúlio Vargas, cigar-smoking "father of the people" and founder of the corporate state.

9 The golden years of Copacabana in the 1950s.

10 Juscelino Kubitschek, the
boundless optimist who built
Brasília.

11 Tanks in Rio's streets as the army
takes power in 1964.

12 General Geisel, the most influential of the military dictators.

13 The car workers' strikes made Lula a national figure.

14 The scourge of inflation: when 500,000 cruzeiros bought next to nothing.

15 The Real Plan conquered inflation and took Cardoso to the presidency.

16 Lula, the first factory worker to become president, at his inauguration in 2003.

17 Dilma Rousseff, elected as Lula's protégée.

18 Droughts in the sertão are no longer fatal.

19 An uneasy peace came to the Complexo do Alemão.

20 The concrete jungle of São Paulo.

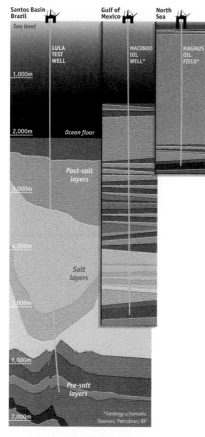

Santos Basin
Brazil

Gulf of
Mexico

North
Sea

Sea level

1,000m

LULA
TEST
WELL

MACONDO
OIL
WELL*

MAGNUS
OIL
FIELD*

2,000m   Ocean floor

Post-salt
layers

3,000m

4,000m

Salt
layers

5,000m

6,000m

Pre-salt
layers

7,000m

*Geology schematic
Sources: Petrobras; BP

21 The pré-sal oil, a bonanza replete with "development risks".

22 Agribusiness conquers the cerrado: harvesting soyabeans in Mato Grosso.

23 Deforestation of the Amazon rainforest continues, but much less rapidly than in the past.

24 A 73km traffic jam of soyabean trucks waiting to load at Paranaguá.

25 The June 2013 protests in São Paulo: the masses demand reform of the state and politics.

26 The day of "national humiliation": Uruguay score a second goal to win the 1950 World Cup final at the Maracanã.

27 The Maracanã, expensively refurbished for the 2014 World Cup.

lined (he went on to become the director of the UN Food and Agriculture Organization in 2011). So was Benedita da Silva, a black PT politician and former domestic servant whom Lula named as social assistance minister, who proved to be a more powerful symbol than administrator. Instead, the government adopted the ideas of Ricardo Paes de Barros, a liberal economist at IPEA, a government-linked economic think-tank, who had written the social policy chapter of *A Agenda Perdida*. This involved unifying the Cardoso government's Bolsa Escola, two other social assistance programmes and Fome Zero into a single scheme called Bolsa Família (Family Fund).[15] Like Bolsa Escola and Mexico's Oportunidades, Bolsa Família was a conditional cash-transfer programme, designed to mitigate poverty in the current generation while providing the next generation with the means to avoid it. It paid mothers a small monthly stipend provided they kept their children in school (as Bolsa Escola had required) and also took them for health checks. By 2006 11 million families received Bolsa Família (and 13.8 million in 2013).

Jeffersonian democracy, Brazilian style

It was in politics and his handling of Congress, rather than economic or social policy, that Lula was most constrained by his party – and this brought his presidency to the brink of disaster. The PT had performed far less well in the election than Lula. It won only ninety-one seats in the lower house, far short of the 257 required for a majority (in the Senate it had fourteen of eighty-one seats). All told, the ten parties of Lula's electoral alliance commanded 250 seats. As political parties multiplied, Brazil had developed what Sergio Abranches, a political scientist, called 'coalitional presidentialism', in which presidents had to form multiparty alliances to govern. This process was usually eased along by the promiscuity of Brazilian parliamentarians: between 1995 and 1998, for example, no fewer than 230 of the 513 congressmen had switched parties, some up to four times. Many of them joined the governing parties in order to win government jobs and secure spending for their states (in 1995–8 the PSDB alone gained forty-seven extra recruits, expanding its delegation by almost half). But the PT had a monkish discipline, requiring a higher level of commitment from its congressmen: it neither attracted nor wanted carpetbaggers (only two joined it in the 2003–6 legislature).[16] It also had a voracious appetite for power, augmented because Lula felt he had to offer top jobs in government to all the party's factions (its left wing comprised about a third of the party's national directorate and more than a quarter of its parliamentary delegation). Dirceu had done a deal which would have secured the PMDB's votes in Congress in return for two choice ministries (transport and regional development, both with juicy public contracts to hand out). But on this Lula felt he had to yield to his own party. 'We decided not to accept the [PMDB's] blackmail,' was how another of Lula's top aides spun it.[17]

The result was that the PT was wildly over-represented in Lula's first Cabinet, with eleven of the twenty-three main ministries. The opportunistic PTB, which after absorbing party-switchers contributed forty-one deputies to the coalition, got just one ministry. To sate the appetite for government posts, Lula massively expanded the federal apparatus, creating a string of Cabinet-level secretariats. When these were taken into account, the PT got 60 per cent of the top jobs in the first Cabinet (the proportions varied only slightly in subsequent ones). In all, Lula added an extra 2,700 patronage appointments to the 20,000 traditionally in the president's gift. A survey of the most senior of these appointees found that two-fifths of them were PT members, who gained jobs irrespective of merit or experience. After years of activism, of endless party meetings and of handing over a chunk of their income to the cause, many believed that a well-paid government job was their just desert.[18]

The smouldering resentment of the PT's congressional allies suddenly exploded in mid-2005, shaking Lula's administration to its foundations. When a videotape surfaced showing a manager at the federal postal service taking a bribe on behalf of his political boss, Roberto Jefferson, the president of the PTB, Jefferson retaliated by unleashing a bombshell in an interview with *Folha de São Paulo*, a newspaper: he said that Delúbio Soares, the PT's treasurer was making cash payments of 30,000 reais ($12,500) to dozens of members of Congress in return for their votes for government bills, as well as funnelling much larger sums to their parties. He called the payments the *mensalão* (big monthly stipend) – a name that stuck for the scandal triggered by his revelations. Jefferson, the former host of a daytime TV show and amateur singer of Italian arias, had been a key ally of Collor, defending him against impeachment. To one of three congressional inquiries set up to look into the ramifications of the *mensalão*, he complained that of the 20 million reais the PT promised his party, he had received only 4 million in two suitcase-loads of cash. Then, in another example of the recurring tendency of Brazilian politics to turn into a *telenovela*, an aide to the brother of the PT's president, José Genoino, was arrested at a São Paulo airport after police found he was carrying $100,000 in dollar bills stuffed down his underpants. The money paid to politicians and parties was channelled through Marcos Valério, a shaven-headed advertising man from Belo Horizonte, who quickly became a household name as Brazil's media devoted exhaustive coverage to a scandal that rapidly acquired baroque dimensions. Investigators found that Valério had eighteen companies and 150 bank accounts. His money came from trans-

fers from two small banks, Banco Rural and BMG; from kickbacks for chan-
nelling deposits from state pension funds to these banks; and from padded
advertising contracts with federal agencies. Valério's accounts suggested he
had made cash payments totalling 55 million reais. His former secretary,
Karina Somaggio, testified that her boss dispatched suitcases of cash on
private planes from Belo Horizonte to Brasília. He had also repaid part of a
bank loan taken out by the PT for the 2002 campaign. As has become the
custom in Brazilian political *telenovelas*, the young woman thrust into the
limelight offered to pose for the local edition of *Playboy*. But Ms Somaggio's
asking price of 2 million reais 'in order to start a political career' was too
high.[19]

Two days after Jefferson's testimony in Congress implicated him in the
mensalão, Dirceu resigned as Lula's chief of staff; along with him went a dozen
other senior officials and the entire top echelon of the PT leadership. Dirceu
himself was a contradictory figure: he could be charming when it suited him
and had worked tirelessly to make the PT electable. But he was also cold,
authoritarian and utterly ruthless. Having been a student leader in the late
1960s, he joined Marighela's Communist guerrilla group and was one of those
flown to Cuba in return for the release of the kidnapped American ambassador. In 1974 he returned to Brazil clandestinely, having had plastic surgery
to disguise himself, and went to live in a small town in Paraná, where he
opened a clothes shop. He married a local woman, to whom he did not disclose
his true identity. When amnesty came, he had his original face restored, separated from his wife and moved to São Paulo to help to found the PT.[20] Criminal
charges were eventually brought against Dirceu, Genoino, Delúbio Soares,
Valério, Duda Mendonça and thirty-three others over the *mensalão*. Because
the PT remained in government, many people assumed that the affair would
'end in pizza', a Brazilian term for a convivial celebration, applied in the
political context to refer to the traditional impunity politicians enjoy. But the
mensalão became a *cause célèbre* for the opposition and the media. In 2012,
after a trial lasting months and followed by many Brazilians on live television,
the supreme court found all the senior defendants guilty, sentencing them to
jail terms of up to eleven years. The verdicts were almost unanimous, even
though most of the justices had been nominated by Lula or Dilma. They owed
much to the dogged determination of Joaquim Barbosa, the lead justice in the
case who was also Brazil's first black supreme court justice.*

---

* In November 2013 Dirceu, Genoino and the others were sent to prison, although the
supreme court had agreed to hear an appeal against the sentences.

The *mensalão* showed that behind the PT's apparent purism lay the cynical Leninist calculations that the end – power – justified any means and that the interests of the party were superior to those of the Brazilian state. The investigations also revealed what many had long suspected: while the PT publicly shunned donations from the private sector, it raised off-the-books cash for campaign expenses. This practice was common enough in Brazilian politics to have a name: *caixa dois* (second till). Indeed, Dirceu and others argued in their defence that the PT had been guilty of nothing more than *caixa dois*. In fact, the PT's version of *caixa dois* involved corrupt illegality far beyond a mere lack of transparency and a violation of electoral law: the party quietly financed itself by levying kickbacks on contracts with bus operators, refuse collection companies and other service providers in municipalities which it ran. It also sought money from illegal bingo and lottery operators. The party's leaders had gone to great lengths to cover this up: when Celso Daniel, the mayor of Santo André (near São Paulo), was kidnapped and murdered in January 2002, the PT passed this off as a common crime. It was alleged by the family of Daniel, who was to have been Lula's campaign co-ordinator, that he was murdered in a dispute about these practices.[21]

Sinister though all this was, the *mensalão* was more than just an illegal party-financing scheme. It seemed to be a systematic attempt to buy support using rent-a-parties. Paulo Delgado, a PT deputy, acknowledged that the government encouraged more than 100 deputies to leave opposition parties and join small pro-government ones. The *mensalão* blew away the PT's sanctimonious claim, based on its municipal administrations and congressional discipline, to command a monopoly of ethical behaviour in Brazilian politics. Some of its more idealistic original members deserted the party. Defenders of the PT pointed out correctly that it was far from possessing a monopoly of political vice, as some in the media implied. And unlike many others in Congress, its officials were not accused of enriching their own pockets (though some may have done). PT sympathizers also pointed to allegations that Cardoso's government had bought votes in Congress to secure the re-election amendment in 1997.* But in that case, which was a one-off, there

---

* In May 1997 *Folha de São Paulo* published allegations contained in audiotapes made by an anonymous source that five deputies from Acre received up to 200,000 reais each from the governor of Amazonas state. *Folha* alleged that the money came from Sérgio Motta, the telcommunications minister and Cardoso's chief political operator. In his memoirs Cardoso stated that it was possible that vote-buying could have happened, but if so it was organized by governors and mayors (who also benefited from the re-election amendment). The tapes did not contain any concrete claim that Motta had promised or asked anyone to pay money, just vague allusions to him. Two of the deputies resigned from Congress. Neither federal prosecutors nor the federal police intervened in the matter. (*Folha de São Paulo*, 31 December 1998; Cardoso (2006b), pp. 299–300.)

was no proof of any involvement by the federal government. Many in the opposition saw the *mensalão* as part of a plan by Dirceu to turn the PT into a party of permanent government, along the lines of Mexico's Institutional Revolutionary Party. But the scheme seemed too hamfisted for that, with its strange mixture of cynicism and naivety. Rather, it looked like an arrogant and improvised response to the exigencies of coalitional presidentialism.

Lula replaced Dirceu as chief of staff with Dilma Rousseff, his minister for energy and mines, who was not part of the PT's founding cohort of leaders. Dirceu's eclipse boosted Palocci's power within the government. He was the most popular of its ministers, and became the *de facto* prime minister (a status he had earlier shared with Dirceu). He began to talk of a 'social accord' to reduce public spending while improving its quality, and to eliminate the fiscal deficit. Palocci rightly sensed that the commodity boom offered the best moment for a fundamental and much-needed reform of the Brazilian state. But his plan was opposed as 'rudimentary' by Rousseff. A crucial opportunity to reform the state while times were good was lost.

In March 2006 Palocci, too, was brought down by misdeeds. Prosecutors in Ribeirão Preto were investigating allegations that the PT got kickbacks from municipal contracts during Palocci's time as mayor. Then the caretaker of a house in Brasília used by Palocci's political friends from Ribeirão to distribute cash and to enjoy the services of female 'receptionists' told *O Estado de S. Paulo*, a newspaper, that the minister had visited the house '10 or 20 times'. That contradicted Palocci's claims that he had never set foot in it. When details of the caretaker's account in a government bank were leaked in an apparent attempt to discredit him as a witness, Palocci was forced to resign.[22]

The waves from the *mensalão* had threatened to sink Lula himself when Duda Mendonça, the PR guru, chose to appear before one of the congressional inquiries. He revealed that he was paid 15.5 million reais for his work for the Lula campaign, all of it under the table and 10.5 million of it from foreign accounts. Since *caixa dois* payments are illegal and the foreign payments involved tax evasion, this implicated the campaign in crimes under electoral law. The next day Lula appeared on television to say that he felt 'betrayed by unacceptable practices of which I have no knowledge'.* In an atmosphere that began to resemble the final months of Collor's presidency, Lula angrily rejected suggestions by aides that he should resign or not run again in 2006. Some in the opposition called for Lula's impeachment. But the PSDB, under Cardoso's influence, drew back from

---

* After Valério, a condemned man, claimed in 2013 that Lula had known of the *mensalão*, prosecutors began an investigation into Lula. But it seemed unlikely that they would find any convincing evidence against him.

that course. The opposition lacked the votes in Congress, which was itself discredited by the scandal. It also lacked the political strength to oust a president who would have portrayed the attempt as a plot by traditional elites. And the PSDB was confident that it could defeat Lula in the election.[23]

That proved not to be the case. Lula learned pragmatic lessons from the *mensalão*. He brought the PMDB into the coalition, giving it three important ministries. Lula was by nature a delegator, who took the big decisions but hated policy detail and paperwork. He began to concentrate even more on promoting his government, in incessant trips around Brazil and abroad. Luckily for Lula, the economy was brightening, thanks to Palocci's reforms and the commodity boom. The government decreed a big increase in the minimum wage, which would rise by 23 per cent in real terms during Lula's first term. Together with Bolsa Família, this reinforced Lula's popularity among poorer Brazilians. In the election on 8 October 2006, Lula fell just short of an absolute majority of valid votes. In a run-off three weeks later, he won 61 per cent of the vote, easily defeating Gerardo Alckmin, the PSDB former governor of São Paulo. This was the same margin as in the run-off in 2002. That similarity concealed a dramatic shift in the source of Lula's support. Because of the *mensalão*, he lost votes among the middle class in the south and south-east. But because of Bolsa Família and the fall in poverty, his vote in the north-east increased substantially. For the first time, Lula received as many votes from women as from men, and his votes among the poorer and less educated reflected their weight in the population as a whole. Lula had torn up the pattern of Brazil's elitist politics, at last giving the lie to the saying that *pobre não vota em pobre* ('the poor don't vote for one of their own'). The PT itself did less well, losing eight of its ninety-one seats in the lower house. Once again Lula's vote-winning ability increased his power over his party.[24]

The drift to state capitalism

Several things allowed and encouraged Lula to adopt a somewhat more statist economic policy in his second term. The economy grew, the current account was in surplus, the real appreciated steadily and investors began to smile on Lula's Brazil. Wages and employment increased, and along with Palocci's credit market reforms, this unleashed a boom in consumption. Though Meirelles remained at the Central Bank, after Palocci's departure economic policy fell under the sway of a group of economists sympathetic to neo-developmentalist thinking who favoured a more active role for the state (harking back to Kubitschek and Geisel). They included Guido Mantega, who had been Lula's personal economic adviser in opposition and who took over from Palocci as finance minister, and Luciano Coutinho, who replaced Mantega as head of the national development bank, the BNDES. Mantega quietly shelved Palocci's plans for reform of the public finances. Lula dropped his earlier talk of reforms to Vargas's labour code or of the tax system. Instead, the government lay back and surfed the commodity boom.[25]

The president launched a programme of public works called the Growth Acceleration Programme (PAC), putting Rousseff in charge. The PAC, with a nominal price tag of 500 billion reais over four years, involved the repackaging of many existing schemes (Cardoso had launched a similar programme, on a smaller scale, in his second term). Some of its projects were worthwhile, such as street lighting, drainage and other works to urbanize favelas in Rio de Janeiro. Others were controversial, such as a vast scheme to irrigate the *sertão* using the waters of the São Francisco river, which ran behind schedule and over budget (see chapter ten). The government also ramped up Luz para Todos, the rural electrification scheme of which Lula talked so expansively at the London conference in 2009, and launched Minha Casa Minha Vida (My House My Life), a low-cost housing scheme. Lula's run of good luck continued when Petrobras in late 2007 announced a huge new oil strike deep below the South Atlantic ocean floor. Lula entrusted Dilma Rousseff, who chaired Petrobras's board, with drawing up a new legal framework for the new fields, known as *pré-sal* ('sub-salt') because they lie beneath a thick and unstable layer of salt. As eventually approved, this declared the new oil to be the property of the state, and went a long way to granting Petrobras a monopoly over its exploitation, while respecting existing contracts and maintaining the previous legal regime for areas outside the *pré-sal*. Strict new rules required up to 70 per cent of the inputs and supplies for the development of the *pré-sal* to be produced in Brazil (see chapter ten).

The oil strikes added to a growing sense of euphoria, extending from Lula to many business people and ordinary Brazilians. Presenting the draft new oil laws in 2009, Lula called the *pré-sal* a 'gift from God' and a 'millionaire [lottery] ticket'. 'Never before in the history of Brazil . . .' Lula would repeat, as he proclaimed yet another social or economic achievement, and sometimes it was true. In January 2008, Brazil became a net foreign creditor – quite a turnaround from the debt-ridden 1980s. A few months later the international credit-rating agencies awarded Brazil an investment-grade credit rating, meaning that its debt was safe enough for foreign pension funds to buy. This is a step that normally leads to a deepening of the capital markets in the country concerned.

The euphoria would briefly be doused by the collapse of Lehman Brothers in September 2008, and the world financial crisis that followed. Lula was at first confident that Brazil would be immune. 'Bush, my son, sort out your crisis,' he urged the American president in March 2008. Six months later he said: 'There [in the United States and Europe], the crisis is a tsunami. Here, if it arrives, it will be a little ripple, not even big enough to [water] ski.' But the ripple became a wave. Brazilian banks suddenly found that credit lines from counterparts abroad to finance imports and exports were cancelled. These trade lines are normally rolled over automatically – they are the barely noticed lubricant that keeps the world economy ticking over. But in the months after Lehman collapsed, the rollover rate of Brazil's trade lines fell from 130 per cent (i.e. they had been expanding) to just 23 per cent, as international banks recoiled from what was traditionally one of the safest forms of lending. This in turn meant that Brazilian firms had to borrow in reais to repay their dollar loans; that helped to drive down the real, from 1.55 to the dollar to 2.40. This sudden depreciation exposed several of Brazil's biggest companies, which discovered that their treasury departments had made huge bets in the derivatives markets. Because they expected the real to continue strengthening, as it had done ever since the 2002 election, they took on dollar credits to pre-finance exports and used them to make short-term investments in reais. Sadia (a big food company), Aracruz (paper and pulp) and Votorantim (an industrial conglomerate) each lost more than $1 billion in this way. Sadia and Aracruz avoided bankruptcy only through shotgun mergers with rivals, while Votorantim's bank, a big provider of loans for car purchases, was rescued by state-owned Banco do Brasil. With tremors coursing through the financial system, Unibanco, the third-biggest Brazilian-owned private commercial bank, agreed a takeover by Itaú, which thus became the largest Brazilian bank.[26]

Despite these events, the world financial crisis served to show Brazil's newfound economic strength. The Central Bank sold dollars from its ample reserves (totalling $220 billion), and loosened bank reserve requirements, pumping some 200 billion reais into the economy. The financial system had wobbled, but not buckled, and inflation remained under control. After a short and mild recession, the economy roared back to life in 2009, as the government injected a large fiscal stimulus. The BNDES expanded its lending by more than half (to 4.5 per cent of GDP), thanks to three capital increases from the government; most of its loans were at less then half the Central Bank's benchmark interest rate. Big chunks of government spending began to be excluded from the fiscal target, as the public accounts became increasingly opaque.

Lula concluded that 'the crisis was caused by the irrational behaviour of white, blue-eyed people, who previously seemed to know everything and now showed that they knew nothing.' The lesson his economic team seemed to draw was that liberal capitalism had failed, and that the future lay with state capitalism, as practised to varying degrees by Brazil's fellow-BRIC countries – China, India and Russia (see chapter eleven). Lula himself told me that the lesson of the crisis was that 'the state must be prepared, that it must have the capacity to intervene when required.' He added:

> I don't want a proprietorial state, or an interventionist state, but I do want the state to have the capacity to regulate and that people know that the state can do this ... This is how I conceive of the state: it mobilizes, oversees, regulates. It does not get involved as an owner, but is equipped to carry out works.[27]

'The problem is that the crisis was seen as a licence to spend,' as Raúl Velloso, a former finance official who is Brazil's foremost expert on the public accounts, put it. Some of the stimulus measures involved a permanent increase in public spending, accelerating a longstanding tendency. Lula continued to push up the minimum wage much faster than inflation, too, which had a knock-on effect on pension spending and some welfare benefits. Spending never got completely out of control, as it did in Hugo Chávez's Venezuela or Cristina Fernández's Argentina. If the government was slow to withdraw fiscal stimulus, it was chiefly because Lula had an election to win.

The triumph of Lulismo

To his credit, Lula resisted suggestions from some of his own supporters that he try to change the constitution to allow him to run for a third term. 'You don't play around with democracy,' he said.[28] But he had a problem: by their misconduct, both of his obvious successors, Dirceu and Palocci, had rendered themselves unelectable. And the *mensalão* had damaged the PT leadership in the public mind. Instead Lula chose Dilma Rousseff as his candidate for the 2010 election. This was a risky move: she had never held elected office, and was a latecomer to the PT. No woman had ever been elected president of Brazil. But Lula, helped by the PT's new marketing guru, João Santana, turned these weaknesses into strengths. He began to associate Dilma with his own achievements. This started in March 2008 with a ceremony in Complexo do Alemão, a large and violent favela sprawling over a hillside in the north of Rio de Janeiro, where some residents had to climb up to 1,200 steps to reach their houses. As part of the PAC, Lula announced that the federal and state governments would collaborate to build a cable car, a scheme copied from Medellín in Colombia. With Dilma at his side, he called her 'a kind of mother of the PAC'. [29]

The two became ubiquitous at government events. When in 2009 Dilma revealed that she had lymphatic cancer which required months of painful treatment, this had the effect of boosting her image as a fighter. She made a full recovery in time for the campaign. As Brazilians became aware that Dilma was Lula's anointed successor, her standing in the opinion polls rose inexorably. The government's stimulus spending helped: the economy grew at an annualized rate of 8 per cent in the fifteen months to mid-2010, while government spending rose at a similar rate.

Dilma duly won 46.9 per cent of the vote, ahead of José Serra for the PSDB (32.6 per cent). The surprise of the election was the strong showing by Marina Silva (19.3 per cent), who stood for the Green Party. A founding member of the PT, as Lula's environment minister she had slowed deforestation in Amazonia. She had resigned over what she saw as the government's increasing opportunism and lack of ethical principle. Dilma duly won a run-off against Serra by 56.1 per cent to 44 per cent. By managing to elect a barely known aide as his successor, Lula scored an almost greater political triumph than if he had been the candidate himself.

Lula had presided over faster economic growth combined with income redistribution and social inclusion, an unprecedented combination for Brazil. The country's regional inequalities declined too. Between 2003 and 2010 the minimum wage rose by 50 per cent in real terms (to the equivalent of US$286 a month in 2010), some 14 million formal-sector jobs were created and some 20 million Brazilians left poverty. As Lula left office, unemployment stood at just 5.3 per cent while around 12 million poor families received between 22 and 306 reais per month under Bolsa Família, depending on their income and the number of children. Lula's governments founded fourteen new federal universities and 214 technical colleges, and created Prouni, a scholarship scheme for poorer students at private universities, which had 700,000 enrolments by 2010.[30]

It was no wonder that Lula left office even more popular than he had entered it, with an approval rating of around 75 per cent. For Perry Anderson, a British Marxist philosopher and eternal optimist for the far left, this reflected 'not appeasement or moderation, but a radicalization in government'.[31] Not really: with the exception of the big increase in the minimum wage, the greater state activism in economic policy in the second term had no tangible effect on Lula's popularity. Rather, this reflected faster economic growth – the result of moderation in the first term and external factors, such as the commodity boom – more ambitious social policies and Lula's status as the champion of the poor. André Singer, a political scientist at the University of São Paulo, was nearer the mark when he suggested that Lula pursued a moderate reformism focused on reducing extreme poverty, without confronting the established economic order. This prompted a political realignment, reflected in the 2006 and 2010 presidential elections, argued Singer, who worked in government as Lula's spokesman in the first term. Poorer Brazilians identified with 'Lulismo' (not the PT specifically), while the mensalão pushed the traditional middle class more firmly into the arms of the PSDB and the opposition.[32]

That coincided with what I encountered on visits to Brazil during Lula's second term. Many in the traditional middle class in São Paulo and Rio were scathing about Lula. It was true that in relative terms, they didn't benefit much from the Lula years. 'There was a perception that "everyone was better off except me", as Claudio Couto, a political scientist in São Paulo, put it.[33] They had to pay more for maids, while social spaces, from shopping centres to roads, became more crowded. Their ostensible worries about the sustainability of spending, the bloated and leaden-footed federal government and lack of reforms of the tax system were valid enough. Indeed, history will judge Lula harshly not so much for what he did as for what he did not do, the fact that he gave up on the structural reforms Brazil needed. As Timothy Power, an American political scientist put it, while Cardoso's was a government of reforms, Lula's was a government of programmes, which involved less expenditure of political capital and thus greater popularity.[34] But behind the complaints of the relatively privileged in Brazil it was not hard to sense an anger and fear at their loss of control over the government. In this there was perhaps a similarity with the UDN's opposition to Goulart and to Vargas in his last, populist term.

This contrasted radically with the way that Lula was seen by Brazilians who lived in poorer areas, where the first group rarely ventured. It was as if they lived in different countries. 'In the [urban] periphery, everyone loves Lula,' said Afonso Gonçalves, a former street vendor and factory electrician who owned a small supermarket in Montanhão, a vast favela in São Bernardo do Campo. 'He focused on the poor. He's the people's president. The poor don't understand politics or socialism. They just want their children to have a better life than them,' Gonçalves told me. I encountered the same sentiments in 2010 in Jardim Iguatemi, an area of favelas tumbling over steep hills on the eastern extremity of São Paulo, an hour and a half's drive from the city centre, out beyond Itaquera, the hardscrabble bairro that was home to Corinthians,

Brazil's most popular football club (of which Lula is a fan). That Jardim Iguatemi shared a name with São Paulo's most chic shopping centre seemed to be conscious self-mockery. I spoke with a group of mothers there, all of whom declared their support for Lula. 'We have to vote for someone who will do something for us, because we live in this place far from the world,' said Quiteria de Souza, a migrant from Alagoas who lived with her three children in a small brick house at the top of a steep hill. According to Milene Ribeiro, a strongly built *mulata* with hair pulled back into a pony tail and similarly a separated mother of three children, Lula 'has made a big effort' and has 'thought a lot about concrete problems'. She mentioned Bolsa Família, and a new technical college in Itaquera. Aged thirty-three, her father was a painter and her mother a maid. She had wanted to become a teacher but had dropped out of university after four months 'because I couldn't afford it'.

Unlike Chávez, Lula never sought socio-economic polarization, nor did he seek to accompany his 'option for the poor' with political radicalization of the kind that occurred under Goulart.[35] He offered Latin America a powerful reformist example – that social change, the widening of active citizenship and the reduction of inequality were possible within the rules of democracy and of economic and financial stability. Some among Brazil's rich understood this. 'They can say what they like about Lula, but he's managing to balance like nobody else the bankers and the MST,' Alvaro Coelho da Fonseca, the owner of an upmarket estate agency in São Paulo told *Piauí*, a Brazilian magazine modelled on the *New Yorker*.[*][36]

A few weeks before the 2010 election, I asked Lula what he saw as the priority for the next government. He answered by summing up his own dream for Brazil:

> We are starting to lay steps so that the poorest begin to rise up to the lower-middle class and then to the middle-middle class. This is the country that I dream that the next president is going to build: a country in which the great majority are middle class, with purchasing power and access to material goods, education and health better than we have today. Brazil is ready for this, people's self-esteem has been raised . . . . I think we managed to move forward and that Brazil sees itself differently now. We have started to like ourselves, we no longer have an inferiority complex.[37]

---

[*] The Movimento Sem Terra or Landless Movement was a radical social movement that specialized in invading farms and public buildings (see chapter ten).

The disappointments of Dilma

Dilma Rousseff came from a comfortable middle-class background, the daughter of a Bulgarian immigrant who prospered as a building contractor in Belo Horizonte and married a much younger primary school teacher. Her father died of a heart attack when she was fifteen. When still a schoolgirl, Dilma began to attend meetings of Polop, a small Marxist group composed mainly of students and academics inspired by the ideas of Leon Trotsky and Rosa Luxemburg. After the 1964 coup, the group would become caught up in growing enthusiasm for armed resistance and Cuban-style guerrilla action. In 1968 Dilma dropped out of her university course in economics, spending a year as a clandestine militant of VAR-Palmares, a short-lived merger of elements of Polop with a group led by Carlos Lamarca, a former army captain. The new group's main action was to steal a safe containing $2.5 million from the house of the lover of Adhemar de Barros, the recently deceased former governor of São Paulo who had boasted that he 'stole but got things done' (see chapter five). Dilma did not take part in the action, but helped to exchange some of the proceeds into cruzeiros. In an internal debate that sundered VAR-Palmares, she was part of a faction which favoured political work aimed at organising the working class, against those, led by Lamarca, who supported guerrilla action. Although she learned how to assemble and dismantle a rifle, she said she never fired one because of her myopia. She was arrested in January 1970, and tortured for twenty-one days at the DOI-CODI in São Paulo. She did not reveal her address, a house in a working-class area which she shared with another militant and where they had hidden six of Lamarca's rifles and other ammunition. She was a prisoner for almost three years, most of that time in the Tiradentes jail, a former slave warehouse in central São Paulo. Convicted by military tribunals of belonging to a subversive organization (but not of any armed actions), she was freed after the Supreme Military Tribunal reduced her sentence. She later said that when she left prison, she felt 'a great loneliness. Everyone I knew was either in jail, or had left Brazil or was dead.'[38]

Dilma went to live in Porto Alegre, home of her jailed partner, Carlos Araújo, where she completed an economics degree. She twice enrolled for (but did not complete) post-graduate study in the economics faculty of the State University of Campinas (or UNICAMP as it is popularly known), the main home of neo-developmentalist thinking, where Luciano Coutinho was among her teachers. She and Araújo joined Brizola's PDT, which would later forge a local alliance with the PT in Rio Grande do Sul. Dilma served as municipal finance secretary in Porto Alegre and then as secretary for energy in the state government, switching to the PT when Brizola broke the local alliance. It was in this job that she caught Lula's attention, armed with a laptop and with the air of authority that came from having negotiated contracts to supply natural gas to local businesses that ensured that Rio Grande do Sul was spared the national electricity blackouts of 2001.

Dilma was thus a survivor, a strong and powerful woman of feminist convictions, respected for her administrative ability, grasp of detail, honesty and appetite for work but feared for her harshness and irascible temper. She was a wooden platform speaker, and lacked political experience and conventional political skills. As president, she did not suffer fools gladly. She would regularly go behind ministers' backs and deal directly with their subordinates whom she thought more competent, a practice which created much resentment on Brasília's Esplanada dos Ministérios. She was more ideological than Lula; she described herself as a 'Brazilian democratic socialist', rather than a (more moderate) social democrat.[39] She had strong democratic convictions: she often repeated that 'I prefer the noise of the free press to the silence of dictatorships', thus distinguishing herself from other left-wing Latin American leaders such as Chávez and Ecuador's Rafael Correa who curbed media freedoms. She repeatedly defended the right of Brazilians to demonstrate peacefully. She explained these convictions by saying they were natural in someone who had struggled against a dictatorship (never mind that she had been struggling for the dictatorship of the proletariat).

Her pragmatism was of a different kind from Lula's; lacking his political dexterity and instinct for consensus, she would change her mind only when reality showed she was in error. She told me that 'you can't be fundamentalist about anything'.[40] Business people who dealt with her as minister or as Lula's chief of staff expressed admiration for her as a tough but fair negotiator, though they would later be much more critical. At an *Economist* conference in Brasília in 2007 I saw some of those qualities for myself when I chaired a breakfast meeting at which she handled questions from a score of business people with aplomb. She was a 'manager-president', according to Luciano Coutinho.[41] But too often this seemed to take the form of meddling and micro-management. Her lack of political experience would lead her into trouble.

On becoming president, Dilma's task was to consolidate Lula's achievement while stepping out of her mentor's shadow. At first all seemed to go well. In her inaugural speech, she proclaimed as her goal that Brazil should become 'one of the most developed and least unequal nations in the world – a country with a solid and entrepreneurial middle class, a vibrant and modern democracy, full of social commitment, political liberty and creativity'. She pledged herself to eradicate extreme poverty and to maintain economic stability 'as a basic value'. She stressed the importance of tax and political reform and of improving the quality of public services and public spending. She promised zero tolerance of corruption and waste.

She soon had to act on that last pledge. With Lula's help she had formed the broadest and most heterogeneous coalition assembled by any president. The PMDB moved to the heart of government: one of its senior leaders, Michel Temer, was her vice-president. Dilma kept many of Lula's ministers, though she added more women. In her first year as president, she sacked seven ministers, in all but one case because they faced claims of graft. The most notable of the early ministerial casualties was Palocci, brought back as Dilma's chief-of-staff, but forced to resign less than six months into her government after revelations that he had enriched himself as a political consultant while serving as a federal deputy between 2006 and 2010. Palocci had pushed through budget cuts after the 2010 spending binge. His departure deprived the government of a powerful counter-weight to the interventionist economic instincts of Dilma, Mantega and the PT's left wing.

Dilma made a cautious start. After the wild overheating of 2010, the government acted to cool the economy. But the real continued to appreciate against the dollar, reaching a high of almost 1.55. Mantega blamed this on the US Federal Reserve's loose monetary policy. Declaring Brazil to be a victim of a 'currency war', he imposed taxes and controls on short-term capital inflows. Others argued that the real's appreciation had as much to do with Brazil's savings shortage and high interest rates and its success in attracting long-term foreign direct investment.

The reality was that the cycle of faster economic growth that had begun with the Real Plan had run its course. Credit was no longer growing as fast; consumers devoted a large chunk of their pay cheques to repaying the loans they had taken out to buy cars and flat-screen televisions. As China's economy decelerated, commodity prices were no longer rising. The commodity boom had pushed up tax revenues while masking Brazil's underlying economic problems of lack of competitiveness. Those were now laid bare: high wages, high taxes, high interest rates and poor infrastructure all pushed up business costs. It was cheaper to import steel made in South Korea from Brazilian iron ore than to buy it locally, complained Carlos Ghosn, the Brazilian CEO of Renault-Nissan. Manufacturers, exposed to foreign competition, found their profit margins squeezed and cut investment.

In speeches Dilma and other officials recognized some of these problems. They accepted that growth would have to come more from investment than consumption. But as a promised economic recovery failed to arrive in 2012, they seemed to panic, engaging in constant, counter-productive meddling.

The Central Bank began to cut interest rates aggressively, seemingly at the president's urging, undermining its credibility. The government announced a bewildering barrage of tax breaks, selective tariff increases and other policy measures. The confusion was summed up by Roberto Setúbal, the chief executive of Banco Itaú:

> The government changes this. They change that. The result is a lot of uncertainty. They have to communicate better the role of government versus the private sector. They are not giving the right incentives, the right returns for the risks that are being offered.[42]

When inflation rose to around 6.5 per cent a year, the top of the Central Bank's target range, the government held down the price of petrol (weakening Petrobras's balance sheet) and bus fares. Even so, as inflation remained stubbornly around 6 per cent and the real began to weaken sharply, the Central Bank had to reverse course in 2013, raising interest rates. 'Lula probably told her that interest rates wouldn't lose her the [2014] election but inflation might,' an opposition economist speculated. To compensate for the tax breaks, the finance ministry began to massage its fiscal target. Its expansionary fiscal policy meant that to control inflation monetary policy had to be tighter than it would otherwise have been. With some justification, officials blamed the problems of the world economy, but Brazil performed less well than the Latin American average. In the first three years of Dilma's presidency growth was set to average only around 2 per cent a year. By undermining the policy tripod at the heart of Brazil's success since 1999 – a floating exchange rate; an independent Central Bank charged with meeting an inflation target; and a responsible fiscal policy aimed at reducing the public debt – Dilma's government had squandered a precious inheritance and lost the trust of the financial markets. The normally diplomatic Organization for Economic Co-operation and Development (OECD), a mainly rich-country research organization, was quietly devastating in its criticisms in a survey of Brazil published in October 2013. It lamented that 'monetary policy credibility risked being undermined by political statements about the future trajectory of interest rates . . . the fiscal rule has also been undermined . . . [by] unusual but legal measures'. It added that development of long-term credit markets had been hampered by 'an uneven playing field' in which the BNDES dominated.[43] In footballing terms, these policy mistakes were own goals. They offered Brazilians no lasting benefit.

The government's political performance was little better. Despite its vast majority it struggled to approve important legislation, such as a new forestry code.* A tax reform aimed at simplifying VAT (levied by the states) foundered. The government failed to get 257 votes in the lower house to approve a measure to reduce the tax on electricity. Henrique Alves, the PMDB president of the lower house, said of Dilma that she is 'exemplary . . . in her rigour, ethics and scrutiny' but that she needed to improve her relations with Congress: 'She needs to exercise the art of listening more, of persuasion and of political conversation with a capital P.'[44]

Opinion polls consistently gave Dilma approval ratings of 70 per cent or more in her first thirty months in office. Her credentials in not tolerating corruption – she made no attempt to block the *mensalão* trial – gave her support in the middle class. Her popularity was based above all on Brazil's record level of employment, combined with a continuing rise in real wages in her first two years in office. She was widely expected to cruise to a second term. But signs of trouble were mounting. As a senior Brazilian politician put it to me in late 2012: Fernando Henrique won two terms because he conquered inflation; Lula won two terms because he lifted millions out of poverty. And Dilma? 'Dilma has opened up many issues but hasn't closed the deal on any of them.' And then the country was taken by surprise by the biggest demonstrations since the *Diretas Já* campaign almost thirty years previously (see chapter thirteen).

---

* Although called thus in Portuguese, it concerns land management in general. It sets out rules for how much of their holdings landowners must keep forested.

CHAPTER NINE

The Long Road to a Middle-class Society

In the mid-1960s Nancy Scheper-Hughes, a young American, was sent by the Peace Corps to be a community health worker in Alto do Cruzeiro, a shantytown of 5,000 rural workers built around an eponymous cross on a hilltop overlooking the town of Timbaúba in Pernambuco's *zona da mata*, the formerly forested area that is its sugar belt. She found what she called a 'Brazilian heart of darkness'. In those days, a third of the residents of Alto do Cruzeiro lived in straw huts and the remainder in small houses of wattle and daub. Their only source of running water was a public standpipe at the foot of the hill. The men and boys worked as cane cutters, earning 40 to 50 (American) cents a day from September to February, and were unemployed for the rest of the year; the women worked as maids or laundresses. In 1965, a year of drought and post-coup disruption, more than 300 babies died in Alto do Cruzeiro, or almost one in two of those born. Each death was marked by the ringing of the bells of the church of Nossa Senhora das Dores (Our Lady of the Sorrows), but was otherwise greeted with resignation. 'The horror was the routinization of human suffering in so much of impoverished Northeast Brazil and the "normal" violence of everyday life,' wrote Scheper-Hughes later.[1]

In the 1980s Scheper-Hughes returned to Timbaúba as an anthropologist and found that while the town had 'all the trappings of modernity', not much had changed in Alto do Cruzeiro. She calculated that the infant mortality rate in the shantytown was still the equivalent of around 200 per 1,000 live births in the late 1980s (while that of Brazil as a whole was forty-eight in 1990). As sugar cane expanded, the cane cutters lost the *roçados* (gardens) where they grew vegetables to supplement their diet. Malnutrition and stunting were commonplace, and contributed to widespread illiteracy. As Scheper-Hughes wrote in her account published in 1992:

The hunger of the *zona da mata* is constant and chronic, not much changed over the 25-year period that I have known the region. It is the hunger of those who eat every day but of insufficient quantity, or of an inferior quality, or an impoverished variety, which leaves them dissatisfied and hungry. By contrast, the hunger of the drought-plagued *sertão*, the backlands and the badlands of Pernambuco, is cyclical, acute and explosive. It descends ruthlessly on people who are generally energetic, self-sufficient and well nourished.[2]

In 2012 traces of that harsh world survived in Alto do Cruzeiro, but a quarter-century had brought much change. The houses were still small, one-storeyed and tightly packed, but were now mainly of whitewashed brick, with satellite dishes sprouting from their red-tiled roofs. There was a well-staffed health clinic, part of Brazil's national health service. Severina da Silva, who worked as a maid and also ran a small shop in her living room in Alto do Cruzeiro, selling sweets, a few staples and ice-creams from a freezer in the corner, said that some people still went hungry. She was forty-eight but looked twenty years older; she was missing several teeth. Her husband, a former alcoholic, got casual work as a cane cutter, but suffered from back problems. Life was less bad for 'Bill' da Silva (no relation), a thirty-one-year-old cane cutter with six children who introduced himself by his nickname. From August to February he worked for a sugar mill, getting a monthly wage of 642 reais (about US$350 at the time). He had a labour contract, with full rights. In the off-season, he got a stipend and a small plot for a *roçado* from the state government. His wife received 234 reais a month from Bolsa Família. He reeled off his ambitions for his children: headteacher, lawyer, engineer or nurse. When I gave him a business card after our conversation, he said he would treasure it: the poor in the north-east now have rights, but their reflexes were formed in a culture in which patronage was all important – and in some ways it still is.[3]

Further inland from Timbaúba lies the *sertão*, the dry lands at the heart of the north-east that are home to around 21 million people, almost half of them from subsistence-farming families. Every few years the *sertão* suffers complete drought. In the past, these droughts, which are related to the El Niño weather pattern, gave rise to banditry, rebellion (as at Canudos), millenarianism or simply a hunger-driven mass exodus to the towns. When a bad drought struck in 1958, Kubitschek wrote in his diary: 'Worrying news arrived. In Pentecostes, in Ceará, shops closed their doors, fearful of looting. In the streets of the town, ten thousand drought-victims wander around, begging for water and bread.'[4] This drought prompted Kubitschek to set up Sudene, a development body for the north-east which attempted to kick-start industrialization in the region through tax-breaks. It was a questionable strategy and had only patchy success.

The climate is pitiless in the *sertão*. In August 1998, during another drought, I set off one morning from Petrolina, a fruit-farming centre on the irrigated bank of the São Francisco, to cross inland Pernambuco to Joazeiro do Norte in Ceará. By mid-morning, the sun had burned off the early, misleading puffs of cloud and started to roast the *caatinga*, the spiny scrub that stretches seemingly without end across the *sertão*. In the hamlets around Ouricuri, a small town 620 kilometres inland from Recife, farmers normally expected 500 millimetres (20 inches) of rain a year, spread from late December to March. That year, they got 250 millimetres in January, half of it unhelpfully in one day, and then nothing. Underfoot, the fawn-grey *caatinga* crackled with dryness. Maize and beans had failed, cattle risked running short of food. As the sun relented towards evening, along country roads women and children trudged home, balancing on their heads cans of water drawn from muddy and fast-disappearing ponds. That year there had been isolated incidents of looting of markets and food lorries, some by the hungry and some by the MST, the far-left landless workers' movement. But a massive relief operation ground into action. The Cardoso government distributed monthly food baskets to 2.6 million families, enlisted a million adults in make-work schemes, and granted 450 million reais (then US$385 million) in cheap loans for wells, small dams and forage. To prevent the aid being pocketed or abused by mayors, at the instigation of Ruth Cardoso the government insisted that each mayor should set up a civic committee to distribute the aid. It wasn't perfect. In Pau Ferro, a hamlet near Ouricuri, I came across Joaquim Carvalho de Souza, who was angry that he hadn't received the emergency credit for feed for his six cows he had applied for. His was one of sixty families depending on a small, slowly vanishing pond. He claimed that only a dozen of the families had received official help. But his wife, Maria, received the *previdência rural* (a non-contributory rural pension equal to the minimum wage). She said they would wait to see if it rained in December, so as not to interrupt their three younger children's schooling.[5]

Brazil's rural north-east has long contained the largest single concentration of poverty in Latin America, a consequence of unequal landholding, frequent droughts, political corruption and backwardness, poor transport infrastructure and lack of education. In the mid-1990s, the typical north-easterner had just 3.3 years of schooling, or half the national average, itself low by international standards. At that time, the nine states of the north-east had a GDP per person of around $2,000, half the national average, and contained half the country's poor. Applying the UN Human Development Index, while southern Brazil approximated the poorer countries of Europe, the north-east rivalled Africa.[6]

The north-east is perhaps where democracy has made the biggest difference. Economically, the region has begun to catch up: in the decade to 2010 the region's GDP grew by 4.2 per cent a year (compared to 3.6 per cent for the country as a whole); household income in the north-east rose by 72.8 per cent, compared to 45.8 per cent in the south-east. In its growth rate, 'the north-east is like India', Marcelo Neri, then a researcher at the Getúlio Vargas Foundation, told me in 2010. Bolsa Família helped: in Timbaúba, for example, some 6,000 of the town's population of 51,000 benefited from the scheme. But more important was the rise in the minimum wage of 60 per cent in real terms in the decade to 2011.

'Drought is a problem of income', as Sergio Moreira, the director of Sudene, explained to me in 1998, echoing the argument of Amartya Sen, the Indian economist who studied famines in his country. 'If the people had income, they would have access to food and water, because it would be worth someone's while to bring them.'[7] In the north-eastern droughts – there was another severe one in 2012 – many animals still die (and the farmer's capital with them). But because they have income, nowadays people do not.

This injection of cash into the north-east attracted investment in commerce and consumer goods factories. Timbaúba boasted new food, textile and shoe factories, as well as car and motorbike dealers and new shops. The expanding consumer market in the region helped Eduardo Campos, the governor of Pernambuco, to lure Fiat to build a car factory in his state. Under Lula, the federal government began several big investment projects in the region. The hinterland of Suape, a newish port south of Recife, has turned into a sprawling industrial complex; when I visited it in 2012, some 40,000 workers were building a vast oil refinery and petrochemical plants for Petrobras. A new shipyard and wind-turbine factories rose above the mangroves. At the other end of the business scale, CrediAmigo, a successful microcredit programme operated by the Banco do Nordeste, a public bank, gave loans to 300,000 microbusinesses.[8] This pattern of industrialization based on the growth of Brazil's potentially huge domestic market – which poverty had long frustrated – was the dream of Celso Furtado, a leading 'developmentalist' economist who was the first head of Sudene and was briefly a minister in Goulart's government. Furtado died in 2004, just as the process got under way. Even so, GDP per person in the north-east remained well below the national average.

Closing the gaps

This modest closing of the regional gap mirrored the wider national picture of sharply falling poverty and income inequality in the first decade of the twenty-first century. The country has no official poverty line, or at least it didn't until

2013 – nothing is ever simple in Brazil. But taking a monthly income per person of 140 reais in 2010 (about US$76) – roughly the cut-off point above which someone becomes ineligible for Bolsa Família – the numbers living in poverty fell from 49.5 million (or 28.5 per cent of the total) in 2003 to 29 million in 2008 (16 per cent of the total) and 24.6 million by mid-2011, according to Neri. Similarly, those in absolute poverty, with insufficient income to feed themselves – fell from 17 per cent in 2003 to 8.4 per cent (or 16.2 million people) in 2010.[9]

Even more remarkably, income inequality fell for the first time since the 1960s. The fall began during Cardoso's second administration and gathered speed thereafter. The GINI coefficient* fell to 0.527 in 2011, down from 0.594 in 2001, according to IPEA. Between 2001 and 2011 the income of the poorest 10 per cent of the population expanded by 91 per cent, while that of the richest 10 per cent by just 16.6 per cent. As Ricardo Paes de Barros, the intellectual architect of Bolsa Família, put it, 'the income of the poorest 10 per cent is growing like China, and that of the richest 10 per cent is growing like Germany'.[10] These figures excluded income derived from capital: at the very top, the rich appeared to thrive, with a growing number of millionaires and billionaires (forty-six billionaires in 2013 according to *Forbes* magazine, up from five in 2003). Brazil produced twenty-two millionaires a day in 2010, according to one count.[11] Nevertheless, the decline in the GINI coefficient was unprecedented. It signalled that democracy was at last doing its job of addressing the deep-rooted unfairness in Brazilian society. The big question was whether the pace of the reduction in inequality could be maintained – or more accurately, what would have to change for this to happen.

To start to answer that question, consider first what lay behind the fall in poverty and inequality. The most important factor was faster growth and job creation, combined with the big rise in the minimum wage. Rising wages accounted for around 60 per cent of the fall in the GINI coefficient. This trend also owed much to the fact that since the return of democracy Brazil had at last begun to remedy its huge shortfall in education: by 2010, the average worker had 8.3 years of schooling, up from 6.1 in 1995, according to Paes de Barros. So the disproportionately large wage premium extracted by educated workers, identified by Langoni in the 1970s, had begun to diminish. Third, government transfers in the form of social programmes, and especially Bolsa Família, accounted for around 40 per cent of the fall in income inequality.[12]

---

* A standard statistical measure of inequality; when applied to income distribution, zero would mean everyone had the same income while 1.0 would mean that one person received all the income.

Its critics claimed that Bolsa Família was old-fashioned political clientelism writ large. 'Bolsa Família is the biggest official vote-buying programme
in the world,' said Jarbas Vasconcelos, a blunt PMDB former governor of
Pernambuco.[13] Certainly it made Lula hugely popular among the poor. But
it was different in important ways from traditional clientelist measures. It
was channelled through municipal governments, not through political
bosses, nor through the PT. The cash payment was made to an electronic card
administered by the Caixa Econômica Federal, a state-owned savings bank.
The money went to mothers. The scheme was both relatively cheap – it cost
just 0.4 per cent of GDP – and far better targeted than most welfare
spending in Brazil. It reached nearly all of the poorest Brazilians (who made
up a quarter of the population). The stipend was too small to constitute a
serious disincentive to work, except perhaps in the poorest areas of the
north-east, where it may have had the effect of forcing up market wages closer
to the level of the minimum wage. (There were complaints among better-off
women that it had become harder to find a maid, for example.) While its
direct impact in reducing overall poverty was small, it accounted for about 15
per cent of the reduction in absolute poverty and had the effect of pushing up
the incomes of the poorest closer to the poverty line, according to Paes de
Barros. By guaranteeing that no Brazilian should starve, Bolsa Família set a
floor without which the notion of democratic citizenship would have been
a mockery.

Dilma Rousseff proclaimed that absolute poverty – which her officials
defined as a monthly income of less than 70 reais per person – would be
eradicated by the end of her government, under a plan called Brasil sem
Miséria (Brazil without Destitution). This involved, firstly, increasing the cash
payments to the poorest families under Bolsa Família to ensure a minimum
income of 70 reais per family member. Second, inspired by a scheme in Chile,
social workers and community health workers were given the task of actively
looking for those among the poorest who had slipped through the social safety
net. They would be added to the Cadastro Único, the single register of welfare
recipients, that had begun in the second Cardoso administration and been
expanded into a crucial tool of social policy. The payments were linked, in
theory at least, to remedial education, training schemes and micro-finance
programmes aimed at ensuring that people entered the labour market and did
not stay hooked on benefits. The scheme was laudable, though some experts
pointed out that 70 reais a month was insufficient for anyone to feed themselves on.[14] And it remained to be seen how effective the programme would
be. The hard core of the destitute were far from monolithic in their situation
and problems: roughly three-quarters of them were in the north-east and

north, and of those around half were rural; the minority of the extreme poor living in the south-east were overwhelmingly to be found on the periphery of the big cities.[15]

New middle class – or new poor?

The fall in poverty swelled what in Brazil is known as social Class C, a term originally derived from market research. Neri defined this as people with a *household* income (not per person) of between 1,200 and 5,174 reais per month in 2011 – or US$690–2,970 at the market exchange rate. According to Neri, between 2003 and 2011 around 40 million Brazilians moved up into Class C. By 2011 this group totalled just over 100 million people, making up 55 per cent of the population and around 47 per cent of total purchasing power. The process had begun under the Cardoso governments, when 20 million joined Class C. Neri, who managed to be both a rigorous economist with a long-standing commitment to social research and a cheerleader for social progress, dubbed Class C 'the new middle class'. He stressed this was 'an economic stratum', not a social class as sociologists understand the term. His findings were the cause of much triumphalism, official and otherwise, and much controversy.[16]

Certainly Class C had disposable income, and proceeded to use it with gusto. The status symbols of Class C were above all *casa e carro* (a house and a car) to which some added *computador, crédito e carteira de trabalho* (computer, credit and a labour contract for a formal job). The expansion in Class C numbers created a mass consumer market in Brazil for the first time, and awoke the interest of local businesses and multinationals alike. José Roberto Mendonça de Barros, an economist who had served in the Cardoso government, pointed out that purchasing power was increased further by the decline in food prices, which, measured in the city of São Paulo, fell by an average of 5 per cent a year in real terms for three decades, thanks to increases in agricultural productivity, improvements in distribution and the opening to imports.

Fuelled by tax breaks and consumer loans, car sales boomed: vehicle production in Brazil almost doubled in the ten years to 2012, to 3.4 million. By 2012 Brazil had overtaken Germany to become the world's fourth-biggest car market (behind China, the US and Japan). Class C took to the skies, too: air-passenger numbers doubled between 1993 and 2000, to 31.3 million, and then almost tripled again, to 87.7 million, by 2011.[17] Azul, a fast-expanding low-cost airline, reported that 85 per cent of its passengers were flying for the first time. They would previously have taken the bus. The number of bank accounts in Brazil rose from 77 million in 2002 to 134 million by 2010. Santander, a Spanish bank that had acquired a big operation in Brazil, opened a branch in 2010 in the Complexo do Alemão, a Rio favela then under the control of drug trafficking gangs. 'This was a gesture,' admitted Fabio Barbosa, its chief executive. 'We want to show these communities that banking is citizenship.' Shopping malls and supermarkets marched across the country, sprouting up in provincial towns and the 'periphery', as Brazilians call it, of the big cities of the south-east.[18]

The biggest segment of Class C was in this urban 'periphery' in places like Montanhão. This took its name, whose literal meaning was 'big heap', from what not so long ago it was: a rubbish dump. On the southern extremity of São Bernardo do Campo, Montanhão's houses of brick and breeze-block straggled over abrupt hills. It was one of the poorest places in Greater São Paulo, but not nearly as poor as it was in the early 1990s. When I visited in 2007 its winding main street bustled with building-materials depots, gift and clothes shops, restaurants and several small supermarkets. One was Mercado Gonçalves. 'This was my dream,' said its owner, Afonso Gonçalves. Arriving in São Paulo from the interior of Ceará when he was eighteen, he began with a fruit stall in the city centre, and then worked for seventeen years as an electrician in a factory. He saved enough to open a small shop, which he expanded more than fourfold into a supermarket, stocking some 12,000 different items, from Nescafé and Colgate to fresh meat, freshly baked bread and, locked in a glass case, Scotch whisky. According to Gonçalves, 'A lot of people here are becoming middle class. A lot have bought new cars. But a lot are very poor as well. It's half and half. A lot get Bolsa Família.' New tower-blocks of flats, of the kind ubiquitous in the smarter parts of all Brazilians cities, jutted up from among the houses of what still resembled a favela. Public services were improving fast: nearly everyone had electricity, piped water and sewerage. Smart new school buses run by the municipal government plied up and down the hillsides. The mood of optimism was palpable. 'Each year has been better than the last,' said Dora Jozina de Arruda, a young woman who ran a small kiosk on the main street selling sweets and grinding keys. Between the profit from the kiosk and her husband's wages as a security guard at a bank, they earned around 2,000 reais a month.[19]

Life in places like Montanhão was still tough. Raw sewage ran in a stream not far from the supermarkets. Up on the hillsides, amid a host of evangelical Protestant churches, a few houses were still wooden shacks. Across Brazil, many in Class C were by any reasonable definition still poor. One such was Angela Cavalcanti, a black office assistant and cleaner in São Paulo, aged fifty-two in 2010. Although she had herself only completed primary schooling, she worked as a teacher near Canudos, in Bahia, before moving to São Paulo in 1986 to escape a violent and drunken husband, with whom she had five children. With a new partner, in 1991 she bought a building plot in Interlagos, a poor district in the south of the city, near the track where Senna once raced. Through relentless hard work and by pooling the resources of the family, she built a small house and acquired a washing machine and dryer, and a second-hand car that she uses to take her grandson to the beach. She has basic health coverage and has had false teeth fitted to replace missing ones. Of the three children who live with her, two are studying to be accountants and the other works as a driver. 'My life has improved a lot,' she said. But nobody in the family earns much more than the minimum wage. 'I'm still poor,' she said. 'If I were middle class . . . I would move to a bigger house in a better neighbourhood.' Her dream was to open a clothes shop. She worried about crime, drug addiction and prostitution in her *bairro*, and felt unprotected by the police. 'We are scared of the traffickers and scared of the police. I am frightened and I have no peace.' But she could move 'only if I win the lottery'.[20]

A similar sense of the sharp socio-economic difference between Class C and the middle class was expressed to me by Francisco Pinheiro, a shrewd community leader in Brasília Teimosa in Recife. Jammed onto a spit of land that juts into the azure Atlantic, Brasília Teimosa was until two decades ago a favela of wooden fishermen's huts. Now its streets are lined with brick houses, some of three storeys and clad in decorative tiles, but others jerry-built. It has seafood restaurants, shops and a couple of bank branches, but also piles of uncollected rubbish. 'Economically, it's much better off than it was,' Pinheiro said. But most people earn less than two minimum wages (around US$600 per month), often shared among a family of four or more. He went on: 'A middle-class person is someone who lives in Boa Viagem' – a smart, beachfront residential suburb of high-rise towers close by – 'with a car, an apartment and income of 3,000 reais ($1,500) a month.'[21]

That characterization happened neatly to fit the more realistic economic definition of the middle class in Latin America deployed by the World Bank in a report published in 2012. The Bank argued that a degree of economic security is inherent to being middle class, and so required a daily income per person of US$10 to US$50 (at purchasing-power parity exchange rates). Using the same definition, Nancy Birdsall of the Centre for Global Development, a Washington think-tank, calculated that 31.6 per cent of Brazilians were middle class in 2009, up from 22 per cent in 1999 and just 14.7 per cent in 1992.[22] That was slightly above the Latin American average of 30 per cent, according to the World Bank. It represented impressive progress, but showed how far Brazil still is from being a middle-class society.

In any event, when sociologists and political scientists consider the issue of social class they look beyond income to matters such as education, occupational status, assets, social capital and so forth. On these criteria, many in Class C clearly fell short. André Singer contended that during the Lula governments what happened was not the creation of a new middle class but rather the incorporation of a sub-proletariat, a large mass of the destitute, into a new working class, via formal employment.[23] That does not quite capture the scale of progress, but it had a large element of truth.

The fall in poverty and inequality was the product of remarkable continuity in the broad outline of economic and social policies under Cardoso and Lula. As Neri put it, 'if Lula is the father of the new middle class, Fernando Henrique Cardoso is the grandfather.'[24] The trouble was that this effort would need to continue much longer – and the going was likely to get tougher. IPEA noted that in 2012 Brazil was still the twelfth most unequal country in the world. For it to match the income distribution of the United States – hardly a paragon of egalitarianism – the GINI coefficient would have to carry on falling at the same rate as in 2001–11 for another two decades.

By 2013 the Furtado-esque strategy of growth through domestic consumption seemed to have run its course. And the policy of driving up the minimum wage above inflation seemed to have reached its limit too, as Neri, who was appointed as minister for strategic affairs in 2013, admitted. That was because wage costs had risen much faster than productivity. It was also because much pension and welfare spending was linked to the minimum wage. And overall, Brazil's social spending served to reinforce, rather than overcome, inequality (see chapter thirteen). That was testament to the survival of the corporate state under the PT governments – indeed it thrived.

The new economic status of the members of Class C looked fragile. As Amaury de Souza and Bolivar Lamounier, two Brazilian political scientists, pointed out, their income was likely to oscillate because of unstable employment or the precariousness of small business, and because of their tendency to take on excessive debt.[25] As Class C rushed to take out loans to buy cars, white goods and flat-screen televisions, consumer loans rose to 13 per cent of GDP in 2009 (up from 6 per cent in 2001). That was almost double the average in the six main Latin American economies. The opposite applied in the case of mortgages, which at just 3 per cent of GDP in 2009 were around half the regional average, according to the World Bank. As the Bank concluded drily, 'Brazilian middle-class households may thus be over-indebted and investing too little in asset accumulation.'[26]

Towards public services for all

The Cardoso and Lula governments started to fulfil the constitution's mandate of universal public services. That applied to health care. The constitution decreed a unified national health service, known as the Sistema Único de Saúde (SUS). Financing was to come from all three levels of government, while the system's management was to be decentralized to municipal health secretaries. How to pay for this was a problem that was partly solved by an earmarked tax on financial transactions (but its renewal was voted down in Congress in 2007). In addition, José Serra, an effective reforming health minister in 1999–2002, pushed through a constitutional amendment earmarking for the SUS minimum slices of revenue from each tier of government. He expanded a family doctor scheme, modelled on Britain's national health service, and a community health worker programme. And he set up a pioneering programme of free anti-retroviral medicines for patients with HIV, winning a battle at the World Trade Organization to allow the licensing of low-cost generic medicines for malaria, tuberculosis and HIV/AIDS.[27]

There were some important advances in health care. Life expectancy has risen by more than ten years since 1980, to 72.8 years in 2010. Across Brazil, infant mortality rates have fallen steeply in the past thirty years – and at last the north-east has almost caught up. The 2010 census reported that nationally 15.6 of every 1,000 children born did not complete their first year of life, down from 29.7 in 2000 and 48.3 in 1990. The figure for the north-east fell from 44.7 in 2000 to 18.5 in 2010. Like many other recent social improvements in Brazil, this one was achieved by a combination of a more responsive state and a more active society. An important role was played by the Pastoral da Criança, a programme of the Catholic Church set up by Zilda Arns, a campaigning doctor, which trained hundreds of thousands of women in basic health care.[28*]

But as Albert Fishlow has observed, 'a totally inclusive national public system of health care does not exist'. Although Brazil's overall spending on health care of around 8 per cent of GDP was in line with international standards, more than half of that went on private health care which benefited only about 25 per cent of the population (including those in labour union schemes).[29] States and municipalities in the north-east and north spent much

---

* Arns was the sister of Cardinal Paulo Evaristo Arns, the Archbishop of São Paulo during the dictatorship, who campaigned against torture; she was killed in the earthquake of January 2010 in Port-au-Prince, Haiti's capital, where she was advising the local branch of Pastoral da Criança.

less than those in the south-east and south, and there was no equivalent for health care of Fundef, the fund to equalize educational spending. Corruption siphoned off some of the health budget, especially at municipal level. In 2007 investigations suggested that up to ninety members of Congress were involved in systematic over-invoicing in the purchase of ambulances. Two-fifths of Brazilians are not reached by the primary care system, and must rely on chaotic hospital emergency services. Even in the big cities, SUS hospitals were often unable to provide timely care of acceptable quality. Hospital beds for inpatients have become relatively scarcer, from 3.3 per 100,000 people in 1993 to 1.9 per in 2009 (lower than all OECD countries except Mexico). Long waiting times were commonplace, with sometimes fatal results. In 2013 the parlous state of public health care was the top public concern, according to opinion polls.[30]

Dilma Rousseff's government pointed to a shortage of doctors: it wanted to raise the current number of 1.95 doctors per 1,000 people (similar to South Korea but below the ratio in most European countries, the US and Mexico) to 2.5 by 2020 by training more and by importing foreign doctors in the interim. That was opposed by the doctors' federation, which fiercely defended their corporate privileges. There was no doubt that doctors were relatively scarce in poorer and more remote areas.[31] In response to the June 2013 street protests, Dilma went ahead and launched a crash programme to recruit thousands of foreign doctors to work in those areas. The government reached agreement with Cuba to import 4,000 doctors. And a law approved by Congress earmarked 25 per cent of royalties from the *pré-sal* oil for health care.

The learning curve

One of the keys to sustaining a more egalitarian society was to improve the quality of public education – perhaps the single most important issue facing Brazil. The New Republic inherited a yawning educational deficit that dated from the Empire. A centralized educational bureaucracy was subject to political interference, rapid turnover of officials, and corruption. That began to change with a clutch of reforms in the mid-1990s under the Cardoso government. They included an education law which decentralized and re-organized the school system, aimed at gradually eliminating overlaps. The law gave municipalities the main responsibility for what Brazilians call *ensino fundamental* or basic education (aged five to fourteen), while also putting them in sole charge of pre-school provision. State governments were required to give priority to *ensino médio* or secondary education. The federal government's role was restricted mainly to higher education, and to regulating and evaluating schools. Municipal governments were required to spend at least 15 per cent of their revenues on primary schools. A constitutional amendment established Fundef, a national fund for basic education, which set a national minimum for spending per pupil and for teachers' salaries, mandating transfers to poorer states and municipalities.

For many rural primary schools in the north-east, some of which were mud-floored huts with untutored teachers who were paid a pittance, this meant a sixfold increase in spending, according to Paulo Renato Souza, Cardoso's education minister.[32] Souza also revamped the primitive school evaluation system: this revealed the yawning regional gap in school performance, showing for example that eighth-grade pupils in Maranhão had learned only as much as fourth-graders in Brasília, underlining the need for Fundef. Souza devolved Fundef money and the funds for school meals and textbooks directly to schools, rather than routing it through the educational bureaucracy. 'Traditionally, books and school meals didn't reach schools because of inefficiency and corruption. Now they do,' Souza told me in 1999. 'Within a decade we'll have figures on quantity and quality [of schooling] which don't make us ashamed as they do today,' he added.[33]

Education is another area in which broad policy continuity has been maintained since 1994. Fernando Haddad, the minister of education in 2005–12, secured a law renewing Fundef, expanding it to cover pre-school and secondary (and changing its name to Fundeb). He strengthened the evaluation system with a national exam to monitor standards and the publication of the results for each school. He also introduced financial incentives for both the best- and worst-performing schools, and a national minimum salary for teachers.

Souza would be right about quantity. The reforms prompted a huge expansion in educational coverage. Between 1992 and 2009 the number enrolled in schools jumped by 19 million (to 57.3 million). Enrolment in basic education is now nearly universal. The biggest leap was in secondary schooling (aged fifteen to nineteen): the net enrolment rate – meaning the percentage of children in the year corresponding to their age – rose from just 15 per cent in 1990 to 51 per cent in 2009. The total proportion of fifteen- to nineteen-year-olds at school was 76 per cent; many had fallen behind by a year or more because of the Brazilian practice of requiring pupils who failed their exams to repeat the year. There was a gap, too, in pre-school education, with only half of under-fives enrolled.

The consequence of this effort was that the workforce gradually became less egregiously uneducated: on average, Brazilians aged twenty-five had almost ten years of schooling. Adult illiteracy gradually declined to 9.6 per cent of the population (but 23.2 per cent in rural areas), according to the 2010 census. But another estimate suggested that 30 per cent of the population was functionally illiterate.[34] The problem was that when they were at school, pupils didn't learn enough. Improving the quality of Brazilian education proved to be a much longer job than Souza had hoped. In an effort to shock Brazilians out of their complacency, Cardoso decided to enter the country in the Programme for International Student Assessment (PISA), an initiative of the OECD, a group of mainly rich countries (of which Brazil is not a member). In the first PISA test in 2000 Brazil duly came last. In subsequent PISA tests it showed steady improvement: in 2009 it came fifty-third (out of sixty-five countries) in reading and science. The OECD highlighted that Cardoso's reforms of school funding in the 1990s had made a huge difference in the poorest areas. Souza pointed out that at least quality had not dropped, despite the huge expansion in the system. But overall school performance remained very poor. Two-thirds of fifteen-year-olds could do no more than basic arithmetic; half could not draw any inferences from what they read, or give any scientific explanation for familiar phenomena.[35]

Visit a school in Brazil, and it is not hard to see what accounts for the poor performance. Take Colegio Recanto Verde Sol, a school offering both primary and secondary education in Jardim Iguatemi in Sao Paulo. Built in 2005, it was clean and reasonably well equipped with a small library, video room and a cafeteria for school meals. But its results were poor. That was partly because its 1,800 pupils studied in three shifts: eleven- to fifteen-year-olds in the mornings, younger ones in the afternoons and over-fifteens in the evening, sometimes not finishing till 11 p.m. Not surprisingly, many older pupils dropped out. 'In secondary, we begin the year with seven classes and end with three or four,' said Angela Regina Rodrigues, the head teacher. Ms Rodrigues was charismatic and committed, but somewhat defensive. Her first problem was getting enough teachers, and then getting them to turn up regularly, since most lived 15 to 20 kilometres away. Classes averaged forty pupils. Lessons mainly seemed to involve teachers writing on the blackboard while many pupils chattered among themselves.[36]

At least there is far more consciousness now that Brazilian schools need to do better. In opinion polls, education has climbed up the list of the country's main problems. The federal government and educational pressure groups are backing a campaign that aims to raise school performance to that of developed countries by 2021, the eve of the bicentenary of Brazil's independence. Meeting that target will require another round of educational reform, focused on schools and teachers themselves.

Grade repetition is one headache: 15 per cent of those completing secondary school were aged over twenty-five. Head teachers get little institutional support to deal with problems of disorderly and violent conduct by pupils, vandalism or the presence of drugs in schools, according to Norman Gall of the Fernand Braudel Institute, a São Paulo think-tank, who has written extensively on the problems of schools. Brazil's teaching unions are organized on a state-by-state basis, and have been unable to run schools as an extractive industry as Mexico's teachers' union long did. But they have often blocked efforts to make the teaching profession more effective and accountable. Teacher absenteeism is such a chronic problem in Brazil in part because in many states teachers are allowed to be absent for forty of the school year's 200 days without having their pay docked. Teacher-training courses tend to be academic, rather than teaching teachers how to teach. 'Brazilian teachers are focused on the sociology of education instead of how to teach ten-year-olds,' as Claudio Costin, the municipal education secretary in Rio de Janeiro, put it. According to Neuza Pontes, a head teacher in Recife, 'teachers think their responsibility is just to take a class, not to ensure that the pupils actually learn.'[37] These observations echoed uncannily those of Richard Feynman, an American physicist who taught a university course in Rio in 1951. His conclusion:

> after a lot of investigation, I finally figured out that the students had memo-rized everything, but they didn't know what anything meant ... I couldn't see how anyone could be educated by this self-propagating system in which people pass exams, and teach others to pass exams, but nobody knows anything.[38]

The main response in Brasília to schooling problems was to promise more money – lots of it. The National Education Plan, discussed in a leisurely way in Congress, proposed raising educational spending to 10 per cent of GDP. Three-quarters of the royalties from *pré-sal* oil are supposed to go to educa-tion. In fact education spending is already fairly high by international stand-ards, at 5.8 per cent of GDP, having risen steadily since 2005. But it was badly distributed. First, public spending on education goes disproportionately to universities, rather than schools. Second, up to half of budgets for schools was spent on pensions, since the constitution allows teachers to retire on full pay after twenty-five years' service for women and thirty for men.[39]

There were two reasons to hesitate before shovelling more money towards education without reforming the way it was spent. The first was that Brazil is going through a swift demographic transition and numbers of young people will soon start falling (see chapter thirteen). The second was corruption. Before Cardoso's reforms, between one-fifth and two-fifths of education spending was siphoned off, according to Marcus André Melo, a political scientist. The reforms, and tighter audit controls reduced that figure. Even so, one audit in five found serious corruption in educational spending.

Across Brazil, there are many examples of innovation in education and pilot projects in school reform – both from above and below. The pioneer was Minas Gerais, which in 1991 approved a law giving much more autonomy to schools to run themselves, through school boards with the power to recruit head teachers (previously nominated by political bosses) and to set investment priorities.[40] São Paulo's state government adopted its own standard curriculum and created a career structure for teachers, including performance-related pay – but this was scrapped in 2011 because of union pressure. The city of Rio de Janeiro has overtaken São Paulo when it comes to school reform. Claudia Costin, the municipal education secretary, not only implemented performance-related pay, a new curriculum and regular testing of pupils but also put more resources into 151 schools in the poorest and most violent areas.[41]

The national school assessment system suggested that the standard in the earlier grades of basic education has improved over the past decade, but not for higher age groups. A scheme pioneered in Pernambuco offered some hope of improvement for secondary schools. It began at the Ginásio Pernambucano, the second-oldest public school in Brazil. Created in 1825 the Ginásio educated many of the north-east's politicians and writers, before declining into mediocrity. By 1999 its fine, red-washed two-storey neo-classical building on the bank of the Capiberibe river in the historic centre of Recife was dilapidated and abandoned. A renaissance occurred thanks to the Institute for Co-Responsibility in Education (ICE), an NGO set up by Marco Magalhães, a former pupil of the school who was then the president of the Latin American division of Philips, the Dutch electronics company, together with a group of businessmen. The ICE restored the building, and in partnership with the Pernambuco state government pioneered a new kind of secondary school, the *escola integral.** This involves a full school day, from 7.30 a.m. to 5.00 p.m., rather than just a four-hour shift. Already by the start of secondary school, the average Brazilian pupil has a three-year learning deficit, according to Magalhães. When pupils arrive at the Ginásio at fifteen, they are tested in Portuguese and maths; only 10 per cent pass, said Neuza Pontes, the head teacher. 'We have three years to try to guarantee they learn what they didn't learn before.' Smaller classes allow teachers to track each pupil's performance individually. About 70 per cent of the Ginásio's

---

* Confusingly, the school that was relocated when the building had to be closed in the 1990s has continued to use the Ginásio name, though it now operates at a different site. It is more troubled.

pupils pass the university entrance exam, a higher percentage than at most private schools. In partnership with ICE, Pernambuco's governor, Eduardo Campos, is adopting this model in all of the state's 700 secondary schools. In 2012, 260 had made the switch. ICE is involved, too, in more than ninety schools in Ceará, and has begun to work in three other states. But whether the kind of improvement made at the Ginásio could be replicated on a large scale is not clear.

Brazil has seen a huge expansion in higher education, too. The number of students increased threefold between 2000 and 2010, to over 6 million. Though Lula created new federal universities, most of the increased demand unleashed by the expansion of Class C has been met by private universities and colleges, which made up around 90 per cent of the 2,400 institutions of higher education in the country. They included two big for-profit companies, quoted on the stock exchange, Kroton and Anhanguera, which agreed to merge in 2013. If the deal is approved by Brazil's anti-trust regulator, the combined company will have 800 campuses, making it the world's largest private provider of higher education.[42] It has managed to keep fees low, compared with private universities elsewhere in Latin America. The government recognized that it needs the private sector's help. It offered private universities tax breaks in return for giving around a tenth of their places free or at discounts to students from poor backgrounds. Some 300,000 students at private universities get low-interest government loans. Even so, more than half of students in higher education drop out before completing their courses, because of money worries, a poor grounding in the basics and the difficulty of combining work and study.

Brazilian universities are the best in Latin America but are poor by the standards of the rest of the world. Research output is unimpressive, teaching techniques are old-fashioned, and rigid rules on hiring, promotion and pay discourage talent. There are some exceptions. The University of São Paulo (USP) was the only Latin American university to figure in the world's top 200 universities (it ranked 158th in 2012) in the list compiled by *Times Higher Education*, a British specialist weekly.* Founded and supported by the São Paulo state government, USP has benefited from a big increase in private funding and in collaborations with foreign institutions. Brazil also has two business schools in the top fifty in the world in the *Financial Times*' executive education rankings.[43] In an attempt to improve both Brazil's skills base and its universities, Dilma implemented a scheme called Science without Borders,

---

* It dropped out of the top 200 in 2013.

under which 100,000 science students would be paid to spend a year at the best universities around the world. A quarter of the 3 billion reais cost was to be contributed by business, and the rest from the federal budget. The official hope was that the students would return full of ideas as to how to shake up their own university.

Brazil's university system embodied an injustice. Brazilians with degrees earned 3.6 times as much as high-school graduates, a differential unmatched anywhere in the OECD.[44] Federal and state universities, most of which were of better quality than most of their private counterparts, were free to students. Public spending on each university student was five times greater per year than for each primary school child. But the vast majority of students at public universities came from better-off families who could afford private schools, and were thus better prepared for the competitive entrance exam. Such students were mainly white. And that prompted a passionate debate about race discrimination and the lack of equality of opportunity.

Affirming a racial divide

In the 2010 census some 51 per cent of Brazilians defined themselves as black or brown.[45] On average their income was slightly less than half that whites, according to a study by IPEA.[46] It found that blacks were relatively disadvantaged in their level of education and in their access to health and other services. For example, more than half the people in Rio de Janeiro's favelas are black; the comparable figure in the city's richer districts is just 7 per cent. Since the days of Gilberto Freyre, the conventional wisdom was that blacks were poor only because they were at the base of the social pyramid – in other words, that society was stratified by class, not race. But a growing number of Brazilians disagreed. The 'clamorous' differences could only be explained by racism, according to Mario Theodoro, a senior official at the federal government's secretariat for racial equality. Black Brazilian activists insisted that slavery's legacy of injustice and inequality could only be reversed by affirmative action policies of the kind adopted in the United States.

Their opponents in what became a passionate debate argued that because the history of race relations in Brazil was different, such policies risked creating new racial problems. Racial mixing and the lack of segregation meant that skin colour in Brazil was a spectrum, not a dichotomy. Few still called Brazil a 'racial democracy'. As Antonio Risério, a sociologist from Bahia, put it: 'It's clear that racism exists in the US. It's clear that racism exists in Brazil. But they are different kinds of racism.'[47] Importing American-style affirmative action risked forcing Brazilians to place themselves in strict racial categories, argued Peter Fry, a British-born, naturalized-Brazilian anthropologist. Having worked in southern Africa, he thought that Brazil's avoidance of 'the crystallizing of race as a marker of identity' was a big advantage in creating a democratic society.

For the proponents of affirmative action, the veiled quality of Brazilian racism explained why racial stratification has been ignored for so long. 'In Brazil you have an invisible enemy. Nobody's racist. But when your daughter goes out with a black, things change,' said Ivanir dos Santos, a black activist in Rio de Janeiro. If black and white youths with equal qualifications applied to be a shop assistant in a Rio mall, the white will get the job, he added.

The debate over affirmative action split both left and right. The governments of Dilma Rousseff, Lula and Cardoso all expressed support for such policies. But they moved cautiously. The main battleground was in universities. From 2001 onwards, more than seventy public universities introduced racial admissions quotas. In Rio de Janeiro's state universities, 20 per cent of places were set aside for black students who passed the entrance exam. Another 25 per cent were reserved for a 'social quota' of pupils from state schools whose parents' income was less than twice the minimum wage – who are often black. Prouni, the big federal programme of student grants and loans, embodied similar quotas for students at private universities. These measures started to make a difference. Although only 6.3 per cent of black eighteen- to twenty-four-year-olds were in higher education in 2006, that was double the proportion in 2001, according to IPEA. (The figures for whites were 19.2 per cent in 2006, compared with 14.1 per cent in 2001.) 'We're very happy, because in the past five years we've placed more blacks in universities than in the previous 500 years,' said Frei David Raimundo dos Santos, a Franciscan friar who ran Educafro, a charity that held university-entrance classes in poor areas. 'Today there's a revolution in Brazil.'

One of its beneficiaries was Carolina Bras da Silva, a young black woman whose mother was a cleaner. As a teenager she lived for a while on the streets of São Paulo. When I met her in 2011 she was in her first year of social sciences at Rio's Catholic University, on a full grant. 'Some of the other students said "What are you doing here?" But it's getting better,' she said. She wants to study law and become a public prosecutor.

Academics from some of the best universities led a campaign against quotas. They argued firstly that affirmative action started with an act of racism: the division of a rainbow nation into arbitrary colour categories. Assigning races in Brazil was not always as easy as the activists claimed. In 2007 one of two identical twins who both applied to enter the University of Brasília was classified by examiners as black, the other as white (on the basis of photos). All this risked creating racial resentment. Secondly, opponents said affirmative action undermined equality of opportunity and meritocracy – fragile concepts in Brazil, where privilege, nepotism and contacts were long the routes to advancement.

Proponents of affirmative action replied that these arguments sanctified an unjust status quo. Formally meritocratic university entrance exams did not guarantee equality of opportunity. A study by Carlos Antonio Costa Ribeiro, a sociologist at the State University of Rio de Janeiro, found that the factors most closely correlated to attending university were having rich parents and studying in private school. That finding was echoed by the World Bank, which found that in Brazil, as in several other Latin American countries, the educational level of a person's parents was much more likely to determine his or her education than in most other countries around the world, though it also found that this correlation had started to weaken.[48]

In April 2012 Brazil's supreme court ruled unanimously that the quotas applied by universities were legal. Four months later Dilma Rousseff signed a law giving all federal universities four years to ensure that half their intake came from public schools, and that the racial make-up of these students should reflect that of the state where they were located. After ten years, the measure would lapse unless renewed. It might have been better had the law simply stuck to social, rather than explicitly racial, quotas. Its implementation was likely to be messy. Nevertheless, it marked an important attempt to try to redress the legacy of slavery.

In practice, many of the fears surrounding university quotas were not borne out. Though still preliminary, studies tended to show that *cotistas*, as they were known, performed academically as well as or better than their peers. That may be because they replaced weaker 'white' students who got in merely because they had the money to prepare for the exam. Nelson do Valle Silva, a sociologist at the Federal University of Rio de Janeiro, said that the backlash against quotas would have been even stronger if access to universities had not been growing so fast, which meant that almost everyone who passed the exam got in somewhere. Peter Fry agreed that affirmative action had 'become a *fait accompli*'. He attributed the declining resistance to guilt, indifference and the fear of being accused of racism.

For black activists, the next target was the labour market. 'As a black man, when I go for a job I start from a disadvantage,' said Theodoro. He noted that the United States, which is only 12 per cent black, had a black president and numerous black politicians and millionaires. In Brazil, in contrast, 'we have nobody'. That was not quite true: apart from footballers and singers, Brazil had a black supreme court justice in Joaquim Barbosa, and senior military and police officers. But they were exceptional. Only one of the thirty-nine members of Rousseff's cabinet – the secretary for racial equality – was black. Stand outside the adjacent headquarters of Petrobras and the BNDES in Rio at lunchtime, and 'all the managers are white and the cleaners are black,' said Frei David. Some private-sector bodies were starting to espouse racial diversity in recruitment. The state and city of Rio de Janeiro both passed laws reserving 20 per cent of posts in civil service exams for blacks, though they had yet to be implemented in 2013. If unemployment rose from today's record low, job quotas were likely to create even more controversy than the battle over university entrance.

Many of the 25 million Brazilians who had left poverty since 2003 were black. Businesses took note: many more cosmetics were aimed at blacks, for example. The mix of passengers on internal flights began to bear some resemblance to Brazil, rather than Scandinavia. Until recently, the only black actors in television soap operas played maids; in 2012 a Globo soap had a black male lead.

Until the invasion of American academic ideas, most Brazilians thought that their country's racial rainbow was among its main assets. They were not wholly wrong. Nelson do Valle Silva, a specialist in social mobility, found that race affects life chances in Brazil but does not determine them. Brazil has had anti-discrimination legislation since the 1950s. The 1988 constitution made both racial abuse and racism crimes. But there were relatively few prosecutions. That was partly because of racism in the judiciary. But it was also because judges and prosecutors thought the penalties were too harsh: anyone accused of racism must be held in jail both before and after conviction. And in Rio de Janeiro the black movement's preference for affirmative action led the state government to lose interest in measures aimed at attacking racial prejudice, according to a study by Fabiano Dias Monteiro, who ran the state's anti-racist helpline before it was scrapped in 2007.[49]

The hardest task was to change attitudes. Many Brazilians simply assumed that blacks belonged at the bottom of the pile. Supporters of affirmative action were right to say that the country turned its back on the problem. But US-style policies might not be the way to combat Brazil's specific forms of racism. If positive discrimination becomes permanent, a publicly funded industry of entitlement may grow up to entrench it and to promote divisive racial politics. Alongside social quotas in universities, a more effective anti-discrimination law might be a better way to establish equality of opportunity and rights

The lack of black Brazilians in leadership positions contrasted with the relative prominence of women. Dilma was a feminist and promoted capable women. Ten of the thirty-nine members of her cabinet in mid-2013 were women. A woman, Maria das Graças Foster, was the CEO of Petrobras;

another, Maria Silvia Bastos Marques, was in charge of the organization of the 2016 Olympic Games, as head of the Municipal Olympic Committee in Rio de Janeiro. Grant Thornton, a consultancy, reported that women made up 27 per cent of senior managers of Brazil's leading companies, compared with a global average of 21 per cent. A higher percentage of women worked outside the home in Brazil (59 per cent) than in Britain or France.[50] One reason was the traditional availability of poorer women to work as maids and childminders. Brazil had around 7 million domestic workers in 2009, nearly all women, according to the ILO. In March 2013 Congress approved a constitutional amendment bringing maids under the protection of the labour laws, with overtime, holiday pay and social security. That would nearly double their total remuneration, and some analysts thought it would lead to many being sacked. Secondly, young Brazilian women had far fewer children than their mothers and were more ambitious in their careers. Around 60 per cent of secondary school pupils and university students are female. Brazil continued to have a macho culture, but it was fraying at the edges.[51]

The *morro* and the *asfalto*

The social divide in Brazil was summed up by the architectural contrast between the serried ranks of tower blocks, which had replaced the detached chalets of the middle class, and the favela, a labyrinth of lanes and passageways between self-built houses of raw brick and corrugated iron, often on steep hillsides or valley bottoms. In Rio de Janeiro, the two were cheek-by-jowl: the *morro* (hill), as *cariocas* refer to the favelas, sometimes overlooked the *asfalto*, the asphalted streets of moneyed districts such as Copacabana, Ipanema and Leblon. The juxtaposition was a constant reminder of Brazil's inequalities that shocked foreign visitors, and was a source of fear and shame to better-off Brazilians. In Rio, favelas did not even appear on maps until the late twentieth century. A product of the way in which urbanization outpaced development, favelas were perhaps less numerous in reality than in the imagination. The 2010 census found 11.4 million favela-dwellers, or less than 6 per cent of the total population. Almost 90 per cent of them were in the big cities and half in the south-east. That compared with 6.5 million in 2000, but IBGE, the statistics agency, said that the introduction of better data-gathering methods meant that the two figures were not comparable.[52]

Under the military government, urban planners forcibly removed some favelas, on occasion to benefit property developers.[53] Since then, official efforts have been directed towards upgrading them, installing basic services and street-lighting, and paving alleys and stairways. There was a strong argument for demolishing favelas built in geologically dangerous areas, and rehousing their inhabitants. But that faced fierce resistance, as Lula admitted to me, referring to his own reluctance to leave a flood-prone favela in São Paulo in 1964: 'People don't like change; even when you want to take someone out of a tumbledown shack in a favela, they don't want to leave.'[54]

Rather than a problem in themselves, favelas were a symbol and symptom of other problems, especially the lack of urban services, and the prevalence of violent crime, drug gangs and inadequate policing. Solve them, and most favelas will evolve into conventional settlements. Brazil was said to have a shortage of 7 million houses. It was scandalous that in a country where the state spent two-fifths of national income, only 55 per cent of homes had a sewerage connection, according to the 2010 census. Though a further 11.6 per cent had a sceptic tank, a third of Brazilian homes had no proper sewerage.[55] The reluctance to leave favelas was often a function of poor public transport. People would not want to move to a distant suburb if it meant a two-hour twice-daily commute on a crowded bus. Conversely, better public transport was a powerful tool of social inclusion.

It was not coincidental that favelas were especially prevalent in Rio, which after losing its status as Brazil's capital suffered economic decline and prolonged misgovernment. The 2010 census found that 1.4 million people, or 22 per cent of the city's population lived in 763 separate favelas.[56] The city's problems were aggravated by the arrival of the illegal drug trade in the 1980s. What at first involved the onward export of Bolivian cocaine to Europe soon developed into a business supplying a local consumer market. Trafficking gangs exploited the vacuum of government authority – Brizola, as governor of Rio state, even banned the police from entering favelas.[57] Three heavily armed gangs came to control the Rio favelas, running extortion rackets involving illegal electricity and satellite television connections, as well as peddling drugs. The gangs were opposed by punitive policing, sometimes involving the army, in murderous invasions followed by swift withdrawals that left the rule of the traffickers undisturbed. In 2006 the Rio police were reported to have killed 1,063 people – more than three times the number killed by all police forces in the United States in the same year.[58] In more recent years former policemen and firefighters (and sometimes serving ones) formed militias, which exercised a counter-terror over many favelas in the west of the city. When Janice Pearlman, an American anthropologist, returned to Rio in the early 2000s to find out what had happened to favela residents she had interviewed in the late 1960s she found that insecurity undermined the dramatic material improvements most had achieved. 'In 1969 the poor living in favelas feared that their homes and communities would be demolished. Today they fear for their lives,' she wrote.[59] That fear was comunicated to an international audience in 'City of God', a film made in 2002 in Cidade de Deus, a rundown housing project in Rio's western suburbs. The Comando Vermelho, Rio's biggest and best-armed trafficking gang, dominated the lives of the 60,000 or so residents of Cidade de Deus and its surrounding favelas.

Then, at last, the state began to approach the problems of Rio's favelas more intelligently. A new governor, Sérgio Cabral, appointed some capable officials. One of them was José Beltrame, an experienced federal police officer named as public security secretary in January 2007. He arrested the incumbent police commanders for corruption and put in place a new strategy whose aim was to recover control of the favelas by establishing a permanent police presence in the form of police stations known as Unidades de Polícia Pacificadora (Pacifying Police Units or UPPs). This effort began with greater stress on intelligence work; then police special forces, and where necessary the army, would go in to disarm or disperse the gangsters; finally, a UPP would be set up, staffed entirely by new and specially trained recruits in an effort to minimize abuses and corruption. Beltrame assigned targets to the whole police force. By getting the city and federal governments to chip in, he managed to double the salaries of front-line policemen (to US$1,200 a month). In 2011 he appointed Martha Mesquita da Rocha as the first woman to head Rio's civil police (detectives), after ordering the arrest of her predecessor on charges of taking bribes from the gangs.[60]

In June 2010 I visited Cidade de Deus, where a UPP had been established nine months previously. The difference was palpable. A force of 318 officers, backed by twenty-five patrol cars, was based in a new police station in a side street between two fetid, litter-strewn drainage channels. In 2008 there were twenty-nine murders in Cidade de Deus; in the first six months of 2010 there was just one. Many residents were appreciative. 'It was horror before,' said Jeanne Barbosa, who ran a small bar on the ground floor of her house. 'Bodies would be thrown out of passing cars, and there were kids with revolvers.' Her niece was killed as she walked home, by a stray bullet from a firefight between the police and traffickers. 'Now the children can play in the street.' A dread-locked unemployed welder who gave his name as Sérgio was more sceptical. He said the police committed abuses. His friend, who had the blank stare of a crack addict, added with deranged precision: '89 per cent of them are corrupt.'

'The big concept is to break the [gangsters'] control of territory imposed by military-style weapons,' Beltrame, a lean man with a driven intensity about him, told me.

When we enter, we disarm. The *bandidos* (criminals) flee; if they resist, they pay a price. I keep a lot of police there for a long time, and they begin to disarm [people] and get information, and crime comes down ... Once I achieve that, this allows society to enter, private business and public services.[61]

In all, Beltrame's plan involved installing forty UPPs covering 500,000 people in 600 favelas by 2014 – a commitment included in Rio's successful Olympic bid. In November 2010, after gangsters in the Complexo do Alemão, a cluster of a dozen favelas containing 140,000 people in the north of the city, began hijacking and burning vehicles, police and troops entered the area in force; after firefights in which at least thirty-seven people died (some bystanders), they took control. Several UPPs then followed in the Complexo; soon after-wards, the same process took place in Rocinha, another large favela where gang control was notoriously brazen. Sceptical *cariocas* were persuaded that something really had changed. The police in Rio did not become spotless over-night: in 2012 forty-six officers working in UPPs were charged with crimes. In a shocking case in 2011 Patricia Acioli, a judge who was investigating police involvement in militias, was gunned down in Niterói; three policemen were arrested for the killing. Gangs were not wholly eradicated from the Complexo do Alemão. But the murder rate in the state of Rio fell dramatically, from forty-two per 100,000 people in 2005 to twenty-four in 2012.[62]

The state, municipal and federal governments began to work together in Rio to try to consolidate security with legality and services. It helped that the city's economy was undergoing a renaissance, too, thanks to the oil boom and a series of big industrial and infrastructure projects on the outskirts. Shortly before I visited, Cidade de Deus had gained its first health clinic. In the Complexo do Alemão, the government built a 4.5-kilometre cable car, blocks of flats and sports pitches. By 2013 rubbish and illegal electricity connections were gradually diminishing, some 500 businesses had formalized and there was talk of a shopping centre. The criminals were still there, but were no longer openly carrying arms.[63]

NGOs were increasingly active in favelas, too. One group, Afroreggae, got favela youths involved in music, dance and theatre as part of a strategy of pacification and local development. In 2010 it opened a big cultural centre in Vigário Geral, a small favela notorious for an incident in 1993 in which a police death squad murdered twenty-one young people in retaliation for the killing of four officers by traffickers. To get there, you crossed a footbridge over the railway from the main avenue. Two young black men on the bridge guarded the entrance to the favela, one with a large revolver tucked ostenta-tiously into the top pocket of his army-style jacket. That represented an improvement, said José Junior, the charismatic founder of Afroreggae, who had a weekly programme about social issues on cable television. In the 1990s a dozen youths with rifles would mount guard, part of the Comando Vermelho's army of 200 men. Now Afroreggae, which obtained financing from big businesses, is the main economic power in Vigário Geral, paying higher wages than the traffickers. The place is much more peaceful. 'Things aren't good yet, but it is no longer complete chaos,' José Junior told me in 2010. 'This is a great moment in Rio.'[64]*

The law and its enemies

The same could not be said for Brazilian policing more generally. The first years of the New Republic saw several other atrocities such as that at Vigário Geral. In 1992 police stormed Carandiru, an overcrowded prison in São Paulo following a riot by inmates, killing 102 prisoners. The following year, eight street children were murdered by police outside the Candelária church in the centre of Rio. In 1996 nineteen members of the MST were gunned down at Eldorado dos Carajás in the south of Pará, when police broke up a demonstration in which they were blocking a highway. That prompted Cardoso to draw up a formal plan to commit Brazilian democracy to uphold human rights, a pledge strengthened by Lula.

The problem was that the police remained unreformed, and Brazil was suffering a wave of violent crime. The chaotic urbanization of the 'miracle' years in the 1970s left a legacy in the urban peripheries of lack of secure land tenure and the absence of effective government. To that, the economic stagnation of the 1980s added a large swathe of under-employed young men. In the 1990s drug dealers moved into the favelas. By 2012 Brazil had become the world's second-biggest market for cocaine; a crack epidemic swept across the country. Guns were in plentiful supply. Although some were smuggled across the Paraguayan border, the vast majority were domestically manufactured; Brazil has a thriving small-arms industry, the second-biggest in the Americas after the US. A careful study estimated that there were 17.6 million guns in the country, of which 57 per cent were not legally registered. Possession of weapons was particularly widespread in São Paulo, Brasília and the states of the agrarian frontiers (such as Mato Grosso, Acre and Roraima).[65] The murder rate climbed steadily during the first years of the New Republic, from 11.7 per 100,000 people, peaking at 28.1 in 2003 before falling to 21 in 2010. This still meant 41,000 Brazilians were killed in that year, and the murder rate was higher than in Mexico, despite that country's well-publicized 'drug war'.[66]

---

* Afroreggae was forced to shut down its activities in the Complexo do Alemão in July 2013 after threats from drug traffickers and a fire at its premises there.

Responsibility for security and policing lies largely with state governors. The Federal Police, while well paid and efficient, is small (around 13,000) and has narrowly defined responsibilities (mainly border security, combating international drug trafficking and investigating federal crimes such as money laundering and cyber crime). Each state has two separate police forces: the military police, as they are called, are responsible for public order, and the civil police for criminal investigation. This structure was a hold over from *coronelismo*, the First Republic and the dictatorship. Although the constitution abolished the subordination of the military police to the armed forces, more ambitious attempts to create unified police forces failed. The system has several flaws. The military police, organized in army-style battalions, had a 'predisposition ... to apply coercion in the streets rather than to arrest', as Anthony Pereira, a political scientist, noted.[67] Relations between the two police forces were often marked by rivalry rather than co-operation. The civil police had few incentives to conduct swift investigations of crime, or to collaborate with prosecutors. The result was that violent crime was rarely swiftly prosecuted. Many police were poorly paid and moonlighted as private security guards. The private security industry grew rapidly: in 2012 it comprised over 2,000 firms employing 690,000 people (plus an unknown number of unregistered firms). The main source of expansion was the demand from better-off Brazilians for security in their apartment blocks, which became vertical gated communities.[68]

The federal government set up a fund as a tool to encourage community policing, and several states adopted at least the rhetoric, and part of the practice, of that approach. This went furthest in São Paulo, with more patrolling and the establishment of permanent twenty-four-hour police posts in the most violent areas, and much stricter rules for the issue of gun licences. The state government's public security secretariat began to give priority to ensuring that murders were solved and punished. The murder clear-up rate went from 20 per cent in 2001 to 65 per cent in 2005.[69] In Diadema, a suburb that in the 1980s was compared to the 'Wild West' of the United States, these initiatives were backed up by the mayor, who set up a municipal police force and restricted alcohol sales. The murder rate there fell from a terrifying peak of 103 deaths per 100,000 people in 1999 to just 9.5 in 2012.[70] In the state as a whole, the murder rate fell from thirty-five in 1999 to ten per 100,000 people in 2011, before rising slightly, to 11.5 in 2012.[71] São Paulo was shaken in 2006 by an uprising by an organized criminal gang, based in the state's prisons, called the Primeiro Comando da Capital (PCC). The PCC mounted 274 attacks on police stations and public buildings, and burnt scores of buses, killing forty-three people (thirty-one of them police). In reprisals that followed, the police killed seventy-four suspected criminals.[72] In the following years, a low-level war continued between the PCC and the police, who responded to the murders of off-duty officers with killings of suspected PCC members in favelas. Elsewhere, the murder rate spiked in several north-eastern states (Alagoas, for example), mainly in response to the arrival of the drug trade. But many smaller cities were peaceful, law-abiding places.

The prison population multiplied relentlessly: by 2011 Brazil's jails held 515,000 inmates, a bigger number than in any country except the United States, China and Russia, and up from just 90,000 in 1990. Like the lack of sewerage, the prisons were another unheralded national scandal. Human rights lawyers reported cells built for eight holding forty-eight; conditions were often filthy and diseases unchecked; in Espírito Santo, prisoners were kept in unventilated metal shipping containers in the baking sun. Around half of prisoners had not received any sentence. A quarter of them were incarcerated for drugs offences. It was the poor (95 per cent of prisoners), the ill-educated (two-thirds had not finished primary school) and the black (two-thirds of prisoners) who were jailed. On the other hand, public-sector workers, politicians, judges, priests and anyone with a degree cannot be held in a common prison while awaiting trial. This is one reason why pressure for prison reform has been so weak.[73]

Opinion polls showed that fear of crime was at the top of Brazilians' concerns. Public opinion tended to take a hard line on crime, and was largely unmoved by the police practice of killing rather than arresting. 'When crime is high, human rights disappear,' commented Patrick Wilcken, Amnesty International's researcher for Brazil.[74] That mood doomed a proposal to ban the sale of handguns, defeated in a national referendum in 2005 by 36 per cent to 64 per cent. Nevertheless, and despite continuing problems, in different ways both Rio and São Paulo showed that better policing was possible.

Brazilian society has changed dramatically over the past two decades. Brazilians are less poor, less unequal and less badly educated than ever before. Above all, the promise of democratic citizenship is starting to be fulfilled at last. But the country still has a long way to go ensure that its democracy protects the lives and rights of all its citizens, and before it can say that it has become the middle-class society to which Dilma aspired.

CHAPTER TEN

Oil, Farming and the Amazon

Getting to Açu Superport, as its promoters call it, involves a seventy-minute helicopter ride north along the coast from Rio, past long sandy beaches and lagoons, then the small oil port of Macaé where a queue of supply ships wait offshore, and finally across gently rolling plains with herds of white Cebu cattle scattered like confetti, before descending to land in the flat and bleak *restinga* (saltmarsh) where Rio de Janeiro state borders Espírito Santo. Everything about the Açu project is superlative. When I visited in May 2012, the bare bones of a giant port were emerging from vast earthworks. Dredges were digging out what will be a long inland elbow of water for an onshore terminal for general cargo. A concrete jetty extended 3 kilometres out into the Atlantic to a future terminal for exporting bulk cargoes of iron ore and oil. When fully operational, the two terminals will have a total of 17 kilometres of wharves, able to receive thirty-nine ships at a time and shift 350 million tonnes a year (congested Santos, Brazil's biggest port, manages just 90 million tonnes a year). A planned oil-handling terminal will be able to take 2 million barrels a day of crude (almost as much as Brazil's output in 2012). The port will be the centre of an industrial complex comprising a power plant big enough to supply electricity to 20 million people, two steelworks, Brazil's biggest shipyard, car plants, a host of other factories and a new town to house up to 250,000 people, all occupying a site the size of Manhattan and signifying a total investment of US$50 billion.

That, at least, was the plan. Açu was the grand vision of Eike (pronounced eye-kay) Batista, Brazil's most flamboyant tycoon, to extract synergies from Brazil's commodity wealth. The son of a former minister of energy and mines, Eike made his first, modest fortune buying up gold mining concessions in the Amazon jungle from *garimpeiros* (wildcat miners) in the 1970s, flying in equipment to mechanize them. With Brazil in the 1980s in a 'mess', as he put it, he left for Canada where he ran a gold mining company. But in 2000, with impeccable timing, he decided to set up once again in Brazil. In his office in an art-deco tower in the centre of Rio restored by his company, sitting at his desk from which he can eyeball the city's emblematic Sugar Loaf mountain, Eike told me the story of what came next.[1] First he bought concessions for iron mines in Minas Gerais. Since 'iron ore is a logistics operation', he set up LLX, the company developing Açu; then came MPX, an energy company to build big coal- and gas-fired power stations on coastal sites to supply his own businesses and sell to the grid. In 2007 he made his boldest move, founding an oil and gas company (OGX) and recruiting experienced former Petrobras managers. OGX bid $1 billion to win a dozen concession blocks just before Petrobras announced its big deep-sea discoveries. Eike claimed that OGX was 'the most successful oil exploration and production company in the world', having found 6 billion barrels of oil (almost twice the total reserves of the United Kingdom).[2] In the Waimea field, in shallow water in the Campos basin, 'we've discovered a whole new oil province' with production costs among the lowest in the world, claimed Eduardo Marques, one of OGX's managers.[3] Then came OSX, an oil-services company intended to become Brazil's biggest shipbuilder. Açu was the hub of Eike's ambition: it is the terminal for a 525-kilometre 'pipeline' or beltway for the export of ore from the iron mines of Minas Gerais and it sits just onshore from the Campos Basin, where 85 per cent of Brazil's oil is extracted.

Dressed in a grey suit and a matching T-shirt, with a smile that switched on and off like a light, Eike dismissed claims that he was a favoured insider who owed his rise to government contacts. 'I'm a truffle-sniffing labrador, an animal that knows how to sniff [out assets],' he said. 'I prefer to own assets rather than money . . . assets that people consume rather than paper.' Unlike Russian oligarchs, 'I won these assets in open competition,' he insisted. When we spoke, in May 2012, the total assets of his EBX holding company – all the Xs were supposed to symbolize the multiplication of value – were worth $1 trillion, he claimed. He used the assets – and his own hyping of them – to raise capital, from the financial markets, the banks and outside investors. A joke in Brazil held that Eike was the only man other than Bill Gates to make billions from PowerPoint presentations; during our interview he watched his own corporate video with apparent wonder, as if seeing it for the first time. By 2012 Eike had become the world's seventh-richest person, with a personal fortune of $30.2 billion, according to *Forbes* magazine. He enjoyed flaunting his wealth. He once kept a Maclaren sports car in his living room; he married Luma de Oliveira, a Rio Carnival queen and *Playboy* model. During our interview, he pointed with approbation to a framed cover on his office wall of *Veja*,

Brazil's leading newsweekly, which portrayed him as 'Eike Xiaoping' with the line 'to get rich is glorious'. His declared intention was to overhaul Mexico's Carlos Slim and become the world's richest individual. After several years of heavy capital expenditure, in 2014 his companies would start paying dividends, he said. 'It's all based on idiot-proofed concepts and underlying assets.'

Except that it wasn't. Scepticism built in the financial markets as several of Eike's companies missed production deadlines. He had sold his iron ore deposit to Anglo American for US$4.8 billion; technical problems caused its development costs to triple to US$8.8 billion and its completion date slipped by several years. Then came the hammer blow: OGX announced in July 2013 that its only producing oil wells, in the Tubarão Azul field (as Waimea was renamed), would probably shut down in 2014 because the technology did not exist to make their challenging geology commercially viable. OGX's shares, which in March 2011 had traded at 20 reais, fell to a few centavos.[4] Faced with debts estimated at over US$13 billion and few sources of cash, Eike called in investment bankers to help him break up his empire. MPX, the energy company, was sold to Germany's EON. In August 2013 EIG Global Energy Partners, an American investment fund, bought a controlling stake in the Açu superport for US$562 million. It may never become the 'Rotterdam of the tropics' that Eike promised, but the port, at least, is likely to be completed, if not all the planned factories. Then in October 2013, in Latin America's biggest-ever corporate bust, OGX filed for bankruptcy, facing debts of US$5.1 billion and having been unable to meet an interest payment of US$45 million. It was followed days later by OSX, the shipbuilding company, with debts of US$2.3 billion.[5] As for Eike, Forbes announced in September 2013 that he was no longer a billionaire. He looked as if he would be lucky to emerge from the wreckage of EBX with much more than a few million dollars and without lawsuits.

Some commentators saw Eike Batista's rise and decline as a metaphor for that of the country, as an exhibit for the argument that Brazil's claim to greatness was a mirage based on a commodity boom.[6] Yet that would be a mistake: the real story of Brazil's commodity industries is both more durable and far more interesting than Eike's hubris and nemesis. To get a sense of why that is, a good place to start is the campus of the Federal University of Rio de Janeiro (UFRJ) at Ilha de Fundão, in Guanabara Bay. A concrete shed at the university's technology park, in the lee of the Rio-Niterói bridge and some rusting shipyards, contains the world's largest and deepest oceanographical research tank.[7] Resembling a huge swimming pool, 25 metres deep in the middle, its machinery allows researchers to simulate the effect of winds, waves and currents on equipment. Its main customer is Petrobras, whose research centre is also sited on the UFRJ campus. The company has put the knowledge gained there to good use.

Petrobras and the *pré-sal*

Founded by Vargas in 1954, Petrobras at first had little luck in finding oil on land. But in the 1960s it began to drill offshore. When the oil price shocks of the early 1970s added urgency to its quest to reduce Brazil's dependence on imported crude, it moved into deeper and deeper water, with increasing success. For decades Petrobras was a company run by engineers, a merito-cratic centre of excellence largely protected from political interference. It became the world's most knowledgeable oil company about deep-sea opera-tions (rivalled in reputation only by BP, at least until the Deepwater Horizon rig exploded in 2010). Cardoso's reforms had subjected Petrobras to competi-tive pressure while also allowing it to enter alliances with multinationals. As a result, Brazil's proven reserves of oil doubled in the decade to 2002, while oil output more than doubled between 1996 and 2005 (when it reached 1.7 million barrels per day).[8]

Then in 2007 came the huge new finds by Petrobras and foreign partners, including Exxon and Britain's BG Group, in what was genuinely a new oil province, up to 300 kilometres offshore from Santos and up to 7 kilometres below the South Atlantic. The oil lay beneath a thick bed of salt laid down when the African and South American continents parted about 130 million years ago, and was thus known as *pré-sal* (sub-salt). The first find was the Tupi field (soon renamed Lula) with up to 8 billion barrels of light crude, an amount equal to Norway's reserves. Further discoveries quickly followed: by 2011, Brazil's proven reserves of oil had risen to 15 billion barrels – more than Mexico's; estimates for the potentially recoverable oil from the new fields ranged from 50 billion barrels (a little less than everything in the North Sea) to 80 billion.[9]

Dilma Rousseff, who as well as being Lula's chief of staff chaired Petrobras's board at the time, hastened to ensure that the state would exercise tight control over the new bounty. Dilma insisted that existing contracts would be respected, including concessions already awarded in the *pré-sal*. But the new legal framework she drew up for future *pré-sal* exploration blocks declared the oil to be the property of a new state company called Pré-Sal Petróleo SA (PPSA). It introduced a production-sharing arrangement, with Petrobras as the sole operator, in place of the previous system of auctioning concessions. As eventually approved, in each block PPSA got half of the oil produced; the other half was split between Petrobras, which was granted a minimum

30 per cent stake in every field, and its partner companies (to be paid according to their costs). Although it did not contribute any capital, PPSA held half the seats on the operating committee set up for each consortium. In a complicated accounting manoeuvre, the government also pre-paid Petrobras for 5 billion barrels of oil to furnish it with extra capital, in effect diluting the owners of the 60 per cent of the company's non-voting shares that were traded on the stock exchange. PPSA's revenues were to be saved in a social fund for education and health care. Another new law distributed royalties from *pré-sal* oil across the country, not just to the producer states as was the custom. It was these last two measures concerning how to spend the bounty (even before it was extracted) that attracted the fiercest political debate in Brasília. Congress festooned the new oil fund with other spending commitments (though Dilma managed to remove these after the 2013 protests); the argument over royalties was not resolved until 2013, holding up the licensing of further exploration blocks.

The government also decreed that up to 70 per cent of the equipment and supplies to develop the *pré-sal*, including drilling rigs and production plat-forms, must be nationally produced. The aims included reviving a ship-building industry that had collapsed after subsidies provided by the military government were withdrawn. Unlike the new legal regime, the national content rule did apply to existing concessions – and added 20 per cent to costs, according to one foreign oilman.[10]

Dilma called the laws 'a passport to the future'. She and Lula justified the more nationalistic rules by arguing that there was no exploration risk – everyone now knew where the oil was. The first sixteen wells Petrobras drilled in the *pré-sal* were all successful, said José Sergio Gabrielli, Petrobras's chief executive. Yet he later admitted that there were large 'development risks'.[11] The oil lies beneath 2 kilometres of water (deeper than the North Sea), and then a further 5 kilometres or more further down, beneath the thick, hot and unstable layer of salt. The difficulty was not so much technology, Gabrielli told me, but rather working out the geological dynamics of the basin to minimize drilling and solving the logistics problems. Petrobras was already transporting 40,000 people a month to the Campos Basin by helicopter; to reach the new, more distant, fields, helicopters would have to carry three times as much fuel as normal.[12] Extracting the oil would require dozens of floating production, storage and offloading vessels (FSPOs) – oil tankers converted into floating platforms, each costing billions of dollars. Other platforms will be needed as helicopter refuelling bases. Rather than piping the oil to shore, it will be ferried in a fleet of about seventy tankers.

Nevertheless, Gabrielli, an affable economist who was an outsider to Petrobras before the PT government appointed him as its finance director, declared that the company would be among the world's top five oil majors by 2020, with total output of 6.4 million b/d, of which 4.9 million would be in Brazil. That was almost two-and-a-half times Petrobras's output in 2010. To get there, he unveiled the largest capital spending plan by any company in the world, worth $224 billion in 2010–14. This was financed partly by a $70 billion share issue in 2010 – the largest-ever public offer, although 43 per cent of the new shares were taken by the government in its pre-payment for future oil.[13]

Yet it quickly became clear that Petrobras had overreached. As well as the *pré-sal*, Lula had lumbered it with building four new refineries, some of them seemingly for political reasons. The Abreu e Lima refinery at Suape in Pernambuco, supposed to be completed by November 2011 at a cost of $2.3 billion, would not be ready until 2014 and would cost $20.1 billion, the company later admitted.[14] Gabrielli's critics claimed that Petrobras had been burdened with political appointees, undermining its efficiency. With the global oil equipment market saturated, Petrobras faced delays in the delivery of some of the thirty-seven rigs and FSPOs it ordered in Asia. Even so, the biggest potential headache was the national content rules. Nobody disagreed that Brazilians should be the main beneficiaries from the oil, and that it should serve to help the country to develop an oil services industry. But many argued that by setting national content so high, and for an indefinite period, the government had not only cocooned Brazilian oil service firms from the need to be internationally competitive but also guaranteed that Petrobras would pay over the odds for equipment and suffer endless delays. Booz & Company, a consultancy, reported that Brazilian suppliers to the oil and gas industry charged 10–40 per cent more than world prices.[15] Costs at Brazilian shipyards were nearly double those in South Korea. The biggest of the new Brazilian shipyards, Atlântico Sul at Suape, won orders for twenty supertankers and seven deep-water floating rigs. It was a joint venture between two Brazilian construction firms, Camargo Correa and Queiroz Galvão, and Korea's Samsung, which was to provide the technical know-how. Although Atlântico Sul received subsidized loans of around US$3 billion from the BNDES, it soon ran into trouble. Samsung pulled out; the yard delivered its first tanker twenty-one months late and at twice the price of the international market. But Dilma celebrated the jobs created in shipbuilding – more than 70,000 of them by mid-2013, she said.[16]

With Petrobras visibly struggling with too many projects, too few qualified staff and equipment delays, Dilma appointed Maria das Graças Foster as its CEO in February 2012. Graça, as Brazilians called her, was a tough engineer and career Petrobras staffer, who had been born in a favela and carried a small tattoo on her forearm. She shook up top management, restoring the meritocracy in the view of insiders, and quickly revised Petrobras's targets.[17] These now called for production in Brazil to reach 4.2 million b/d by 2020, a mere doubling in a decade. 'We've taken a corporate decision to be extremely pragmatic,' she told me. 'We have to reduce Petrobras's operational costs.'[18] But even these targets were going to be tough to meet: although output from the *pré-sal* fields had reached 295,000 b/d by April 2013, production was falling in mature fields elsewhere, and the company admitted that total output was unlikely to increase by much before 2015. Of the Pernambuco refinery, Graça declared: 'This is a story to be learned from, to be written and read by the company, so that it is not repeated.'[19]

Petrobras also faced a new problem. To restrain the inflation resulting from its loose monetary and fiscal policies, Dilma's government held down the price of petrol. Because of the setbacks in refining and production, Petrobras had to import petrol, which it was obliged to sell at a loss.[20] Despite high oil prices, in the second quarter of 2012 the company posted its first quarterly loss since 1999. That meant it had to issue more debt to finance its capital spending, despite selling off assets outside Brazil. After peaking in the spring of 2008, when it was worth almost $300 billion, Petrobras's market capitalization had plunged to $82 billion by July 2013; by then it was worth only a third as much as Chevron, whose proven reserves and refining capacity were similar.[21]

Several industry experts questioned whether it had been wise for the new laws for the *pré-sal* to have abandoned the concession model which continued to serve Brazil well in other areas. In May 2013 the first auction for exploration licences in five years produced record bids from both national and foreign companies. On the other hand, the first *pré-sal* auction under the new rules, for the giant Libra field, held in October 2013 produced only one bidder, a consortium made up of Petrobras (40 per cent), Shell and Total (20 per cent each) and two Chinese firms (10 per cent each).

The government pointed to Norway as an example of a country that had used state regulation to develop a world-class oil and oil services industry. Norway's Statoil, like Petrobras, is a publicly quoted national oil company. The difference, according to Helge Lund, the company's CEO, is that Statoil doesn't have automatic rights in exploration areas. In addition, while in the industry's first decade Norway required the local purchasing of 60 per cent of equipment, it gradually reduced this to zero.[22] No doubt some foreign suppliers might not have manufactured equipment in Brazil without the national content rule; some Brazilian companies will acquire exportable technological knowledge that they might not have done. But many suppliers would have come anyway, given the size of the *pré-sal* market and its technical challenges. At the technology park on Ilha de Fundão, GE is building what will

be only its fourth research centre outside the United States, with an investment of $250 million over five years. Part of the attraction is the opportunity
to work with Petrobras in developing equipment for the *pré-sal*, using the
UFRJ's oceanographical tank for testing kit such as hoses and the like,
according to Ken Hurd, the centre's director.[23] One of GE's neighbours will be
BG Group's first worldwide Technology Centre; it expects to invest up to
$2 billion in Brazil in research and development by 2025.[24] That is a conse-
quence of a more enlightened public policy, one that required oil and gas
companies to spend 1 per cent of their revenues on research and development.

In a characteristic piece of boosterism, Lula told *Le Monde* that 'Brazil in
20 or 30 years time will be the greatest energy power on the planet'.[25] He cited
not just oil and gas but also the country's competitive advantage in ethanol. In
this prediction, he might even have been right. The questions were when, at
what cost in resources that might have been deployed elsewhere, and whether
Brazil would be overtaken by the shale gas boom in the United States.

The *gaúchos* and Embrapa lead an agricultural revolution

Like deep-sea oil, Brazilian farming marries natural endowment with state-
sponsored research and a skilled and specialized workforce. Brazil is already
an agricultural superpower, the sole tropical country to have achieved that
status. It is the world's third-largest exporter of farm products, behind only
the US and the EU: in 2009 it was the world's top exporter of coffee, sugar,
orange juice, beef and poultry and the second-biggest of soya beans and maize
(corn) and fourth-biggest of cotton and pork.[26] Yet this prowess is very recent.
Until the 1970s Brazil was still a food importer. The military dictatorship,
preoccupied with feeding the swelling urban masses, controlled food exports
and prices. (It was only in 1997 that the Cardoso government abolished export
taxes on food commodities.) The past twenty years have seen a surge in
production: output of grains and oilseeds increased from 58 million tonnes in
1990–91 to 166 million tonnes in 2011–12 (with a record harvest of 186
million tonnes forecast for 2012–13).[27] Overall, Brazil's share of world agricultural exports climbed from 2.4 per cent in 1990 to 5.2 per cent in 2011, when
they were worth $86 billion.[28]

Brazil has, of course, always enjoyed an abundance of sun and rainfall,
which in some areas allow up to three harvests a year. The big change was the
opening up of the *cerrado*, whose poor soils were previously seen as too acidic
for commercial farming. Brazil's 'green revolution' began in 1973 when the
Geisel government founded the Empresa Brasileira de Pesquisa Agropecuaria
(Embrapa), an agricultural research institute. It sent 1,200 agronomy students

abroad to get PhDs. The returning scientists treated the *cerrado*'s soils with lime, developed improved kinds of pasture and new varieties of soyabeans adapted to the tropics. Soyabeans, previously a temperate crop, have displaced coffee as Brazil's largest single agricultural export.[29]

The second vital ingredient in the green revolution was the farmers. The opening up of the *cerrado* coincided with demographic pressures in the family-farming belt in the southern states. In some cases the family property had become too small to divide up further; in others smallholders or labourers were driven off the land by the expansion of mechanized commercial farming. These people faced a choice. A few founded the militant Movimento Sem Terra (MST) of landless would-be farmers in Rio Grande do Sul in 1979, to fight for land reform. But most got on the bus and made the long trek north-west to Mato Gross and Goiás, or north to Bahia and beyond, in a Brazilian epic known as the *gaúcho* migration (though they were from Paraná and Santa Catarina as well as Rio Grande do Sul, and are of course not to be confused with Argentine cowboys). Many were skilled, entrepreneurial farmers. They brought with them innovative techniques, such as 'no-till' farming. Now widely adopted in Brazil and Argentina, this was invented in the 1970s by farmers in Paraná who faced a problem of soil erosion; they discovered that they could plant directly on top of the rotted straw of the previous harvest, thus avoiding ploughing and retaining more nutrients in the soil. This required the development of a new planting machine, now manufactured in Brazil.[30]

One Friday evening in 1999 I sat down with a group of *gaúcho* farmers (and a migrant New Zealander) in Rondonópolis, a modern market town in the middle of nowhere in Southern Mato Grosso. Over beers in a large outdoor bar they complained, as Brazilian farmers often do, about the lack of credit and about NGOs which blamed them for the rape of Amazonia, which was at least 200 kilometres further north. But they were irrepressibly bullish. 'The world's biggest agricultural future is here,' said Adilton Sachetti, whose family of *gaúcho* origin had nine big farms scattered around the state. The next day I drove south with Sachetti across mile after mile of flat tableland stretching to the far horizon, carpeted with swelling crops of soyabeans and cotton. This is Brazil's prairies. The monotony of the landscape was broken only by the artefacts of modern agri-business: a crop-dusting plane swept low over the fields to release its chemical cloud, while giant harvesting machines lined up in the yards beside the occasional farmhouses. Sachetti's television at home was tuned to the Weather Channel; his agronomists plotted rain maps on their computers. In Primavera do Leste, a trim little town out on the prairie, I met Wilson, who had worked as a jobbing tractor driver back home in Rio Grande do Sul. Arriving in Primavera in 1984, when 'there were only a few houses and a petrol station', he bought and sold land, planting rice and then cotton; his friends said he had become a millionaire. In 2011 Mato Grosso over took São Paulo to become the top state for agricultural production (by value). Rondonópolis's population has almost doubled since 1999, to 200,000; it now has an airport with a daily flight to Paraná.

In 2013 a railway from São Paulo and Santos reached Rondonópolis, potentially easing the soya farmers' transport problems. These were acute. Brazil's neglect of infrastructure meant that in 2010 a soya grower in Mato Grosso had to spend 38 per cent of gross income on transport to the port of Paranagua, leaving profits low, according to José Roberto Mendonça de Barros, the economic consultant. Another study found that Brazilian soya farmers had caught up with Americans in farm productivity, but paid an average of US$128 per tonne to get their crops from farm to port compared with US$38 in the United States. A record harvest in 2013 prompted record transport congestion and port delays. In March, eighty ships waited off Santos at a reported cost of $25,000 a day, while the tailback of trucks outside the port stretched for 30 kilometres. Delays in shipments prompted Sunrise Group, a Chinese importer, to cancel an order for 2 million tonnes of soya.[31]

Thanks to Embrapa's research and the *gaúcho* migration, the driving force of Brazil's agricultural revolution has been a sustained increase in productivity. Land planted with grains and oilseeds expanded from only 38 million hectares in 1990–91 to 51 million hectares in 2010–11, while output per hectare rose from 1.2 tonnes to 3.3 tonnes over the same period. Much of the recent increase in productivity comes from the adoption of seeds that grow more quickly, developed by multinational biotechnology companies, allowing two harvests a year of corn and soyabeans.[32] Brazil has enthusiastically adopted genetically modified crops. While the farm lobby is politically powerful, and farmers get privileged access to credit through Banco do Brasil, a state-owned bank, they are relatively unsubsidized compared with their counterparts in Europe, the US or Japan – or with many Brazilian manufacturers. Although the *cerrado* now accounts for 70 per cent of Brazil's grain harvest, there is plenty of agricultural innovation in other areas of the country too. That applies especially to sugar, an industry unrecognizable from the days of the *casa grande* and slavery in the north-east.

In a large, sloping field overlooking Piracicaba in upstate São Paulo, one morning in 2010 I climbed aboard a mechanical harvester with Ananias Farias, its driver. He manoeuvred the machine skilfully along the edge of a stand of 3-metre-high cane, fat and juicy from months of sunshine. The harvester sliced up the cane into 20-centimetre chunks, regurgitating them into a 30-tonne trailer keeping pace alongside. The harvester juddered tiringly, but Farias told me he enjoyed the work. It certainly beat cutting cane by hand. The harvester cuts up to 600 tonnes of cane a day; a manual cane cutter, of whom few are left in São Paulo's sugar industry, can manage 10 tonnes at most in a day's back-breaking labour. The trailers took the cane to the Costa Pinto mill operated by Raizen, a joint-venture between Brazil's Cosan and Royal Dutch Shell. There it was automatically weighed, washed, crushed and then, depending on world market prices, either crystallized into sugar or distilled into ethanol. The woody residue – the *bagaço* – was burned in two high-pressure boilers that, according to the flickering needle in the control room, were supplying around 50 megawatts of electricity to the local grid – enough to power half of Piracicaba, a city of 370,000 people.

Biofuels, mainly derived from sugar, are Brazil's most important source of energy after oil. Ethanol has acquired a bad reputation in the United States, because of its heavy subsidies and diversion of corn from use as food. But Brazilian sugar-based ethanol is environmentally friendly: per unit of energy it generates only two-fifths of the carbon emissions of petrol and half those of corn-based ethanol. And Brazil has plenty of spare arable land – some 70 million hectares in fact – into which sugar and other crops can expand without touching an acre of rainforest or competing with food production.[33]

Like the opening up of the *cerrado*, the state had a hand in the birth of Brazil's ethanol industry – and again the motive was the oil price shock. Geisel's government created Pró-Álcool, a programme which used subsidy and regulation to encourage cars fuelled by ethanol. This collapsed with the fall in oil prices in the 1980s. The modern ethanol industry was reborn through private initiative. Engineers at the Brazilian subsidiaries of multina-tional car parts firms developed the technology for flex-fuel engines, capable of running on either petrol or ethanol, or a mixture of the two; by 2012 these were fitted in 80 per cent of the 3.4 million cars manufactured in Brazil that year.[34] In addition to supplying this market, Brazil has the potential to become the world's biggest exporter of ethanol, especially after the Obama administra-tion in 2011 allowed an import tariff of 54 cents a gallon to lapse.[35] Yet in 2012 Brazil had to import the stuff from the US. The industry has suffered from poor harvests, the after-effects of the 2009 credit crunch, and especially from the government cap on the price of petrol. To export on a large scale, it needs to make expensive investments in pipelines, some of which are under way. The potential is enormous. 'But the long-term future of the ethanol industry depends on government policies,' according to Marcos Jank, then the presi-dent of the sugar producers' association.[36] That is because Petrobras is at once the industry's biggest customer (by law, petrol in Brazil is sold in a blend of

three or four parts to one of ethanol), an important investor in ethanol plants
– and ethanol's mightiest competitor.

In different ways, the *cerrado* and the sugar industry give the lie to the
notion – prevalent among some economists – that commodity production is
a low-tech, low-value affair, unbecoming of a rising economic power. As
Mendonça de Barros noted, 'natural-resource chains are being transformed
by technology into more industrialized businesses; sugar cane is now a diversified industry rather than just farms. A huge industrial complex is being built
on this.'[37] As well as ethanol, sugar is also the feedstock for bioplastics, a
greener alternative to petrochemicals. Around Campinas, several high-tech
joint-ventures between American and Brazilian firms are poised to turn cane
into soft drink bottles and the like. Brazil has become a world leader in some
branches of biotechnology and genetic sciences. Agribusiness may provide
relatively few direct jobs, but it supports a constellation of small service firms,
providing well-paid professional work in computer and veterinary services
and so on.

There were two other common criticisms of Brazilian farming: social and
environmental. Land ownership is highly unequal. A mere 1.1 per cent of
farms occupy around 45 per cent of the land (though some of those are vast
holdings in the Amazon of questionable legality).[38] Agrarian reform was a
longstanding demand of the left. In the name of opposition to the feudal
latifúndio (large estate), the MST embarked on a campaign of land invasions
in the 1980s and 1990s, prompting a few landowners to form armed self-
defence groups in response. Then came the massacre of nineteen MST
members by police during a protest on a road near Eldorado dos Carajás in
Pará. For a while the MST became a symbol of Brazil's social injustices and
inequalities. Perhaps the peak of public sympathy for the landless came with
their favourable portrayal in a Globo telenovela, *O Rei do Gado* ('The Cattle
King'), which aired in 1996.

Cardoso responded by launching the biggest land reform programme in
Brazil's history. He described this as 'an unpaid debt from the past', assumed
for social and political reasons, rather than economic ones. A new law
approved a summary procedure for the expropriation of idle land. The
government also bought land for redistribution. Since 1995 successive governments have settled a total of more than 900,000 families on 90 million
hectares. The MST would set up roadside camps of makeshift tents of black
plastic, whose members would eventually be allocated a plot of land in land
reform settlements, as they were called. Yet the MST proved to be better at
protesting than farming. At one settlement, at Pirituba near São Paulo's
southern border with Paraná established in 1984, farmers were making only

around $150 a month (plus much of their own food) when I visited in 1997. That was partly because of MST pressure to farm collectively and partly because, the north-east excepted, many of the movement's recruits were from the unemployed underclass in the urban periphery, with no experience of farming.

The MST attracted the support of impressionable foreigners, such as Noam Chomsky, a linguist at the Massachusetts Institute of Technology, who singled it out as one of 'the most important popular movements anywhere'. But it became increasingly discredited in Brazil. Its original cause became largely redundant: today, Brazilian farms, however large, are highly produc-tive, a world away from feudal *latifúndia*. Farming the *cerrado* demands capital investment and technology and involves economies of scale, making large holdings inevitable. It is indisputable that in Brazil's past, gross inequality of access to land bequeathed broader socio-economic inequality, but it was far less relevant in the overwhelmingly urbanized society of the twenty-first century. Indeed, full employment in the cities and the scale of the settlement programme dried up the flow of the MST's recruits. Faced with irrelevance, it degenerated into a quasi-paramilitary organization, engaged in social banditry and anti-capitalist vandalism against agribusiness. It seemingly had no interest in helping the beneficiaries of land reform to become prosperous farmers, preferring to keep them as clients of its grip on state aid. In the view of many, land reform had become a gigantic and inefficient welfare programme. The MST was also accused of ecological depredation in Amazonia – though that criticism was also targeted at farming in general.[39]

The trees and the people

On 7 September 1908 at a camp on the river Juruena, deep in the jungle of northern Mato Grosso, Colonel Cândido Mariano da Silva Rondon marked Brazil's independence day by playing the national anthem to his assembled troops on a gramophone lugged to the spot for the purpose.[40] In the evening, he projected slides of the President of the Republic and other authorities. On other occasions he took photographs of friendly Indians parading with the Brazilian flag. Rondon was a fervent positivist. Supremely incongruous though the surroundings rendered these civic rituals, for Rondon they were a conscious exercise in binding together a nation from Brazil's vast territory. His exhausted troops were laying a telegraph line from Cuiabá, the capital of Mato Grosso, north-westwards to the river Madeira. They suffered desertions and deaths from malaria, poor food and Indian attacks. The Rondon commis-sion, as it became known, was prompted by concern among the authorities, dating back to the Paraguayan war, that poor communications made the country vulnerable to attack. It was an endeavour that would take eight years; it involved clear-cutting a 30-metre-wide swathe through almost 1,300 kilometres of virgin jungle, crossing numerous large rivers. Rondon was further delayed by accompanying Theodore Roosevelt, the former American president, his son and their inappropriately voluminous baggage, on a five-month expedition to the Rio da Dúvida (the River of Doubt), an unexplored tributary of the Madeira. By the time the telegraph line was inaugurated in 1915, radio communication had rendered it largely redundant; after a brief moment of utility during the *tenente* rebellion in São Paulo in 1924, it fell into disuse.

Rondon became the first director of Brazil's Indian Protection Service (today known as the National Indian Foundation, or Funai). A native of Mato Grosso and of partly Indian blood himself, Rondon respected the Indians, instructing his troops: 'Die if necessary, never kill'. His approach was 'to protect and assimilate' by example, rather than by force. Revisionist anthropologists have pointed out that this was a contradiction: assimilation meant the loss of culture. And it was contradictory, too, that Rondon defended the Indians' right to their land while simultaneously working to open it up for development.[41] Nevertheless, his approach was far more enlightened than that of many other countries towards their indigenous peoples at the time. It would be carried on by the Villas Bôas brothers, whose decades of work for Funai and its predecessor included the creation of Brazil's first indigenous reserve (in the upper Xingu in 1961). And the rainforest would resist development for a while longer.

Traversing the area in the 1930s, Lévi-Strauss described Rondon's telegraph posts as being as isolated as if they were on the moon. Their operators were

> left behind by one of those waves of colonization, so frequent in the history of central Brazil, and which sweep groups of adventurers or restless, poverty-stricken individuals on a great surge of enthusiasm into the interior and then immediately leave them stranded there, cut off from all contact with the civilized world.[42]

The Amazon was a place which bewitched outsiders and where, like Colonel Percy Fawcett, a British explorer in 1925, they sometimes disappeared. Fortunes were lost more often than made there. In 1930 Henry Ford allowed himself to be talked into setting up a vast rubber plantation in Pará. The Ford Motor Company built a replica of an American suburban town on the Tapajós

river, which Brazilians dubbed Fordlândia. But the best conditions for rubber
were in Acre, thousands of kilometres further west, and Ford's rubber trees
suffered repeated blights. After fifteen years and an investment of almost
$10 million Ford abandoned the venture without having tapped any rubber.[43]
This failure and the earlier one of a group of Confederate settlers who moved
to Santarém after the American Civil War led Vianna Moog, writing in the
1950s, to conclude that 'in Amazonia, nature has implacably routed everyone,
up to the present'. Only the *caboclos*, the tough descendants of mixing
between Amerindians, Portuguese and Africans, adapted to the forest and
survived.

But nature would soon find itself outgunned by two innovations, the
chainsaw and the bulldozer, and 'suddenly the great rain forests were pros-
trate at the feet of man', as John Hemming notes.[44] Kubitschek ordered the
building of a 1,900-kilometre highway north from Brasília to Belém, known as
the BR-153/010; in the 1960s another road, the BR-364, was built from Cuiabá
to Porto Velho on the Madeira, following the line of Rondon's telegraph and
opening up what is now called the state of Rondônia. Both these highways
crossed open savannahs, but brought the forest within easy reach of lateral
penetration roads. The military dictatorship created the Superintendency for
the Development of the Amazon (Sudam), modelled on the north-east's
Sudene. One of its first actions was to decree a free-trade zone in Manaus. Tax
breaks, repeatedly renewed until today, lured screwdriver plants assembling
consumer electronics to the heart of the rainforest, turning Manaus into a city
of 2 million with almost 600 factories and 100,000 manufacturing jobs.

Since Rondon's day the army had feared that what it saw as the emptiness
of the Amazon rendered Brazil's sovereignty over it vulnerable to challenge,
especially by the United States. In the glow of the 'economic miracle' General
Médici abruptly launched an ill-considered plan to drive a trans-Amazonian
highway through the heart of the forest from the north-east to the Peruvian
border, along a line a few hundred kilometres south of the Amazon river. He
saw this as the solution to two problems: 'men without land in the Northeast
and land without men in Amazonia'.[45] The rains and the forest soon reclaimed
long stretches of the Transamazônica, but other roads would follow, such as
one from Cuiabá to Santarém. These highways – and especially the BR-153/010
and BR-364 – unleashed a chaotic land rush; by 1980, some 500,000 settlers
had moved along the BR-364, many of them *gaúchos* like those who opened
up the *cerrado*. Along with them came *garimpeiros* (wildcat miners), land
speculators known as *grileiros* (who create false land titles), prostitutes and
other adventurers.[46] Like much else in Brazil in the 1980s and early 1990s, the
Amazon seemed to have spun completely out of control. A frontier gold rush

reached its apogee in the huge crater dug by thousands of *garimpeiros* at Serra Pelada near Marabá, a modern-day rendering of Hieronymus Bosch's vision of hell. Many people, Indians and settlers alike, died in land wars. In Acre, Chico Mendes, a charismatic leader of a union of rubber-tappers, was murdered by the sons of a local rancher who wanted the union's land.

As the chainsaws went into action, the forest came under attack from three directions. The first was cattle ranchers. Driving from Belém along the BR-101 to Paragominas, a town about 300 kilometres to the south in 1999, I passed through a landscape dominated by rough pasture dotted with Cebus and white egrets, with occasional fire-blackened tree stumps the only evidence that this had been rainforest not long before. The ranchers removed the forest by clear-cutting and/or burning, taking the topsoil in the process. The degraded pasture that grew back supported only one cow per hectare – a grossly inefficient form of farming. About 75 per cent of deforested land is occupied by cattle ranches, mainly in large or medium holdings, according to the World Bank.[47]

The second predatory force were the loggers who prized the forest's hardwoods and often worked hand-in-glove with the ranchers. Having reduced the Atlantic rainforest to only 7 per cent of its original extent by the 1960s, the loggers moved to the Amazon, and especially Pará, where by the late 1990s there were around 1,000 sawmills. It was a wasteful process: using tractors, loggers damaged 27 trees for each one they cut down and only used around 30 per cent of the wood they felled, according to a study in the late 1990s by Imazon, an NGO based in Belém.[48] The lumber industry provided around a quarter of the jobs in the Amazon. Much of its product went for charcoal or to wooden floors and furniture for apartments in Brazil's cities. Only about 15 per cent of the hardwood was exported.[49] Paragominas became the logging capital of eastern Pará. Giant trailers carrying tree trunks fed its sawmills. They all claimed to practise managed forestry, but none of them did back then, according to Imazon. Ibama, the federal environmental agency, had cancelled 80 per cent of their forest management plans – but that was on paper. Many sawmills continued to operate in defiance of the law.

The third wave of the assault against the forest was the smallholders and colonists. While in theory large landowners could deforest only 20 per cent of their land, that figure was 50 per cent for smallholders. They practised slash-and-burn farming, and quickly moved on, just as the Portuguese had in the Atlantic forest four centuries earlier. Land reform played a role too: 80 per cent of the land given out in Amazonia was forest, according to a congressional report.[50] While some NGOs blamed the soya farmers, their impact was mainly indirect, in pushing cattle ranching deeper into the forest. (It is true that the opening up of the *cerrado* for farming has caused widespread damage to its ecology, but most Brazilians would argue that the economic return and the world's need for food justifies this.) All told, between 1960 and 2000 the population of the Amazon expanded tenfold, to 20 million (and to 25 million today). Around 18 per cent of the original forest has been razed. Most of the losses occurred in an 'Arc of Deforestation' along the southern rim of the forest, from Rondônia and northern Mato Grosso to Pará.

Two opposing Brazilian visions of the Amazon and its future began to come into ever-sharper conflict in the late 1990s. One held that the aim of policy should be economic development. 'Amazonia is like any other part of the world . . . and has to be thought of as a material base to sustain the people who live there,' an official in the Pará state government told me. But Brazilians 'from Brasília southwards' want 'the whole of Amazonia protected as a gigantic reserve', as Eduardo Martins, the then head of Ibama, put it. 'The deforestation rate for the environment minister is the same as the inflation rate for the finance minister – it's what he's judged on.'[51] Other ministries, such as planning, backed the view that the Amazon had to be developed.

Over the past fifteen years, gradually the conservationist view has gained the upper hand. One factor was growing international pressure, manifested in the 1992 Earth Summit held in Rio de Janeiro. Yet perhaps the main, unnoticed, consequence of that gathering was to start a national conversation in Brazil. As the country has urbanized, many Brazilians have acquired greater environmental consciousness – indeed far more so than in most countries. A 2010 poll by the Pew Global Attitudes Survey taken in twenty-two countries found that Brazilian respondents were the most likely to say that the environment and climate change were 'very serious' issues; eight out of ten of them said that preserving the environment should be a priority even if this meant slower economic growth. Another study, this one of 25,000 people in five countries by Ipsos, found that more Brazilians understood correctly terms such as biodiversity and biopiracy than Americans or Europeans. Perhaps this is because Brazilians know they have more 'environmental capital' to lose than almost any other country.[52]

The Amazon is not just by far the world's biggest rainforest and its single biggest 'carbon sink', vital to the prospects for slowing global climate change. It is also a treasure trove of biodiversity: half of the world's species are believed to live in rainforests. While globally, deforestation and land use change account for 18 per cent of carbon emissions, they are responsible for 75 per cent of Brazil's emissions. In addition, the rainforest holds the key to Brazil's own climate, and the rainfall it needs if it is to remain an agricultural superpower. In recent years, several parts of the country have suffered severe flooding, which some Brazilians link to climate change. Floods and landslides in the mountains inland from Rio de Janeiro in January 2011, which killed more than 1,200 people, were widely held to be the worst natural disaster in Brazil's history.* The Amazon is itself vulnerable to climate change. According to a World Bank study in 2009, the loss of a further 2 per cent of the forest could start to trigger dieback in its drier southern parts, making it vulnerable to destruction by fire. If that is true, the forest is perilously close to disaster. Climatic models suggest that the Amazon will dry out at some time in the next thirty to eighty years because of a combination of deforestation and changing global temperatures.[53]

In the past decade Brazil has at last acquired the tools to control deforestation. On the one hand, the National Space Agency (INPE), based at São José dos Campos in São Paulo, uses its own satellites, together with remote sensing data bought from NASA and the European Space Agency, to monitor deforestation in real time. When INPE detects something suspicious it alerts local Ibama agents.[54] On the other hand, the federal government has designated 42 per cent of the Amazon as protected areas, either as indigenous reserves or natural parks. This process received a decisive push from Marina Silva, Lula's environment minister in 2003–8. Born in a rubber-tapping community in Acre, Silva's life-story rivals that of Lula as a triumph over adversity. She contracted malaria half a dozen times and suffered poisoning from drinking water contaminated with heavy metals. She was sixteen before she learned to read. She wanted to be a nun, but became a teacher and union activist instead. She worked with Chico Mendes, and was a founding member of the Workers' Party, being elected a senator. As environment minister she formulated a comprehensive plan to halt deforestation. This involved declaring more reserves and toughening up enforcement. Federal police arrested dozens of officials for trafficking in fraudulent logging licences. In 2008 Silva persuaded Lula to send troops to Tailândia, which replaced Paragominas as Pará's logging capital, after sawmill workers had expelled Ibama inspectors. A new law declared that no public forest can be privatized. Ibama agents on the ground now have the power to levy fines, confiscate equipment and blacklist farmers, which bars them from receiving bank credit. Another new law attempted to clean up, partly through an amnesty, the murky land titles which bedevilled forest management. At the same time, Brazilian and foreign NGOs put pressure on ranchers and soya farmers to stop deforestation by organizing boycotts by retailers and consumers. In 2005 Greenpeace gave its 'Golden

---

* That seemed like an urban view which ignored the slow agony of past droughts in the *sertão*.

Chainsaw' award to Blairo Maggi, whose family company is Brazil's largest soya producer and who was elected governor of Mato Grosso. Apparently stung, Maggi had a change of heart, beginning to work with NGOs to preserve the forest.[55]

Use it, not to lose it

The result of all these efforts was that the rate of deforestation fell dramatically, though with some upward spikes which seemed to be related to rises in commodity prices. In the year to July 2012, INPE's data showed that only 4,656 square kilometres of forest had been cut down, a dramatic fall from the peak of almost 30,000 square kilometres in 2005. Environmentalists began to be optimistic that Brazil could reach zero net deforestation (taking into account replanting of trees) within a couple of decades. Lula had gone to the UN summit on Climate Change in Copenhagen in 2009 armed with an ambitious promise that Brazil would unilaterally cut the rate of deforestation by 80 per cent from its average level of 1996–2005 by 2020. The Copenhagen pledge was a victory for the environment ministry. Lula had previously backed the foreign ministry's view that Brazil should line up with China and India in arguing that slashing carbon emissions was the responsibility of developed countries alone.

Meeting and bettering Lula's pledge required further improvements in enforcement, which remained patchy. Large stretches of Amazonia remained a wild frontier, where the presence of the state was weak and those who defended the forest sometimes did so at risk to their life. Labour inspectors would periodically unearth cases of debt peonage – modern slavery – in the region. Consolidating the gains also required strengthening incipient attempts to provide economic incentives to keep the forest standing, and to change the way farming is conducted in already cleared areas. Lula dropped Brazil's traditional hostility to any outside involvement in the Amazon, proposing an international fund to help pay Brazil for the forest's environmental services to the planet. Norway pledged an initial $1 billion to this fund by 2015 under an international scheme known as Reduced Emissions from Deforestation and Forest Degradation or REDD. Brazil has used the money for schemes that promote sustainable uses of the forest (such as rubber-tapping and the harvesting of fruit and nuts), as well as managed forestry and better farming practices. Embrapa was promoting mixed agro-forestry schemes for degraded pasture in the Amazon. All these initiatives have begun to have a visible effect, as ranchers begin to replant forest and fertilize their pasture, to make it more productive. By 2013 deforestation and logging had all but stopped in

Paragominas, thanks to a combination of tougher enforcement, pressure from NGOs and economic logic. Only fourteen of the city's sawmills, which had once numbered 240, were still working.[56]

The Indian tribes had some successes at last. Around 1960 their total population had fallen below 100,000 and they faced possible extinction. But thanks to a combination of better health care (including the measles vaccine) and, above all, greater security for their lands, many tribes bounced back. For the first time since the sixteenth century, their numbers grew, reaching over 800,000 in the 2010 census. But joining mainstream Brazilian society on their own terms was fraught with complications. Take the Suruí people of Rondônia. On first coming into contact with the outside world in 1970, they suffered a hecatomb: disease and deforestation of their territory cut their numbers from 5,000 to fewer than 300, according to Almir Narayamoga, the Suruí's chief. The population has now risen to 1,300; they have a protected reserve of 240,000 hectares; and have drawn up a long-term plan for education, health, the protection of their culture and the provision of sources of income. Indian tribes take much better care of the forest than others, because they depend on it for hunting and the gathering of fruit, according to Chief Almir. The Suruí have a partnership with Google to use technology to monitor their land. They are replanting the 10 per cent of it that was deforested before they gained control over it. 'The forest helps us and we're going to have to help the forest,' said Almir.[57] There were still three dozen or so uncontacted tribes in Brazil, living in more or less voluntary isolation. Since the 1980s Funai's policy has been to create 'exclusion zones' for these groups. But it was hard to see this as anything more than a temporary expedient. The future for these tribes looks bleak.[58] And Funai itself has been accused of corruption and incompetence in its stewardship of Indian tribes, many of whose members are among the poorest of Brazilians.

Conserving Brazil's environment while seeking to develop its resources sustainably involved difficult trade-offs. One example of this was the long battle in Congress over a new national Forest Code. On one side stood the farmers' lobby led by Kátia Abreu, a tough and politically astute senator who had taken over the running of her husband's large *fazenda* in Tocantins when she was widowed. On the other were greens, inspired among others by Marina Silva. The farmers argued that the existing code, which dated from 1965, was anachronistic and unenforceable. Indeed, less than 1 per cent of the fines levied for failing to observe it were paid. Greens argued that weakening it amounted to a licence to deforest. In the end, a compromise was struck with the help of the veto of nine articles by Dilma Rousseff. This granted an amnesty to those who deforested before 2008, provided they replant on a scale that rose with the size of the property. If it was properly enforced and backed up with loans, the new code ought to lead to an overall increase in forest cover.[59] But greens blamed the new code for a rise in deforestation in the year to July 2013, to 5,843 square kilometres.

The noisiest battle over whether Brazil can enjoy environmentally friendly development involved the building of hydroelectric dams in Amazonia – and particularly a giant one at Belo Monte, on the lower reaches of the Xingu where it forms a huge bend and drops 90 metres in 140 kilometres. This had become Brazil's biggest building site, with 20,000 labourers working round the clock, when I visited in October 2012. On a shoulder of land above the river, flocks of excavators were pecking away at the rock and loading it into trucks that filed down into the crater like ants. Here will be installed Belo Monte's main turbines, fed by a 20-kilometre canal being dug from the other side of the bend, where the river is being partially dammed. When complete, Belo Monte will have an installed capacity of 11,233 megawatts, making it the world's third-biggest hydroelectric scheme, after China's Three Gorges and Brazil's own Itaipu. According to a vocal international protest campaign, backed by American NGOs and Hollywood stars, at Belo Monte Brazil's government was practising ecocide against the forest and cultural genocide against Amazonian Indians. A short film by James Cameron likened the project's backers to the rapacious destroyers of nature depicted in his film *Avatar*.[60]

Yet much of the criticism seemed misplaced. The government had abandoned the dictatorship's scheme to build six dams on the Xingu, flooding much of its valley including Indian territories. Belo Monte was redesigned as a run-of-river dam, using the Xingu's natural flow and the purpose-built canal to power its turbines, obviating the need for a reservoir. The building works are on land that was largely deforested by the Transamazônica in the 1970s. No Indian villages or land will be flooded. While the river's flow and fishery will be disrupted at the bend itself, only some 200 Indians were directly affected. Most of the Indian protesters lived in villages several days' travel upstream. While any large project has an impact on local people, the Belo Monte consortium was committed to compensation projects costing billions of dollars, including a fish ladder and new homes, schools and health centres. The real risk from Belo Monte is a different one: that it might prove to be a white elephant paid for by taxpayers whose chief beneficiaries would be the country's politically powerful construction companies. The project's estimated costs have almost doubled (to 29 billion reais) since it was approved. It was being built for a consortium of state-owned electricity companies with a record loan of 22.5 billion reais from the BNDES, after private companies withdrew, believing that the government had set an uneconomic price for its electricity. Because Belo Monte has no reservoir to store water, in the dry season its turbines will be almost still.

What made the issue so complicated was that there were environmental arguments on both sides. Notwithstanding its deep-sea oil, Brazil's energy matrix is remarkably green, thanks partly to ethanol but mainly because the country gets almost 80 per cent of its electricity from hydro plants. Because of Brazil's growing prosperity, electricity demand was rising by 6,000 megawatts a year – the equivalent of a Belo Monte every two years. Most of Brazil's untapped hydropower potential lies in the Amazon (there were plans for up to thirty dams, and two were recently built on the Madeira in Rondônia). With run-of-river schemes now the norm – for good environmental reasons – their seasonal variations in generation mean they will have to be backed up with carbon-emitting thermal plants. Even so, unless and until solar power becomes a viable alternative, dams like Belo Monte probably represented the least bad compromise between meeting energy demand and limiting environmental damage.

CHAPTER ELEVEN

Brazil's Guided Capitalism

Embraer's main factory beside the small commercial airport of the industrial city of São José dos Campos, 100 kilometres (60 miles) north-east of São Paulo, encompasses fifteen giant hangars totalling 400,000 square metres – the size of sixty football pitches. Many of them weren't there when I first visited Embraer a couple of years after its 1994 privatization. Founded in 1969 as a state-owned aircraft-maker, Embraer enjoyed two decades of success in both military and civilian markets with sturdy turbo-props, such as the Bandeirante and the Tucano. Then it flew into deep trouble, because of shrinking defence budgets, recession and mistakes by its government managers. Its last new plane in state hands was an over-designed turbo-prop that cost US$1.5 million more than its rivals: not a single one was sold.

Since being privatized, Embraer has prospered, becoming the world's third-largest maker of commercial jet aircraft, and the market leader in jets with fifty to 120 seats. To do so, it has had to be nimble. Its first commercial jet, the fifty-seater E-145, sold mainly to North American regional airlines keen to skirt union restrictions on the crewing of larger planes. With its bigger E170–190 range (of seventy to 129 seats) the company broke out of that niche. When I returned to the factory in June 2010, workers were completing the final assembly of planes for airlines from Europe (Lufthansa and Lot), Bahrain's Gulf Air, China's Tianjin, Argentina's Austral and Brazil's Azul. Embraer has ventured abroad, too. In 2002 it set up a joint venture in China to manufacture the E-145, and later opened factories in Florida and Portugal.

The 2008–9 global economic slowdown hit the aircraft industry hard, forcing Embraer to mothball a production line and lay off several thousand workers. The firm's revenues of US$6.2 billion in 2012 were still slightly below the 2008 peak.[1] But at over 18,000 in 2013, the workforce was growing again – and was well above its peak when in state hands of 12,700 in 1990. The company faced growing competition, too. As well as Canada's Bombardier, a long-standing rival, companies from Russia, China and Japan have launched, or were working on, small commercial jets. But Embraer's planes are reliable and the company has an established brand. Rather than develop bigger planes, which would pit it against Boeing and Airbus, the company has decided to revamp its existing commercial jets to make them more fuel-efficient while diversifying in other ways. The production lines at São José dos Campos and at Harbin in China that used to make the smaller E-145, rendered uneconomical by higher oil prices, were reconfigured to make executive jets. Embraer's defence business is growing too. It is developing a new military transport plane, and has forged a partnership with Boeing to market this. Embraer has sold its SuperTucano ground-attack aircraft to a score of air forces around the world. In 2013 it won a US$427 million contract from the US Air Force for twenty Super-Tucanos, to be assembled at a new factory in Jacksonville, Florida. Between them, executive jets, defence and maintenance contracts will grow to account for half the company's sales, Frederico Curado, Embraer's CEO, told me.[2]

This ability to adapt to changing market conditions was the hallmark of Embraer. Curado argued that the company's competitive advantages were its know-how (of composite materials, for example), its highly skilled workforce (a third of them engineers) and its network of local suppliers. Two things lay behind these achievements. The first was the foundation at São José de Campos in 1950 of the Instituto Tecnológico da Aeronáutica (ITA), a technical school modelled on the Massachusetts Institute of Technology where many of Embraer's engineers were trained. This was the brainchild of Air Marshal Cassimiro Montenegro, who argued: 'to make planes, we first have to make competent engineers.'[3] Secondly, the need to compete in the global market means that Embraer has trusted in innovation rather than government protection. This has included its use of 'reverse outsourcing': it turned suppliers such as GE and Honeywell into risk-sharing partners, who have invested some US$270 million in the E-jets (or about 27 per cent of the total investment) in return for a share in the profits.[4] The Super-Tucano is an example of 'frugal innovation' of the kind that management gurus often identify with India and China. Adapted from a training aircraft, it can deliver smart bombs and is highly effective against lightly armed insurgents.* It costs only US$1,000 an hour to operate, compared with US$10,000 an hour for an F-16 fighter-jet.[5]

---

* The Super-Tucano was used to devastating effect by the Colombian air force in a series of pinpoint bombing raids that killed several senior leaders of the FARC guerrillas. These were instrumental in changing the strategic balance of Colombia's internal conflict, persuading the FARC to start peace talks with the government in 2012.

Curado insisted that Embraer has been strengthened by adversity. 'The best protection against change is productivity,' he told me. For Embraer, since 2009 that meant small changes, like switching lights off during the lunch hour, while also pressing ahead with more automation. The firm carried on investing in research and development, launching new executive jets. The strength of Brazil's currency for much of the period between 2003 and 2012 made that productivity drive all the more important.

In other words, Embraer is much like any other high-tech global company. It is also Brazil's third-largest exporter, after Petrobras and Vale. It gave the lie to the notion that the country's recent economic success was merely a function of the commodity boom. True, Embraer is a relative rarity in Brazil. But it is not unique. One of the successful Brazilian industrial companies that 'nobody has ever heard of' is Weg.* Founded by three engineers of German descent in Santa Catarina in 1961, Weg has grown to become one of the world's top three makers of electric motors, along with two European giants, Siemens and ABB. It also manufactures generation and transmission equipment, industrial automation systems and paints, and is moving into wind turbines. When I visited its huge factory in Jaragua do Sul, 60 megawatt electric generators weighing some 30 tonnes were packed up ready for dispatch to customers in Germany, Australia and the United States. In 2012, for the first time, slightly over half of Weg's total revenue of around 6.2 billion reais came from outside Brazil. Although in recent years it has acquired businesses and factories in Mexico, India and China, around four-fifths of its foreign orders were fulfilled from its Brazilian factories, most of them in Santa Catarina.

When I sat down with Harry Schmelzer, Weg's CEO, in his large but utilitarian office at the Jaragua factory, I asked him how his company had managed to increase exports despite the recent strength of the real and Brazil's high costs. 'There's not a secret, nor a single formula,' he replied. Echoing Embraer's Curado, he stressed that the main factor was a permanent search for productivity gains through investment in technology and innovation: 'We're in a mature market, that doesn't involve new technology like the iPad, but it evolves technologically a lot every year.' Motors become ever quieter and more efficient. Weg's quest for competitiveness goes back a long way. It began exporting in the 1970s. 'The intention to be a global company dates from that period because we always competed against global companies,' said Schmelzer, who joined the company in 1981.[6] Though also of German descent, he is not related to the founders and his elevation to the top job

---

* As Roger Agnelli put it at the conference in 2009 at London's Marriott Hotel (see page 3).

marked a milestone in the evolution of a family company into a Brazilian multinational. Like Embraer, Weg's success is built on the quality of its workforce. It operates a German-style apprenticeship system; in a corner of the factory at Jaragua do Sul, young recruits are taught mechanics and electronics while continuing at secondary school in the evenings. The firm shares 12.5 per cent of its profits each year with its workers, whose numbers have grown to 26,000. The result is that in a country where labour churn had recently become frenetic, it retained its staff for seven to eight years on average. It is tempting to see Weg as a remote outpost of the German *Mittelstand* of medium-sized engineering firms. But it shows that Brazilian manufacturers can compete globally if they go about it the right way.

Debating de-industrialization

That was an important lesson. In recent years Brazil has been gripped by fears that it is losing its manufacturing industry to a triple whammy of cut-throat Chinese competition, an overvalued currency and high costs. Certainly manufacturing's share of the economy has declined, from a peak of 25 per cent of GDP in 1985 to 15 per cent in 2011. Similarly, manufactured products made up 55 per cent of Brazil's exports in 1985 but accounted for only 36 per cent in 2011.[7] After recovering from a brief slump in 2008–9, industrial production stagnated. But there was no consensus as to whether this decline was permanent, or indeed whether it should be cause for worry. In part the relative decline of manufacturing was simply the consequence of the newfound success of Brazil's commodity sectors. Nevertheless, most economists would say that an economy of Brazil's size will not manage to become developed without a flourishing manufacturing industry, even if this represents a smaller share of the economy than it did in the past. And certainly, some of the macroeconomic policies that Brazil has pursued in the past two decades had negative consequences, direct or indirect, for manufacturing. The trade opening of the 1990s exposed the shortcomings of the cosseted industries engendered by the 'national-developmentalist' state. The Real Plan – or more specifically, the high, and sometimes astronomic, interest rates deployed to defend the currency peg until 1999 – inflicted collateral damage on manufacturers. Yet these policies brought great benefits to Brazilian consumers and the Brazilian economy as a whole. The biggest problem was the soaraway strength of the real, first in the 1990s and then even more so from 2003 to 2012. The exchange rate made it even harder for industries like shoes, textiles, toys and furniture, which had been based on cheap labour, to compete with cheap Chinese imports. Even so, a careful study of imports of Chinese manufactured goods showed that these had largely displaced imports from elsewhere rather than Brazilian production. China had a more significant impact in displacing Brazilian exports of manufactured goods to Latin America, though this had only a limited impact on total industrial output and employment.[8]

The government's response to the appreciation of the real and the fear of de-industrialization was a more interventionist industrial policy. This involved a combination of selective subsidies and protection. Under Luciano Coutinho, the BNDES became both a more explicit instrument of industrial policy and a nurturer of French-style 'national champions'. Coutinho believed that the country needed more big Brazilian multinationals; he thought that big, locally owned firms offered some inherent benefits as sources of innovation and local supply chains.[9] Only ten Brazilian firms ranked in the *Financial Times* list of the top 500 global companies by market capitalization (and three of those were subsidiaries of foreign companies). In fact, that was not so bad: India only had twelve on the list and Mexico just five. Similarly, eight Brazilian companies, eight Indian ones and only three from Mexico made it to *Fortune's* list of the top 500 global companies ranked by sales.

The BNDES's traditional role was to offer long-term funding for infrastructure projects or large industrial developments. Now the bank began to sponsor 'national champions' in food and agribusiness, telecoms, construction and pulp and paper, some of them created through more or less voluntary mergers. The BNDES also took minority stakes in many companies, through BNDESPar, its equity arm. It was trying to create a big Brazilian pharmaceutical company and a semiconductor firm. In 2011 it would even offer to help Abilio Diniz, Brazil's supermarket king, to merge his Pão de Açucar company with Carrefour's Brazilian assets; it did so even though Diniz's manoeuvre was an unlawful attempt to renege on a deal he had previously signed under which control of Pão de Açucar was due to pass to France's Casino. The BNDES also gave big loans to state-owned electricity companies (revived by Lula) and to Petrobras, to help finance its expanded role in the *pré-sal* fields. In addition, it was a lender to Eike Batista's empire.

Some economists believed that the BNDES crowded out private lending, and that it was a means of exercising undue influence over the private sector. That was a 'conservative fiction', according to Coutinho.[10*] But the BNDES

---

* The government did use its influence over pension funds to force out Vale's boss, Roger Agnelli, in 2011 because he resisted official pressure to turn his company from a multinational mining giant into something resembling a Brazilian iron and steel industrial conglomerate. Agnelli had to go because he had been 'impolite' in not telling Lula before Vale laid off workers during the downturn in 2008–9, one of the state-backed shareholders later told me.

certainly appeared to distort the credit market. Much of the development bank's lending was at a low or even negative real interest rate. Commercial banks could not match that. Indeed, a legacy of inflation was that bank deposits tended to be unusually short term, and though commercial bank lending expanded greatly much of it involved fairly short-term consumer loans. Coutinho talked about the need to provide incentives for commercial banks to make longer-term loans. But the BNDES continued to play the dominant role as lender to corporate Brazil. The result was that the state, rather than the market, allocated many financial resources. All told, the three big public banks (the others were the Banco do Brasil and the Caixa Econômica Federal, a savings bank) accounted for over half of all outstanding credit by mid-2013, up from a third in 2008. The BNDES's lending represented a hidden subsidy while failing to boost overall investment. As Armando Castelar Pinheiro, an economist, noted, the BNDES's total lending rose from 1 per cent of GDP in 1995 to 4.6 per cent of GDP in 2010 but investment's share of GDP remained constant over that period at just over 18 per cent.[11]

Officials, including Dilma Rousseff herself, did talk much about the need to increase private-sector investment and boost productivity and competitiveness. But they thought that the government could and should induce this. 'She firmly believes that every problem has a government solution,' commented José Roberto Mendonça de Barros.[12] In 2011, when the real's appreciation was at its height, Rousseff unveiled a bundle of measures aimed at helping industry, called Brasil Maior. Some of these were sensible, such as incentives for universities and companies to collaborate on research and Science without Borders, Dilma's scheme for Brazilians to study abroad. But the plan included two controversial measures: the tax on cars imported by manufacturers who lacked a plant in Brazil was yanked up by 30 percentage points, and the government eliminated the payroll tax for the clothing, shoe, furniture and software industries. Rather than picking winners, as industrial policy aims to do, this looked like succouring losers (though the payroll tax-cut was subsequently broadened to other industries).

Coutinho insisted that the government's industrial policy was different from the protectionist developmentalism of the 1960s and 1970s. 'We have to support competitive sectors,' he told me. 'The market is imperfect. The state also makes mistakes. A model in which we do industrial policy in the crucible of an open economy reduces the margin for error. We're following the Asian model of openness.'[13]

But its critics accused the government of a fashionable drift towards state capitalism. According to Arminio Fraga, Cardoso's Central Bank chief, this had never wholly disappeared in Brazil. 'It's a model which emphasizes benefiting selected companies, rather than letting the market work. It's a bad model. Combined with protectionism it's even worse,' he said.[14] The government began to use state companies to regulate markets in oil, electricity and banking, causing them to register losses, pointed out Sergio Lazzarini of INSPER, a business school.[15] By contrast, South Korea's successful industrial policy, invoked by Coutinho and other officials, was aimed above all at boosting exports, forcing companies to compete abroad, and was ruthless in cutting off subsidies after a limited period.

Cardoso's trade opening in the 1990s had been radical by Brazilian standards, but not when compared to many other countries in Latin America and beyond. Brazil's economy remained relatively closed: average tariffs were higher than those in South Korea, China and Taiwan, for example, and rose after 2008. The cost of importing a container to Brazil was exceptionally high, and national content rules applied to public procurement and to many industries.[16] Imports were equal to just 13 per cent of Brazil's GDP in 2012, the lowest figure among the 176 countries tracked by a World Bank study. South Korea, the industrial and technological powerhouse admired by Dilma Rousseff's economic team, was far more open, with exports and imports equal to 58.5 per cent and 54 per cent of GDP respectively. The protectionist impulse ran deep among officialdom. Edmar Bacha, one of the fathers of the Real Plan, pointed out the flaws in this approach:

It's pathetic when you see so much complaining against importing . . . We have something very peculiar in Brazil, which is an enormous openness to foreign investment which doesn't generate exports. I am astonished when I hear our president say 'we're going to protect our market' and those who are exploiting our market are multinationals, who make extraordinary profits here. We are protecting multinationals to exploit Brazilian consumers.[17]

Without the specialization, productivity and technology that come from greater integration with the world economy, Brazil would find it hard to make the leap from being a middle-income country to a rich one, according to Bacha.[18]

Brazil's car industry was a good example of Bacha's argument. In the 1980s it churned out antiquated cars in small volumes at high prices; Volkswagen and Ford saw so little point in competing in the Brazilian market that they merged their operations in a joint-venture called Autolatina. The opening of the economy and the Real Plan prompted a radical shake-up of the industry. Autolatina was dissolved in 1995. The four main incumbent manufacturers – Volkswagen, Fiat, General Motors and Ford – poured billions into upgrading their factories to produce something resembling the models and engines they made in Europe. Half-a-dozen new entrants built assembly plants. The industry moved away from its São Paulo heartland, with new plants springing up across the country. Many Brazilian car parts makers, some of them household names, were bought up by multinationals. In some respects, Brazil became a pioneering location for the global car industry: Fiat used its vast Betim plant as the launch site for the Palio, a new model designed specifically for the developing world; both Fiat and General Motors, at a new plant in Rio Grande do Sul, adopted a method known as lean or modular manufacturing, in which suppliers bolt on components inside the factory. In 2009 the 9,400 workers at Fiat's Betim plant made 730,000 cars while the company's 22,000 workers at its five plants in Italy managed just 650,000.[19]

All Brazilian governments since the 1950s have paid special attention to the car industry. That was partly because of its weight: in 2012 it accounted for a fifth of manufacturing industry and 150,000 direct jobs and, the industry claimed, 1.5 million jobs in all.[20] Its strong unions are a pillar of the PT. The industry's investment splurge meant that, as in Europe, it suffered overcapacity. By 2012, the country's fifty-seven vehicle plants (belonging to twenty-eight different manufacturers) could churn out 4.5 million vehicles. Production oscillated around 3.5 million vehicles a year in 2010–12. Lula and Dilma repeatedly suspended sales taxes on cars to boost demand. There was no economic logic to this special treatment: its perverse results were to clog Brazil's unimproved roads with traffic – the vehicle fleet more than doubled in the decade to 2012, to 79 million – and to increase Petrobras's import bill for petrol.

Although Brazil was the world's fourth-largest vehicle market (by volume) in 2012, it was only the seventh biggest producer. The government was especially sensitive to the industry's complaints about imports from companies that did not manufacture in the country. These surged to 200,000 in 2011, mostly from South Korea and China, up from just 13,000 in 2007. This prompted the tariff hike, with the aim of forcing the importers to make their cars in Brazil. National content rules meant that Brazil has a fully integrated car industry, rather than screwdriver plants assembling imported kits. But this heavily cosseted industry produced fairly expensive cars that struggled to compete internationally. The starting price for Volkswagen's Fox, a Brazilian-made small car, was US$18,660 but it was sold in Britain for $11,100. Imported Chinese cars were being sold for 22,000 reais in 2011 while comparable cars from VW or Fiat cost 31,000.[21] On paper the industry had a creditable export record, selling more than 750,000 vehicles abroad in 2010; but more than three-quarters of these sales involved managed-trade agreements with Argentina and South Africa. Its balance of trade moved sharply into deficit in recent years. Contrast that with Embraer. While on paper only around 20 per cent of what went into its planes was made in Brazil, national content was a misleading yardstick, according to Curado. Around 50–60 per cent of the value added by the company is generated in Brazil, he told me. Embraer was a net foreign-exchange contributor to the tune of around US$2 billion a year.

Schumpeter, shoes and sensors

Even in its relatively diminished state, Brazil retained a large and diversified manufacturing base. The Federation of Industries of São Paulo (FIESP), the most powerful industrial lobby, has 132 different sectoral associations. Travel around the country revealed plenty of evidence that Brazilian industry was going through a Schumpeterian process of creative destruction and change, rather than outright decline. True, that was not much consolation for those firms being destroyed. But it suggested that behind de-industrialization – to the extent that it was in fact happening – multiple and complex factors were at play, and that elements of the industrial policy deployed by the governments of Lula and Dilma to try to halt this process were misguided.

Take the shoe industry. In the Sinos Valley, around the town of Novo Hamburgo, in Rio Grande do Sul, a local footwear industry grew up, based originally on the availability of hides. As was so often the case in Brazil, the building of a new transport link – in this case a highway (the BR-116) linking Porto Alegre to São Paulo – allowed local businesses to expand by selling to the national market. Exports followed, especially of women's leather shoes to the United States; a separate footwear industry specializing in men's leather shoes developed along similar lines in Franca, in upstate São Paulo. Brazil's shoe exports peaked temporarily at $1.8 billion in 1993. They were mainly of cheap sandals, and were subsequently hit by Asian competition and the strength of the real.[22] Those competitive challenges intensified in the new century. In response, the industry began to reorganize.

When I went to Novo Hamburgo in 1998, that process was well under way. Many firms moved production of cheap plastic shoes to new, bigger factories in the north-east. By then, Grendene, one of Brazil's four main shoe firms, employed almost 10,000 people in the north-eastern state of Ceará. Around 1,500 of them worked in a big shed of a factory in Crato, deep in the *sertão*, making plastic flip-flops and trainers. Nilton Vebber, the factory manager, explained to me that production costs were 30 per cent lower than in Rio Grande do Sul, because of tax breaks and cheaper labour.[23] The second shift was the outsourcing of some production to China. That began when international footwear-buying agents recruited designers and specialist technicians from Rio Grande do Sul to go and work in Dongguang, the shoe capital of Guangdong. By 2007 about 1,700 Brazilians were working in the city; the Porto Alegre football teams, Grêmio and Internacional, had fan clubs in Guangdong.[24] These émigrés became the channel through which Brazilian shoe firms contracted Chinese production. A third shift was to rely more on the growing domestic market. As they acquired more disposable income, one of the first things Brazilian women bought was more shoes: overall, demand averaged four pairs per person by 2010. Total shoe production remained fairly constant between 2000 and 2010, at about 800–900 million pairs, meaning that Brazil was still the largest shoemaker outside Asia. But exports fell in that period to 127 million pairs, down from 200 million in 1993.[25]

A fourth change was the most promising one: Brazil's shoe industry found different ways to add value. The Sinos Valley was home to a large cluster of small firms, including modern tanneries and specialist fashion designers, backed by a private-sector-funded institute for research and development. These firms were extremely flexible, able to respond swiftly to demands for new models. In other words, they were well adapted to the needs of 'fast fashion'. While the average export price of a Brazilian shoe was $10 per pair, meaning that they competed with Indonesia and India, the average price of shoes exported from Rio Grande do Sul doubled in the decade to 2010, to $22. The Sinos Valley now competes internationally with shoes from Spain and Germany.[26]

The bigger firms have invested in branding, marketing and vertical integration, developing their own branded retail outlets. Vulcabras exported to thirty countries, mainly under its Azaleia brand. Grendene turned its Melissa thermoplastic 'jelly' shoes for women into an international brand. Perhaps the best-known example was Alpargatas, which through its Havaianas brand managed to turn the humble flip-flop into a fashion statement, exported to eighty countries and retailing at up to US$200 a pair. This success was the result of a considered strategy, not the government's industrial policy: the company hired leading designers, expanded the range of colours and designs to appeal to foreign consumers, and invested heavily in marketing. Because it promoted its flip-flops as a colourful and joyful expression of Brazilian culture, consumers abroad were happy to pay the price for them to be made in Brazil, not China.[27] What the shoe industry showed was that some segments of Brazilian industry could no longer compete internationally on cheap labour, and that the solution to their problems was successful adaptation, rather than the protection of decline.

I came across a similar story of successful evolution in Santa Rita de Sapucaí, a bucolic town of 40,000 people and red-tiled houses spreading up the slopes above a slow-moving river in the south-western corner of Minas

Gerais.[28] Coffee farms sprawled over the rolling hills; a local co-operative made cheese and *doce de leite* (caramel). This was the unlikely setting for a cluster of electronics companies, comprising 142 mainly small firms which employed 10,000 people and had total sales of 1.7 billion reais in 2011. As so often in Brazil, it owed its existence to a far-sighted initiative to create an educational institution. In this case it was INATEL, a technical college teaching electronics and telecoms founded in 1959 as a philanthropic project by Luiza Moreira (whom everyone called 'Sinha'), the niece of a former governor of Minas Gerais who was briefly president of Brazil in the First Republic. The teachers at INATEL began to set up their own small firms. According to Elias Kallas, a former IBM manager who works at INATEL, this process then got an inadvertent boost when Telebras, the state telecoms monopoly, stopped investing and recruiting in the 1980s because of the military government's financial difficulties. The school has a hundred or so specialist engineers working in laboratories. It has a tradition of encouraging its students, present or past, to turn ideas into products via two incubators, which offer space and facilities and hatch about seven to ten new businesses each year. The 'electronics valley', as Santa Rita calls itself, mainly produces components for telecoms systems, alarms and security devices. Around 15 per cent of the cluster's output is exported; much of the rest substitutes for imports. Its small firms collaborate to produce a finished component. A lot of what they do is to adapt existing products by incorporating new foreign technology. When I visited, the president of the local business association was at a trade fair in China seeking new ideas. The vice-president, Luiz Carlos Paduan, has set up a successful business designing and manufacturing standardized wiring kits for house builders.

A dozen or more bigger firms have set up in Santa Rita, attracted by the skilled workforce and the inevitable local tax breaks. One of them is Sense, Brazil's leading manufacturer of proximity sensors and automation-control valves for industrial processes. Founded by two graduates of INATEL, it operates from a large factory on a hilltop overlooking the town, surrounded by gardens frequented by small birds of brilliant orange and yellow plumage. Its sales (of 60 million reais in 2011) were still growing though more slowly, mainly because of the strong real and the slowdown in industrial investment in Brazil. But it was still exporting to the United States and Britain among other countries. It invested up to 10 per cent of its sales in developing new products; it had a 3-D printer in the factory, used for making new sensors, according to Sérgio Augusto Bertolini, the company's development manager. This focus on innovation, and a reputation for quality, enabled Sense to survive in a harsh climate.

The Brazil cost

The problem was that most Brazilian businesses were unable to raise their productivity. The OECD found that around 40 per cent of Brazil's economic growth of the past decade was a result of the expansion of the labour force; only 19 per cent was the result of labour becoming more productive, while the equivalent figure for China, Korea and Taiwan was 85 per cent. What economists call total factor productivity (the efficiency with which labour, capital and technology are combined) actually fell in Brazil after 2000; in several other Latin American countries it grew slightly over the same period, while in a sample of Asian countries it grew by 2.4 per cent a year.[29] Brazilians had a term for their failure to keep pace with the rest of the world in efficiency: *o custo Brasil* – the Brazil cost. There were half a dozen elements to it: taxes, labour laws, red-tape, interest rates and high transport costs deriving from parlous infrastructure, in addition to a poorly educated workforce. And businessmen argued that it has strangled their best efforts to be competitive.

The total tax take (including social security and other compulsory contributions) rose relentlessly, from around 25 per cent of GDP in the mid-1980s to 36 per cent in 2008 (and 37 per cent by 2012).[30] That figure was slightly above the equivalent in the United Kingdom and the average for the OECD group of mainly developed economies; it was the highest for any large developing country in the world, with the recent exception of Argentina. The tax system was poorly designed. A recent exhaustive study found that in 2010 indirect taxes on goods and services accounted for 45 per cent of the total tax take, compared to around 34 per cent in the OECD countries.[31] Taxes on income and profits accounted for only 19 per cent of the total, compared with 33 per cent in the OECD. So Brazil's system was unusually regressive (i.e. it hit the poor unduly hard). Some tax experts argue that indirect taxes are economically more efficient. In Brazil's case they were not: some were cumulative (i.e. producers pay taxes on taxes) and they penalized investment and exports. Although the federal government collected around two-thirds of taxes, VAT (known as the ICMS) was levied by the states, and not all used the same rate. In a 'fiscal war', state governors offered exemptions from ICMS to attract firms to set up in their states, or to encourage importers to use their ports. About 26 per cent of the total tax take comprised payroll taxes (including pension and social security contributions). These were much higher than in most developing countries; roughly speaking, they meant that employing someone cost double their salary.

The tax system was extraordinarily complicated. Between 1988 and 2012 almost 30,000 separate tax rules were issued by the federal government (or more than three per day); include rules issued by states and municipalities, and the total rose to thirty per day, according to the Brazilian Institute of Tax Planning, a pressure group.[32] It took more time to comply with the requirements of the tax system in Brazil – 2,600 hours a year for an average company – than in any other country in the world, according to a study by PwC, an accountancy firm, and the World Bank.[33] All this added unnecessarily to firms' costs. 'Brazil is a tax hell,' was how Roberto Giannetti, FIESP's foreign trade director, summed it up. The tax authority – the Receita Federal – adopted a penalty-oriented system, rather than one based on guidance. This generated much litigation. 'There's something wrong in this country that we have millions of lawsuits between the Receita and companies,' Giannetti told me.[34] There have been some attempts at reform. Around 5 million small and micro businesses have signed up for a simplified tax regime. This has encouraged small businesses to join the formal economy, though it may also provide a perverse incentive for them not to grow. Efforts to harmonize the ICMS to discourage the 'fiscal war' failed in Congress.

Then there were the labour laws, still based on Vargas's Consolidação das Leis do Trabalho (CLT), the labour code inspired by Mussolini. This comprised more than 900 articles, some written into the 1988 constitution. Many of them were rigid: for example, holidays could only be taken in one or two chunks, neither of less than ten days. Workers and bosses cannot negotiate their own agreements. It was almost impossible to comply with the code in full. In 2009 alone, 2.1 million Brazilians opened cases against their employers in the labour courts. These almost always sided with workers. That may have represented a refreshing change from the exploitative norm in some developing countries, but it added unduly to firms' costs. Even workers dismissed for clear examples of gross misconduct could expect to win their cases.[35] The CLT was a big reason why many workers in Brazil were in the informal economy (i.e. with no formal rights). Lula talked of reforming the labour laws – and was perhaps the only leader who had the political capital to do so. Then the economy started creating a lot of formal jobs, although that was mainly because of the greater availability of bank credit and the simplified tax regime for small businesses (and despite the labour laws). Formal workers formed 45 per cent of the urban workforce by 2008, up from 38 per cent in 2003.[36] So Lula gave up – and an important opportunity to make the system fairer and more efficient was lost.

From the vantage point of business, these problems became more acute with the rise in wages and the achievement of full employment. Higher incomes boosted demand for services, what economists call 'non-tradables' (such as most forms of retailing, or personal services, such as hairdressing) which do not face competition from imports. But this bid up the price of labour for manufacturers, who did. According to the OECD, over the decade to 2013, labour costs for Brazilian industry rose twice as fast as in the country's trading partners; only slightly more than half of the increase was due to the appreciation of the real.[37] Skill shortages and the strong real meant that salaries for some posts in Brazil were higher than in the US. Generous and badly designed severance pay encouraged workers to move jobs frequently, and discouraged employers from investing in training. Bigger companies found they had to invest in extra schooling for their workers. Vale taught maths and Portuguese to some of its workers in railway carriages converted into mobile classrooms, for example.[38] The construction industry saw a big increase in formalization, with around 30 companies joining the stock market. But house-builders found their productivity fell as they had to hire barely literate workers.[39]

The cost of capital was another millstone for business. For much of the past two decades Brazil has had some of the highest interest rates in the world. Better macroeconomic policies and the conquest of inflation brought their reward in a gradual and long-term fall in the Central Bank's policy rate in real terms, from about 40 per cent in the 1980s to 20 per cent in the second half of the 1990s, and to an average of 8 per cent in the period after inflation targeting was adopted in 1999. That still meant that the policy rate was about four percentage points above the average for emerging countries that practised inflation targeting.[40] Brazil's history of debt defaults and inflation, and the resulting uncertainty, may originally have been one of the reasons for this. But the main explanation seemed to be Brazil's persistently low level of savings: at around 16.5 per cent of GDP, they were below the levels in other Latin American countries such as Mexico, Peru and Chile, and far below the 30 per cent or so that was common in East Asian countries. This reluctance to save had complex roots. Eduardo Giannetti argued that it was one of several expressions of Brazil's desire to live in the present, noted by Machado de Assis, and reflecting the habits of mind generated by slavery as well as by widespread poverty, neglect of education and the lack of the rule of law.[41] The savings shortage was exacerbated by the public sector's chronic deficit – one of the costs of Lula's and Dilma's rejection of Palocci's plan to eliminate the deficit was that Brazilian companies and families and the government itself had to pay more for credit.

In addition, the spread between loan and deposit rates was very high, so the interest rates actually paid by borrowers ranged from high to astronomic. The loan rate averaged 47 per cent in 2011, rising to up to 200 per cent on credit card debt.[42] Although Palocci's financial reforms reduced credit risks for banks, other factors kept the spread high: banks were required to park between 45 per cent and 60 per cent of their deposits at the Central Bank. This made for a banking system that was admirably safe and solid, but which lent relatively little and expensively. Taxes added to the cost of credit. As the commercial banking system consolidated, it came to be dominated by two large public banks (Banco do Brasil and Caixa Econômica Federal) and four private banks (Itaú, Bradesco, Spain's Santander and, with a smaller presence, Britain's HSBC). Greater competition would have forced a cut in spreads and bank profit margins.

Another problem for businesses was the forest of regulations and red tape. The World Bank ranked Brazil 130th out of 185 countries for the ease of doing business, worse than places like Argentina, Honduras, Pakistan, Russia and Yemen. (It was ranked 156th for the ease of paying taxes and 143rd for insolvency proceedings.)[43] For example, imagine that Maria and João want to open a small shop in São Paulo.[44] First they have to register with the state commerce board and take this registration document to the federal tax authority, in order to obtain the legal registration of the business and its inscription in the federal Social Security Institute. Then Maria and João must get a permit from the state finance secretariat, a safety certificate from the fire brigade and an operating licence from the city government. These bodies will require a photocopy of their property tax receipt, a notarized copy of the rental contract for the premises, a notarized photocopy of their identity cards and of their CPF or tax identity card (a separate document), notarized proof of their address and of the certificate from the state commerce board. No wonder that many Marias and Joãos don't bother and operate in the informal sector, or that many Brazilians who can't afford to hire a *despachante* (a professional navigator of the bureaucracy) have to spend hours hanging around in *cartórios* (notaries), or that being a *cartório* is a lucrative profession in Brazil.

Red tape was just as big a problem at the top as at the bottom. The average turn-around time for a container at Santos was twenty-one days, compared with the international norm of a day or two. Shipping companies said that much time could be gained merely by simplifying customs procedures. As Kátia Abreu, the feisty farmers' leader, remarked 'in the rest of the world ports operate twenty-four hours a day; here, they stop for lunch.' The cost of loading a container in Santos was US$2,215 compared with US$580 in Shanghai.[45]

A degree of regulatory complexity is inevitable in a federal country. Fortunately, Brazil is not China, where gleaming new infrastructure can be railroaded through, overriding all objections. Projects have to obtain environmental licences; scrutiny of public spending by independent federal and state audit bodies has exposed, and doubtless deterred, corruption and waste.

But in practice the regulatory labyrinth could strangle both private and public investment. A project to expand the port at Angra dos Reis near Rio de Janeiro, which Technip, a French oil services company, had spent years developing with the backing of the state government and had obtained many permits, was blocked when a single permit was denied.[46] Lula expressed a similar frustration to me:

> What most surprises me about Brazil is the extent of the difficulties that we create for ourselves ... Suppose a president with a mandate for four years wants to carry out some big infrastructure project. Between him conceiving of the project, doing the basics, the planning, getting the environmental licence, getting the licence to start work, dealing with the tender, dealing with the judiciary and the lawyers – his mandate is over and he does not get the job done.[47]

The neglect of transport infrastructure was palpable. Brazil's ports and airports were choked. According to a study commissioned by the government from McKinsey, Brazil needed to more than double its airport capacity in the twenty years from 2010 to meet growing demand, at a cost of around US$ 19 billion.[48] Many highways were two-lane, rather than dual carriageway; they were blocked by files of slow-moving lorries. Brazil had the third-longest road network in the world, at 1.7 million kilometres, but only 10 per cent of it was asphalted. The farmers' lobby calculated that up to 10 million tonnes of grains, worth 2.7 billion reais, were lost each year on the journey along bumpy and insecure roads from farm to port.[49] Tens of millions of Brazilians lost thousands of hours each year stuck in traffic jams in the cities. Only around two-fifths of the country's scant road network was in a reasonable state of repair. The cost-efficient concept of just-in-time supply was a distant dream for many businesses. 'We have to have stocks in case of a customs strike,' Sérgio Augusto Bertolini of Sense told me. Casas Bahia, a large white goods retailer, held lots of expensive stock at its distribution centre outside São Paulo, and opted to own its own distribution network. 'In Brazil you can only sell what you already have. What you are about to receive is an unknown,' Michael Klein, its CEO, told the *Financial Times* in 2006.[50]

Apart from red tape, there was a more fundamental reason why infrastructure – and especially transport links – was so neglected in Brazil. Although the state had expanded massively since the 1980s, public investment collapsed, squeezed out by the huge rise in current spending. It recovered gradually, but only to 2.4 per cent of GDP by 2011.[51] Even when the money was available, some state agencies were weak in executing projects: the

McKinsey study found that Infraero, the state airport operator, spent only 819 million reais of its investment budget of 2.84 billion reais in 2007–9. According to press reports, only a third of the planned investment in transport under Lula's Growth Acceleration Programme (PAC) was disbursed in 2007–9.[52] A north–south railway line across the *cerrado* from Maranhão to Goiás was begun under Sarney but was still not finished in 2013. Lula launched a grandiose project to divert water from the São Francisco along more than 600 kilometres of canals to irrigate the *sertão*. Budgeted to cost 4.5 billion reais and be concluded in 2010, by mid-2013 the project was 'just a clutch of disconnected canals, rusty pipes of twisted metal and a pumping station that resembled a concrete ghost', according to *O Globo*. The cost estimate had risen to 8.2 billion reais; the government promised to finish it by 2015.[53]

The PT was suspicious of inviting private investors to improve transport infrastructure. In São Paulo the PSDB-run state government had no such qualms: the result was that the state had an impressive network of toll motorways. All told, investment in infrastructure, both public and private, fell from an average of 5.2 per cent of GDP in the 1980s to just 2.1 per cent by the early 2000s. To catch up with the infrastructure enjoyed by East Asian countries, and to match their faster rate of economic growth, Brazil would need to invest between 5 per cent and 7 per cent of its GDP in infrastructure over the next twenty years, according to one group of economists.[54]

The Brazil cost did not just apply to industry. It affected farmers and service businesses too. But farmers had a powerful competitive advantage. And service businesses were protected from foreign competition, either because they produced non-tradable goods or explicitly (as in the case of lawyers, who fought to prevent foreign law firms from setting up shop in Brazil). The appreciation of the exchange rate made the Brazil cost even more painful for manufacturers and farmers. Apart from a brief fall in 2008–9, the real climbed steadily against the dollar from 2003 onwards, peaking in 2011 at 1.54 reais to the dollar. In 2010 Guido Mantega, the finance minister, declared Brazil to be the victim of a 'currency war' unleashed by the central banks in the developed world, which were desperately trying to revive their moribund economies by injecting money into them.[55]

Some of this cheap money leaked into emerging-market economies, in search of higher returns. That helped to push up the value of the real, as it did with other Latin American currencies. But there were domestic factors at work too. In part, the real appreciated because Brazil was becoming richer. The commodity boom meant that the country ran a current account surplus (until 2008). The growing economy sucked in foreign direct investment. The oil strikes excited notions in financial markets that the real would become a petro currency. And high interest rates encouraged foreign financial investors to buy Brazilian assets.

Magnified by the strong real, the Brazil cost made the country phenomenally expensive. Many imported consumer items, from designer clothes to smartphones, cost roughly twice as much in São Paulo as in New York.[56] Taking all these cost pressures into account, it was no wonder that investment in Brazil remained so sluggish, at around 17–18 per cent of GDP, eventually prompting a slowdown in growth; in the faster-growing economies of Peru and Chile that figure was in the high twenties. Luciano Coutinho recognized that if the economy were to return to growth of around 5 per cent a year, investment needed to rise to about 24 per cent of GDP.

When industrial production and investment failed to respond to the Brasil Maior industrial policy, government officials began to accept that the country had a competitiveness problem. They took a few steps to try to address aspects of the Brazil cost. Some were more successful than others. By imposing taxes and controls on foreign investment in financial assets and derivatives, Mantega succeeded in reversing the excessive appreciation of the real. When money began to drain out of emerging financial markets in 2013, he scrapped these measures. As the real plunged to below 2.40 to the dollar, official satisfaction with the currency depreciation turned to alarm. Alexandre Tombini, the Central Bank president, stepped in with a currency swap arrangement that smoothed the currency's fall.

Although some commentators objected to the temporary financial controls, they looked justified – though tighter fiscal policy would have reduced the need for them. If they damaged investors' trust in Brazil, it was mainly because they coincided with clumsier government interventions. Industry complained about high electricity prices. Dilma announced that she would drive them down by forcing a lower rate of return for generating contracts when these came up for renewal. That prompted a collapse in the share price of electricity companies, and generated much uncertainty. Critics have pointed out that heavy taxes on electricity were one reason why tariffs were high.

After much hesitation, Dilma's government announced that it would award contracts to private investors to operate and upgrade airports and ports, and to build new roads and railways. It created a new ministry of civil aviation to wrest control of the airports from the air force. Deals for expanding three of the main airports were agreed. At São Paulo's Guarulhos international airport, a grim and overcrowded facility of brutalist concrete, work began on building a long-needed new terminal. The government pushed through a new ports law which it hoped would open the gates to more private investment in building and operating container terminals. At last, in 2013 the government began to auction contracts to upgrade federal highways. Officials expressed confidence that they would sign contracts that would ramp up spending on transport infrastructure to 100 billion reais a year in both 2014 and 2015.[57]

The birth of Brazilian multinationals

Industrial policy revealed the longstanding lack of faith among officials in the capacity of Brazil's private businesses and entrepreneurs to develop the country or to flourish without state aid (which was naturally sought by many of them). This lack of faith might have been justified in the past, given their huge difficulties in gaining access to capital and markets (because of poor transport links). It was true that Brazilian companies often seemed to lack the ambition to expand abroad. I asked Luiz Carlos Paduan why Santa Rita hadn't produced anything like a Brazilian Huawei, the Chinese telecoms giant. His answer was that 'It would need a big investment from the government, or having the technology already here. We can't compete with foreign technology because costs are too high here.'

Another reason was the rich pickings to be had in the domestic market, especially once companies realized that they could sell to the masses of the India element in Bacha's Belindia, rather than restrict themselves to the Belgium, as they had traditionally. For example, Brazil became the world's third-biggest market (after the United States and Japan) for a series of consumer goods, such as pet food and skincare products, it was the fourth-biggest cement consumer (after China, India and the US) and was set to become the fifth-biggest grocery market (after the above plus Russia) by 2015. It was the second-biggest market in the world (behind the US) for Sweden's Electrolux.[58] That was why Brazil pulled in so much foreign direct investment.

Nevertheless, the past decade has seen the rise of Brazilian multinationals. Vale was by most measures the leader, after its US$18 billion purchase of Inco, a Canadian nickel miner, in 2006 and a series of other foreign acquisitions. Top of the *FT*'s list of Brazil's biggest companies was Ambev, part of Anheuser Busch-Inbev, the world's biggest brewer. Formally based in Belgium, AB-Inbev was the creation of a group of hard-driving Brazilian entrepreneurs led by Jorge Paulo Lemann, a former Brazilian tennis champion and the son of a Swiss immigrant who set up Banco Garantia, an investment bank. Garantia was modelled on Goldman Sachs; like Goldman, it was a partnership. After trading losses occasioned by the Asian devaluations of 1998 prompted him to sell the bank to Credit Suisse in 1998, Lemann and his longtime partners, Marcelo Telles and Carlos Alberto Sicupira, set up what would become

Brazil's biggest private equity firm, GP Investimentos. But long before that, Lemann and his partners had bought a controlling stake in Brahma, a Brazilian brewer, for US$60 million in 1989. His ambition, he told people in São Paulo, was to turn it into the world's biggest brewer, through foreign acquisitions.[59] With AB-Inbev, he achieved precisely that. Having sold their stake in GP Investimentos in 2004, the three Brazilians founded 3G Capital, an international investment fund which bought Burger King for US$3.3 billion in 2010 and then teamed up with Warren Buffett to buy Heinz, an icon of US business, in 2013 (for US$23 billion). The combined market value of the companies run by the three Brazilians was greater than that of Citigroup.[60] Lemann both preceded and succeeded Eike Batista as Brazil's richest man. Aged seventy-four, he was as patrician, discreet and austere as Eike was flamboyant. After a failed kidnapping attempt against his children in a São Paulo street as they were being driven to school in 1999, he relocated to Switzerland, commuting to Brazil on a private jet. Like Buffett, whom he had long admired, he was personally frugal (private jet apart). He and his Swiss second wife brought up their own children without a nanny; Lemann was known to drive himself to his office at Banco Garantia in a Gol, a small Brazilian Volkswagen.[61]

Lemann's global ambition was matched by that of André Esteves, a very different personality. A systems analyst from a lower middle-class background in Rio de Janeiro's gritty *zona norte*, Esteves worked as a trader at Pactual, a small Brazilian investment bank, before wresting control of it. He sold it to Switzerland's UBS for $3.1 billion in 2006 only to buy it back again for $2.5 billion three years later. He went on to turn BTG-Pactual, as it is now called, into Latin America's biggest investment bank, with operations in Chile, Peru and Colombia. Aged forty-four, Esteves is boyish and bright-eyed, and relentlessly upbeat. 'We as Latin Americans should think big because the quality of our economies allows us for the first time to do so,' he told a meeting in the City of London in September 2012. Esteves made it clear that he expected his bank to become a global force, starting with its asset management business. Although listed on the Bovespa, the São Paulo stock exchange, BTG-Pactual is a partnership, a model that seems to work in the relatively freewheeling and non-hierarchical business culture that has taken root in the country's newer businesses.[62]

Itaú turned itself into Latin America's leading commercial bank, buying the retail operations of BankBoston in Chile and Uruguay and those of HSBC in Chile. Other Brazilian companies that went multinational included JBS, which began as a butcher's shop in Goiás half a century ago and became the world's biggest meatpacking firm. Gerdau, a steel firm from Rio Grande do

Sul, is one of the world's biggest makers of specialist steel, with factories in fourteen countries including the US. Brazilian construction firms, such as Odebrecht, had begun operating outside the country in the 1970s. Marcopolo, a bus maker, began to go abroad in the 1990s when it saw little prospect of growth in Brazil where it already had a 70 per cent market share. It now has joint ventures in China, Russia and India, as well as factories in Argentina, Colombia, Mexico and South Africa. Typical of a newer crop of Brazilian multinationals was Natura, a manufacturer of cosmetics and beauty products sold door to door by sales reps. It first took on and beat Avon, which had a powerful presence in Brazil, and then expanded into a dozen markets abroad.

In 2006, for the first time, outward investment by Brazilian firms outstripped inward foreign direct investment, though the former fell away at least temporarily after the 2008–9 financial crisis. While *multilatinas* from other countries in the region tended to expand in neighbouring countries, Brazilian multinationals often chose to invest in the United States, as well as elsewhere in Latin America and Europe (but rarely in Asia).[63] It was reasonable to suppose that more Brazilian multinationals would emerge. Some of the constraints on international expansion had loosened. It was much easier for companies to raise capital than in the past. Even if the banks were unable or unwilling to make long-term loans, the country's capital market developed swiftly after the Real Plan. The number of companies listed on the São Paulo stock exchange (known as the Bovespa) rose to over 350. The exchange's average daily trading volume surged from US$420 million in 2004 to over US$3.5 billion in 2010–12; its total market capitalization increased from an average of $341 billion in 2004 to a peak of US$1.5 trillion in 2010, before falling back to US$1.2 trillion by 2012.[64] The exchange encouraged reforms of corporate governance so that minority shareholders were protected from the discrimination they had suffered in the past. Many quoted companies abolished their previous practice of maintaining a separate class of voting shares, restricted to the controlling family and their friends. In 2008 the Bovespa merged with the São Paulo Commodities and Futures Exchange, which thanks to Brazil's agricultural strength was the biggest of its kind outside Chicago and London. Pension funds and mutual funds provided a big pool of institutional investors: there were 10,500 mutual funds with net assets totalling US$1 trillion in 2012, forming the sixth-biggest fund industry in the world, similar in size to that in France.[65] Brazil suddenly became knee-deep in private-equity and venture-capital funds. Foreign financial giants, such as Blackstone and JPMorgan Chase, bought into Brazilian private-equity and hedge funds. Some of these funds took minority stakes in medium-sized companies, and then guided them to the stock market so they could cash out their stake. Brazilian regulators welcomed them, but imposed higher standards of transparency on their operations than was the case in New York or London before the crash.[66]

Nevertheless, Brazilian capitalism had much room to grow. Though the shares of around seventy companies were actively traded on the Bovespa, eight companies accounted for more than 50 per cent of the market's value. State-controlled companies made up about a quarter of the market's value. According to Paulo Oliveira of Brain Brasil, a capital market association, there were a further 2,000 companies that could list on the stock market over the next few years. Several Brazilian banks – notably Bradesco, the biggest commercial bank until Itaú and Unibanco merged – were big equity investors on their own account. In many cases they combined with pension funds to form controlling groups of shareholders. Partly because of the relative lack of bank lending, Brazil seemed to be developing a distinctive kind of capitalism, one that married family companies and bank holdings (in Lombard or German fashion) with a lively public equity market.

From industrial policy to innovation policy

The depreciation of the real in 2013 was likely to lift a lot of the short-term pressure on industry. But Brazil's competitiveness problem was deep-rooted. As Embraer's Curado told me, the best protection against change is indeed to focus on productivity. Instead of micro-managing subsidies to favoured sectors and to losers, a more effective industrial policy would aim to promote competition and productivity-enhancing innovation across the board, partly by a much more aggressive effort to tackle the 'Brazil cost'.

Brazil had plenty of entrepreneurs. According to one study, 27 million Brazilians in 2011 either already owned a business or were starting one – the third-highest figure in the fifty-four countries studied. The problem was that few small businesses went on to become big ones, either because of their owners' lack of ambition or because this would involve growing too big to qualify for the simplified regulations and taxes.[67] There was a danger that the BNDES's focus on 'national champions' and big companies would create oligopolies. Fortunately, Congress approved a law in 2012 endowing Brazil with a modern competition authority.

But there were some examples of upstarts successfully shaking up an industry. One was airlines. When I lived in São Paulo in the 1990s and used Congonhas, the city's commuter airport, I would often find my boarding pass collected in person by Rolim Amaro, a former air-taxi pilot whose TAM airline challenged Varig, the leisurely national flag-carrier, by offering efficient service and modern planes. TAM, which in 2012 merged with Chile's LAN to form

Latin America's largest airline group, was in turn taken on by Gol, a low-cost carrier that was the creation of Constantino de Oliveira, a farmer's son from Minas Gerais who built Brazil's biggest bus company. Gol took over the remains of the bankrupt Varig. The TAM-Gol near-duopoly was then shaken up by David Neeleman, a Brazilian-American entrepreneur, who in 2008 founded Azul, a budget airline that did well by basing itself at Viracopos, Campinas's uncrowded airport, by flying new routes linking mid-sized cities and by introducing yield-management technology to price seats.

The creation of specialist education and training institutions had played a crucial role in encouraging manufacturing, as well as in adding value to commodity production. There was scope for much more of that, as well as for improving the schools and universities. For example, a lack of English speakers was one reason why Brazil was a net importer rather than net exporter of software, according to Alfredo Behrens, a management theorist in São Paulo.[68] The country has been wise in fostering scientific research. By 2010 it produced 10,000 PhDs a year, ten times more than in 1990. Between 2002 and 2008 its share of the world's scientific papers rose from 1.7 per cent to 2.7 per cent, a creditable figure. It spent 1 per cent of its GDP on research, half the rich world share but almost double the average in the rest of Latin America. In São Paulo, the state constitution required its government to pass 1 per cent of its tax revenues – amounting to US$450 million in 2010 – to FAPESP, a research fund.[69] Other states such as Minas Gerais as well as the federal government have similar arrangements. This effort has made Brazil a world leader in research in tropical medicine, bioenergy and plant biology. It was at the root of the construction of a new value chain around sugar cane.

'The culture of innovation has finally arrived in Brazil', according to Fernando Reinach, a research scientist who was science secretary in Cardoso's government and set up several companies before becoming a venture capitalist in São Paulo. But he argued that the government's conception of innovation was that it was something that happened inside big companies, as in the United States in the 1950s. That was not wholly mistaken, he said, but it ignored that nowadays big companies buy in (or buy up) innovation from start-up firms. Valuable research was being conducted in Brazil's public universities, where there were islands of excellence. Missing was a law allowing university researchers to take this intellectual property to companies, Reinach told me. A lot of the venture capital funds that have sprung up in Brazil have money from the BNDES or the pension funds, and behave in practice like risk-averse private equity funds. 'It's very hard for a centralized state to organize the ecosystem of innovation,' Reinach said. 'We have to create the conditions to let it flourish.'

PART III

Prospects

CHAPTER TWELVE

Global Ambitions and Frustrations

In May 2010 Lula flew to Tehran for a meeting with Iran's president, Mahmoud Ahmadinejad, and Turkey's prime minister, Recep Tayyip Erdogan. After almost eighteen hours of negotiations, the three leaders announced an agreement concerning Iran's controversial nuclear programme: Iran would send 1,200 kilos of low-enriched uranium to Turkey within a month and would in exchange receive fuel rods to power its research reactor; in addition, it would put this commitment in writing to the International Atomic Energy Authority (IAEA). In front of the cameras, Ahmadinejad raised the arms of Lula and Erdogan in triumph, as if commemorating victory in a boxing match. Lula called it 'a victory for diplomacy'.[1]

In explaining this initiative to try to resolve one of the world's thorniest conflicts – and one that was a long way from their own neighbourhood – Brazilian officials made clear their country's ambition to be a global power. 'We're assuming our responsibilities in a more multi-polar world,' Antonio Patriota, Amorim's deputy and soon to be his successor as foreign minister, told me shortly afterwards. The world was changing: the US and its allies were weakened by failure in Iraq and by the financial crisis. Brazil's socio-economic success endowed it with 'more political capital to invest in foreign policy'. Both Brazil and Turkey were non-permanent members of the UN Security Council in 2010. In negotiating the Tehran accord, Brazil was 'assuming our responsibility in terms of not waiting for someone else to design policy and then say you are either with us or against us', according to Patriota.[2]

Yet Lula's diplomatic victory proved a Pyrrhic one. Within hours of him leaving Tehran, Iran stated that it would carry on enriching uranium regardless. The United States and other western governments slammed the deal as being no advance on an agreement Iran had reached with the IAEA in October 2009 and quickly resiled from. A dissenting view in Washington, propounded by Thomas Pickering, a senior retired diplomat, held that the Tehran accord was worth considering and that it was an advance on the October 2009 proposal, under which Iran would have exchanged its 1,200 kilos of low-enriched uranium for fuel rods in small batches and inside the country. But many western diplomats portrayed Lula as having naively walked into Ahmadinejad's trap.[3]

Hillary Clinton, the US Secretary of State, told Celso Amorim, Brazil's foreign minister, that 'buying time for Iran, enabling Iran to avoid international unity with respect to their nuclear program makes the world more dangerous, not less.'[4] Amorim responded somewhat petulantly that 'many people are disappointed because this produced results, because they didn't expect that to happen.' He and Marco Aurélio Garcia, Lula's influential foreign policy adviser, stressed that they had consulted the Obama administration and European powers in the run-up to the Tehran trip. Officials in Brasília even took the extraordinary step of leaking a private letter that Obama sent to Lula in April, suggesting that they had US approval for the negotiation and the deal. But American officials responded that the letter was just one of many communications and was taken out of context. According to a senior official in the American administration, the day before Amorim went to Tehran Clinton had told him in a half-hour phone call that the fuel swap and letter to the IAEA would not be enough for the US to abandon sanctions and that the crucial step – missing in the accord – was for Iran to agree to halt enrichment of uranium to 20 per cent.[5]

Even worse for Lula and Amorim, just three weeks after the Tehran Accord, their newfound partners in the BRICs, China and Russia, joined the US, Britain and France in voting at the UN Security Council for new, tougher economic sanctions against Iran because of its defiance of international norms in its nuclear programme. Brazil and Turkey were alone in voting against the resolution. According to the American official, Turkey had been inclined to abstain, but was persuaded to vote against by Brazil.[6] The decision to vote against, rather than abstain, marked a rupture with Brazil's own diplomatic tradition: on none of the ten occasions since 1946 on which Brazil had sat on the Security Council had it ever voted against a resolution that had majority support.

'If anyone has the illusion that sanctions will bring Iran to the negotiating table, they will lose that illusion,' Marco Aurélio Garcia told me.[7] Yet history would prove him wrong: the impact of sanctions on Iran's economy prompted a new president, Hassan Rouhani, to seek negotiations with the United States in September 2013. More than the Tehran gambit itself, Brazil's subsequent behaviour – the leaking of the letter and the vote against sanctions – sowed mistrust in Washington and in some European capitals as to Brazil's intentions and allegiances.

The Iran initiative illustrated the limitless ambition of Lula's foreign policy. Many outside commentators, especially in Europe and Latin America, and some in Brazil, rejoiced at the country's embrace of 'South–South' alliances and rejection of what they saw as a past subservience to Washington. At home, the political establishment and the media largely closed ranks behind the government. But a number of former senior Brazilian diplomats were sharply critical of the Iranian enterprise, seeing it as an expression of Lula's voluntarism and hubris and of his party's ideological approach to foreign policy.

It was certainly true that Brazil had at last become more assertive, shedding some of its previous ambivalence about throwing its weight around in the world. But what does Brazil really stand for, and what does it want? Does it see itself as primarily a 'western' or a 'southern' power? In the great ideological battles between democracy and authoritarianism, between universal values (such as human rights) and moral relativism, which side is Brazil on?

In search of a foreign policy

The most elegant of the ministerial buildings that march in formation along the broad esplanade that sweeps northwards from the Praça dos Tres Poderes in Brasília houses Itamaraty, as the foreign ministry is known, after its original home in Rio de Janeiro. The building is a modernist palace of concrete and glass crafted by Niemeyer, the grounds created by Burle Marx. The entrance hall on the ground floor is interrupted only by a broad half-spiral staircase, unsupported by columns or banisters, that leads to an open mezzanine. The effect is of light and effortless grandeur. The colonnaded building is surrounded by a mirror lake – a moat that seemed to symbolize what was until recently Brazil's condition, one of splendid isolation. Indeed, when Henry Kissinger visited as the US secretary of state in the mid-1970s and was asked by his host, Antonio Silveira, for his impression, he replied, 'It's a magnificent building, Antonio, now all you need is a foreign policy to go with it.'[8]

Brazilian policymakers have long believed that their country is destined to be a great power, because of its continental scale and wealth of resources. They equipped themselves with what is widely regarded as one of the world's most competent and professional diplomatic services. Yet the country long stood apart, seemingly self-absorbed. While outsiders see Brazil as the largest country in Latin America, that is a description which most Brazilians traditionally rejected. Under the monarchy, Brazil looked to Europe rather than to its own region. Brazilian intellectuals saw their country as part of the Atlantic world, rather than Latin America. The leaders of the First Republic favoured Pan-Americanism, the notion intermittently pushed by the United States that the Americas as a whole should co-operate. Brazil was the only Latin American country to help the US during the Spanish–American War of 1898: it sold to the US two cruisers which it had ordered from a British shipyard, and allowed the US Pacific Fleet to use its ports for bunkering and repairs en route to the Caribbean. These impulses led Brazil to declare war on the Allied side in both the world wars of the twentieth century.

But frictions with the United States began to emerge in the aftermath of the Second World War and with the start of the Cold War. Vargas was frustrated that Brazil's support for the Allies was not rewarded either with a permanent seat at the Security Council of the newly founded United Nations, or with an equivalent of the Marshall Plan for Europe. Kubitschek wrote to Eisenhower proposing such a scheme, which he called 'Operation Pan-America', arguing that the best way to combat Communism in Latin America was to support economic development. But the Americans were not interested; they would only pursue this approach after the Cuban Revolution when Kennedy launched the Alliance for Progress, which closely resembled Kubitschek's plan.[9] When the generals took power in Brazil in 1964 with US support, the two governments were once again united by anti-Communism, as they had been under Dutra in 1945–50. Henry Kissinger, the foreign policy supremo in the Nixon and Ford administrations from 1969 to 1975, saw Brazil as one of a clutch of rising regional powers around the world to which the US could delegate the conduct of the Cold War.[10] Geisel and his foreign minister, Silveira, were both intrigued and alarmed by this courtship. They pursued a more nationalist and more ambitious foreign policy that combined Brazil's longstanding preoccupation with economic development with a more independent international stance. The dictatorship built an arms industry and began to proclaim Brazil's status as a 'great power'. Although Brazil never joined the Non-Aligned Movement it shared many of its stances, and forged new trade and diplomatic ties in Africa and the Middle East. Kissinger's initiative ended in frustration: tensions with the United States arose over trade – Brazil objected to US tariffs on its sugar, orange juice and steel – and Geisel's pursuit of nuclear technology (in a deal with Germany). Under Jimmy Carter, the US also began to criticize the regime's human rights abuses, prompting Geisel to cancel a military co-operation agreement.

Brazil's contemporary international identity thus has complex origins, as Andrew Hurrell, an international relations professor at Oxford University, has written. Brazil's elites have seen themselves as part of the West in cultural and religious terms, and the country has a strong tradition of western ideas about international law and society. Yet on the other hand, Brazil has been shaped by the legacy of colonialism, slavery and poverty and by the imperatives of development.[11] Under Geisel, and again under Lula, Brazil asserted its 'southern' gene more than the 'western' one. The world-view of Brazilian diplomats assigns paramount importance to defending economic and political sovereignty. It follows from this that Brazil usually upholds the principle of non-intervention in the internal affairs of other countries, and that it favours multilateralism and the peaceful resolution of conflicts. (Brazilian diplomats are proud that their country has not fought a war with any of the ten countries with which it shares a border for almost 140 years.) These were indeed natural positions for a country whose past relative weakness meant that it was a follower rather than a leader.

Underlying Brazil's view of the world is a deep-rooted suspicion that the United States is set on blocking Brazil's advance, and even that it has designs on the Amazon or the new South Atlantic oilfields. Yet as Matías Spektor of the Fundação Getúlio Vargas has pointed out, this mistrust sits oddly with the fact that Brazil 'benefited enormously from existing patterns of global order', which have allowed its peaceful rise to modern industrial nation and contemporary economic giant. This gives rise to an ambiguity and a pragmatic moderation at the heart of Brazilian foreign policy: while it is uncomfortable with the prevailing world order, it wants to reform rather than up-end it.[12] The ambiguity, in turn, is a source of frustration to the United States and European countries, which often find Brazil prickly and awkward in ways they find surprising in a large market democracy that is fortunate to face no obvious security threats. Outsiders who are enchanted by Brazilians' warm-hearted embrace often underestimate their nationalism because it is not xenophobic. It has nevertheless intensified with the country's greater success in recent years.

In the decades since the advent of the New Republic and the end of the Cold War, Brazilian foreign policy has evolved in several directions. First, the region has become the top foreign policy priority; while that is normally defined as South America, it has increasingly become Latin American and the Caribbean as a whole. Second, Brazil has given growing importance to seeking alliances with other rising powers in what is sometimes called the 'global South', in Asia and Africa as well as in Latin America. Third, Brazil has sought to expand its worldwide diplomatic presence and has been an increasingly vocal supporter of changes to global institutions – from the UN Security Council to the IMF and world trade negotiations – with the aim of occupying a more prominent place in the world's councils.

Circumstances played a part in Brazil's increasing assertiveness. On the one hand, a much stronger economy meant that the country was no longer dependent on bail-outs from the IMF and the US Treasury. Cardoso, a poly-glot academic, was naturally at home on the world stage. And Lula, through his personality, his biography and his instinct as a negotiator, sought and obtained a bigger international role. On the other hand, the moment of American hyperpower following victory in the Cold War proved brief, curtailed by political defeat in Iraq and Afghanistan and the aftermath of the 2008 financial crisis. Europe fell into prolonged slump, while the economies of China, India and other emerging countries raced ahead (at least until 2013). Brazil was not alone in distancing itself from the US agenda in the IMF and the World Trade Organization. While no other country comes close to rivalling US military power, the world in many ways has become more polycentric.

Although there have been continuities in Brazil's foreign policy since 1985, there have also been changes of emphasis. Cardoso pursued a policy of 'autonomy via participation' in the global economy and said that 'to provoke friction with the United States is to lose'.[13] It was an irony that Lula in foreign policy – as well as in his reinvention of 'national developmentalism' – harked back to Geisel, the president against whom he had led the metalworkers' strikes. Many of Lula's initiatives abroad commanded consensus, but others did not. In the view of his critics, who would come to include several of Itamaraty's most distinguished retired ambassadors, foreign policy became 'radicalised, contaminated by ideological and party-political motivations', according to Rubens Ricupero, who was one of them.[14] Especially towards the end of his second term, Lula was seen by them as following the PT's foreign policy preferences, a sop for his failure to follow the party line on the economy. Dilma Rousseff drew back from Lula's personal protagonism, and put slightly more stress on promoting human rights, but otherwise followed a broadly similar policy to her predecessor.

Celso Amorim, a capable and experienced professional diplomat who was Lula's foreign minister for eight years, became a PT member. His deputy for much of that time was Samuel Pinheiro Guimarães, a left-wing intellectual whom Cardoso had sacked as Itamaraty's director of research in 2001 for being too anti-US. Marco Aurélio Garcia, the senior PT official who acted as foreign affairs adviser to both Lula and Dilma Rousseff, took the lead on Latin American issues, leaving Amorim to direct formal diplomatic negotiations and policy towards the rest of the world. Garcia, a historian whose natural habitat was Paris's Left Bank, had been the PT's international relations secretary for ten years before moving into the Planalto, and had close ties with left-wing parties across the region.

'Mercosul is our destiny'

Apart from its longstanding interest in the river Plate region which had led it into the Paraguayan war, until recently Brazil paid little attention to its neighbours. Baron Rio Branco, the foreign minister from 1902 to 1912 and the father of Brazilian diplomacy, settled border disputes with Argentina, Uruguay and Colombia. Rio Branco arranged the purchase of Bolivia's Acre province (for £2.5 million) after Brazilian migrants had moved in during the rubber boom, prompting violent clashes. He thus definitively fixed Brazil's borders.[15] Yet Brazil remained inward-looking. As Bethell notes, Brazil only became part of Latin America when the rest of the world decided that Latin America existed as an entity, after the Second World War, when several regional organizations were established.[16] No Brazilian ruler had ever visited another South American country until Campos Salles went to Argentina in 1900. Rio Branco laid the groundwork for a treaty of co-operation with Argentina and Chile, signed in 1915 (but never ratified by Argentina). Getúlio Vargas made short trips to Argentina, Uruguay, Paraguay and Bolivia. When Juscelino Kubitschek stopped off in Ecuador and Peru on his way back from a gathering of presidents from across the Americas in Panama in 1956, he was the first Brazilian president to visit either country. Until 1985, no Brazilian president had set foot in Colombia or Venezuela. Apart from a couple of border encounters, only three presidents had ever visited Argentina and only two Argentine rulers had made the trip the other way. The two countries' rail networks were built to different gauges.[17]

In the 1970s and early 1980s Brazil and Argentina eyed each other with deep suspicion. Both were ruled by military dictatorships, and both were working on developing nuclear weapons. But then democracy came, first to Argentina with the election of Raúl Alfonsín in 1983 and then to Brazil. José Sarney's main foreign policy achievement was détente with Brazil's largest neighbour. Both agreed to renounce nuclear weapons, and to inspect periodically each other's nuclear facilities; they also negotiated bilateral trade preferences. Carlos Menem, who replaced Alfonsín in 1989, and Fernando Collor both began to tear down the protectionist policies that each country had pursued for half a century. In 1991 they came together with their counterparts from Paraguay and Uruguay to sign the Treaty of Asunción, creating Mercosul – the Common Market of the South (known as Mercosur in Spanish). For Brazil, this was a big change. According to Alfredo Valladão, an international relations specialist at Paris's Sciences Po university, it was driven partly by the peopling of the country's interior in the course of the twentieth century. Brazil could no longer ignore its neighbours: its borders had become conduits for migration and crime as well as trade.[18]

Past regional integration schemes in Latin America had been designed to expand protected markets for import-substitution industrialization. Mercosul was different: it was based on 'open regionalism', the idea that tearing down barriers between them could help countries to participate more effectively in a globalized economy. At first, Mercosul made rapid progress. By 1995, most trade in goods between the four members was tariff-free. The group agreed to create a customs union, in which as in the European Union members apply a common external tariff to imports from third countries (this saw average tariffs fall from 37.2 per cent in 1985 to a low of 11.5 per cent in 1994). They set a five-year deadline to complete their free-trade area and customs union. With a combined GDP of US$985 billion in 1995, Mercosul aspired to be the world's fourth-largest integrated market after the North American Free-Trade Area (NAFTA, linking Mexico to the United States and Canada), the European Union and Japan.* Trade among the four members grew swiftly, rising from just US$4 billion in 1990 to $20.7 billion in 1997. Multinationals, such as Unilever and Nestlé as well as carmakers, began reorganizing their operations, concentrating manufacture of a particular product-group for the whole sub-region at a single factory. Mercosul became an effective brand that helped to put its members on the world business map. Chile and Bolivia joined as associate members, and the group's leaders agreed to expand cross-border infrastructure, such as roads and powerlines. They also saw Mercosul's role as being to defend democracy. After Brazil and Argentina took the lead in defusing a coup attempt in Paraguay in 1996, Mercosul formally included a 'democracy clause' as a condition for remaining a member of the group. Argentina and Brazil declared a 'strategic alliance' and began to stage joint military exercises.[19] 'Mercosul is our destiny,' Cardoso stated.

Yet it quickly ran into trouble. The most visible problem was macroeconomic instability: first Brazil's 1999 devaluation and then the collapse of Argentina's currency board (which had pegged the peso at par to the dollar) in 2001–2 upset trade patterns between the group's key members. This led each country, but especially Argentina, to throw up 'temporary' barriers to the other's trade. The underlying problem was that even before the Brazilian devaluation, Mercosul ceased to make progress in deepening its common market. Although a dispute settlement mechanism was at last adopted in 1999, in practice most quarrels were handled by presidential diplomacy. Although officials from the member governments frequently boasted that their project embodied a deeper level of integration than NAFTA, a mere free-

---

* This was before China had become the world's second-biggest economy.

trade area, in practice this was not so. A common customs code, to prevent goods from outside the bloc being subject to duties a second time if they crossed an internal border, was not approved until 2010 and was yet to be implemented in 2013. And the Common External Tariff was punctured by more and more exceptions.

These flaws were symptomatic of deeper stumbling-blocks. Mercosul suffered from far greater asymmetry than the EU, with Brazil accounting for almost four-fifths of its founding members' population and roughly 70 per cent of their GDP. Brazil was reluctant to pool sovereignty. For it, Mercosul was primarily a geopolitical project, pushed by Itamaraty rather than by businesspeople (except those in the southern states, who were enthusiastic). It was Itamaraty that insisted that Mercosul should be a customs union: this required the other three members to raise their tariffs on capital goods, helping to provide a captive market for segments of Brazilian industry. Argentina would have benefited from a 'deeper' Mercosul, which would have offered guaranteed access to the huge Brazilian market. But under Néstor Kirchner, elected in 2003, and his wife and successor Cristina Fernández, Argentine policy became more nationalist and inward-looking. In contrast Uruguay, with a small, open economy, chafed at Brazilian and Argentine protectionism, even after the left took power there in 2004.

Under Cardoso, Brazil also began to seek a broader role in the region, beyond Mercosul. In 2000 he organized the first of what would become regular South American summits, which agreed to develop cross-border infrastructure and set the goal of merging Mercosul and the five-country Andean Community. Cardoso successfully mediated a conflict between Peru and Ecuador, which had featured brief border wars in 1981 and 1995. And Brazil pursued, albeit with many misgivings, talks for a thirty-four-country Free Trade Area of the Americas (FTAA), an initiative of President George H.W. Bush and launched at the first Summit of the Americas held in Miami in 1994.

'Nossa América Latina'

Lula came into office stating that he wanted to give greater priority to regional integration. Under the auspices of Marco Aurélio Garcia, what that meant was building a Brazilian-dominated political bloc in South America, as a more or less explicit counterweight to the influence of the United States in the region. Towards the end of Lula's governments, Brazil became increasingly involved in Central America and the Caribbean, where it opened many new embassies. As for Mercosul, Lula said he wanted to revive and deepen it;

he was more explicit than Cardoso in seeing it as a primarily political grouping.

The circumstances were propitious for this project. The United States was distracted first by the 'war on terror', and then by financial crisis. It has been a less active player in Latin America than in the past. On the other hand, during and after a period of economic stagnation or worse in the region in 1998–2002, left-wing leaders came to power in a string of countries in South America.

In a retrospective analysis, Amorim claimed 'remarkable results in the economic, commercial, infrastructural and political spheres' of South American 'solidarity and integration'. On paper, at least, there were certainly some successes for Brazil's strategy. Largely at Brazilian insistence, Mercosul was widened to include Venezuela and Bolivia as full members (and Ecuador applied to join). Cardoso's South American summits evolved into first the South American Community in 2004 and then in 2008 the South American Union (UNASUL in Portuguese). With Brazilian guidance, UNASUL mediated in political conflicts between government and opposition in Bolivia and Ecuador; it provided an umbrella under which Ecuador and Venezuela restored ties with Colombia after temporarily suspending them over disagreements about Colombia's war against the FARC guerrillas. In 2008 Brazil organized a get-together of the leaders of all thirty-three Latin American and Caribbean countries at Sauípe, a resort near Salvador. It was the first time they had all met without the presence of outsiders. Out of this came the Community of Latin American and Caribbean Nations (CELAC), a body whose main purpose was to include Cuba and to exclude the United States and Canada. Though CELAC was inspired mainly by Venezuela's Hugo Chávez and by Mexico, the message seemed clear: it was Brazil and not the US under the discredited George W. Bush that was the leading power in the region. Brazil began to give less importance to the Organization of American States (OAS), which the US saw as the main regional body.

Chávez had his own, rival plans for the region, embodied in the Bolivarian Alternative for the Americas or ALBA (which also means 'dawn' in Spanish), an explicitly anti-American club joined by Bolivia, Cuba, Ecuador, Nicaragua and several small Caribbean island-states. 'Brazil is not going to adhere to ALBA but it respects it,' García told me.[20] Brazil claimed to be a moderating influence on Chávez. But it also intervened to bolster him. The Lula government's first foreign policy act was to send an oil tanker to Venezuela to break an oil workers' strike against Chávez. García justified this on the grounds that Chávez was legitimately elected, and Brazil supported constitutional rule. Brazil also set up a Group of Friends to mediate between government and opposition in Venezuela.

Chávez and ALBA were in some ways functional for Brazil; to the US, the Lula government portrayed itself as the moderate and responsible alternative in the region, and in many ways it was. Brazilian diplomats were masterful at politely stalling Chávez's more madcap schemes, such as the Bank of the South and a proposed gas pipeline from Caracas to Buenos Aires. But they embraced others. At Chávez's suggestion, UNASUL set up a defence council. 'To defend against what?' asked Cardoso. The implicit answer was the United States. 'The United States isn't attacking Latin America. Chávez threatens, he's not being threatened,' Cardoso told me.[21] At least until the revelations in 2013 about US espionage, Brazilian officials were rarely explicit about the ways in which they thought the US was a threat to South America (even in the Cold War, its direct interventions were confined to Central America and the Caribbean). When Colombia's conservative president, Álvaro Uribe, updated a military co-operation agreement which granted the US facilities at seven military bases, Lula echoed Chávez's anger. But Brazil then signed a similar, if more modest, agreement of its own with the US. Samuel Guimarães argued that the Defence Council should sponsor a South American arms industry – another example of *saudade* for Geisel.

Amorim declared that Brazil should be more 'generous' to its smaller Mercosul partners in minor disputes. This approach was tested when Evo Morales, Bolivia's socialist president, with Chávez at his side, sent troops to nationalize Petrobras's operations in his country. Lula's response looked feeble. He held a meeting with Morales and Chávez, and emerged to say that Bolivia was acting within its rights. Inviting Venezuela, with its state-dominated and dysfunctional economy, to join Mercosul underlined Brazil's changing conception of the group. It acquiesced, too, in Argentina's growing protectionism, and in the serial weakening of the bloc's trade rules. 'We support Argentina's re-industrialization,' García told me. Mercosul arose out of a 'liberal vision' that he did not share.

Lula increasingly began to talk about 'nossa América Latina' (our Latin America), going beyond Brazil's traditional South American focus. Early in his rule, Brazil agreed to lead the UN peacekeeping mission in Haiti, set up after the chaotic overthrow of Jean-Bertrand Aristide, a demagogic left-wing president. Though disliked by the PT, this was widely seen in the outside world as an example of Brazil assuming constructive regional responsibilities. Brazil staked out an increasingly important role in Cuba. With loans from the BNDES, Odebrecht built a deep-water port at Mariel, west of Havana, and signed a contract to modernize and run a sugar mill. Brazil also took the lead in opposing a bloodless coup in Honduras in 2009. It insisted, though without success, on the restoration to power of Manuel Zelaya, an ally of Chávez who was ousted by the Honduran army, acting on the orders of the country's Congress and judiciary, after he tried to organize an unconstitutional referendum that might have allowed him a second consecutive term.

Inside Brazil, the main criticism of Lula's policy towards the region was that it was politically partisan and inconsistent, and gave insufficient importance to the defence of democracy and human rights. Dropping Brazil's tradition of non-intervention, Lula sometimes sided openly with other left-wing Latin American leaders in their domestic political battles. When Chávez was campaigning for a referendum abolishing term limits in 2008, Lula gave an interview to Germany's *Der Spiegel* in which he called him 'Venezuela's best president in the past 100 years'.[22] Brazil was silent when Chávez violated his own constitution by packing the judiciary and harassing opponents. 'We don't want to be like other countries [i.e. the US], giving lessons and judging. We think in the fundamental things those [democratic] values are protected in Venezuela,' Garcia told me. In comments after a Cuban dissident died while on hunger strike when Lula happened to be visiting Havana, he appeared to equate political prisoners in Cuba with common criminals in Brazil.[23] Brazilian diplomats insist that they raised the issue of human rights in private with Raúl Castro's government, and that this was more effective than public lecturing. Their critics were not so sure.

Cardoso argued that 'Brazil can't be the gendarme of Latin America, but it can play a pedagogical role with reference to democracy . . . Lula is very indulgent with Chávez. The region has recovered the machinery of democracy, but not its soul.'[24] In 2012 Fernando Lugo, the ineffectual left-wing president of Paraguay, was ousted in a lightning impeachment. This was unfair and reprehensible, but it was constitutional (and popular). Yet Dilma Rousseff and Marco Aurélio Garcia responded by instigating the suspension of Paraguay from Mercosul, citing the democracy clause. The not-coincidental result of this was that Venezuela was formally admitted to Mercosul (the last obstacle to its admission had been the refusal of Paraguay's Congress to ratify it). To many, this looked like blatant political intervention in the internal affairs of a neighbour. A senior source at Itamaraty told me later that the suspension was opposed by Antonio Patriota, Dilma's foreign minister (who was sacked in 2013). It sometimes seemed that Brazil's notion of promoting democracy and human rights in the region went no further than solidarity with left-wing presidents, however autocratically they behaved.

Yet Brazil remained ambivalent about assuming leadership in the region. Many Brazilians, especially more conservative ones, still found it hard to see their country as part of otherwise Spanish-speaking South America, let alone Latin America. In an article in *El País*, a Spanish newspaper, João Ubaldo Ribeiro, a Brazilian novelist, ranted:

There is practically nothing in common in the culture, history and ethnic composition of Brazil and Peru ... An Argentine considers himself as similar to a Brazilian as a German to a Turk. A Latin American essence doesn't exist, beyond geographical contiguity.[25]

Unlike most other Latin American countries, Brazil continues to think it can play a global role independently of its region, as Valladão notes. Secondly, Brazil's self-image was (and remains) that of a gentle giant; it likes to think it imposes its will in its region through grandeur rather than war, according to Sérgio Buarque.[26] 'We've eliminated from our dictionary any hint of hegemony,' Lula said in 2006. 'Brazil doesn't want to lead anything but be the partner of all countries.'[27]

In practice, Brazil was often unable or unwilling to provide the kind of support or co-operation that some of its neighbours wanted or needed. Take Colombia, the second most populous country in South America. Brazil and Colombia had long had distant relations marked by mutual incomprehension, partly because they are separated by the formidable natural barrier of the Amazon rainforest.* By the 1990s, Colombia was in danger of becoming a failed state, its democracy assailed by the FARC guerrillas (financed by drug money and large-scale kidnapping) and right-wing paramilitaries. Uribe's predecessor, Andrés Pastrana, turned to the US for help, in the form of Plan Colombia, a military aid scheme. Cardoso's government was unsympathetic: Plan Colombia seemed to trigger atavistic fears in Brazil of US military involvement in the Amazon. Brazil claimed to be neutral between a democratic government and the FARC – an extraordinary position. Uribe was furious at Chávez's ill-disguised sympathy for the FARC, which included allowing the guerrillas to buy arms through Venezuelan officials. Rather than show solidarity with a democratically elected president faced with subversion, Lula chose to triangulate between Uribe and Chávez. Relations improved when Juan Manuel Santos replaced Uribe and sought a rapprochement with Chávez and began peace talks with the FARC.

Brazil's ambivalence about regional leadership, and the limitations of a policy focused on political camaraderie, proved costly when it came to the fundamental task of boosting trade, investment and economic ties. Despite the government's claims, Mercosul languished. According to Rubens Barbosa, a former Brazilian ambassador to London and Washington who had helped to negotiate the Treaty of Asunción of 1991, 'the founding idea that Mercosul would be an instrument of trade liberalization has disappeared. What we have

---

* But also parhaps because they are quite similar: like Brazil, Colombia is a decentralized country with a diversified manufacturing industry and was long inward-looking.

today is a political and social forum, and micromanagement of trade.' In absolute terms, trade among the members grew, but as a share of Brazil's total
trade, its trade with the other three peaked at 17 per cent in 1997 and fell to
only 9 per cent in 2010, according to Barbosa.[28] Although that was partly
because the commodity boom boosted Brazil's exports to the rest of the world,
it was also because the group no longer served to intensify its members'
economic linkages. Ricupero lamented that Mercosul summits had become
'empty media spectacles, with the inappropriate presence of foreign guests,
long speeches and an almost total absence of any real and substantive discussion of the difficult items on the agenda.'[29] By choosing as its main allies
Argentina and Venezuela whose economies were largely closed and dysfunctional, Brazil gained captive markets, in some cases for businesses that otherwise could not compete. Brazilian construction firms gained contracts worth
several billion dollars in Venezuela. Brazilian companies bought up significant
chunks of Argentine industry. Yet this strategy was vulnerable to an eventual
change of political leadership in those countries.

Trade headwinds

For Brazil, there was an opportunity cost in all this. During the 2002 election
campaign Lula had denounced the idea of the FTAA as representing the
'economic annexation' of Latin America by the US. Brazil had legitimate
concerns about the FTAA talks. The things it was most interested in were
greater access to the US market and the elimination of American subsidies to
farmers. The US response was that under an FTAA market access would be
granted to smaller countries in the Americas first (and Brazil last) and that
subsidies were a matter for the WTO global trade talks. Brazil was also
concerned that US insistence on opening up government procurement while
tightening intellectual property rules would constrain its freedom to practise
industrial policy. And the US's dogmatic and unjustified insistence on
inserting a prohibition on capital controls into trade agreements would have
made it hard for Brazil to respond to the 'currency war' after the financial
crisis. At a meeting in Miami in 2003 Amorim proposed a watered-down
version that would have left many issues to the WTO. Thereafter, the US lost
interest in the talks, which quietly died. At the same time, Brazil's deference to
Argentina's extreme protectionism was a factor in Mercosul's failure to
conclude a trade agreement with the European Union, for which negotiations
had begun in 1999. Between 2002 and 2013 the only trade deals concluded
by Mercosul – and thus Brazil – were with Peru, Israel and the Palestine
Authority, and neither of the latter two took effect.

Many other Latin American countries considered the benefits of a trade deal with the US to outweigh the drawbacks. The Bush administration responded to the demise of the FTAA with 'competitive liberalization'. Chile had already turned away from Mercosul and signed a bilateral trade deal with the US. Central America, the Dominican Republic, Peru, Colombia and Panama followed suit. Brazilian business began to become more anxious about its isolation. That anxiety was crystallized by the formation in 2011 of the Pacific Alliance, comprising Chile, Colombia, Mexico and Peru. These countries all had open free-market and mainly fast-growing economies, which had embraced globalization with a web of bilateral trade agreements, including with Asian countries. Their combined GDP was similar to that of Brazil. The Pacific Alliance was a hard-nosed businesslike affair, a return to the open regionalism of Mercosul's origins. After two years of negotiations, the Alliance's members reached an agreement to eliminate tariffs on 92 per cent of their trade, with the rest to follow gradually. They also talked of harmonizing the rules of origin under which goods qualify as nationally made. The Alliance was an effort to insert its member countries in global value chains. Its formation was a tacit rejection of Brazil's approach to regional integration.

For its part, Brazil insisted on the primacy of multilateral trade negotiations, in the shape of the WTO's Doha Round. It emerged as a key player in the talks, thanks to its initiative in 2003 in organizing a bloc of big developing countries known as the G20 (not to be confused with the group of large economies formed in 2008) which insisted on a 'development round', blocking any deal that did not include action to dismantle farm subsidies in the US and the EU. Again, Brazil was justified in this. But the problem was that Doha got nowhere. Amorim blamed 'ineffective leadership in richer nations' for this. While that was true, it was also the case that when a deal was almost clinched in 2008, it foundered on the demands of India and China to protect their farmers.[30] Brazil underlined its clout in world trade by securing the election in 2013 of one of its diplomats, Roberto Azevêdo, as the director-general of the WTO, and he quickly secured a limited agreement. But by then the US had begun bilateral trade talks with the EU and a group of Pacific countries, bypassing the Doha Round. However, Brazil did become adept at using the WTO's robust dispute-settlement mechanism; it secured a ruling that US subsidies on cotton were illegal.

Ever since the 1970s Brazil had been a global trader, its exports divided more or less evenly between the US, Europe, the Americas and the rest of the world. That changed a bit over the past decade, as trade with China grew rapidly. Total trade between the two countries rose seventeen-fold between 2002 and 2011, and China displaced the United States to become Brazil's biggest export market and supplier of imports. The government initially hailed this as a success for its strategy of diversifying trade and intensifying 'South–South' economic links. But there was an imbalance: around 85 per cent of Brazil's exports to China were raw materials (mainly iron ore, soya beans and crude oil), while its imports from China were overwhelmingly of manufactures. As Paulo Skaf, the president of FIESP, São Paulo's industrialists' lobby, pointed out, around 70 per cent of Brazil's manufactured exports went to the Americas, north and south. Yet its rejection of the FTAA and its refusal to open its markets more widely to the Pacific Alliance countries meant that it lost ground in these markets to both China and to the United States. And though the commodity boom helped to boost Brazil's share of world exports, at just 1.3 per cent in 2012 this remained smaller than in the 1970s, and small for a country which accounted for 3.3 per cent of the world economy. Brazil was only the world's twenty-second-biggest exporter.[31]

Multinationals flocked to Brazil to take advantage of a protected market, but not to integrate the country to global value chains, as the Pacific Alliance was seeking to do. A dispute with Mexico about cars illustrated the difference. Since 2002, a bilateral agreement allowed free trade in cars between the two countries, initially to Brazil's advantage. But in 2011 Mexican exports under the accord surged by 40 per cent to US$2 billion, while Brazil exported cars worth just US$372 million. Brazil demanded that only cars with at least 40 per cent local content (up from 30 per cent) should benefit from the agreement. It complained that Mexico's car exports were in essence Asian cars (something Mexico rejected). This apparently petty dispute revealed contrasting philosophies about how to be a successful manufacturing economy.

Though their criticism remained timid, some Brazilian industrialists began to become alarmed by the country's isolation from world trade. Paulo Skaf of FIESP told me in 2007 that he would favour Brazil joining an FTAA – a reversal of the organization's position of a decade earlier.[32] 'The world is not going to wait for Brazil,' wrote Rubens Barbosa, who was the president of FIESP's foreign trade council. 'Either Brazil makes up for lost time and reformulates its trade-negotiation strategy, or it will become ever more isolated in the real world of global trade and investment.'[33] Sérgio Amaral, another senior former ambassador who headed the Brazil–China business council, a private-sector group, argued that the right response to the growth in Chinese imports was for Brazil to lead a move to tear down trade barriers across Latin America.[34] There was no sign that Dilma was prepared to do that, though the government did belatedly show more interest in the trade talks with the EU.

Spreading diplomatic wings

The country's greater prominence in world trade diplomacy – if not in world trade – was part of a bigger push to make Brazil count in the world. Under Lula, Brazil opened thirty-three new embassies, fourteen of them in Africa and many of the rest in the Caribbean. The annual intake of new diplomats increased from thirty-five or forty to around 100.[35] As president, Lula himself visited more than seventy-five countries. Much of this effort involved strengthening Brazil's ties with the 'South'. One of Amorim's first initiatives, on which he was particularly keen, was to establish a formal dialogue with India and South Africa, bringing together three large multi-racial southern democracies in a club known as IBSA. Lula was also the prime mover behind regular South American summits with both African and Arab countries.

Then came a Russian initiative to hold annual summits of the BRIC countries. Brazil basked in the new status that attendance at these summits gave it. The four countries shared a vague consensus that they should be given a bigger say in the institutions of world governance, especially on economic matters. They began to co-ordinate their positions in the economic G20. But more things divided than united them. Brazil quickly came to see China as an economic threat as much as a partner.

Perhaps the greatest success of Lula's foreign policy was in Africa. In this, too, he was echoing Geisel and Silveira. Lula visited twenty-five African counties as president, doubled the number of embassies there and helped to boost two-way trade, from $3.1 billion in 2000 to $26 billion in 2012. Brazil recognized the contribution that African slaves had made to the country, and tapped into a shared cultural heritage. Brazil was generally well received in Africa because it was not a former colonial power, and it trod much more lightly than China. Unlike China, Brazilian companies relied on local labour rather than bringing in their own workers. Africa was the main focus of Brazil's small but growing foreign aid programme. Embrapa set up a research station to provide technical help on cotton-growing in West Africa. Nevertheless, Brazilian investment in Africa, at around $10 billion between 2003 and 2009, was much smaller than China's. It was dominated by Vale, Petrobras and Odebrecht, and concentrated particularly in Portuguese-speaking Angola and Mozambique, as well as South Africa and Nigeria.[36]

Lula's embrace (literally, and often) of authoritarian rulers in Africa, the Middle East and Asia attracted the same criticism as his friendship with the Castros in Cuba and with Hugo Chávez. He flew to Tripoli, and called Muammar Qaddafi a 'friend and brother'. He used the same language of Iran's Ahmadinejad, welcoming him in Brazil and disregarding his Holocaust-denying thuggishness. At the UN Human Rights Council, Brazil generally opposed calls for investigations or condemnations of abuses in particular countries. This was 'not the way we work', Amorim told me. 'It's not by being a loudspeaker that you change things.'[37] But Dilma was somewhat less fond of tyrants. In her first month as president, she told a Jewish group in Porto Alegre, to a standing ovation, that she would be 'a tireless defender of equality and human rights everywhere in the world'.[38] In 2011 Brazil voted for the first time in eight years to condemn Iran at the Human Rights Council. 'There's no foreign policy that makes me not condemn the brutal stoning of a woman,' Dilma said.[39]

One of the Lula government's main objectives in expanding its diplomatic alliances was to gain recognition of its claims to be a global power. Amorim and Lula spoke repeatedly of their desire to reshape the rules of world governance, as exemplified in the IMF, the G20 and above all the UN Security Council, a body whose composition reflected the balance of power in the world in 1945 rather than in the twenty-first century. Cardoso had pressed Brazil's claim for a permanent seat at the Security Council, but Lula did so more insistently. Although Brazil did gain slightly more weight at the IMF as part of a modest reform of the Fund's shareholdings, the prize of Security Council reform eluded it. That was partly because China, despite the BRIC link, gave Brazil no support; it opposed reform since this would involve the admission of Japan. The United States was lukewarm. Whereas Barack Obama endorsed India's aspiration for a Security Council seat, when he visited Brazil in March 2011 he merely expressed 'appreciation' for his hosts' claim. That reflected the underlying mistrust in relations between Brazil and the United States, exacerbated by the Iran imbroglio.

The awkward friendship

'Everyone wants to know how a Texan like me is going to get on with someone like you,' George W. Bush told Lula, then newly elected as Brazil's president, at the start of a fifty-minute meeting in the White House's Oval Office on Monday, 10 December 2002. The conservative former oilman and the trade unionist indeed formed an odd couple. But they got on well. 'The chemistry between the two presidents was immediate,' according to Rubens Barbosa, who as Brazil's ambassador to Washington was present. 'The conversation flowed easily.' Whatever their other differences, both men were down to earth and direct. Bush spoke of the security threats the United States faced following the terrorist attacks of 11 September 2001. Lula said Brazil would only support the US in any military venture that had the full backing of the United Nations, that it would pursue a 'more ambitious' foreign policy and would take on a leadership role in South America. He said that he and the Workers' Party had been misunderstood in some quarters in the US, that they were committed to democracy and social change. 'What I want is that by the end of my government every Brazilian can eat three meals a day: breakfast, lunch and dinner,' he concluded. This remark reportedly stayed with Bush, who told aides after the meeting, 'I like this guy'.[40]

There was mutual interest as well as personal rapport. For American business, Brazil was more important than many European or Asian markets. Bush was also interested in Brazil's potential as an energy producer. For Lula, good relations with the US were important for his political balancing act between business and the left, between Davos and the World Social Forum. The two governments agreed to hold regular ministerial and presidential meetings. Thanks to Lula's directness and affability, the relationship did not suffer serious damage either from Brazil's opposition to the Iraq war (partly because Brazil was not on the UN Security Council at the time) or from its reservations about the FTAA. Lula acted as a friend to Bush in a South America where anti-American leaders such as Chávez and Morales were making all the noise. At a discordant summit of the Americas at Mar del Plata, an Argentine seaside resort, in 2005, aides to the host, Néstor Kirchner, organized a rally at which Chávez said he had come to 'bury' the FTAA and 25,000 people chanted 'Bush, fascist, Bush terrorist'.[41] Bush flew on from Mar del Plata to Brasília where Lula, who had left the summit early, entertained him with a barbecue. Oddly, Lula would never establish this kind of personal rapport with Barack Obama, a colder and more cerebral figure. As well as differences in personality, that may have been because Obama, who was wildly popular in Latin America, did not need Lula to act as his guide or friend in the way that Bush appreciated.[42]

For all the diplomatic statements that relations between the two largest countries in the Americas had never been better, in fact they were marked by a deep undercurrent of frustration and misunderstanding, and occasional episodes of friction. As Peter Hakim of the Inter-American Dialogue, a Washington think-tank, has written: 'Brazil and the US are, and will remain, friends. But they are not likely soon to emerge as partners or allies.'[43] That is because Brazil has grown in stature in the world partly by acting on its own and regularly disagreeing with the US. This in turn has made the US increasingly wary of a more powerful Brazil, according to Hakim. It does not help that Washington collectively knows and understands little about Brazil. Exceptions such as Thomas Shannon, a fluent Portuguese-speaker who served as the top State Department official for Latin America under Bush and as ambassador to Brasília under Obama, only served to prove the rule. Brazilians have not forgotten that Ronald Reagan began a 1982 visit by saying, 'It's nice to be in Bolivia'.* George W. Bush once asked Cardoso whether there were many black people in Brazil (though Condoleezza Rice quickly cut in with detailed information on the subject).[44]

From the American viewpoint, trade and economic issues form the core of the relationship. The US is the largest single buyer of Brazilian manufactured exports and source of foreign capital and technology. When Obama visited Brazil in March 2011 he brought about fifty CEOs from top American businesses and met several hundred Brazilian business leaders. Yet mutual interest has not produced any significant economic co-operation agreements. There are many disagreements: Brazil complains about US farm subsidies and the US about Brazilian protectionism in general; the US wants tighter, and Brazil looser, protection of intellectual property; and Brazil accused the US of waging a 'currency war' against it. While the US, under both Bush and Obama, acquiesced in Brazil's more assertive role in Latin America, the two countries have found it hard to co-operate in the region. As Hakim notes, while not acting as antagonists, they disagreed about, for example, how to resolve the impasse after the coup in Honduras and how to put into practice the 2001 Inter-American Charter protecting democracy and the rule of law.

Two issues have provoked particular friction. One is nuclear technology. Brazil, which has the world's sixth-largest uranium deposits, mastered the technology of nuclear power by the 1980s. It is building a third nuclear power station at Angra dos Reis, on the coast south of Rio de Janeiro. Cardoso signed the Nuclear Non-Proliferation Treaty (NPT), which Brazil had long seen as discriminating in favour of established nuclear powers. For that reason it has defended Iran's right to enrich uranium, choosing to believe Ahmadinejad's assurances that its plans were purely peaceful. The US is irritated by Brazil's refusal to sign the NPT's additional protocol, which allows for more intrusive inspection of nuclear facilities. Because Brazil has renounced nuclear weapons, some American officials would like to see it act as a proselytizer for the NPT, pressing Iran to abandon enrichment and accept nuclear fuel for its research reactor from the IAEA.[45] Brazil's reasonable answer to all this is that it fully complies with the NPT, and its facilities are regularly inspected both by the IAEA and by Argentina. It thinks that the US and Russia should reduce their nuclear stockpiles, as the NPT requires, before insisting on other measures.

---

* A Brazilian newspaper answered him the next day with a headline stating 'The people of Bolivia welcome the president of Canada'.

Nevertheless, by distancing herself from Iran, Dilma Rousseff tried to repair the damage to relations. She pushed for, and was granted, the rare accolade of a state visit to Washington, scheduled for October 2013. Then came the revelations from Edward Snowden, the former contractor for the US National Security Agency, that the US had monitored Dilma's emails and phone calls. Given Brazil's sensitivities about its oil and its technology, subsequent revelations that the NSA had spied on Petrobras caused an even bigger storm in Brazil. With a presidential election only a year away, Dilma decided that being seen to waltz in an evening dress with Obama was too risky. Before announcing the cancellation of the trip, she consulted Lula and her political marketer, João Santana, rather than Itamaraty. She also proposed laws to require Brazilians' internet data to be hosted onshore, and to regulate internet companies, prompting opposition from Google, Facebook and the like.

The big misunderstanding in the relationship was that the two countries wanted different things out of it. The US was interested in trade, investment and energy, and in co-ordinating policy with Brazil in Latin America. Brazil wanted the US to treat it as global power, rather than as a Latin American one. And it strongly resisted any suggestion that it might act as a South American sheriff on behalf of Washington. Yet the US did not see Brazil as being quite in the same league as China, Russia and India. That was partly because Brazil enjoys the good fortune not to lie in a troubled part of the world.

The soft-power power

Passengers landing or taking off from Rio's commuter airport in the late 1990s got a close view of the Brazilian Navy's flagship, the *Minas Gerais*, berthed at a wharf in Guanabara Bay. A light aircraft carrier built for Britain's Royal Navy at the end of the Second World War, she was at that time the oldest working aircraft carrier in the world and rarely left port. Brazil lacked planes that could fly from her decks; an early result of Mercosul was that the navy borrowed Argentine fighters for occasional exercises. Such was the parlous state of Brazil's military power. This has never been great – its military dictatorship resisted the splurge on arms spending indulged in by many of its Latin American counterparts. That was sensible, since uniquely for a country of its size and its numerous borders, Brazil faces no plausible military threat of any strategic significance.

With 190,000 troops, Brazil's army is smaller than Colombia's. The armed forces are conservative and retain a degree of veto power over some issues. The three separate military ministries were merged into a single defence ministry under civilian control only in 2000 – a decade or more after most

Latin American countries took that step. Only in 2010 did the three services accept a joint chief of staff, reporting to the defence minister.[46] Two years earlier, the government published a first-ever National Defence Strategy. Over the past two decades the army has transferred three battalions to the Amazon. That is the most vulnerable part of Brazil's territory, but the threats are from drug-traffickers, illegal loggers and, in the 1990s, the occasional spillover from Colombia's internal conflict, rather than the American incursion of Brazilian myth. Even so, there are only 25,000 troops in the Amazon – fewer than in Rio de Janeiro state.[47]

Cardoso began the task of re-equipping the armed forces. The *Minas Gerais* gave way in 2000 to the *São Paulo*, a larger French aircraft-carrier built in the late 1950s; it was matched with a squadron of second-hand Skyhawk A-4 fighter-bombers. Lula launched a big procurement programme, potentially worth $86 billion, between 2010 and 2015.[48] Much of this involved upgrading or replacing clapped-out kit, such as tanks, frigates and transport aircraft. There were two big new purchases. In December 2013, the defence ministry announced that it would buy thirty-six Gripen advanced fighter jets from Sweden's Saab, at a cost of $4.5 billion. The government had earlier agreed to build a nuclear-powered submarine to a French design. This was ostensibly to protect the new deep-sea oilfields. But it also involved a further step in Brazil's nuclear ambitions. The failure to achieve a Security Council seat led a few Brazilians such as José Alencar, Lula's vice-president, to argue that the country should develop nuclear weapons if it wanted the world to take it seriously as a great power. Officials insisted that was out of the question. But there seemed little doubt that Brazil wanted to become a 'threshold state', as Japan is, reaching the point where it could quickly develop a nuclear warhead if required.

Brazil had little incentive, and few spare resources, to invest in military hardware. Instead, to further its claim to be treated as a global force, it would have to rely almost exclusively on 'soft power' – the ability to get what you want through attraction rather than coercion or payments, as Joseph Nye, who coined the phrase, defines it.[49] In this Brazil was well endowed. Its culture – music, dance, football and way of life – was immensely attractive to outsiders. Its combination of a market economy, democracy and social progress was a powerful example to the developing world. Brazil made more effort to deploy soft power. Lula stepped up its tradition of participating in UN peacekeeping missions. Leading the Haiti mission involved active peace enforcement, under chapter seven of the UN Charter, rather than peacekeeping by consent under chapter six. That was at the intersection of soft and hard power, and blurred Brazil's previous commitment to non-intervention.[50] Under what Amorim called 'the diplomacy of generosity' Brazil became a significant aid donor (though it still received concessional loans from the World Bank and Inter-American Development Bank). Its small official aid programme was augmented by big contributions to various UN agencies.[51] Its technical co-operation was aimed especially at improving social programmes and farming in African countries. Embrapa had projects in four African countries, as well as in Venezuela (for political reasons) and Panama. The government ran seminars about Bolsa Família for visiting delegations from Africa and Asia. It was symptomatic of Brazil's soft power that Bolsa Família became a synonym for conditional cash-transfer schemes, which were adopted by dozens of countries around the world, even though Mexico's Oportunidades was the first large-scale scheme of this kind. And Brazil's leadership in committing to a unilateral cut in carbon emissions at the Copenhagen summit gave it moral authority on issues of climate change and the environment.

In a memoir published in 2012, Ricardo Lagos, a former Chilean president, offered an admiring assessment of Brazil's soft power.

> Brazil today is perhaps the most coveted example of a middle power. Its markets are booming, its people are diverse and cosmopolitan, and its government is the exemplar of multilateralism. In diplomatic circles, Brazil is the most wanted representative on every panel or commission – allies of the West and also friends of the global South. In short, Brazil is objectionable to no one.[52]

But was being 'objectionable to no one' enough to achieve the global status Brazil craved? How many real partners and allies did it have? The list more or less stopped at Argentina, Uruguay, Venezuela, Bolivia, South Africa, Angola and Portugal. And having asserted its right to be heard on the world stage, it was less clear just what Brazil wanted to say. Ricupero complained of 'gestural diplomacy'. Another of the diplomatic critics told me: 'China is concerned with being, not with appearing. Brazil is obsessed with appearing, not being.' Brazilian officials said they wanted to help to make the rules, rather than just follow them. But what kind of global order would they prefer? Many would argue that Brazil was right to oppose military intervention in Iraq, and more recently in Syria. But was non-intervention always the answer to the world's conflicts and problems?

If economic growth picks up again and Brazil makes the leap towards developed status, it is possible to see the country being accepted as a global power on its own terms. But that may take a while. Until then, Brazil's conundrum is that it is half-hearted about exercising real leadership in South

America, restrained by its defensiveness and protectionism. The emergence of the Pacific Alliance showed that, contrary to Amorim's claims, the region was more divided in 2013 than it had been in 2002. This half-hearted regional leadership in turn reduced Brazil's appeal for the United States. And its frictions with the United States, in many ways a more natural ally than its fellow-BRICs, in turn reduced Brazil's sway with some of its neighbours. Globalization and the current world order had brought Brazil more benefits than problems. It might gain in stature by recognizing that.

CHAPTER THIRTEEN

An Unreformed Leviathan

On a cold Thursday afternoon, on 6 June 2012, a couple of thousand people gathered near the Municipal Theatre in the centre of São Paulo to protest against an increase in bus fares of 20 centavos, taking the fare to 3.20 reais (US$1.50). The march ended in clashes with the police. The Free Fare Movement, a small far-left group which organized it, called for daily protests which slowly grew in size and involved some acts of vandalism. For a week nobody took much notice. But that changed on 13 June when the São Paulo military police used brutal tactics to repress a march: videos showed officers firing stun grenades and rubber bullets seemingly indiscriminately at fleeing protesters and bystanders; several journalists were injured, two shot in the face with rubber bullets at close range. This prompted something to snap in a large segment of Brazilian society. The protests flowered into a spontaneous outpouring of discontent, night after night, peaking on 20 June when a total of more than a million people demonstrated in eighty cities across the country.[1]

What marketers call social classes C, D and E, who make up more than 80 per cent of the population, spend an average of three to four hours a day on public transport, in many cases on crowded buses or suburban trains. No wonder they were angry about the fare rise.[2] But if the protests echoed the *vintém* riots of 1880 in Rio de Janeiro in their immediate cause, discontent quickly went much wider than fares. It included anger at police forces that were better at brutalizing demonstrators than preventing or investigating crime. The fading of the economic boom and higher inflation added to the disgruntlement. But at its core was frustration at the poor quality of health care, public transport and schools, and anger that too much public money was squandered by politicians on corruption and waste. The protests were leaderless and resolutely non-party, organized through social media, of which Brazilians are avid users. Polls suggested that many of the demonstrators were from the middle class (old or new), but also that they enjoyed the sympathy of broad swathes of society.

The focus of popular frustration quickly turned from bus fares to the Confederations Cup – the warm-up tournament for the World Cup. The budget for the twelve stadiums for the World Cup – six new and six refurbished – stood at over \$3.5 billion (and counting), three times more than South Africa spent in hosting the previous tournament in 2010. They were some of the world's 'best and most modern stadiums', Dilma Rousseff boasted, built to the exacting requirements of FIFA, world football's discredited but self-important governing body. On Saturday, 15 June Dilma had been soundly booed when, flanked by Sepp Blatter, FIFA's president, she officially opened the Confederations Cup at the Mané Garrincha stadium in Brasília, newly built at a cost of 1 billion reais. The Brasília stadium, along with those being built in Cuiabá, Manaus and Natal, were widely derided as white elephants. None of these cities had clubs in the top division of the Brazilian football league, and matches in them rarely drew more than a few thousand spectators. In violation of an earlier pledge, the government footed most of the bill for the stadiums, while promised public transport and urban renewal projects for the World Cup were delayed or dropped. Brazilians had noticed that the government seemed to give more importance to satisfying FIFA's exacting demands than their own needs: during the protests, demonstrators held up placards demanding 'FIFA-standard' hospitals and schools.

Ironically, Dilma had set as one of her objectives improving public services. But she had done too little to achieve this. Although they faded after a few weeks, the protests catalysed a change in the public mood. In the opinion polls, Dilma's approval rating plummeted to the low thirties; though it then recovered slowly, this throws the 2014 presidential election wide open. But mayors and state governors were just as much targets of public anger as the federal government; Marina Silva was almost the only politician whose ratings rose as a result of the protests. All this came as a visible shock to the left and, to a lesser extent, the right (the establishment press quickly changed its tune from condemning the protesters as vandals to embracing them as heroes). The protests caught the PT and its allied social movements, accustomed to a monopoly of the Brazilian 'street' over the past three decades, completely off-balance; they struggled to come up with a narrative to explain them. Once the protests had outgrown the Free Fare Movement, the PT and far-left parties were jeered when they displayed party banners. One march in Brasília ended with an attempt to trash Itamaraty (the initial target was the Planalto Palace itself). Spokespeople for the PT were reduced to lamenting that the protests had been hijacked by 'fascists' or 'the right'. 'The right didn't manage to co-opt them, nor the left to interpret them,' according to Bruno Torturra, one of the founders of Mídia Ninja, a network of independent journalists whose coverage of the protests, distributed through social media sites, attracted 11 million hits a week during June, July and August 2013.[3] A less kneejerk argument by the PT held that the demonstrations were an attempt by the traditional middle class to defend its privileged status in the face of the invasion of road space, hospitals and universities by 'Class C'. That may indeed have been one strand of discontent. But it was far from being the only one. At the first big demonstration in São Paulo, on 17 June, the main banner proclaimed, 'it's not for a few cents, it's for rights', and there were cries of 'it's the revolt of the periphery'. 'Stop saying that it's about fares, it's for a better Brazil,' one young demonstrator declared.[4] 'Everyone was on the streets, it was a psychodrama, a collective catharsis,' according to Torturra. Comparisons with Occupy Wall Street, Spain's *indignados*, the Turkish protests and the Arab Spring seemed wide of the mark: Brazil had not recently suffered the excesses of finance capitalism, or authoritarian leadership. Fernando Henrique Cardoso saw a resemblance to the events of May 1968 in Paris, which he had observed as a visiting professor at the University of Nanterre: 'The street is saying: consumption is not enough, I want more . . . it's a generic dissatisfaction . . . the demonstrators don't feel represented by the parties, and I don't know if they even want to be.'[5]

In response, Dilma floundered at first. She rushed to confer with Lula and João Santana, the marketing guru who had run her 2010 campaign. Her initial response was to propose a Constituent Assembly – as if she had just woken up after falling asleep in 1984. This was widely rejected as unconstitutional – including by Vice-President Temer, a constitutional lawyer. After a meeting with governors and big-city mayors, Dilma then proposed five 'pacts'. These included promises to spend more on public transport and education and to import foreign doctors to work in remote areas while adding an extra 11,000 places at medical schools by 2017. (The mayors of São Paulo and Rio were leaned on to cancel the fare increases, just as Dom Pedro obliged his finance minister to cancel the *vintem*.) Somewhat contradictorily, another of the 'pacts' restated the government's commitment to fiscal responsibility. The most important proposal was a referendum on political reform. But this was fraught with complexity. Not only was there no sign that Congress would give its approval, but there was no consensus as to how the political system should be changed. Yet there was no doubt that many Brazilians thought that their politicians had become a self-serving and predatory class, a development that went hand in hand with a state that was both expensively bloated and yet incapable of providing the services they needed. In other words, the underlying demands from the protests were reform of the state and of the political system.

In some quarters, there was incredulity that Brazil had reached this impasse after a dozen years of PT rule. *Piauí* magazine reported that Miguel Lago, a twenty-five-year-old activist in Rio with a masters degree in political science from Sciences Po in Paris, found himself required to explain the protests to French journalists. 'When I spoke of the crisis of representation, more than one journalist asked me: "How so?" Lula, Dilma, aren't you advancing a lot?'[6] Lula himself recognized in an op-ed published under his name in the *New York Times* that the protesters wanted political institutions that are 'cleaner and more transparent'. The PT, he declared, 'needs profound renewal. It must recover its daily links with social movements and offer new solutions for new problems.'[7] But was it capable of doing this? As Marina Silva put it, the problem was that 'those who were transformers and revolutionaries later became conservative'.[8] The PT, whose leaders had begun their political lives by rebelling against Geisel's corporate state, had ended up reproducing it, becoming both its beneficiary and its prisoner.

The high price of patronage politics

In the early years of the New Republic, many political scientists both in Brazil and abroad looked at the country's political system and despaired. It was, wrote one, 'an exceptional case of party weakness'.[9] Parties multiplied, many lacked any ideology beyond the pursuit of power for its own sake, and politicians promiscuously switched between them. Yet just when Brazil's democracy seemed to be descending into chaotic ineffectiveness, political leaders came up with a formula to make the system work. Under Cardoso, Lula and Dilma, 'coalitional presidentialism' has provided stable government. Presidents have assembled multi-party, multi-regional coalitions in something akin to an informal parliamentary system.[10] In their voting record in Brasília, parties were more disciplined than outward appearance suggested. Brazil avoided both the political instability and populism that several other Latin American countries suffered over the same period.[11] But this success papered over flaws in the political system whose cost has risen inexorably.

Over the past two decades Brazil's democratic politics has been anchored at national level by the competition between Lula's PT and Cardoso's PSDB. Of the two, only the PT can claim a mass membership; the PSDB has the character of a club of middle-class technocrats and professionals. But both parties have a clear programme and an ideology, though these have changed over time. As he steered his party towards the centre, Lula covered his tracks in part by trying to polarize debate between himself and the PSDB, which he caricatured as right-wing and 'neo-liberal'. In fact, it is a managerial and modernizing centrist party that is fairly liberal on economics while supporting progressive social policy.

Neither the PT nor the PSDB has ever held more than a fifth of the seats in Congress. The 513 seats in the Chamber of Deputies (the lower house of Congress) were shared between twenty-one different parties in October 2013 (twenty-three until several merged that month). Brazil boasted the world's most fragmented political system, with 11.5 'effective parties' according to an international index which takes into account both the absolute number of parties and their relative weight in the legislature.[12] This was more even than Israel (7.3), whose party system was notoriously dysfunctional. The number of effective parties had risen from 8.7 in 1990 and 7.1 in 1998. Most of them were what political scientists call 'catch-all parties' run by professional politicians with few policy ideas but whose aim was to command a slice of the state and practise the politics of patronage in the form of government jobs and control over public contracts, and to extract federal money for public works in their districts. It is a symptom of the relative weakness of parties that cross-bench lobbies can often be as important in shaping the legislative agenda in Congress. The most important include the lobby groups for farmers (known as the *ruralistas*), evangelical Protestants, mayors, and the health care and football industries.

The PMDB, a party which has not sought the presidency since humiliating defeats in 1989 and 1994 but which is highly influential in the federal Congress and in state governments, has become the archetype of this kind of politics, though it was also practised by a slew of smaller parties. Jarbas Vasconcelos, a former governor of Pernambuco who was one of a few holdovers from the PMDB's golden era as a reforming opposition to the dictatorship, was withering about his colleagues in an interview in *Veja* in 2009:

> Today the PMDB is a party without banners, without proposals, without any bearings. It's a confederation of regional leaders, each with his own interest, and 90 per cent of them practice clientelism, with an eye mainly on official posts. [They want these posts] to do business, to earn commissions. Some still seek political prestige. But the majority of *pemedebistas* specialize in those things for which governments are denounced: manipulation of tenders, guided contracts, corruption in general.[13]

Marcos Nobre, a philosopher, has argued that *pemedebismo* is the dominant political culture in Brazil, and that its core is a 'system of vetoes', and 'the permanent postponement of definitive solutions'.[14] This has served as a force for moderation and consensus-seeking, but it can also lead to paralysis. And it constitutes a powerful obstacle to reform – especially of public spending and of politics itself. It is not hard to see in the PMDB a continuation of the PSD of the 1950s, or of Brazil's tradition of patronage politics dating back to the monarchy. The influence of this political culture may help to explain the otherwise puzzling absence in Brazil of a powerful and ideologically coherent party of the right.

The PMDB has one foot in *coronelismo* and the other in modernity. Its conservative face is symbolized by José Sarney. He has controlled the state of Maranhão for almost fifty years, representing it as federal deputy (twice), governor and senator (twice). More recently, Sarney has been senator for Amapá, a nearby newly created mini-state, while passing Maranhão to his daughter, Roseana, its governor in 1994–2002 and again since 2010, and one of its senators in 2003–9. Other relatives hold positions in Maranhão's courts and state bureaucracy. A loyal lieutenant, Edison Lobão, is Dilma's minister of energy and mines; when he took the job, he passed his seat in the Senate to his son, while his wife sits in the lower house. Sarney's family owns Maranhão's biggest media company. Far from bringing progress to Maranhão, Sarney has ruled over its continuing backwardness: it is one of the two poorest states; 61 per cent of those aged over ten who attended the state's schools, 161 of which are named after members of his family, did not complete basic education; tens of thousands of *maranhenses* migrate each year for seasonal work as cane cutters or building workers. With Lula's backing, Sarney was president of the federal Senate for six of the ten years to 2012, a post which confers influence over the government's legislative agenda and opportunities for patronage. He survived a scandal in which it was revealed that the Senate passed secret resolutions granting perks to its members and that one of his grandchildren received business from the Senate (though Sarney was not its president at the time).[15]

In fact Sarney is almost the last of his breed. His counterparts who imposed dynastic rule on other north-eastern states have given way to younger, more modern, more-or-less reformers. More typical of today's PMDB is Sérgio Cabral, Rio de Janeiro's governor since 2006. On the one hand he brought better government to the state. He appointed a capable team, who sorted out the state's chaotic finances and launched the UPP community-policing scheme. He won a second term with 66 per cent of the vote in 2010. But on the other hand he turned out to possess some traditional political vices. He enjoyed frequent foreign junkets. Of middle-class background with no career outside politics, he was revealed to be the owner of a lavish beach house worth 5 million reais (he claimed the money came from political consulting). According to a profile by Daniela Pinheiro in *Piauí* magazine, Cabral celebrated his second marriage in 2001 (to Adriana de Lourdes Ancelmo, a lawyer) with a reception for 900 guests at the Copacabana Palace, Rio's legendary luxury hotel, decorated with 4,000 dozen roses for the occasion, followed by a honeymoon in Paris.[16] His problems began in 2011 when he borrowed Eike Batista's private jet to take family and friends to Trancoso, a chic resort in Bahia, for the birthday party of Fernando Cavendish, a construction magnate. This escapade was exposed in tragic circumstances when a helicopter taking some of Cabral's group on the last leg of the trip crashed, killing seven people. A congressional investigation found that Cavendish both had close ties to *bicheiros*, as the mafia types behind Rio's illegal numbers racket are known, and had accumulated contracts worth 1 billion reais with the Rio state government, some awarded without tender. Then Cabral became the object of revenge by Anthony Garotinho, a former Rio governor who also faced corruption claims and whom he had used in his political ascent only to break with him as soon as he was elected to the governorship. Garotinho released photos of various festivities when Cabral took 150 people, including Cavendish, to Paris to celebrate his receipt of the Légion d'Honneur. In one picture, Cavendish was seen fooling around at a dinner with several secretaries (ministers) in the state government, all with napkins tied around their heads. Garotinho then claimed that Cabral's wife's law firm derived 60 per cent of its fees from work for suppliers to, or organs of, the state government, up from 2 per cent before her husband took office. All this turned Cabral into Brazil's most unpopular politician: when the protests broke out in June 2013, demonstrators camped outside his flat in Leblon, Rio's most expensive district, for fifty days. Although many Brazilian politicians have the hide of an alligator, it seemed unlikely that Cabral would dare show his face at the World Cup final in the expensively revamped Maracanã stadium.

The PMDB was far from alone in practising patrimonialism and patronage politics. It was simply the biggest among a large number of such outfits. It had joined Cardoso's government as a junior partner. After the *mensalão*, it became a mainstay of Lula's coalition. Its status was reinforced by Dilma's choice of Michel Temer, a wily PMDB politician from São Paulo (and unofficial leader of that city's influential Syrian–Lebanese community) as her vice-president. Following Lula's doctrine of isolating the PSDB and the opposition, Dilma built the largest governing coalition ever assembled since 1985, comprising twelve parties (of which seven held ministries) ranging from communist to right-wing populist with a total of 400 deputies, or almost four-fifths of the lower house.[17] The incongruity of this kind of alliance-building was highlighted in the 2012 municipal election, when an uncomfortable Lula posed for a photograph with Paulo Maluf, the corrupt conservative protégé of the dictatorship, to support the successful campaign of the PT's Fernando Haddad for mayor of São Paulo.

The high price of coalitional presidentialism taken to these extremes was symbolized by the ever-expanding size of the Cabinet under Lula and Dilma. In May 2013 Dilma appointed Guilherme Afif Domingos to run the newly created ministry for small and micro business. With this, the number of ministries in the federal government rose to thirty-nine. That was almost double the average number of ministries that the mainly developed countries of the OECD manage to make do with, and double the size of the Cabinet in China. As well as small business, Dilma had separate portfolios for ports, fishing, sports, tourism, civil aviation, women's rights and human rights. With no apparent irony, she said Afif's job was to cut red tape. In accepting, Afif's sense of irony seemed to have deserted him too: in a long career in politics in conservative and liberal parties, he had campaigned against Brazil's high tax burden, to which his new ministry was now adding. A senior adviser to Dilma insisted to me that cutting the number of ministries wouldn't reduce the size of the federal bureaucracy.[18] But the baroque contraption that was the Brazilian Cabinet did multiply the number of senior patronage posts and magnified the pressures to spend in ways which are not socially useful.

Spend, spend, spend

Factor in the chronic fiscal deficit, and total government spending in Brazil was around 40 per cent of GDP. Given the country's level of economic development, this was an unusually high number.* Brazil's drama was that it taxed and spent like a European country but the quality of its schools, hospitals, public transport and police was distinctly Latin American. (Chile managed to provide better public services than Brazil with a tax take of 21 per cent of GDP, though admittedly it is a much smaller country and its health care and pension systems are largely privatized.) To make matters worse, the state was not investing enough in things that would boost productivity and economic growth, such as infrastructure (see chapter eleven). And to cap it all, neither the tax system nor public spending served to reduce income inequality – as they do in most developed countries – but rather they reinforced it. In other words, Brazil's income distribution would be less unfair if the state did not intervene in it at all.[19]

---

* Irrespective of political preferences concerning the size of the state, the global trend is for public spending to grow as a share of the economy as countries become more developed. That is mainly because development usually requires the provision of more sophisticated public goods (such as infrastructure, basic scientific research and good policing) but also because richer countries tend to be democracies, whose citizens demand public provision of health care, education and welfare.

How had this situation come about? In the 'national-developmentalist' era between 1930 and 1985, from Getúlio Vargas to the military dictatorship, the state became more and more involved in the economy but provided education and social benefits only for a relatively privileged minority. Democratization mobilized popular demands for public services and a welfare state. These demands were embodied in the 1988 constitution, with its declaration of a universal right to free health care and education and its creation of a much broader and deeper social safety net. But rather than reforming the old corporate state, which was generous to its limited number of beneficiaries, the rudiments of a democratic welfare state were grafted on to it. And since the constitution reflected the political weakness of the federal government and the relative strength of the state governors in the late 1980s, it decentralized revenue more than it did responsibilities, leading to duplication, waste and lack of accountability. The result was a horrendously expensive and inefficient arrangement. Contrary to many gloomy judgements in the early years of the New Republic, the Cardoso and Lula governments managed to achieve economic and political stability and to expand social provision, despite the demands of the constitution. But the slowdown in economic growth made this balancing act more difficult.

Cardoso began partially to dismantle and reform the corporate state. Privatizations reduced taxpayer subsidies for economic activities. Decentralization was partially reversed by fiscal reforms. Lula took important steps towards making public services universal, and to strengthen the social safety net. But in giving something to the have-nots, he didn't take away the privileges of the haves. And Lula's second government and Dilma's resurrected the discretionary subsidies to business (as well as unions) that underlay the corporate state of Vargas and Geisel. By allying with the PMDB in the aftermath of the *mensalão*, Lula allied with 'the heart of the corporate state', according to Nobre.[20]

The main problem was not so much that the federal bureaucracy was hugely swollen in itself. The rudiments of a professional, meritocratic civil service put in place by Vargas survive. Federal civil servants, in particular, have become increasingly well qualified, and the same goes for some states and bigger municipalities. A study by the Inter-American Development Bank found that Brazil has the most meritocratic and effective government bureaucracy in Latin America.[21] This included some centres of excellence, such as Itamaraty – one used to come across diplomats in key administrative posts in other ministries, in the manner of French *énarques*, though the practice has declined under the PT. Other examples are the Banco do Brasil; the national statistics institute (IBGE), and IPEA, a government-linked economic think-tank which survived an attempt by the PT to politicize it. Brazil produces one of the best household surveys in the Americas, according to statisticians.[22]

But meritocracy was disfigured by the large number of patronage appointments at senior levels of government. Under Cardoso the presidency had no fewer than 20,000 senior jobs in the bureaucracy in its gift. That number expanded under Lula and Dilma. They were divided up among political parties in return for their support for the government. Although the politicians usually appointed technically qualified supporters to these jobs, they were often not the best available.[23] And the PT governments were generous to the federal bureaucracy, whose unions supported the party. Between 2003 and 2009 the number of federal employees increased by around 10 per cent, but the total federal wage bill more than doubled in nominal terms (while inflation over the period was less than 50 per cent).[24]

It is transfer payments of various kinds that are at the heart of the misplaced priorities of Brazilian public spending. The federal government collects most of the taxes, but it transfers much of the money to the states (which got 25 per cent of the total tax pie in 2010) and municipalities (18.3 per cent). So public spending in Brazil is quite decentralized: after transfers, the federal government gets 58 per cent of total revenues and states and municipalities 42 per cent.[25] It is also very rigid. Add in other mandatory items of federal spending (on wages, pensions and debt service for example), and not only is there little left over for public investment but the government has relatively little fiscal flexibility. If budget spending has to be held back to meet fiscal targets, it is discretionary items that bear the brunt. So for example, in 2013 Brazil's recently expanded army of diplomats found their travel budgets slashed, reducing their usefulness.

The pension time-bomb

If public spending is to meet the needs of a changing society, the government needs to devote more resources to health and a bit more to education, and less to the machinery of government and to privileged interest groups. It also needs to be less generous to pensioners. That is because Brazil is ageing fast. The decline in mortality that prompted rapid population growth for much of the twentieth century has now been outpaced by a dramatic fall in the fertility rate: the average Brazilian woman had more than six children in the 1960s, but now has fewer than two. The country is enjoying what researchers call a 'demographic bonus', in which the working-age population is at its largest in relation to dependants (children and old people). But the demographic bonus will run out as early as 2018, according to an estimate by IBGE.[26] From the mid-2020s, the working-age population will start to shrink in absolute terms, according to the World Bank. The elderly population will increase dramatically. While it took more than a century for France's elderly population (aged sixty-five or above) to increase from 7 per cent to 14 per cent of the total, the same change will take place in Brazil in just two decades (2011–31), the Bank reckons.[27]

The problem is that youthful Brazil already spends almost as big a share of national income on pensions as the geriatric societies of southern Europe. Only 11 per cent of Brazilians are over sixty-five, and yet pensions command almost as big a slice of GDP as in Greece, where the elderly make up 29 per cent of the population.[28] That is mainly because of the generosity of the 1988 constitution when it came to pensioners. Many Brazilians, especially those working in the public sector, are allowed to retire early on a large percentage of their final salary, and to draw their pension even if they get another government job. In practice, the average retirement age is fifty-four, and the average pension is equal to 70 per cent of final salary. Brazil is also uniquely generous in allowing bereaved spouses to collect almost the full pension of their deceased partner for the rest of their lives (and in some cases, such as the armed forces, even the children of the deceased may claim). And pensions are automatically raised in line with the increase in the minimum wage. The result of all this is that pension spending rose from 2 per cent of GDP in 1988 to 11.2 per cent in 2010. The National Social Security Institute (INSS), which provides pensions to formal private-sector workers, collected 5.8 per cent of GDP in contributions in 2010 but paid out pensions and benefits equal to 7.3 per cent of GDP. The federal government and states and municipalities pay out around 4 per cent of GDP each year to former public-sector workers, of which 1.7 per cent of GDP is unfunded.[29] In other words, the pension system already requires a taxpayer subsidy of 3.2 per cent of GDP.

The partial pension reforms of 1999 and 2003 (eventually implemented in 2012) capped bigger pensions and eliminated some of the pension privileges of civil servants, but only for new entrants. They have served only to slow the rate at which the pension burden will increase. Even so, the World Bank reckons that pension spending will double as a share of GDP (to 22.4 per cent) by 2050. The number of pensioners will grow at 4 per cent a year for the next decade, which is now faster than the rate of economic growth. Further reform is essential, especially curbing early retirement and survivor benefits, and raising the retirement age (currently sixty-five for men and sixty for women) in line with rising life expectancy. Though it would be politically tricky to do, breaking the automatic link between the minimum wage and pension benefits would do much to trim the increase in pension spending. As Fabio Giambiagi, one of Brazil's leading pension specialists, points out, for each increase of 5 per cent in the minimum wage, INSS spending rises by 2 per cent on top of its vegetative growth.[30]

The non-contributory minimum pension for rural workers and the elderly poor enshrined in the constitution have been important in reducing poverty and income inequality. Nevertheless, pension spending taken as a whole is wildly skewed to the better-off. The preponderance of pensions in total spending is the main reason why the richest 20 per cent of Brazilians receive 3.6 times more from public social spending – defined as including education, health care, pensions and Bolsa Família – than the poorest 20 per cent, according to the World Bank. The pension bonanza is also unfair in another way: Brazil spends far more on its old people than on its children. Net public transfers per capita to the over-sixty-fives are almost ten times more than to under-fifteens, compared with around twice more in Sweden, Spain and Finland, the Bank finds.[31]

While spending less on pensions, Brazil needs to spend a bit more on education, especially in expanding pre-school coverage and in improving the quality of secondary schooling. But demographic change also means that the number of Brazilians of school age has already started to fall. So it is insane for the Congress and government to have written into law a requirement to expand public spending on education as a proportion of GDP from the current figure of 5.2 per cent to 10 per cent by 2020. Brazil needs to spend its education budgets more effectively; health care deserves to get a bigger slice of any extra spending. As Brazilians get older, they will require more, and more expensive, health care. Infectious diseases have given way to rich-world ailments – heart disease and cancer – as the most common cause of death. Yet the share of public health-care spending in Brazil is well below the norm in rich countries.

Other transfer payments are less obvious, but equally unfair. They involve a series of more or less hidden subsidies, a tradition dating from the 'national-developmentalist' state, as Marcos Lisboa (the economist who advised Palocci) and Zeina Latif have recently argued.[32] These range from the subsidies on earmarked loans to favoured businesses by public banks, to tax breaks for the Manaus Free Trade Zone and to industries singled out by Dilma's government, to the financing of labour unions through a compulsory payroll tax. Business groups are complicit in these arrangements. The argument of Lisboa and Latif echoes that of the late Mario Henrique Simonsen, Geisel's finance minister, who in a long cover essay in *Veja* in 1987 lambasted Brazil's *capitalismo cartorial* ('capitalism of notaries'), which he feared with some reason was being entrenched in the new constitution. He saw this as the state seeking to resolve the problems of a political, economic and financial elite using taxpayers' money and pretending that it is promoting the public good. They dance in line to be able to continue drinking champagne. In this deception, curiously, the extremes of right and left meet, like the cobra that bites its own tail.[33]

Simonsen argued that the state always publicized its giveaways but hid the fact that it is the taxpayer who pays the bill for this generosity.

Cupidity and corruption

Apart from pensions and hidden subsidies, a third big misallocation of public money involves the voracious cupidity of a predatory class of professional politicians, which results in generous benefits for insiders as well as in outright corruption. These politicians and their retainers were the heirs to Brazil's long tradition of patrimonialism – of eliding private and public interests – and the beneficiaries of an incomplete political and judicial framework for accountability. The Congress and the judiciary set a poor example to the nation. The constitution fixed as a ceiling for public-sector pay the salary of a supreme court justice. This was generous, at 26,700 reais (around US$13,000) a month in 2013 (plus extra perks). In December 2010 Congress voted to raise its own salaries by 62 per cent, bringing them into line with those of the supreme court. Members of Congress get fifteen monthly instalments a year, taking their total salary to a third more than their counterparts in the US and more than four times that of Spanish parliamentarians.* In addition, they get 80,000 reais a month with which to pay staff, 34,000 reais a month for office expenses, a housing allowance, subsidized flights and free health insurance.[34] Many politicians employ relatives in their offices, at public expense. After the approval of a freedom of information law in 2012 it emerged that the federal Congress employed 25,000 staff, of whom 1,500 were paid more than the ceiling. There were plenty of individual cases of plunder: a court clerk in Brasília received the equivalent of US$226,000 a year; a judge in São Paulo was found to have received payments totalling US$361,500 in a *month*. State legislators in Sarney's Maranhão paid themselves eighteen monthly salaries a year (of US$10,000 each).[35]

The total public payroll expanded by 30 per cent in the decade to 2012, to 9.5 million. Two-thirds of this increase took place in state and municipal governments. Founding new municipalities was a particularly lucrative

---

* The 14th and 15th salaries were abolished in late 2013, except for the first and last years of a legislator's mandate.

industry. Almost 1,200 new ones have been created since 1990 by dividing existing ones, taking the total to 5,568. Although this increase of 27 per cent was broadly in line with the increase in the population over the same period, the United States, with half as many people again as Brazil, manages with 3,141 counties. Municipal legislatures alone (i.e. councillors and their staff, but not municipal officials) comprise almost 230,000 people, all lavishly rewarded by the taxpayer. For the 90 per cent of municipalities that contain fewer than 50,000 inhabitants, transfers from the federal government account for 85 per cent of their budgets. Nearly all the newly created municipalities fall into this category. Though the supreme court made an effort to halt the creation of new municipalities, the process goes on: in October 2013 the Senate approved a law allowing 188 new municipalities (and regularizing another fifty-seven), creating an extra 30,000 public-sector jobs.[36]

On top of this legal exploitation of the taxpayer, there was much siphoning off of public money at all levels of government. Some of this was trivial, but revealing: Marco Maia, the PT president of the chamber of deputies in 2011, invented an expenses-paid meeting in Spain so that he could watch Real Madrid play Barcelona; he paid for the trip only after being found out. Then there were systematic schemes, such as payments of several million reais from ministries to shell companies or fake NGOs, which prompted the fall of agriculture and labour ministers at the start of Dilma's government. In 2006 the federal police revealed a scam (colourfully dubbed in the press *Sanguessuga* or 'bloodsucker') under which a ring of officials and former parliamentarians had sold more than a thousand ambulances to municipalities across the country at more than double their cost. Though it attracted less publicity, corruption was probably more prevalent in local government than in Brasília. Sometimes it was for private gain, sometimes to raise money for party funds and election campaigns. Government contractors (especially construction companies) which paid bribes were just as guilty as the politicians and officials.

Brazilian politicians, as a class, enjoyed a deep-rooted sense of entitlement and a tradition of impunity. They could only be tried by the higher courts. Those accused would often resign to avoid expulsion from Congress, only to stand again at the next election. They could often count on the solidarity of their colleagues. In 2013 Natan Donadon, a PMDB deputy from Rondônia, became the first parliamentarian to be imprisoned since 1985 when he was convicted by the supreme court of stealing 8 million reais when finance director of the Rondônia state legislature in 1988–95. Nevertheless, the chamber in a secret vote decided against expelling him. In the same year, José Roberto Arruda, a former governor of the Federal District, was sentenced to five years in jail for padding a contract.

Society fights back

Yet it would be a gross exaggeration to imagine that Brazilian politics was irredeemably corrupt and clientelistic. There were plenty of examples of reforming state and city governments. One, dating back to the late 1980s, was the north-eastern state of Ceará. When Tasso Jereissati, a young reformer from the PSDB, was elected as its governor in 1987, he broke with the north-east's clientelistic tradition. He began by cleaning up the state's finances, eliminating 40,000 jobs (out of a total payroll of 146,000) held by non-existent 'phantom' workers. He launched a far-reaching community health programme, hiring and training 8,400 women as community health promoters, and invested heavily in education.[37] The PSDB and its allies continued to run the state for the next twenty years, though the reformist impulse eventually petered out amid political squabbles. More recently, the PSDB has been successful in running Minas Gerais. When Aécio Neves was elected as governor in 2002, the state was nearly bankrupt. He appointed a team of public management specialists under Antonio Anastasia, an academic, who boosted tax revenues, streamlined procurement and cut costs in what they called a 'management shock'. After two terms of Neves, *mineiros* elected Anastasia, who is stolidly uncharismatic, to succeed him. Businessmen rate Minas Brazil's best-run state, according to one survey; the state spends over 8 per cent of its budget on public investment; poverty has fallen faster than in the country as a whole, and Minas has the best-performing schools.

In Pernambuco Eduardo Campos of the centrist Brazilian Socialist Party (PSB) achieved something similar. The grandson of Miguel Arraes, Pernambuco's old-fashioned socialist governor both before and after the dictatorship, Campos combines a faint air of a traditional political boss with a large dose of modern management-speak and a drive to create a knowledge-based economy. As governor, not only did he face down the labour unions over school reform but he brought in private managers to run state hospitals and formed private–public partnerships for infrastructure. Curitiba under Jaime Lerner, an architect and planner who was three times its mayor and twice governor of Paraná for different parties, became legendary for urban innovation, having invented the bus rapid-transit system widely copied elsewhere across Latin American and the world. The PT was often effective in city governments. In Porto Alegre it promoted (though did not invent) participatory budgeting, a scheme whereby the budget was drawn up by the mayor in consultation with elected community delegates. This was much copied elsewhere in the world. But participatory budgeting was not without flaws. It was sometimes a means to bypass a politically hostile council chamber, while the community elections suffered from dwindling participation.[38]

Above all, Brazil's media and a growing number of civil society watchdogs and NGOs kept a close watch on the abuse of public money and power. The country possesses the most effective public-audit bodies in Latin America, of comparable quality to those in developed countries.[39] They regularly turned up evidence of wrongdoing. Despite their footdragging, the courts started to act. While there was some anti-PT bias in the media's hysteria over the *mensalão*, the case was widely seen as establishing an important precedent, that those in power were not above the law. That rule, however, should also have been applied to a number of transgressors from the PMDB and other parties. And while the national media enjoy political independence, that is not always true at local level. The share of media owned by politicians ranged from 6 per cent in Rio Grande do Sul to 100 per cent in Rondônia.[40]

Nevertheless, Brazil suffered a vicious circle in which fear of corruption led to the imposition of self-defeatingly rigid conditions for public contracts. 'The excess of controls has reached the point that [government] action atrophies,' Antonio Anastasia complained. 'Officials think it's better to do nothing, so as not to run risks.'[41] This was allied to a general lack of capacity in project planning that afflicted governments at all levels, and contributed to the country's failure to expand and renew its infrastructure. While accepting that this 'cult of control' had come about for understandable reasons, Anastasia argued that a system of retrospective scrutiny would be more effective.

One of the best antidotes to corruption would be a more effective judiciary. The judiciary is fairly politically independent; the 1988 constitution empowered public prosecutors, many of whom have showed zeal. But the courts are hopelessly slow and inefficient. They have abused their independence to create a gravy train. Spending on the judiciary's staff rose fivefold between 1988 and 1997, compared with a 78 per cent increase in the federal government payroll in that period. The courts in Rio de Janeiro alone employ 20,000 people. The Labour Courts are another example of featherbedding: their annual running cost was 10 billion reais in 2010.[42]

Despite this surplus of staff, the average length of time for a case to be completed is around ten years. The courts are clogged: there were around 36 million ongoing cases in 2006.[43] A modest reform in that year made supreme court decisions, if agreed by eight of the eleven justices, binding on lower courts; another restricted the court's brief to cases of public interest. This has helped to speed up the work of the supreme court, but not by much. Apart from the slowness of justice, the other main complaint is its partiality.

Those able to afford top lawyers can delay a case almost endlessly. According to Joaquim Barbosa,

> Brazil is a country that punishes many poor people, black people and people without connections. People are treated differently according to status, skin colour and the money they have ... A powerful person can hire a powerful lawyer with connections in the judiciary, who can maintain contacts with judges without any control by the public prosecutor or by society. And then surprising decisions follow.[44]

In a notorious case, Antonio Pimenta Neves, a prominent journalist, who in 2000 murdered a much younger subordinate when she broke off their affair, managed to avoid going to prison for ten years. According to *Folha de São Paulo*, when it comes to investigations involving politicians, the federal police took an average of two years to complete an investigation, double the norm for other cases; similarly, cases opened against politicians by the supreme court typically dragged on for more than ten years without a verdict. *Folha* found that of 258 cases involving politicians (166 of them federal legislators) at the supreme court, only two were ready for trial.[45]

Another defence against corruption would be if the electoral system did more to promote the accountability of politicians to voters. On the whole, Brazilian voters do tend to reward good governments and punish corruption. But this is harder when it comes to legislatures. The Congress is elected under proportional representation, but each state constitutes a single electoral district. São Paulo, for example, has seventy deputies, each in theory representing all of the state's 45 million people. They are chosen under an 'open list' system: deputies are elected according to the share of the total vote of each party or alliance, but who is selected from each party list depends on the votes they accrue as an individual. Several problems flow from this. First, because of the size of the electoral district, people have much less idea of who their deputy is than their mayor, governor or president. Perversely, this system encourages both candidates from organized interest groups (e.g. the police or the evangelical churches) and celebrities: in 2010 a clown and comic who called himself Tiririca and stood as an anti-politician was the legislative candidate with the most votes (1.3 million) in São Paulo and Brazil.

Second, such large multi-member districts encourage the multiplication of parties. In addition, the judiciary has been consistently accommodating of party fragmentation. When Congress approved a law introducing a threshold of 5 per cent of the national vote for a party to obtain seats in the legislature, due to come into effect in 2010, the supreme court inexplicably struck it down. In another bizarre decision, the electoral tribunal ruled that new parties could inherit party funds and free television time at elections – a crucial campaign tool – in proportion to the number of deputies they attracted.

A third drawback of the system is that it makes campaigning hugely expensive to reach such a large group of potential voters. Money is as central to Brazilian elections as it is in the United States. Although parties get free television time in proportion to their votes at the previous election, they still spend massively on campaign events, on producing their television commercials and on paying people to stand around at road junctions waving flags and handing out leaflets. In such a large country, a presidential candidate also incurs huge travel costs. The best estimates are that a presidential campaign costs anywhere from 100 million to 200 million reais. Much of this comes from corporate donations, especially from construction companies and banks, not all of which are declared. Of the ten biggest donors to the PT, six were construction companies with contracts in Venezuela, *Veja* noted.[46] Companies tend to spread their donations around, offering smaller sums to the opposition.

A fourth problem was that unlike other federal states, such as the United States and Germany, Brazil over-represents sparsely populated states not just in the Senate but in the lower house too (as does Argentina). According to population, São Paulo should have 110 seats, rather than its current seventy, in the Chamber of Deputies, while several states should have just one, rather than the minimum of eight (up from six under the military regime). To make matters worse, the 1988 constitution created three new sparsely populated states: the former federal territories of Amapá (population: 700,000 in 2012) and Roraima (470,000 in 2012) and, more justifiably, Tocantins (1.4 million) carved from Goiás. The small (in population) states of the north and north-east tend to elect more conservative backwoodsmen than the south and south-east. This over-representation was by common consent almost impossible to reverse.

The most logical reform would be to split larger states into several electoral districts, each of six to eight members, and to combine this with a threshold for representation in the lower house of 5 per cent of the national vote. This would reduce the number of parties, cut the cost of campaigning and bring a greater sense of accountability. But the PT had other ideas: it places more importance on requiring campaigns to be financed exclusively from public funds, and it wants a closed list of candidates (i.e. their order on the ballot determined by the party leadership). Others want to extend the presidential term to five years but ban re-election, at least for a consecutive term.

The question raised by the protests was whether the beneficaries of the existing system would be capable of changing it. Some reform seemed possible, though it is likely to be brought in gradually. Already, some important changes have been introduced since 1988, including the alignment of the presidential and congressional elections in the same year. The introduction of electronic voting in the late 1990s eliminated electoral fraud: the kind of shenanigans that happened in Florida in the US presidential election of 2000 would be impossible in Brazil. Following a grass-roots campaign, in 2010 the Congress approved a law (dubbed *ficha limpa* or clean record) barring politicians found guilty of crimes or misdemeanours by a higher court from standing for office, even if they had yet to exhaust the appeal process. However, the supreme court ruled that this would apply only in future. It meant that some thoroughly discredited politicians got a new, but perhaps final, lease of life in the 2010 election. They included Jader Barbalho, a PMDB senator accused of siphoning off more than 1 billion reais in public funds. Paulo Maluf was convicted in a lower court of over-invoicing on public works (and faces an Interpol arrest warrant on charges of money laundering should he ever leave Brazil), yet was still elected as a federal deputy for São Paulo with 497,000 votes. Having initially been barred, Anthony Garotinho was elected a deputy for Rio with 605,000 votes.

The campaign for the *ficha limpa* law, led by NGOs and ordinary Brazilians acting through social media, seemed like a sign of things to come. It was true that more Brazilian households received transfer payments – including pensions, Bolsa Família and other benefits, the figure was around 40 million – than paid income tax. But the protests of June 2013 suggested that Brazil's social transformation of the past two decades has generated much more demanding citizens. That was not before time.

CHAPTER FOURTEEN

Brazil's Century?

The only previous time that Brazil hosted the football World Cup, in 1950, it proved to be a national humiliation. On paper, Brazil had the best team in the world. The government of what was then the Federal District built the Maracanã stadium for the big occasion. Brazil duly reached the final, where it faced Uruguay. On Sunday, 16 July the Maracanã's vast open terracing was packed to overflowing: the official attendance of 173,850 paying spectators was a world record for a sporting event, never mind the officials and other free-loaders who pushed the total close to 200,000. At the start of the second half, Brazil scored a goal. Then the unthinkable happened: in the space of thirteen minutes, late in the game, Uruguay scored twice to win the tournament.

Nelson Rodrigues, the playwright and journalist, summed up the outcome in characteristically hyperbolic terms: 'Everywhere has its irremediable national catastrophe, something like a Hiroshima. Our catastrophe, our Hiroshima, was the defeat by Uruguay in 1950.' Roberto DaMatta, the anthropologist, has echoed that view in more sober terms, describing that day as

> perhaps the greatest tragedy in contemporary Brazilian history. Because it happened collectively and brought a united vision of a loss of a historic opportunity. Because it happened at the beginning of a decade in which Brazil was looking to assert itself as a nation with a great future.[1]

Eight years later, when Brazil's squad set off for the 1958 World Cup in Sweden, it did so amid a climate of national pessimism about its prospects, which Rodrigues attributed to that fateful day in 1950, 'a national humiliation that nothing, absolutely nothing, can cure'. He insisted that Brazil had the best players in the world. 'Only one thing trips us up,' he concluded, a 'mongrel complex . . . a problem of faith in ourselves'.[2] His phrase *complexo de vira-latas* ('mongrel complex') entered the language. So when Lula talked repeatedly of Brazil as a country that had recovered its self-esteem, and that the award of the Olympics to Rio meant that Brazil was recognized by the world as a 'first-class country', he was declaring that the *complexo de vira-latas* had at last been overcome.

That rang true. Over the past twenty years Brazil has gone a long way towards meeting the challenges it faced when it emerged from dictatorship, those of creating a robust democracy, a stable and more dynamic economy and of reducing its yawning social inequalities. In the process Brazil has avoided some of the pitfalls to which its neighbours have succumbed. Liberal economic reform under Cardoso was the result of a broad political consensus and was negotiated democratically. It was not the work of a Pinochet, or a messianic strongman such as Argentina's Carlos Menem or Peru's Alberto Fujimori. That made it harder to achieve but harder to unpick. Lula's social policies avoided the unsustainable redistributive populism of a Chávez, or even of Argentina's Cristina Fernández. Brazil's leaders have worked within the rules and institutions of democracy. They have set a welcome example to Latin America and the world that progressive social change, representative democracy and the market economy are compatible. Given his popularity at the time, Lula might have secured a constitutional change to allow him to run for a third time in 2010. It was to his credit that he did not seek to do so.

Nevertheless, there were clear signs that the cycle of economic reform and social progress unleashed by the establishment of democracy and by the Real Plan had run its course. As they celebrate the World Cup in June and July 2014 and the Rio Olympics two years afterwards, the country's leaders can no longer be as confident as they might have been a few years ago that these events will serve to showcase Brazil's arrival on the world stage as a new global power. Rather, Brazil's growing pains and frustrations are likely to be on display alongside its achievements and its rise. Felipe Scolari, the manager of the national team, is surely right when he says that the country will put on a good party, and that the vast majority of visiting fans will enjoy themselves.[3] But it would be surprising if many of the visitors do not run into problems with public transport. And many Brazilians expect further protests in the period between the World Cup and the presidential election of October 2014.

The election seemed likely to be a close contest. Dilma Rousseff and the PT were counting on popular satisfaction with full employment and the increase in wages over the past decade as well as popular gratitude towards Lula to secure her another term. Fast forward a further four years, and the government was likely to be able to count on a significant increase in oil revenue. This was the case for André Singer's contention that Lulismo had created a lasting realignment in Brazilian politics. Yet the protests of June 2013 suggested an alternative reading of the popular mood. After twelve years in office the PT looked tired and bereft of ideas. Its rapprochement with the corporate state had rendered it incapable of providing the improved public services and better infrastructure that Brazilians were demanding. That poses the question as to whether the PT's attachment to corporatism has become the main obstacle to the continued success of Lulismo. Certainly, the opposition – in the person of Eduardo Campos, Marina Silva or Aécio Neves – had a chance of winning.

Look a bit further ahead, and DaMatta's evocation of 'a loss of a historic opportunity' in 1950 has a haunting relevance today, not just for events on the football pitch. For evidence that countries can miss historic opportunities, Brazilians have only to look at their neighbour further south, Argentina. In 1913 its income per head was on a par with that of France and Germany, and far ahead of Italy's or Spain's. That was thanks to three decades of growth averaging 5 per cent a year, driven by exports from the Pampas, foreign (mainly British) investment, especially in railways, and immigration. Since then, Argentina has lost ground against western Europe almost continuously. Uniquely, it had development in its grasp and then squandered it. Growth slowed partly as the Pampas became fully exploited, because of Argentina's difficulties in industrializing and because a weakened Britain cast the country adrift after the Second World War. But Argentina's decline was mainly a result of the distributional conflicts and political instability that accompanied the emergence of Peronism – an inward-looking, populist movement – as the country's dominant political force. Fortunately Brazil has several padlocks against this kind of political inversion. They include the diversity of the economy, its long (if sometimes truncated) tradition of representative government, its consensual political culture, its open society and the strength of its independent judiciary and media.

Brazil has amassed some formidable economic strengths. They include its farming, its oil, gas and ethanol industries, and a growing base of science and research. And the reforms of Cardoso and Lula's first government, together with the income from the commodity boom, have endowed the country with stronger defences against economic turbulence in the wider world. Despite the recent weakening of the macroeconomic framework, international reserves stand at a record level (of US$376 billion in mid-November 2013, equal to almost two years' worth of imports), the country is a net foreign creditor and public debt, though rising, is manageable. But none of this is a reason for complacency.

Will the twenty-first century be 'Brazil's century', as Lula proclaimed? That, of course, grants the country many decades in which to achieve its potential at last. Nevertheless, the starting point must be to recognize that Brazil once again has a problem of low economic growth. And faster growth is vital if the country is to continue the task of narrowing its still intolerable socio-economic inequalities and providing opportunities to all its citizens. The faster expansion of 1994–2010 owed much to the pay-off from stabilization, to the commodity boom induced by China's industrialization, to the world liquidity glut and to the incorporation into the formal labour force of millions of under-occupied Brazilians. All of those motors are slowing, if not sputtering.

In 2013 FIESP, the São Paulo industrialists' lobby, published a blueprint for the next fifteen years that set as a goal doubling the country's income per head – to US$22,000, or roughly that of Portugal, Poland or Chile today – and to raise its health and education indicators to those of developed countries. It reckons this would require growth averaging 5.3 per cent a year and an increase in investment (private and public) from its current level of 18 per cent of GDP to 24 per cent. Raising Brazil's game in this way is almost inconceivable without a new round of structural reform. From now on, faster growth will depend increasingly on improving the country's dismal productivity. That requires greater efforts to improve education and infrastructure. But it also means more capital investment, and thus more savings. André Lara Resende, one of the economists of the Real Plan, points out that from the 1950s onwards all the periods of rapid growth in Brazil were a result of an increase in public investment, financed either through forced savings (extracted from the population through inflation) or external savings (in the form of foreign debt or foreign investment).[4] That was because private savings were always low. And the public sector continues to be a net dis-saver (its debt payments are higher than public investment). Since neither inflation nor a return to large-scale foreign indebtedness is palatable, and since foreign investment can always slow, this suggests the need to raise savings, either private or public or both. Unless oil revenues come to the rescue, that in turn points to the need to lower the tax burden (or at least prevent it from rising further) and to reallocate public spending so that more goes to investment and less to current spending. This means reviewing the kind of state the country needs in the twenty-first century. Mario Covas's speech in the Senate of twenty-five years ago has an uncanny relevance today:

> Enough of spending without having the money. Enough of so many subsidies, so many tax breaks, so many unjustified privileges. Enough of jobs for the boys. Enough of notaries … Brazil doesn't just need a fiscal shock. It needs, as well, a capitalist shock, a shock of free initiative subjected to risk and not only rewards.

It is hard to see Brazil succeeding in raising its growth rate without tax and fiscal reforms – preferably an overarching grand bargain that simplifies the tax system, makes lower tiers of government responsible for raising more of their own revenues, and reins in the growth of pension spending and the subsidies that Covas referred to. If the government is to spend more on health care, education, better policing, sewerage and infrastructure, as it should, it will have to spend less on other things. Similarly, Brazil needs to rebuild the state's capacity to carry out project planning and execution. At the same time, the country can ill afford not to pursue labour and union reforms, which would balance the rights of workers and employers, and allow more flexibility to negotiate the relationship between the two. That ought to have the effect of continuing to reduce the proportion of the labour force that works in the informal economy, devoid of all legal protection. And Brazil's companies are unlikely to become more competitive unless more is done to open the economy to international trade.

The positivists versus the citizens

Brazil has an allergy to liberalism. Roberto Campos, one of the country's more important liberal economists, wrote that 'admitting to liberalism, explicitly, is as outlandish in a country with a *dirigiste* culture as having sex in public' (and even he cut his teeth in public life as an official in Kubitschek's dirigiste government).[5] There were reasons for this – and they are why Brazil is different than the United States, with which it so often likes to compare itself.

From colonial times until the dictatorship, an abiding preoccupation of Brazil's leaders was to hold together a vast territory of difficult geography, where establishing communications and the conditions for prosperous and healthy human life was enormously difficult. As a result, in Brazil it was the state that created the nation, rather than the nation creating the government, as happened in the United States. It also meant that unlike in Spanish America, the rulers of the state were ever conscious of the need to consult local notables in order to conserve national unity and prevent secession. Slavery – and the fear of slave revolt – was another reason for the need for a united front. It also distorted the priorities of the state in ways that set back Brazil's development for centuries, and condemned it to the status of the country of the eternal future. The tragic consequence of a society of masters and slaves was that the state, even as it set about developing the economy, failed to invest in the education, health and safety of the great mass of poorer Brazilians. And it is only since 1988 that Brazil has even proposed to become a society in which the rule of law should apply equally to all.

Against this background, when liberalism did emerge in the nineteenth century it was quickly bastardized by positivism and patrimonialism. From the Portuguese crown, to the empire, to Getúlio Vargas and to the dictatorship, Brazil has been made from 'the top downwards', as Getúlio himself proclaimed; its state has been colonized by insiders, by relatively privileged interest groups, be they private businessmen, labour unions or indeed, recently, some social movements. Cardoso was able to start to remake this corporate or 'national developmentalist' state because he encountered it at a moment of historic weakness, and because Brazilians were so utterly fed up with inflation. But he had no illusions about the difficulty of his task. In a revealing passage in his memoirs, he unburdened himself of a heartfelt warning to Arminio Fraga before the latter's Senate hearing for the job of Central Bank president:

Brazil doesn't like the capitalist system. The congressmen don't like capitalism, the journalists don't like capitalism, the academics don't like capitalism ... They don't know they don't like capitalism, but they don't like it. They like the state, they like intervention, controls, exchange controls, whatever might be conservative is better than what is liberal. This is an immense difficulty that we have, because we are proposing the integration of Brazil into the international system. They don't even like national capitalism, still less the international version, they mistrust our link with the international system. The ideal, the assumption, that is at the back of their minds is a regime that is non-capitalist and isolated, with a strong State and ample social welfare. All this is utopian, people are not conscious of that.[6]

Partly because it was broadly successful for so long in developing the economy, the 'national developmentalist' state put down deep roots in Brazil's collective consciousness. It is deeply imbued in the psyche of many political and business leaders. It is not wholly surprising that it is making a comeback, albeit in much diluted form, although given its lamentable record on education and health care, it is in some ways surprising that these ideas have returned under a party of the left. On a good day Brazil's current policymakers seem to envisage the country as a tropical France (on a bad day, they are tempted by China). But as Zaki Laïdi, a professor of international relations at Sciences Po in Paris, has warned: 'France has had a strong aversion to liberalism for more than two centuries, but has not succeeded in building an alternative model that would allow it to adapt to globalization without rejecting its history.'[7]

This is not an argument that Brazil has to imitate the United States. Ever since Tiradentes yearned for a Jeffersonian republic in Minas Gerais, Brazilians have contrasted their country with its *alter ego* to the north. Many have lamented, with Vianna Moog, that Brazil produced extractivist *bandeirantes*, rather than toiling pioneers. But Brazil cannot change its history or, at least in the short term, its culture. Indeed, Eduardo Giannetti, a rare Brazilian liberal, argues that if his country did not become like the United States 'it was essentially because it did not want to'. It was not prepared to sacrifice *alegria* and an easy-going approach to life for capital accumulation and future prosperity.[8] He proposes that Brazil can offer the world a different and less materialistic set of values from the American way, exemplified in the country's recent commitment to environmentalism. Certainly, the shift in the past two decades towards policies that do more to protect the environment marks the end of a long march of more than four centuries to occupy Brazil's vast territory that began with the Jesuits and the *bandeirantes*. The country's agriculture is already relying more on raising productivity than on incorporating more land. But Brazil still has too many poor people for it to renounce the pursuit of economic growth for a good while yet.

Nor is the critique of the rebirth of national developmentalism an argument for a 'neo-liberal' (i.e. neo-conservative) minimal state. Brazil is no Singapore: it is too big a country with too many social and regional inequalities for that to be an option (though it could learn much from that island state's commitment to innovation, openness and social insurance). Rather, it is a call for Brazil to return to the social-democratic consensus that achieved so much success in 1994–2006, and that combined broadly liberal economics with a greater emphasis on social policy and the reduction of inequalities. Unless Brazil abandons its recent dalliance with a revival of the corporate state and returns to trying to create an effective regulatory one, it will not be able to meet the demands of its increasingly empowered citizens for more opportunities, better services and a better quality of life.

It was unfortunate, but perhaps inevitable, that the debate within the opposition movement that raged in São Paulo in the late 1970s led to the foundation of two rival parties, the PT and then later the PSDB. In different ways, both have been modernizing forces but they became the opposing poles of Brazilian politics, each obliged to ally with the archaic forces of *pemedebismo* and its like. As Mario Henrique Simonsen argued in 1987, 'the great national debate is not between left and right, but between the modern and the archaic'.[9] That remains true. The 2014 election may produce a change of political direction. But whether or not it does, the Brazilian people, who are gradually becoming better educated and in some ways more entrepreneurial, may take a hand in the direction of public policies.

Three times in the past quarter of a century Brazilians have taken to the streets in large numbers in peaceful protests against the status quo. Though they failed to achieve the direct presidential election they demanded in 1984, they fairly quickly got democracy. In 1993 they saw Collor chased from office, though not punished, for his contempt for the rule of law. Will they get the better public services and greater political accountability they demanded in 2013? This will form the main thread of political debate in the country in the years leading up to the bicentenary of independence in 2022. For almost the first time in their history, Brazilians are now demanding to remake their country from the bottom up, as a country of equal citizens rather than patrimonial privilege. That has placed the corporate state on the defensive. It gives grounds to hope that the achievements of the past two decades will be built upon and extended in a new phase in the Brazilian story.

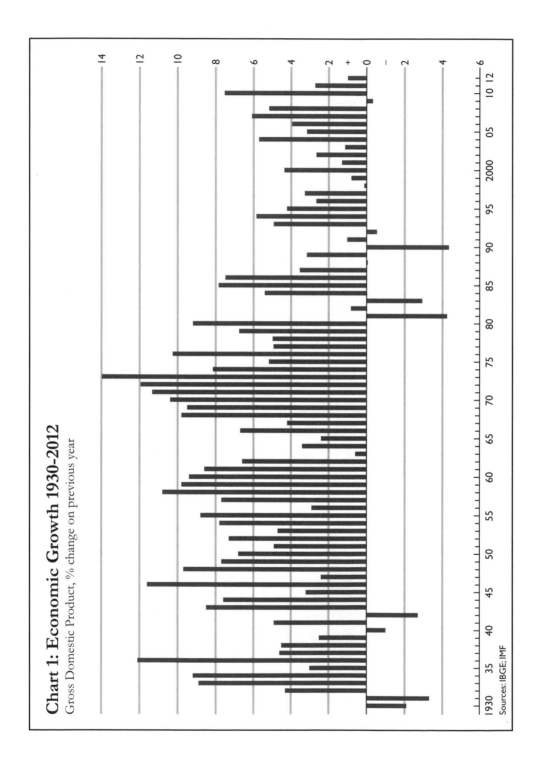

Chart 1: Economic Growth 1930-2012

Gross Domestic Product, % change on previous year

Sources: IBGE; IMF

Notes

Unless otherwise stated, the place of publication is London.

Chapter One: Brazil's Troubled Rise

1. Interview with Lula, Brasília, September 2010.
2. www.internetworldstats.com, accessed on 4 August 2013; *Financial Times*, 12 October 2013.
3. Edward Luce, *In Spite of the Gods: The Strange Rise of Modern India*, Little, Brown, 2006.
4. *Folha de São Paulo*, 20 May 2010.
5. As quoted by Timothy Garton Ash in the *Guardian*, 8 April 2010.
6. Fernando Henrique Cardoso with Brian Winter, *The Accidental President of Brazil: A Memoir*, Public Affairs, New York, 2006, p. 26.
7. Stefan Zweig, *Brazil: A Land of the Future*, Ariadne Press, Riverside, California, 2000 (first published in English in New York in 1941).
8. We went on to spell some of these out:

   > Government spending is growing faster than the economy as a whole, but both private and public sectors still invest too little, planting a question-mark over those rosy growth forecasts. Too much public money is going on the wrong things. The federal government's payroll has increased by 13 per cent since September 2008. Social-security and pension spending rose by 7 per cent over the same period although the population is relatively young. Despite recent improvements, education and infrastructure still lag behind China's or South Korea's . . . The government is doing nothing to dismantle many of the obstacles to doing business – notably the baroque rules on everything from paying taxes to employing people (*The Economist*, 14 November 2009)

9. See, for example, Arminio Fraga and Eduardo Amadeo, 'O Fim da Herança Bendita', *O Globo*, 16 December 2012.

Chapter Two: The Brazilian Way of Life

1. Castro, Ruy, *Rio de Janeiro: Carnival under Fire*, Bloomsbury, 2004, p. 56.
2. Mario Sergio Conti, *Notícias do Planalto: A imprensa e Fernando Collor*, Companhia das Letras, São Paulo, 1999, p. 363.
3. Quoted in Claudio Bojunga, *JK: O artista do impossível*, Editora Objectiva, Rio de Janeiro, 2001, chapter 1.
4. Quoted in Alex Bellos, *Futebol: The Brazilian Way of Life*, Bloomsbury, 2002, p. 27.

Chart 2: Inflation 1939–2012

FIPE index of consumer prices in São Paulo, annual % change

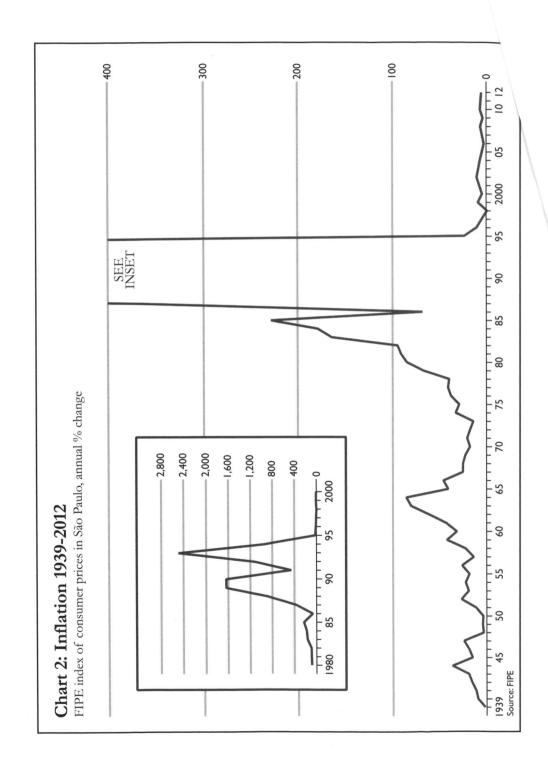

SEE
INSET

Source: FIPE

5. I am grateful to Alfredo Behrens for this point.
6. Roberto DaMatta, *Explorações: Ensaios de Sociologia Interpretiva*, Editora Rocco, Rio de Janeiro, 2011, p. 90.
7. Author visit to Embraer factory, São José dos Campos, June 2010.
8. Castro (2004), chapter 2.
9. Roberto DaMatta, *O Que Faz o brasil, Brasil?*, Editora Rocco, Rio de Janeiro, 8th edition, 1995, p. 75.
10. *Financial Times*, 13 February 2012.
11. *Financial Times* magazine, 23 February 2013.
12. Larry Rohter, *Brazil on the Rise: The Story of a Country Transformed*, Palgrave Macmillan, New York, 2010, chapter 2.
13. See Ruy Castro, *O Anjo Pornográfico: A Vida de Nelson Rodrigues*, Companhia das Letras, São Paulo, 1992.
14. 'Public Morality in Brazil: Hemlines and Headlines', *The Economist*, 12 November 2009.
15. Joseph A. Page, T*he Brazilians*, Addison-Wesley, Reading, Massachusetts, 1995, chapter 14.
16. See David Lehmann, *Struggle for the Spirit: Religious Transformation and Popular Culture in Brazil and Latin America*, Polity Press, Cambridge, 1996.
17. 'Brazilian Billionaire Bishop is now a Banker too', *Forbes*, 22 July 2013.
18. 'Religion in Brazil: Earthly Concerns', *The Economist*, 20 July 2013.
19. Interview in *Valor Econômico*, 2 December 2011.
20. 'Television in Brazil: Soaps, Sex and Sociology', *The Economist*, 14 March 2009.
21. Arnaldo Jabor, 'Avenida Brasil está acabando', *O Estado de S. Paulo*, 9 October 2012.
22. Sérgio Buarque de Holanda, *Raízes do Brasil*, Companhia das Letras, São Paulo, 1996, p. 82.
23. Alfredo Behrens, *Culture and Management in the Americas*, Stanford University Press, 2009, p. 122.
24. Maílson da Nóbrega, *Além do Feijão com Arroz: Autobiografia*, Civilizacão Brasileira, Rio de Janeiro, 2010, pp. 25–6.
25. Quoted in *Financial Times* Business Education Special Report, 31 January 2011.
26. *O Estado de S. Paulo*, 10 October 2012.
27. Ricardo Batista Amaral, *A Vida quer é Coragem: A Trajetória de Dilma Rousseff, a Primeira Presidenta do Brasil*, Primeira Pessoa, Rio de Janeiro, 2011, p. 115.
28. Vianna Moog, *Bandeirantes and Pioneers*, George Braziller, New York, 1964, p. 115.
29. Claude Lévi-Strauss, *Tristes Tropiques*, Penguin, 1992, p. 182.
30. DaMatta (1995), chapter 2.
31. Remarks at *The Economist* Brazil Business Summit, São Paulo, November 2010.
32. Claude Lévi-Strauss, *Saudades de São Paulo*, Companhia das Letras, São Paulo, 1998, p. 7.
33. Machado de Assis, *Papéis Avulsos*, Martins Fontes, São Paulo, 2005, pp. 191–205. I am grateful to Eduardo Giannetti for pointing me to this story and for stressing to me Brazil's secular failure to build an adequate capital base.

Chapter Three: The Forging of a People

1. Stuart B. Schwartz, 'The Economy of the Portuguese Empire', in Francisco Bethencourt and Diogo Ramada Curto (eds), *Portuguese Oceanic Expansion 1400–1800*, Cambridge University Press, 2007; Darcy Ribeiro, *O Povo Brasileiro*, Companhia das Letras, São Paolo, 1995, pp. 34–8.
2. Several medieval maps marked 'Brasil' among apparently mythical islands in the Atlantic. Vicente Yañez Pinzón, who sailed with Columbus in his first voyage, may have landed briefly at what is today Cabo Santo Agostinho, south of Recife, four months before Cabral reached Brazil. N. P. Macdonald, *The Making of Brazil: Portuguese Roots 1500–1822*, The Book Guild, Lewes, Sussex, 1996, chapter 4.
3. Jorge Caldeira (ed.), *Brasil: A Historia Contada Por Quem Viu*, Mameluco, 2008, pp. 26–9; John Hemming, *Red Gold: The Conquest of the Brazilian Indians*, Papermac, 1978, chapter 1; Macdonald (1996), chapter 4.

4. Ribeiro (1995), pp. 28–34; Warren Dean, *With Broadax and Firebrand: The Destruction of the Brazilian Atlantic Forest*, University of California Press, Berkley, 1997, chapter 2.
5. On Vespucci, see Felipe Fernández-Armesto, *Amerigo: The Man who Gave his Name to America*, Weidenfeld & Nicolson, 2006. Vespucci had earlier acted as a pilot in a small Spanish fleet commanded by Alonso de Hojeda which appears to have explored Brazil's north coast from Maranhão to Cabo Orange (close to the present-day border with French Guiana) around the same time as Cabral landed at Porto Seguro (Fernández-Armesto, 2006, pp. 67–71).
6. Vianna Moog, *Bandeirantes and Pioneers*, George Braziller, New York, 1964, p. 102.
7. Accessible accounts of colonial Brazil include Leslie Bethell (ed.), *Colonial Brazil*, Cambridge University Press, 1987; Boris Fausto, *A Concise History of Brazil*, Cambridge University Press, 2006.
8. Sergio Buarque de Holanda, *Raízes do Brasil*, Companhia das Letras, São Paulo, 1996, p. 53.
9. Quoted in Ribeiro (1995), p. 75.
10. For the story of *La France Antarctique*, see Jean de Léry, *History of a Voyage to the Land of Brazil*, University of California Press, Berkley, 1992.
11. Darlene J. Sadlier, *Brazil Imagined: 1500 to the Present*, University of Texas Press, Austin, 2008, chapter 1; Hemming (1978), chapter 1.
12. Ribeiro (1995), p. 47; Hemming (1978), p. 148.
13. Quoted in Hemming (1978), p. 151.
14. Stuart B. Schwartz, 'Plantations and Peripheries *c.* 1580–*c.* 1750', in Bethell (1987); Caldeira (2008), pp. 166–8; Buarque de Holanda (1996), pp. 126–7.
15. Quoted in Fernando Rosas Moscoso, *Del Rio de la Plata al Amazonas: El Perú y el Brasil en la Época de la Dominació Ibérica*, Editorial Universitaria, Universidad Ricardo Palma, Lima, 2008, p. 107.
16. On Vieira, see Ronaldo Vainfas, *Antônio Vieira*, Companhia das Letras, São Paulo, 2011.
17. Quoted in Hemming (1978), p. 156.
18. Dean (1997), p. 88; Hemming (1978), p. 172.
19. Dauril Alden, 'Late Colonial Brazil, 1750–1808', in Bethell (1987); David Birmingham, *A Concise History of Portugal*, Cambridge University Press, 2008, pp. 82–8; Hemming (1978).
20. Hemming (1978), Appendix.
21. Ribeiro (1995), p. 110.
22. The following paragraphs draw heavily on Herbert S. Klein, *The Atlantic Slave Trade*, Cambridge University Press, 2010; and Robin Blackburn, *The Making of New World Slavery: From the Baroque to the Modern, 1492–1800*, Verso, 2010.
23. Blackburn (2010), p. 170; Klein (2010), p. 132.
24. Schwartz (1987), p. 74.
25. Schwartz (1987), p. 81.
26. Gilberto Freyre, *Casa-grande & senzala: Formação da família brasileira sob o regime da economia patriarcal*, Global Editora, São Paulo, 51st edition, 2006, p. 36.
27. Quoted in Schwartz (1987), p. 81.
28. Klein (2010), Appendix.
29. Klein (2010), chapter 4.
30. Caldeira (2008), pp. 127–30.
31. Moog (1964), p. 18.
32. Charles Darwin, *The Voyage of the Beagle*, Dent Dutton, New York, 1961, p. 11.
33. Moog (1964), p. 223.
34. Dean (1995), pp. 107–11.
35. Quoted in Dean (1995), p. 108.
36. Blackburn (2010), p. 163.
37. Schwartz (1987), p. 67; Caldeira (2008), p. 144.
38. Robert Edgar Conrad, *Children of God's Fire: A Documentary History of Black Slavery in Brazil*, Princeton, 1983, pp. 163–74.
39. Vainfas (2011), p. 275.

40. Freyre (2006), p. 33.
41. Foreword to Freyre (2006).
42. Conrad (1983), Part Two, pp. 55–111.
43. Klein (2010), chapters 6 and 7.
44. Conrad (1983), p. xviii.
45. Klein (2010), p. 177; Fausto (2006), p. 20.
46. Dauril Alden, 'Late Colonial Brazil', 1750–1808', in Bethell (1987), table p. 290; Klein (2010), p. 36; Conrad (1983), p. 317.
47. Conrad (1983), pp. 210–16.
48. Quoted in Conrad (1983), p. 56.
49. Conrad (1983), p. 233.
50. Evaldo Cabral de Mello (ed.), *O Brasil holandês*, Penguin/Companhia das Letras, São Paulo, 2010, chapter 11.
51. Many of Post's canvases were painted on his return to the Netherlands from sketches made in Brazil. Prince Maurits gave eighteen of Post's canvases to France's Louis XIV; they are now in the Louvre. Some of Eckhout's images of Brazilian Indians were used by the Gobelins tapestry factory of Paris, and became popular tapestries. See Sadlier (2008), pp. 71–83; Pedro Corrêa do Lago and Blaise Ducos, *Frans Post: Le Brésil à la cour de Louis XIV*, Exhibition catalogue, Louvre, 2005.
52. Frédéric Mauro, 'Political and Economic Structures of Empire, 1580–1750', in Bethell (1987); Blackburn (2010), pp. 187–96.
53. Vainfas (2011), p. 157.
54. These paragraphs draw heavily on A. J. R. Russell-Wood, 'The Gold Cycle, c. 1690–1750', in Bethell (1987). See also Fausto (2006), pp. 49–54.
55. Alden (1987), p. 289.
56. Quoted in Blackburn (2010), p. 489.
57. Alden (1987).
58. Fausto (2006), pp. 54, 59–63; Alden (1987), pp. 336–43; Kenneth Maxwell, *Naked Tropics: Essays on Empire and Other Rogues*, Routledge, 2003, chapter 7.
59. Ivo Mesquita, 'Brazil', in Edward J. Sullivan (ed.), *Latin American Art in the Twentieth Century*, Phaidon, 1996.
60. Leslie Bethell, 'The Independence of Brazil', in Bethell (ed.), *The Cambridge History of Latin America*, Vol. III, Cambridge University Press, 1985, p. 163.
61. Buarque de Holanda (1996), chapter 4; Fausto (2006), p. 58; J. H. Elliott, 'Modernizing the Marranos', *New York Review of Books*, 11 March 2010; Vainfas (2011); Isabel dos Guimarães Sá, 'Ecclesiastical Structures and Religious Action,' in Bethencourt and Curto (2007), pp. 265–7.
62. Alden (1987), p. 292.
63. Ribeiro (1995), p. 17.
64. Moog (1964).
65. Freyre (2006), p. 114.
66. Buarque de Holanda (1996); on Faoro's notion of the patrimonial state in Brazil, see André Botelho and Lilia Moritz Schwarcz, *Un Enigma chamado Brasil*, Companhia das Letras, São Paolo, 2009, pp. 364–77, and Fernando Henrique Cardoso, *Pensadores que inventaram o Brasil*, Companhia das Letras, São Paulo, 2013, pp. 227–62.

Chapter Four: From Monarchy to Coffee Republic

1. Patrick Wilcken, *Empire Adrift: The Portuguese Court in Rio de Janeiro 1808–21*, Bloomsbury, 2004, chapters 1 and 2.
2. Maxwell (2003), chapter 8; Dean (1997), chapter 6.
3. Bethell (1985), p. 185; Marshall C. Eakin, *Brazil: The Once and Future Country*, St Martin's Press, New York, 1997, pp. 28–9.
4. Bethell (1985), p. 195.
5. Fausto (2006), p. 77.

6. Leslie Bethell and José Murilo de Carvalho, 'Brazil from Independence to the Middle of the Nineteenth Century' in Bethell (1985), chapter 16, p. 684; Fausto (2006), p. 80.
7. Bethell and Carvalho (1985), pp. 691–2.
8. José Murilo de Carvalho, *D. Pedro II*, Companhia das Letras, São Paulo, 2007, p. 9.
9. On Dom Pedro, see Carvalho (2007).
10. Bethell and Carvalho (1985), pp. 691–717.
11. Richard Graham, 'Brazil from the Middle of the Nineteenth Century to the Paraguayan War', in Bethell (1985), pp. 775–8; Gabriela Nunes Ferreira, 'Visconde do Uruguai: Teoria e prática do estado brasileiro', in Botelho and Schwarcz (2009).
12. Bolívar Lamounier, *Da Independência a Lula: Dois séculos de política brasileira*, Augurium Editora, São Paulo, 2005, pp. 30–31 and 84–5.
13. Emilia Viotti da Costa, 'Brazil: the Age of Reform 1870–1889', in Leslie Bethell (ed.), *The Cambridge History of Latin America*, Vol. V, Cambridge University Press, 1986, p. 742.
14. Graham (1985), pp. 775–7.
15. Stephen Topik, 'The Hollow State: Effect of the World Market on State-Building in Brazil in the Nineteenth Century', in James Dunkerley (ed.), *Studies in the Formation of the Nation State in Latin America*, Institute of Latin American Studies, 2002, pp. 112–32.
16. José Bonifácio quoted in Conrad (1983), pp. 418–27.
17. 'Our Expiring Commercial Treaty with the Brazils', *The Economist*, 2 September 1843. The article argued that 'the conditions insisted on by the Brazilians for a continuation of our trade [i.e. steep tariff reductions on British imports of Brazilian sugar, coffee and cotton] – instead of being onerous to us . . . would . . . be of the greatest benefit' to Britain.
18. Victor Bulmer-Thomas, *The Economic History of Latin America since Independence*, Cambridge University Press, 1994, p. 142.
19. Nathaniel H. Leff, 'Economic Development in Brazil 1822–1913', in Stephen Haber (ed.), *How Latin America Fell Behind: Essays on the Economic Histories of Brazil and Mexico, 1800–1914*, Stanford University Press, 1997.
20. 'Evolution', in Machado de Assis, *A Chapter of Hats and Other Stories*, Bloomsbury, 2009, p. 109.
21. Colin M. Lewis, *Public Policy and Private Initiative: Railway Building in São Paulo 1860–1889*, Institute of Latin American Studies Research Papers No. 26, University of London, 1991, p. 12.
22. Topik (2002), pp. 122–6.
23. Interview with Tânia Andrade Lima and visit to Valongo site, November 2011.
24. Bethell (1985), p. 192.
25. Bethell and Carvalho (1985), pp. 729–37.
26. Bethell and Carvalho (1985), pp. 743–6; Graham (1985), p. 751.
27. Warren Dean, 'The Brazilian Economy 1870–1930', in Bethell (1986), pp. 701–2; Fausto (2006), p. 107.
28. Lewis (1991); William Summerhill, 'Transport Improvements in Brazil and Mexico', in Haber (1997), p. 113.
29. This paragraph draws heavily on Fausto (2006).
30. Marcos Augusto Gonçalves, *1922: A semana que não terminou*, Companhia das Letras, São Paulo, 2012, p. 68.
31. Peter Burke and Maria Lúcia Pallares-Burke, *Gilberto Freyre: Social Theory in the Tropics*, Peter Lang, Oxford, 2008, p. 61.
32. Carvalho (2007), chapter 15; Graham (1985), pp. 784–7.
33. Raymond Aron, *Main Currents in Sociological Thought*, Penguin, 1965, pp. 63–109; Todd A. Diacon, *Rondon*, Companhia das Letras, São Paulo, 2006, chapter 4; Carvalho (2007), chapters 17 and 25.
34. Viotti da Costa (1986), p. 747.
35. Viotti da Costa (1986), p. 739.
36. Carvalho (2007), chapter 30.

37. Joaquim Nabuco, *Essencial*, Penguin/Companhia das Letras, São Paulo, 2010, p. 38.
38. Robert M. Levine, *Vale of Tears: Revisiting the Canudos Massacre in Northeastern Brazil, 1893–1897*, University of California Press, Berkley, 1995, p. 43.
39. Fausto (2006), p. 129.
40. Luiz Felipe D'Avila, *Os Virtuosos: Os Estadistas que Fundaram a Repúublica Brasileira*, A Girafa Editora, São Paulo, 2006, chapter 3; Marco Antonio Villa, *A História das Constituiçoes Brasileiras*, Leya, São Paulo, 2011, chapter 2.
41. Fausto (2006), p. 17.
42. Euclides Da Cunha, *Rebellion in the Backlands*, Picador, 1995, p. 414.
43. Levine (1995); da Cunha (1995); Ronald M. Schneider, *Brazil: Culture and Politics in a New Industrial Powerhouse*, Westview Press, Boulder, Colorado, 1996, p. 49.
44. Da Cunha (1995), p. 695.
45. Da Cunha (1995), p. 231.
46. Da Cunha (1995), p. 612.
47. Boris Fausto, 'The Social and Political Structure of the First Republic', in Bethell (1986), pp. 779–829; José Murilo de Carvalho, *Cidadania no Brasil: O longo caminho*, Civilização Brasileira, Rio de Janeiro, 14th edition, 2011, pp. 56–7; Levine (1995), pp. 91–7.
48. Dean (1986), p. 690.
49. Dean (1986), p. 697.
50. Menotti conference in Caldeira (2008), pp. 480–2; on modernism, see Gonçalves (2012) and Beatriz Resende, 'Brazilian Modernism: the Canonised Revolution', in Vivian Schelling, *Through the Kaleidoscope: The Experience of Modernity in Latin America*, Verso, 2000, pp. 199–216.
51. Resende (2000); Nádia Battella Gotlib, *Tarsila do Amaral: A modernista*, Editora Senac, São Paulo, 1997.
52. *Financial Times* magazine, 7 June 2003.
53. Gonçalves (2012), p. 326.
54. David Rock, 'Society and Politics in Argentina 1880–1916', in Leslie Bethell (ed.), *Argentina since Independence*, Cambridge University Press, 1993, p. 89.
55. Fausto (2006), pp. 166–90; Leslie Bethell, 'Politics in Brazil under Vargas 1930–1945', in Bethell (ed.), *The Cambridge History of Latin America*, Vol. IX, Cambridge University Press, 2008, pp. 9–10; Domingos Meirelles, *As Noites das Grandes Fogueiras: Uma História da Columna Prestes*, Editora Record, Rio de Janeiro, 1995, chapters 1–7.
56. Alain Rouquié, *The Military and the State in Latin America*, University of California Press, Berkley, 1987, chapters 3 and 4 (quote, p. 113).
57. Alfredo Behrens, *Culture and Management in the Americas*, Stanford University Press, 2009, p. 113.

Chapter Five: Getúlio Vargas and 'National Developmentalism'

1. Boris Fausto, *Getúlio Vargas*, Companhia das Letras, São Paulo, 2006; Leslie Bethell, 'Politics in Brazil under Vargas 1930–45', in Bethell (ed.), *Brazil since 1930, Cambridge History of Latin America*, Vol. IX, Cambridge Univerty Press, 2008. Quote from diary in *Veja*, 23 May 2012; quote from Tancredo Neves in Claudio Bojunga, *JK: O artista do impossível*, Editora Objetiva, Rio de Janeiro, 2001, p. 184.
2. Jorge Ferreira, *João Goulart: Uma Biografia*, Editora Civilizacão Brasileira, Rio de Janeiro, 2011, p. 25.
3. Fausto (2006b), chapter 1; Ruben Oliven, *Tradition Matters: Modern Gaúcho Identity in Brazil*, Columbia University Press, New York, 1996, Introduction.
4. Fausto (2006) chapter 2; Marcelo Paiva de Abreu, 'The Brazilian Economy 1930–80', in Bethell (2008); Baer (2008), chapter 3.
5. Bethell, 'Politics in Brazil Under Vargas 1930–45', in Bethell (2008), pp. 27–30; Roberto Pompeu de Toledo, 'O Que Foi a Revolução de 1932', *Veja*, 4 July 2012. The Constitutionalist Revolution, as the *paulistas* called it, is still much recalled in São Paulo, marked by a state public holiday on 9 July, the day the uprising started; two of

the city's main avenues carry the names of 9 July and 23 May, when four young *paulista* demonstrators were killed in a clash with *tenentes*. The civil war is largely forgotten elsewhere in Brazil.

6. Diary quotes in Fausto (2006b), p. 68.
7. Michael L. Conniff (ed.), *Latin American Populism in Comparative Perspective*, University of New Mexico Press, Albuquerque, 1982 (see the chapter on Brazil by Conniff himself).
8. Bethell, *op. cit.*, pp. 35–51; Fausto (2006b), pp. 70–81. Like Góes Monteiro, Dutra's ties to Vargas dated from his studies at the military academy in Porto Alegre; as a general, Mourão Filho began the coup in 1964 that overthrew democracy.
9. Quoted in Fausto (2006b), pp. 81–2.
10. Bethell (2008), p. 56.
11. See Howard Wiarda, *The Soul of Latin America: The Cultural and Political Tradition*, Yale University Press, New Haven and London, 2001, chapter 9.
12. Bethell (2008), pp. 90–114.
13. Quoted in Fausto (2006b), p. 82.
14. Bethell (2008), pp. 61–5.
15. Populism is a slippery and controversial term, but one that is unavoidable for the analyst of Latin American politics. I mean by it a brand of politics in which a strong leader seeks to organize, from above, a multi-class mass electoral coalition, claiming to represent 'the people' (*o povo* in Portuguese or *el pueblo* in Spanish) against 'the oligarchy' or presumed foreign foes. These leaders have characteristically weakened or eliminated institutional checks and balances on executive power. Populism has normally been associated with unsustainable economic policies that have given priority to redistribution at the expense of price stability and fiscal balance. I explored the subject of populism at greater length in Michael Reid, *Forgotten Continent: The Battle for Latin America's Soul*, Yale University Press, 2007. On Vargas as a populist and populism in Brazil, see Leslie Bethell, 'Populism, Neo-populism and the Left in Brazil: From Getulio to Lula', in Cynthia Arnson and Carlos de la Torre (eds), *Populism in Twenty-first Century Latin America*, Johns Hopkins University Press, Baltimore, 2012, and Michael L. Conniff, 'Brazil's Populist Republic and Beyond', in Conniff (ed.), *Populism in Latin America*, University of Alabama Press, Tuscaloosa, 1999.
16. Gomes and the UDN, who had expected to win, managed only 35 per cent, while the PCB gained almost 10 per cent.
17. Bethell (2008), p. 92.
18. Thomas Skidmore, *Politics in Brazil 1930–1964: An Experiment in Democracy*, Oxford University Press, 1967.
19. Fausto (2006b), chapter 4.
20. Fausto (2006b), pp. 195–6; Bethell (2008), pp. 116–19; Skidmore (1967), chapters 3 and 4. This letter was dictated by Vargas in early August at his request to José Soares Maciel Filho, a journalist and friend of the president, and was intended as a political testament. The full text was incorporated into the programme of the PTB. Vargas himself wrote a shorter, more personal note shortly before he died.
21. Janice Pearlman, *Favela: Four Decades of Living on the Edge in Rio de Janeiro*, Oxford University Press, 2010, p. 152.
22. The UDN's Juarez Távora, a former *tenente*, won 29 per cent, and Ademar de Barros 24 per cent.
23. Bojunga (2001), p. 16.
24. Bojunga (2001), p. 166.
25. Quotes, Bojunga (2001), p. 329 and 296.
26. The Portuguese is: 'Deste Planalto Central, desta solidão que em breve se transformará em cérebro das mais altas decisões nacionais, lanço os olhos mais uma vez sobre o amanhã o do meu país e antevejo esta alvorada, com fé inquebrantável e uma confiança sem limites no seu grande destino.'
27. Bojunga, pp. 391–9, 419–29, 553–69 and 732.

28. Raymundo Faoro, *A Democracia Traída: Entrevistas*, Editora Globo, Porto Alegra, 2008, p. 150.
29. Skidmore (1999), p. 148; Marcelo Paiva de Abreu, 'The Brazilian Economy 1945–1964', in Bethell (2008), p. 343.
30. Quoted in the *Guardian*, 2 October 2013.
31. Mario Sergio Conti, *Notícias do Planalto: A imprensa e Fernando Collor*, Companhia das Letras, São Paulo, 1999, p. 52.
32. Mesquita in Sullivan (1996).
33. Quote, Bojunga (1996), p. 573.
34. Bethell (2008), p. 136.
35. Bethell (2008), pp. 133–40 and Ferreira (2011), chapter 6.
36. Ferreira (2011), chapter 7.
37. Skidmore (1967), pp. 234–53; Bethell (2008), pp. 140–47.
38. Ferreira (2011), pp. 425–8.
39. Elio Gaspari, *A Ditadura Envergonhada*, Companhia das Letras, São Paulo, 2002, p. 51.
40. Skidmore (1967), chapter 8; Bethell (2008), pp. 148–59; Maria Celina D'Araujo and Celso Castro (eds), *Ernesto Geisel*, Fundação Getúlio Vargas, Rio de Janeiro, 1997, chapter 9. The March 1964 naval mutiny was instigated by Corporal José Anselmo, who was later discovered to have been an agent of naval intelligence.
41. Bethell (2008), pp. 159–63.
42. Thomas Skidmore, *The Politics of Military Rule in Brazil 1964–85*, Oxford University Press, 1988, pp. 27–9; D'Araujo and Castro (1997), chapter 9.
43. Skidmore (1967), pp. 325–9; Bethell (2008), pp. 152–64; Lincoln Gordon, Supplement to *Brazil's Second Chance: En Route Toward the First World*, Brookings Institution, Washington DC, 2003 (see Appendix B, p. 57, for the 26 March telegram from Gordon to Washington quoted); second Gordon quote footnoted in Rouquié (1987), p. 439.
44. Bojunga (2001), p. 261.

Chapter Six: The Long Dictatorship

1. Gaspari (2002), pp. 123–4.
2. Rouquié (1987), p. 286; D'Araujo and Castro (1997), pp. 75 and 141.
3. D'Araujo and Castro (1997); Rouquié (1987), chapter 9, Cardoso quote p. 286.
4. I have drawn heavily on Skidmore (1988) and D'Araujo and Castro (1997) for this account of the dictatorship.
5. Tropicália was the name of an installation by Hélio Oiticica, a concretist artist. See Caetano Veloso, *Verdade Tropical*, Companhia das Letras, São Paulo, 1997.
6. Data on repression from Carvalho (2011), p. 164.
7. Quoted in Bojunga (2001), p. 664.
8. Skidmore (1988), p. 150, military justice study, p. 132.
9. Gaspari (2002), pp. 21–41.
10. Conti (1999), pp. 38–9.
11. Ricardo Batista Amaral, *A Vida quer é coragem: A trajetória de Dilma Rousseff, a primeira presidenta do Brasil*, Primeira Pessoa, Rio de Janeiro, 2011, p. 46.
12. Fernando Henrique Cardoso with Brian Winter, *The Accidental President of Brazil: A Memoir*, Public Affairs, New York, 2006. On Dilma Rousseff, see Amaral (2011), chapter 6.
13. Abreu (2008), pp. 283–92; Angus Maddison and Associates, *Brazil and Mexico: The Political Economy of Poverty, Equity and Growth*, World Bank and Oxford University Press, 1992, chapter 1.
14. Marcelo de P. Abreu, Afonso S. Bevilaqua and Demosthenes M. Pinho, 'Import Substitution and Growth in Brazil, 1890s–1970s', in Enrique Cardenas, Jose Antonio Ocampo and Rosemary Thorp, *An Economic History of Twentieth-Century Latin America, Vol. 3: Industrialization and the State in Latin America, the Postwar Years*, Palgrave, 2000, chapter 6, pp. 154–76.

15. This definition is by Luciano Martins, a sociologist, quoted in Bojunga (2001), p. 350.
16. D'Araujo and Castro (1997), pp. 249 and 287.
17. Abreu (2008), pp. 294–5; Baer (2008), chapter 4.
18. Miriam Leitão, *A Saga brasileira: A longa luta de um povo por sua moeda*, Editora Record, 2011. *Donatários*, p. 232; BNDES study quoted p. 89.
19. Mailson da Nóbrega and Gustavo Loyola, 'The Long and Simultaneous Construction of Fiscal and Monetary Institutions', in Lourdes Sola and Laurence Whitehead, Centre for Brazilian Studies, Oxford, 2006, pp. 57–83.
20. Miriam Leitão, *Saga Brasileira: A longa luta de um povo por sua moeda*, Editora Record, Rio de Janeiro, 2011, pp. 88–9; Faoro (2008), p. 63.
21. Paraná (2002), pp. 45–60; 'Dona' is a widely used honorific denoting a married woman and/or mother.
22. Quoted in Carlos Melo, *Collor: O Ator e Suas Circunstâncias*, Editora Novo Conceito, São Paulo, 2007, p. 39 footnote; Francisco Vidal Luna and Herbert S. Klein, *Brazil Since 1980*, Cambridge University Press, 2006, chapter 6.
23. The report was published under the auspices of the São Paulo Catholic archdiocese and translated as *São Paulo: Growth and Poverty*, Catholic Institute of International Relations and the Bowerdean Press, 1978.
24. Carvalho (2011), p. 169.
25. Maddison and Associates (1992), p. 52 and pp. 86–9; *Revista Piauí*, November 2012.
26. See Bacha (2012), pp. 33–8.
27. This was the opening sentence of Cardoso's political platform for the 1994 presidential campaign.

Chapter Seven: From Disorder to Progress under Cardoso

1. Quoted in the documentary film *Senna* (2010).
2. Gallup poll in Faoro (2008), p. 181; on Senna's death and funeral, see the documentary film *Senna* (2010) and Richard Williams, *The Death of Ayrton Senna*, Penguin, 1995, p. 17; Peter Robb, *A Death in Brazil*, Bloomsbury, 2004.
3. Maílson da Nóbrega, *Além do Feijão com Arroz: Autobiografia*, Civilizacão Brasileira, Rio de Janeiro, 2010, pp. 380–81, 396.
4. On the constitution, see Villa (2011), chapter 7; Carvalho (2011), chapter IV; and Bethell (2008), pp. 237–46. Martins quote in Nóbrega (2010), p. 370.
5. Kirk Weyland, 'The Brazilian State in the New Democracy,' in Peter R. Kingstone and Timothy J. Power (eds), *Democratic Brazil: Actors, Institutions and Processes*, University of Pittsburgh Press, 2000, p. 40.
6. Timothy Power, 'Political Institutions in Democratic Brazil: Politics as a Permanent Constitutional Convention', in Kingstone and Power (2000), p. 21.
7. I have drawn heavily on Conti (1999) for Collor's rise and fall; pp. 9–29 for Alagaos background.
8. Cardoso (2006), pp. 131–5.
9. Quoted in Conti (1999), p. 166.
10. Melo (2007), chapter 1; Bethell (2008), pp. 246–7; Conti (1999), pp. 231–75. Conti largely absolves Globo TV, though not its director of news bulletins, Alberico Sousa Cruz, of the commonly made charge of bias towards Collor. But he states that the report of the final television campaign debate on Globo's flagship news programme, *Jornal Nacional*, was edited to be clearly favourable to Collor (who was generally reckoned to have won the debate).
11. Leitão (2011), chapter 9.
12. For Farias and Collor, see Conti (1999), part 2.
13. Bethell (2008), p. 254.
14. Baer (2008), chapter 6.
15. Cardoso with Winter, (2006), pp. 186–8; Fernando Henrique Cardoso, *A Arte da Política: A História que Vivi*, Editora Civilização Brasileira, Rio de Janeiro, 2006, chapter 3; Leitão (2011), chapter 12; Baer, p. 130.

16. Cardoso with Winter (2006), p. 193; inflation statistics in Ministry of Finance, *The Brazilian Economy: The Challenge of Stability and Sustained Growth*, Brasília, 1996, and Baer (2008), p. 410.

17. Leitão (2011), p. 299

18. Michael Reid, 'The Disorders of Progress: A Survey of Brazil', *The Economist*, 27 March 1999. Author interview with Vilmar Faria, January 1999.

19. Robert M. Levine and John J. Crocitti (eds), *The Brazil Reader: History, Culture, Politics*, Duke University Press, Durham, North-Carolina, 1999.

20. Cardoso (2006), p. 279.

21. Francisco Anuatti-Neto *et al.*, 'Costs and Benefits of Privatization: Evidence from Brazil', in Alberto Chong and Florencio López de Silanes (eds), *Privatization in Latin America: Myths and Reality*, Stanford University Press, 2005.

22. Roberto Macedo, 'Distribution of Assets and Income in Brazil: New Evidence', in John Nellis and Nancy Birdsall (eds), *Reality Check: The Distributional Impact of Privatization in Developing Countries*, Center For Global Development, Washington DC, 2005.

23. Author interviews with Cardoso, 31 March 1999, and with Jereissati, February 2003; Cardoso (2006), p. 370.

24. Author interview, April 1996.

25. Author interviews with Malan, 9 April and 16 October 1996, 22 July 1997 and 15 September 1998; Baer (2008), Table 7.5, p. 138. In this period the Brazilian government still used a concept called the 'operational' fiscal deficit, which didn't count the impact of indexation and devaluation on government debt.

26. Speech to the UN Economic Commission for Latin America and the Caribbean, Santiago, Chile, 3 March 1995.

27. Roberto Pompeu de Toledo, *O Presidente segundo o sociólogo: Entrevista de Fernando Henrique Cardoso*, Companhia das Letras, São Paolo, 1998, chapter 6.

28. Gustavo H. B. Franco, 'A inserçao externa e o desenvolvimento', a 1996 paper provided to the author.

29. Reid (1999); Leitão (2008), chapter 18.

30. Author interview, 31 March 1999.

31. Cardoso (2006), pp. 485–9.

32. Author interview, January 1999; Cardoso (2006), pp. 521–9.

33. Author interview, January 1999.

34. *O Estado de S. Paulo*, 7 February 2010.

35. See, for example, *Veja*, 17 January 1996.

36. Monica de Bolle, *O Globo*, 9 April 2013; *O Estado de S. Paulo*, 2 May 1999; *Veja*, 17 April 2002.

37. Cardoso (2006), pp. 12–13.

Chapter Eight: Lulismo and the Brazilian Dream

1. On the foundation of the PT see Margaret Keck, *The Workers' Party and Democratization in Brazil*, Yale University Press, 1992, chapters 4 and 5; and Lincoln Secco, *História do PT*, Ateliê Editorial, São Paulo, 2011, chapter 1.

2. Faoro (2008), pp. 157–8.

3. Interview in *Veja*, 22 September 2004.

4. *Veja*, 2 November 2005.

5. Luiz Inacio Lula da Silva, *Carta ao povo brasileiro* (available at http://www.pt.org); *Veja*, 27 February 2013; *O Estado de S. Paulo*, 4 May 2013.

6. 'Let the People Decide', *The Economist*, 3 July 2002.

7. 'A Matter of Faith', *The Economist*, 15 August 2002.

8. 'Brazil's Presidential Election: The Meaning of Lula', *The Economist*, 3 October 2002.

9. Available at http://www.biblioteca.presidencia.gov.br/ex-presidentes/luiz-inacio-lula-da-silva/discursos

10. *Veja*, 6 November 2002.

11. Marcos de Barros Lisboa, *A Agenda perdida*, Rio de Janeiro, September 2002; Rafael Cariello, 'O Liberal contra a miséria', *Revista Piauí*, No. 74, November 2012.
12. Author interview, February 2003; detail of pension reform in Albert Fishlow, *Starting Over: Brazil since 1985*, Brookings Institution Press, Washington DC, 2011, p. 126.
13. Meeting attended by the author, September 2003.
14. For terms of trade, see ECLAC, *Economic Survey of Latin America and the Caribbean*, Santiago, 2012, Table A11.
15. Cariello (2012).
16. Reid (1999); Wendy Hunter, *The Transformation of the Workers' Party in Brazil*, Cambridge, 2010, p. 161.
17. Hunter (2012), chapter 6; interview with Luiz Dulci, February 2003.
18. Hunter (2012), chapter 6.
19. *The Economist*, 23 June and 14 July 2005; Norman Gall, *Lula and Mephistopheles*, Fernand Braudel Institute of World Economics, São Paulo, 2005; *Folha de São Paulo*, 5 August 2005.
20. *Newsweek*, 2 December 2002.
21. *The Economist*, 14 July 2005; Gall (2005).
22. *The Economist*, 23 March 2006.
23. *Valor Econômico* weekend magazine, 21 May 2010.
24. Wendy Hunter and Timothy Power, 'Rewarding Lula: Executive Power, Social Policy and the Brazilian Elections of 2006', *Latin American Politics & Society*, Vol. 49, No. 1, Spring 2007.
25. 'Lazy, Hazy Days for Lucky Lula', *The Economist*, 30 June 2007.
26. Lula quotes from *O Globo*, 28 March 2009; Leitão (2011), chapters 3 and 20.
27. Author interview, Brasília, September 2010.
28. Lula first said this in 2007, and repeated it several times: http://radioagencianacional. ebc.com.br/node/65890.
29. Ricardo Batista Amaral, *A Vida quer é coragem: A trajetória de Dilma Rousseff, a primeira presidenta do Brasil*, Primeira Pessoa, Rio de Janeiro, 2011, pp. 175–6.
30. Author interview with Lula, Brasília, September 2010.
31. Perry Anderson, 'Lula's Brazil', *London Review of Books*, 31 March 2011.
32. André Singer, *Os Sentidos do Lulismo: Reforma gradual e pacto conservador*, Companhia das Letras, São Paulo, 2012, pp. 9–22.
33. Author interview, São Paulo, October 2013.
34. Talk at Rising Brazil conference, Institute for the Study of the Americas, London, October 2011.
35. Singer makes this distinction in Singer (2012), p. 36.
36. *Revista Piauí*, May 2008.
37. Author interview, Brasília, September 2010.
38. For Dilma's life story, see Amaral (2011).
39. Author interview, London, November 2009.
40. Author interview, London, November 2009.
41. Remarks at press breakfast, London, May 2011.
42. Interview in *Financial Times* Weekend Magazine, 23 February 2013.
43. OECD, *Economic Surveys: Brazil*, Paris, October 2013.
44. Interview in *Veja*, 12 June 2013.

Chapter Nine: The Long Road to a Middle-class Society

1. Nancy Scheper-Hughes, *Death Without Weeping: The Violence of Everyday Life in Brazil*, University of California Press, Berkley, 1992, pp. 1–20.
2. Scheper-Hughes (1992), p. 137.
3. Author interviews, Timbaúba, October 2012.
4. Bojunga (2001), p. 517.
5. Author interviews, August 1998. I wrote up this trip in 'The North-East: Politics, Water and Poverty', *The Economist*, 27 August 1998.

6. *The Economist*, 27 August 1998.
7. Author interview, Brasília, July 1998.
8. IPEA, 'A Década inclusiva (2001–2011): Desigualdade, pobreza e políticas de Renda', *Comunicado*, No. 155, 25 September 2012; 'Brazil's North-East: Catching up in a Hurry', *The Economist*, 19 May 2011; Marcelo Neri (ed.), *Microcrédito: O Mistério nordestino e o Grameen brasileiro*, Fundação Getúlio Vargas, Rio de Janeiro, 2008.
9. Author interviews with Marcelo Neri and Ricardo Paes de Barros, São Paulo and Rio de Janeiro, May 2010; Marcelo Neri, *A Nova classe média: O lado brilhante da base da pirâmide*, Editora Saraiva, São Paulo, 2011, p. 26.
10. IPEA (2012).
11. *Financial Times*, 21 April 2012.
12. IPEA (2012); interview with Paes de Barros.
13. *Veja*, 18 February 2009.
14. See Plano Brasil Sem Miseria, www.gov.br; discussed at http://www.bbc.co.uk/portuguese/noticias/2013/03/130307_abre_pobreza_brasil_jp_j f.shtml and 'Social Spending in Brazil: The End of Poverty?', Americas View, *The Economist*, 28 February 2013.
15. Author interview with World Bank official, Brasília, November 2011.
16. Neri (2011), chapters 1 and 3.
17. Data from the World Bank.
18. Anfavea, *Anuario Estadístico*, São Paulo, 2012; interview with Fabio Barbosa, São Paulo, June 2012.
19. Author visit and interviews, July 2007; Patricia Mota Guedes and Nilson Veira Oliveira, 'Democratization of Consumption', *Braudel Papers*, No. 38, Braudel Institute, São Paulo, 2006.
20. Interview by Emma Raffo on the author's behalf, São Paulo, June 2010.
21. Autor interview, Recife, October 2012.
22. World Bank, *Economic Mobility and the Rise of the Latin American Middle Class*, by Francisco G. Ferreira *et al.*, Washington DC, 2012; Nancy Birdsall, 'A Note on the Middle Class in Latin America', Center for Global Development Working Paper 303, São Paulo August 2012.
23. Singer (2012), p. 16.
24. Neri quote in *O Estado de S. Paulo*, 15 May 2010; see also Marcus André Melo, 'Unexpected Success, Unanticipated Failures: Social Policy from Cardoso to Lula', in Peter R. Kingstone and Timothy J. Power, *Democratic Brazil Revisited*, University of Pittsburgh Press, 2008.
25. Amaury de Souza and Bolívar Lamounier, *A Classe Média Brasileira: Ambições, valores e projetos de sociedade*, Elsevier Editora, Rio de Janeiro, 2010, p. 158.
26. World Bank (2012), Box 5.1, p. 141.
27. See Fishlow (2011), pp. 105–15.
28. Data from IBGE and Ministry of Health; *Guardian*,14 September 2010.
29. Fishlow (2011), Table p. 114.
30. *Financial Times*, 30 June 2013; 'Health Care in Brazil: Flying in Doctors,' *The Economist*, 31 August 2013.
31. *O Globo*, 8 April 2012.
32. Author interview, Brasília, January 1997.
33. Author interviews with Paulo Renato Souza and with Maria Helena Guimaraes de Castro, director of Instituto Nacional de Estudos e Pesquisas Educacionais (INEP), Brasília, January 1999.
34. Data from Barbosa Filho, Fernando de Holanda and Pessoa, Samuel Abreu, 'Metas de Educação para a Próxima Década', in Fabio Giambiagi and Claudio Porto (eds), *2022: Propostas para um Brasil Melhor no Ano do Bicentenário*, Elsevier Editora, Rio de Janeiro, 2011, pp. 189–202. Functional illiteracy from Naercio Menezes Filho, 'Educação, Produtividade e Inflação', *Valor Econômico*, 19 April 2013.
35. 'Education in Brazil: No Longer Bottom of the Class', *The Economist*, 9 December 2012; author interview with Souza, São Paulo, June 2010.

36. Author visit and interview, June 2010.
37. *The Economist*, 9 December 2012; Norman Gall, *School Reform in New York and São Paulo*, Braudel Institute, São Paulo, 2007; Costin remarks at an *Economist* conference, Sao Paulo, October 2012; author interview with Pontes, Recife, October 2012.
38. Richard P. Feynman, *'Surely You're Joking, Mr Feynman!' Adventures of a Curious Character, as to told to Ralph Leighton*, W. W. Norton & Company, New York and London, 1985, pp. 494 and 506 (iBook edition). I am grateful to Eduardo Giannetti for pointing me to Feynman's observations.
39. Gall (2007); Americas View, *The Economist*, 28 October 2012.
40. Author interview with João Batista dos Mares Guia, former state education secretary, Belo Horizonte, January 1999.
41. http://www.economist.com/blogs/americasview/2011/09/education-brazil.
42. 'Higher Education in Brazil: The Mortarboard Boom', *The Economist*, 15 September 2012; *Financial Times*, 9 February 2012 and 25 April 2013.
43. 'Universities in Latin America: The Struggle to Make the Grade', *The Economist*, 8 October 2012; *Financial Times* Executive Education magazine, 13 May 2013.
44. 'Education in Brazil: Studying the World', *The Economist*, 17 March 2012.
45. This section is an updated and edited version of an article I reported and wrote for *The Economist* ('Race in Brazil: Affirming a Divide', 28 January 2012). Apart from where separately referenced, those quoted were interviewed in Rio de Janeiro and Brasília in October and November 2011.
46. IPEA, *Boletim de Politicas Socias*, No. 16, 2008, pp. 247–55.
47. Antonio Risério, *A Utopia Brasileira e os Movimentos Negros*, Editora 34, São Paulo, 2007, p. 17.
48. World Bank (2012), pp. 6–9.
49. Fabiano Dias Monteiro, 'Do Anti-racismo criminal às ações afirmativas: Um estudo sobre o debate político racial no Rio de Janeiro (2000–2007)', Unpublished doctoral thesis, Universidade Federal de Rio de Janeiro, 2010.
50. 'Schumpeter: Redeemers of a Macho Society', *The Economist*, 15 June 2013.
51. *Brazil Focus*, a newsletter published by David Fleischer, 29 March 2013; *Financial Times*, 30 March 2013.
52. *Veja*, 21 December 2011.
53. See Janice Pearlman, *Favela: Four Decades of Living on the Edge in Rio de Janeiro*, Oxford University Press, 2010.
54. Author interview, Brasília, September 2010.
55. *Folha de São Paulo*, 29 April 2011.
56. *O Globo*, 21 December 2011.
57. *Veja*, 21 April 2010.
58. Anthony W. Pereira, 'Public Security, Private Interests and Police Reform in Brazil', in Kingstone and Power (2008), p. 196.
59. Pearlman (2010), p. 165.
60. 'Security in Brazil: A Magic Moment for the City of God', *The Economist*, 20 June 2012; *Guardian*, 18 February 2011.
61. Author interview, Rio de Janeiro, June 2010.
62. See *Veja*, 13 March 2013, for police crimes; *New York Times*, 9 January 2012; murder rates as reported by the Overseas Security Advisory Council of the US Department of State.
63. *Veja*, 13 March 2013.
64. Author visit to Vigario Geral and interview with José Junior, June 2010.
65. Pablo Dreyfus *et al.*, 'Small Arms in Brazil: Production, Trade and Holdings', *Small Arms Survey*, Geneva, 2010.
66. Organization of American States, *Report on Citizen Security in the Americas*, Washington DC, 2012; 1980 figure from Pereira (2008), p. 188.
67. Pereira (2008), p. 196.
68. *Valor Econômico*, 20 March 2013.

51. According to Raul Velloso, writing in *O Estado de S. Paulo*, 8 October 2012.
52. *O Estado de S. Paulo*, 3 May 2010.
53. *O Globo*, 23 June 2013.
54. Raul Velloso, César Mattos, Marcos Mendes and Paulo Springer de Freitas, *Infraestructura: Os caminhos para sair do buraco*, Instituto Nacional de Altos Estudos, Rio de Janeiro, 2012, pp. 11–12.
55. *Financial Times*, 28 September 2010.
56. *Financial Times*, 21 September 2012.
57. *Financial Times*, 19 August 2013.
58. *Valor setorial: Higiene, perfumes e cosméticos*, November 2011; *Financial Times*, 1 January, 26 May and 26 November 2012; Reuters, 18 June 2013.
59. *Revista Exame*, 7 October 1998.
60. *Bloomberg Businessweek*, 29 August 2013.
61. *Revista Exame*, 7 October 1998.
62. Meeting attended by the author.
63. Lourdes Casanova and Julian Kassum, 'Brazilian Emerging Multinationals: In Search of a Second Wind', Insead Working Paper, New York, 2013.
64. Data from http://www.bmfbovespa.com.br/enus/download/BMFBOVESPA_Products_Facts_Fig_January2013.pdf.
65. Presentations by Francisco Santos, Commissão de Valores Mobiliários, and Joaquim Levy, Bradesco Asset Management, *Economist* Conference, Paris, July 2012.
66. 'Alternative Investments in Brazil: The Buys from Brazil', *The Economist*, 19 February 2011.
67. *Financial Times*, 9 May 2013.
68. Author interview, São Paulo, May 2010.
69. 'Science in Brazil. Go South, Young Scientist', *The Economist*, 8 January 2011.

Chapter Twelve: Global Ambitions and Frustrations

1. *O Estado de S. Paulo*, 17 May 2010.
2. Author interview, Brasília, June 2010.
3. Ambassador Thomas Pickering *et al.*, 'US Shouldn't Dismiss Turkish–Brazilian Nuclear Deal', *Huffington Post*, 1 June 2010.
4. AFP, 27 May 2010.
5. Author interview, June 2010.
6. Author interview, June 2010.
7. Author interview, Brasília, June 2010.
8. Rohter (2010), p. 246.
9. Skidmore (1967), pp. 173–4.
10. See Matias Spektor, *Kissinger e o Brasil*, Editora Zahar, Rio de Janeiro, 2009.
11. Andrew Hurrell, 'Lula's Brazil: A Rising Power, but Going Where?', *Current History*, February 2008.
12. Matías Spektor, 'Eyes on the Global Prize', *Americas Quarterly*, Spring 2011.
13. Hurrell (2008).
14. Rubens Ricupero, 'O Brasil e o mundo: A política exterior após Lula', *Braudel Papers*, Instituto Fernand Braudel, São Paulo, 2010.
15. Fausto (2006), p. 152.
16. Leslie Bethell, 'Brazil and Latin America', *Journal of Latin American Studies*, Vol. 42, Issue 3, August 2010, pp. 457–85.
17. Boris Fausto and Fernando J. Devoto, *Brasil e Argeninta: Um ensaio de história comparada (1850–2002)*, Editora 34, São Paulo, 2004, pp. 227–35; Michael Reid, 'Remapping South America: A Survey of Mercosur', *The Economist*, 12 October 1996.
18. Presentation at Rising Brazil conference, King's College Brazil Institute and ILAS, London, November 2010.
19. Reid (1996) and Michael Reid, 'Mercosur: A Critical Overview', unpublished paper for Chatham House, London, January 2002.

69. Author interview with Tulio Kahn, adviser to the Public Security Secretariat, São Paulo, June 2010.
70. Agência Brasil, 15 June 2012; 'Diadema', *Braudel Papers* No. 36, Fernand Braudel Institute of World Econmics, São Paulo, 2005.
71. Globo.com, 26 January 2013.
72. Pereira (2008), p. 203.
73. 'Prisons in Latin America: A Journey into Hell', *The Economist*, 22 September 2012.
74. Talk at the Brazil Institute, King's College, London, October 2011.

Chapter Ten: Oil, Farming and the Amazon

1. Author interview, Rio de Janeiro, May 2012.
2. BP Statistical Review of World Energy, June 2013.
3. Author interview, Rio de Janeiro, May 2012.
4. *Financial Times*, 4 July 2013.
5. Reuters, 30 October and 11 November 2013.
6. *Financial Times*, 7 August 2013.
7. Author visit, October 2012.
8. BP (2013).
9. 'Brazil's Oil Boom: Filling up the Future', *The Economist*, 5 November 2011.
10. Private conversation with the author.
11. Norman Gall, *Oil in Deep Waters*, Fernand Braudel Institute of World Economics, São Paolo, 2011.
12. Interview with the author, London, February 2009.
13. 'Petrobras's Record Share Issue: Now Comes the Hard Bit', Americas View, *The Economist*, 24 September 2010.
14. *Revista Piauí*, No. 72, September 2012.
15. *The Economist*, 5 November 2011.
16. Petrobras news release, 11 September 2013.
17. *Valor Econômico*, 26 June 2012.
18. Interview with the author, São Paulo, October 2012.
19. *Revista Piauí*, No. 72, September 2012
20. Reuters, 3 August 2012.
21. *Wall Street Journal*, 7 July 2013.
22. Interviewed in *Veja*, 13 February 2013.
23. Author interview, Rio de Janeiro, October 2012.
24. Information at http://www.bggroup.com/MediaCentre/LatestNews/Pages/Global TechnologyCentre, accessed on 20 August 2013.
25. *Le Monde*, 25 May 2006.
26. *The Economist*, 28 August 2010.
27. Data from www.conab.gov.br.
28. Data from the World Trade Organization's *International Trade Statistics* 2012, Table II.15, p. 66, World Trade Organization.
29. See 'Brazilian Agriculture: The Miracle of the Cerrado', *The Economist*, 28 August 2010.
30. Interview with Pedro Arraes, Embrapa, Brasília, June 2010.
31. Author interview with J. R. Mendonça de Barros, São Paulo, May 2010; *Veja*, 27 March 2013.
32. *Financial Times*, 30 August, 2013.
33. 'Energy in Brazil: Ethanol's Mid-Life Crisis', *The Economist*, 4 September 2010.
34. Anfavea, *Anuário Estatística*, 2012.
35. *Financial Times*, 9 April 2012.
36. Interview with the author, São Paulo, May 2010. Jank resigned from the post in 2012.
37. Interview, May 2010.
38. Baer (2008), p. 292.

39. 'Agrarian Reform in Brazil: This Land is Anti-Capitalist Land', *The Economist*, 28 April 2007; Xico Graziano, 'O Pais sem o MST', *O Estado de S. Paulo*, 6 August 2013.
40. Todd A. Diacon, *Rondon*, Companhia das Letras, São Paulo, 2006, chapters 1 and 2.
41. Diacon (2006), chapter 5.
42. Lévi-Strauss (1993), p. 273.
43. John Hemming, *Tree of Rivers: The Story of the Amazon*, Thames and Hudson, London, 2009, pp. 265–8.
44. Hemming (2009), p. 291.
45. Skidmore (1988), pp. 145–7.
46. Hemming (2009), p. 293.
47. World Bank (2006), p. 92.
48. Author interview with Paulo Amaral, Imazon, Belém, April 1999.
49. Interview with Eduardo Martins, director of Ibama, Brasília, April 1999.
50. Interview with Garo Batmanian, World Wildlife Fund, Brasília, April 1999.
51. Author interview, Brasília, April 1999.
52. *Valor Econômico*, 21 May 2010.
53. James Astill, 'Seeing the Wood: A Special Report on Forests', *The Economist*, 25 September 2010; talk by Anthony Hall, London School of Economics, November 2010.
54. *Financial Times* magazine, 23 February 2013.
55. Unger (2007); 'Brazil and Climate Change: Dancing with the Bear', *The Economist*, 16 April 2009.
56. Emma Duncan, 'All Creatures Great and Small: Special Report on Biodiversity', *The Economist*, 14 September 2013.
57. Remarks at an Economist conference, Rio de Janeiro, May 2012; 'Protecting Brazil's Forests: Fiddling while the Amazon Burns', *The Economist*, 3 December 2011.
58. John Terborough, 'Out of Contact', *New York Review of Books*, 5 April 2012.
59. *New York Times*, 24 January 2012; *Valor Econômico*, 19 October 2012.
60. Author visit, with Helen Joyce, *The Economist*'s Brazil correspondent, October 2012; 'Dams in the Amazon: The Rights and Wrongs of Belo Monte', *The Economist*, 4 May 2013.

Chapter Eleven: Brazil's Guided Capitalism

1. Data at www.embraer.com.br.
2. Author interview, São José dos Campos, June 2012.
3. *Valor Econômico*, 8 November 2011.
4. Interview with Carlos Eduardo Camargo, director of external communications, Embraer, São José dos Campos, June 2012.
5. *Financial Times*, 17 April 2012.
6. Author interview, Jaragua do Sul, October 2012.
7. Edmar Bacha and Monica Baumgarten de Bolle (eds), *O Futuro da indústria no Brasil: Desindustrialização em debate*, Editora Civilização Brasileira, Rio de Janeiro, 2013, p. 13.
8. 'Brazilian Manufacturing in the Face of Chinese Competition', DEV Research Briefing, University of East Anglia, July 2011.
9. Author interview, São Paulo, May 2010.
10. Author interview, São Paolo, May 2010.
11. 'Brazil's Development Banks: A Ripple Begets a Flood', *The Economist*, 19 October 2013; *Valor Econômico*, 4 November 2011.
12. Author interview, São Paulo, October 2012; for Rousseff on the government's role in stimulating competitiveness, see e.g. 'Dilma defende governo pragmático', interview with *Valor Econômico*, 4 December 2012.
13. Author interview, São Paulo, May 2010.
14. Interview in *Veja*, 19 October 2011.
15. Telephone interview with the author, October 2012.

16. OECD (2013), pp. 68–70.
17. Interview with *O Globo*, 20 October 2012.
18. Edmar Bacha, 'Abrir ou abrir, eis a questão', *Valor Econômico*, 27 September 2013.
19. 'Latin America's Car Industry: Revving up', *The Economist*, 27 April 1996; author visit to Betim, May 1997; *Wall Street Journal*, 25 February 1999; *Financial Times*, 23 December 2010.
20. Data in these paragraphs from Anfavea Statistical Yearbook 2012.
21. *Financial Times*, 21 February 2012; author interview with Sérgio Amaral, chair of the Brazil–China Business Council, São Paulo, October 2011.
22. Author interview with Ricardo Wirth, Abicalçados, Novo Hamburgo, November 1998.
23. Author interview, Crato, August 1998.
24. Macauhub, 12 March 2007, accessed on 30 August 2013; interview with Alessandro Teixeira, Ministry of Development, Industry and Commerce, Brasília, October 2011.
25. Achyles Barcelos Da Costa, 'The Footwear Industry in Vale do Sinos (Brazil): Competitive Adjustment in a Labour-Intensive Sector', *CEPAL Review*, No. 101, August 2010, UN Economic Comission for Latin America, Santiago; Vinicius Licks *et al.*, 'Leather Footwear in Brazil: The Rio Grande do Sul Cluster', 5 April 2012, available at http://www.isc.hbs.edu/pdf/Student_Projects, accessed on 30 August 2013.
26. Licks *et al.* (2012).
27. Dominique Turpin, 'How Havaianas Built a Global Brand', *Financial Times*, 3 September 2013.
28. Author visit and interviews, October 2012.
29. OECD (2013), pp. 46–7.
30. José Roberto Rodrigues, Julia Moraies Soares Afonso and Kleber Pacheco de Castro, 'Avaliaçao da estrutura e do desempenho do sistema tributário brasileiro', *Documento para Discussão*, Banco Interamericano de Desenvolvimento, January 2013, p. 11.
31. *Rodrigues et al.* (2013), p. 13.
32. Gilberto Luiz do Amaral *et al.*, *Quantidade de normas editadas nos Brasil*, IBPT, São Paulo, 2012.
33. 'Paying Taxes 2013: The Global Picture', available at www.pwc.com.
34. Author interview, São Paulo, October 2012.
35. 'Brazil's Labour Laws: Employer, Beware', *The Economist*, 10 March 2011.
36. Luis A. V. Catão, Carmen Pagés and Maria Fernanda Rosales, 'Financial Dependence, Formal Credit and Informal Jobs: New Evidence from Brazilian Household Data', Discussion Paper, IZA, Bonn, December 2009.
37. OECD (2013), pp. 48–9.
38. *Newsweek*, 20 September 2010.
39. Author interview with José Roberto Mendonça de Barros, São Paulo, October 2012.
40. Alex Segura-Ubiergo, 'The Puzzle of Brazil's High Interest Rates', IMF Working Paper, Washington DC, February 2012.
41. Eduardo Giannetti, *O valor do amanhã*, Companhia das Letras, São Paulo, 2005, chapter 20.
42. *Financial Times*, 14 September 2011.
43. http://www.doingbusiness.org/rankings.
44. This example is adapted from an article in *O Estado de S. Paulo*, 9 December 2012.
45. *Financial Times*, 23 August 2013; Abreu interview with the author, São Paulo, October 2012; *Veja*, 27 March 2013.
46. Presentation by Frédéric Delormel, Technip, Economist Brazil Business Summit, Paris, July 2012.
47. Interview with the author, Brasília, 9 September 2010.
48. McKinsey & Company, *Estudo do setor de transporte aéreo do Brasil: Relatório consolidado*, Rio de Janeiro, 2010.
49. Antonio Luiz Leite, 'Malha rodoviária brasileira é a terceira do mundo, mas seu estado é precaria', *Valor Econômico*, 6 November 2009.
50. *Financial Times*, 29 August 2006.

20. Author interview, Brasília, June 2007.
21. Author interview, São Paulo, July 2009.
22. www.dw.de, 10 May 2008.
23. News.bbc.co.uk, 11 March 2010.
24. Interview in *El País*, 16 June 2010.
25. 'El Mito de América Latina', *El País*, 6 October 2001.
26. Buarque (1996), p. 177.
27. Interview in *El País*, 3 November 2006.
28. 'South American Integration: Mercosur RIP?', *The Economist*, 14 July 2012; Rubens Barbosa, column in O *Estado de S. Paulo*, 12 April 2011.
29. Ricupero (2010).
30. 'Trade Talks: Doha Round . . . and Round . . . and Round', *The Economist*, 31 July 2008.
31. 'Balança comercial brasileira: Dados consolidados', http://www.mdic.gov.br, accessed on 2 October 2013.
32. Author interview, São Paulo, June 2007.
33. Rubens Barbosa, 'O Brasil fora das Cadeais produtivas globais', *O Estado de S. Paulo*, 26 February 2013.
34. Author interview, São Paulo, November 2012.
35. Interview with Antonio Patriota, June 2010.
36. Reuters, 23 February 2011; *Financial Times*, 9 February 2010.
37. Author interview, Brasília, August 2009.
38. *El País*, 29 January 2011.
39. *Veja*, 30 March 2011.
40. Rubens Barbosa, *O Dissenso de Washington: Notas de um observador privilegiado sobre as relaçoes Brasil–Estados Unidos,* Agir, Rio de Janeiro, 2011, pp. 130–35.
41. 'Anti-US Protests Flare at Summit', *Washington Post*, 5 November 2005.
42. Author interview with senior American official, June 2010.
43. Peter Hakim, article on US–Brazil relations for *International Affairs*, forthcoming.
44. Barbosa (2011), p. 109.
45. See, for example, op-ed by Bernard Aronson, *International Herald Tribune*, 5 April 2012.
46. www.forte.gov.br, 6 September 2010.
47. *Veja*, 19 January 2011.
48. 'Navigating the Emerging Markets: Federal Republic of Brazil', IHS, Janes, 2011.
49. Joseph S. Nye, *Soft Power: The Means to Success in World Politics*, Public Affairs, New York, 2004, p. x.
50. 'Brazil and Peacekeeping: Policy, not Altruism', *The Economist*, 25 September 2010.
51. 'Brazil's Foreign-Aid Programme: Speak Softly and Carry a Blank Cheque', 15 July 2010.
52. Ricardo Lagos, *The Southern Tiger: Chile's Fight for a Democratic and Prosperous Future*, Palgrave Macmillan, 2012, p. 228.

Chapter Thirteen: An Unreformed Leviathan

1. *Revista Piauí*, No. 82, July 2013; 'Protests in Brazil: The Streets Erupt', Americas View, *The Economist*, 18 June 2013.
2. This according to research by Globo TV, which was planning to develop content for cellphones with this in mind; see *Valor Econômico*, 2 December 2011.
3. Author interview, São Paulo, October 2013.
4. *Valor Econômico* 18 June 13; *O Estado de S. Paulo*, 19 June 2013.
5. Interview in *Folha de São Paulo*, 22 June 2013.
6. Claudia Antunes, 'Nova York chamando', *Revista Piauí*, No. 82, July 2013.
7. *New York Times*, 17 July 2013.
8. *Valor Econômico*, 21 June 2013.
9. Scott P. Mainwaring, *Rethinking Party Systems in the Third Wave of Democratization: The Case of Brazil*, Stanford University Press, 1999, p. 5.

10. Lamounier (2005), p. 227.
11. Timothy J. Power, 'Continuity in a Changing Brazil: The Transition from Lula to Dilma', draft paper kindly provided to the author.
12. *Valor Econômico*, 21 October 2013.
13. *Veja*, 18 February 2009.
14. Marcos Nobre, 'O Fim da polarizaçao', *Revista Piauí*, No. 51, December 2010. See also Marcos Nobre, *Imobilismo em movimento: Da abertura democrática ao governo Dilma*, Companhia das Letras, São Paulo, 2013.
15. 'A Brazilian Political Boss: Where Dinosaurs Still Roam', *The Economist*, 5 February 2009; 'Brazil's Scandal-Plagued Senate: House of Horrors', *The Economist*, 9 July 2009; *O Globo*, 7 May 2012.
16. Daniela Pinheiro, 'Na Boca do Povo', *Revista Piauí* No. 85, October 2013. This paragraph draws heavily on this profile by one of Brazil's most outstanding journalists.
17. David Fleischer, Brazil Focus, 25 May–7 June 2013.
18. Author interview in Brasília, October 2011.
19. Marcelo Medeiros and Pedro H. G. F. Souza, 'The State and Income Inequality in Brazil', 2013, available at SSRN: http://ssrn.com/abstract=2257857 or http://dx.doi.org/10.2139/ssrn.2257857.
20. Nobre (2010).
21. Inter-American Development Bank, *The Politics of Policies*, Harvard University Press, 2006.
22. Catão, Pagés and Rosales (2009).
23. Author interview with Claudio Couto, Fundação Getúlio Vargas, São Paulo, October 2013.
24. 'Brazil's Booming Economy: Flying too High for Safety', *The Economist*, 20 May 2010.
25. Mailson da Nóbrega, *Veja*, 1 May 2013.
26. See IBGE's population projections based on the 2010 census at http://www.ibge.gov.br/home/estatistica/populacao/projecao_da_populacao/2013/.
27. World Bank, *Growing Old in an Older Brazil*, 2011, p. xxvi.
28. Helen Joyce, 'Grounded: A Special Report on Brazil', *The Economist*, 28 September 2013.
29. World Bank (2011), chapter 3.
30. Author interview, Rio de Janeiro, June 2010.
31. World Bank (2011), chapter 1.
32. Marcos de Barros Lisboa and Zeina Abdel Latif, 'Democracy and Growth in Brazil', Insper Working Paper, WPE311/ 2013.
33. Mario Henrique Simonsen, 'O Brasil na Contramão', *Veja*, 14 October 1987. I am grateful to Eduardo Giannetti for providing me with this article.
34. *Veja*, 22 December 2010.
35. *New York Times*, 10 February 2013.
36. Eduardo Giannetti, 'O Manifesto de Simonsen revisitado', unpublished manuscript kindly provided to the author; Brazil Focus, 12–18 October 2013.
37. The Ceará reforms are the subject of Judith Tendler, *Good Government in the Tropics*, Johns Hopkins University Press, Baltimore and London, 1997.
38. Marcus André Melo, 'Democratising Budgetary Decisions and Execution in Brazil: More Participation or Redesign of Formal Institutions', in Andrew Selee and Enrique Peruzotti, *Participatory Innovation and Representative Democracy in Latin America*, Woodrow Wilson Center Press and Johns Hopkins University Press, Washington DC and Baltimore, 2009.
39. Remarks by Marcus André Melo, 'Democratic Brazil Ascendant' conference, Brazil Institute, King's College, London, February 2013.
40. Remarks by Melo (2013).
41. Remarks at *The Economist*'s Brazil conference, São Paulo, October 2013.
42. Armando Castelar Pinheiro, 'A Reforma do judiciário: Uma análise econômico', BNDES, Nota Tecnica, 1998; John Prideaux, 'Getting It Together at Last: A Special

Report on Business and Finance in Brazil', *The Economist*, 14 November 2009; 'Brazil's Labour Laws: Employer, Beware', *The Economist*, 10 March 2011.
43. *Veja*, 13 December 2006.
44. Speech reported in *O Estado de S. Paulo*, 3 May 2013.
45. 'A engranagem da impunidade', *Folha de São Paulo*, 26 February 2012.
46. *Veja*, 13 March 2013.

Chapter Fourteen: Brazil's Century?

1. Quoted in Alex Bellos, *Futebol: The Brazilian Way of Life*, Bloomsbury, 2002, chapter 3.
2. Nelson Rodrigues, 'Complexo de vira-latas', in Joaquim Ferreira Dos Santos, *As Cem Melhores Crônicas Brasileiras*, Editora Objetiva, Rio de Janeiro, 2005
3. Remarks at *The Economist* Brazil conference, São Paulo, October 2012.
4. André Lara Resende, 'Além da conjuntura', *Valor Econômico*, 21 December 2012.
5. 'Liberalism in Brazil: The Almost Lost Cause of Freedom, *The Economist*, 28 January 2010.
6. Cardoso (2006b), p. 428.
7. Zaki Laïdi, 'Sarkozy's Failure Reflects France's Identity Crisis', *Financial Times*, 24 April 2012.
8. Eduardo Giannetti, 'Brazilian Culture in the 21st Century', *Bulletin du Bibliophile*, forthcoming.
9. Mario Henrique Simonsen, 'O Brasil na contramão', *Veja*, 14 October 1987.

Bibliography

Abreu, Marcelo de P., Afonso S. Bevilaqua and Demosthenes M. Pinho, 'Import Substitution and Growth in Brazil, 1890s–1970s', in Enrique Cardenas, Jose Antonio Ocampo and Rosemary Thorp, *An Economic History of Twentieth-Century Latin America, Vol. 3: Industrialization and the State in Latin America, the Postwar Years*, Palgrave, 2000

Amaral, Ricardo Batista, *A Vida quer é Coragem: A Trajetória de Dilma Rousseff, a Primeira Presidenta do Brasil*, Primeira Pessoa, Rio de Janeiro, 2011

Anderson, Perry, 'Lula's Brazil', *London Review of Books*, 31 March 2011

Anuatti Neto, Francisco, Milton Barossi Filho, Antonio Gledson de Carvalho and Roberto Macedo, 'Costs and Benefits of Privatization: Evidence from Brazil', in Alberto Chong and Florencio López de Silanes, *Privatization in Latin America: Myths and Reality*, Stanford University Press, 2005

Aron, Raymond, *Main Currents in Sociological Thought*, Penguin, 1965

Bacha, Edmar, *Belíndia 2.0: Fábulas e ensaios sobre o país dos contrastes*, Civilizaçao Brasileira, Rio de Janeiro, 2012

Bacha, Edmar and Monica Baumgarten de Bolle (eds), *O Futuro da indústria no Brasil: Desindustrialização em debate*, Editora Civilização Brasileira, Rio de Janeiro, 2013

Baer, Werner, *The Brazilian Economy: Growth and Development*, Sixth Edition, Lynne Rienner, Boulder, Colorado and London, 2008

Barbosa, Rubens, *O Dissenso de Washington: Notas de um observador privilegiado sobre as relaçoes Brasil–Estados Unidos*, Agir, Rio de Janeiro, 2011

Bellos, Alex, *Futebol: The Brazilian Way of Life*, Bloomsbury, 2002

Bethell, Leslie (ed.), *The Cambridge History of Latin America*, Vol. III, Cambridge University Press, 1985.

—— (ed.), *Colonial Brazil*, Cambridge University Press, 1991

—— (ed.), *The Cambridge History of Latin America*, Vol. IX, *Brazil Since 1930*, Cambridge University Press, 2008

——, 'Populism, Neo-populism and the Left in Brazil: From Getúlio to Lula', in Cynthia Arnson and Carlos de la Torre (eds), *Populism in 21st Century Latin America*, Johns Hopkins University Press, Baltimore, 2012

Bethell, Leslie and José Murilo de Carvalho, 'Brazil from Independence to the Middle of the 19th Century', *Cambridge History of Latin America*, Vol. III, 1985, chapter 16

Bethencourt, Francisco and Diogo Ramada Curto (eds), *Portuguese Oceanic Expansion 1400–1800*, Cambridge University Press, 2007

Birdsall, Nancy, *A Note on the Middle Class in Latin America*, Center for Global Development Working Paper 303, Washington DC, August 2012

Blackburn, Robin, *The Making of New World Slavery: From the Baroque to the Modern 1492–1800*, Verso, 1997

Bojunga, Claudio, *JK: O artista do impossível*, Editora Objetiva, Rio de Janeiro, 2001

Botelho, André and Lilia Moritz Schwarcz (eds), *Um Enigma chamado Brasil*, Companhia das Letras, São Paulo, 2009
Bourne, Richard, *Lula of Brazil: The Story so Far*, Zed Books, 2008
Buarque de Holanda, Sérgio, *Raízes do Brasil*, Companhia das Letras, São Paulo, 1996
Bulmer-Thomas, Victor, *The Economic History of Latin America since Independence*, Cambridge University Press, 1994
Burke, Peter and Maria Lúcia Pallares-Burke, *Gilberto Freyre: Social Theory in the Tropics*, Peter Lang, Oxford, 2008
Busch, Alexander, *Brazil: Emerging Giant*, Hanser/ING, Munich, 2011
Cabral de Mello, Evaldo (ed.), *O Brasil holandês*, Penguin and Companhia das Letras, São Paulo, 2010
Caldeira, Jorge (ed.), *Brasil: A historia contada por quem viu*, Mameluco, São Paulo, 2008
Caldeira, Jorge, *História do Brasil com empreendedores*, Mameluco, São Paulo, 2009
Cardoso, Fernando Henrique, *A Arte da política: A história que vivi*, Editora Civilização Brasileira, Rio de Janeiro, 2006
——, *Pensadores que inventaram o Brasil*, Companhia das Letras, São Paulo, 2013
——, with Brian Winter, *The Accidental President of Brazil: A Memoir*, Public Affairs, New York, 2006
Cariello, Rafael, 'O Liberal contra a miséria', *Revista Piauí*, No. 74, November 2012
Carvalho, José Murilo de, *D. Pedro II*, Companhia das Letras, São Paulo, 2007
——, *Cidadania no Brasil: O longo caminho*, Civilização Brasileira, Rio de Janeiro, 14th edition, 2011
Castro, Ruy, *O Anjo Pornográfico: A Vida de Nelson Rodrigues*, Companhia das Letras, São Paulo, 1992
——, *Rio de Janeiro: Carnival under Fire*, Bloomsbury, 2004
Catão, Luis A.V, Carmen Pagés and Maria Fernanda Rosales, 'Financial Dependence, Formal Credit and Informal Jobs: New Evidence from Brazilian Household Data', Discussion Paper, IZA, Bonn, December 2009
Conniff, Michael L. (ed.), *Latin American Populism in Comparative Perspective*, University of New Mexico Press, Albuquerque, 1982
——, *Populism in Latin America*, University of Alabama Press, Tuscaloosa and London, 1999
Conrad, Robert Edgar, *Children of God's Fire: A Documentary History of Black Slavery in Brazil*, Princeton, 1983
Conti, Mario Sérgio, *Notícias do Planalto: A imprensa e Fernando Collor*, Companhia das Letras, São Paulo, 1999
Corrêa do Lago, Pedro and Blaise Ducos, *Frans Post: Le Brésil à la cour de Louis XIV*, Exhibition catalogue, Louvre, Paris, 2005
D'Araujo, Maria Celina and Celso Castro (eds), *Ernesto Geisel*, Fundação Getúlio Vargas, Rio de Janeiro, 1997
D'Avila, Luiz Felipe, *Os Virtuosos: Os Estadistas que Fundaram a República Brasileira*, A Girafa Editora, São Paulo, 2006
Da Cunha, Euclides, *Rebellion in the Backlands*, Picador, 1995
DaMatta, Roberto, *O Que Faz o brasil, Brasil?*, Editora Rocco, Rio de Janeiro, 8th edition, 1995
——, *Explorações: Ensaios de sociologia interpretiva*, Editora Rocco, Rio de Janeiro, 2011
Darwin, Charles, *The Voyage of the Beagle*, Dent Dutton, New York, 1961
Dean, Warren, *The Brazilian Economy 1870–1930*, in Leslie Bethell (ed.), *The Cambridge History of Latin America*, Vol. V, Cambridge University Press, 1986
——, *With Broadax and Firebrand: The Destruction of the Brazilian Atlantic Forest*, University of California Press, Berkley, 1997
Diacon, Todd A., *Rondon*, Companhia das Letras, São Paulo, 2006.
Dias Monteiro, Fabiano, 'Do Anti-racismo criminal às ações afirmativas: um estudo sobre o debate político racial no Rio de Janeiro (2000–2007)', Unpublished doctoral thesis, Universidade Federal de Rio de Janeiro, 2010

Dos Santos, Joaquim Ferreira (ed.), *As Cem Melhores Crônicas Brasileiras*, Editora Objetiva, Rio de Janeiro, 2005

Dreyfus, Pablo *et al., Small Arms in Brazil: Production, Trade and Holdings*, Small Arms Survey, Geneva, 2010

Duncan, Emma, 'All Creatures Great and Small: A Special Report on Biodiversity', *The Economist*, 14 September 2013

Eakin, Marshall C., *Brazil: The Once and Future Country*, St Martin's Press, New York, 1997

ECLAC (UN Economic Commission for Latin America and the Caribbean), *Economic Survey 2012*, Santiago.

Faoro, Raymundo, *A Democracia traída: Entrevistas*, Editora Globo, 2008

Fausto, Boris, *A Concise History of Brazil*, Cambridge, 2006a)

——, *Getúlio Vargas*, Companhia das Letras, São Paulo, 2006b)

Fernández-Armesto, Felipe, *Amerigo: The Man who Gave his Name to America*, Weidenfeld & Nicolson, 2006

Ferreira, Jorge, *João Goulart: Uma biografia*, Editora Civilizacão Brasileira, Rio de Janeiro, 2011

Feynman, Richard P., '*Surely You're Joking, Mr Feynman!' Adventures of a Curious Character, as told to Ralph Leighton*, W. W. Norton & Company, New York and London, 1985

Fishlow, Albert, *Starting Over: Brazil since 1985*, Brookings Institution Press, Washington DC, 2011

Freire, Antonio de Abreu, *Padre Antonio Vieira: Educador, estratega, politico, missionário*, Portugália Editora, Lisbon, 2008

Freyre, Gilberto, *Casa-grande & Senzala: Formação da família brasileira sob o regime da economia patriarcal*, Global Editora, São Paulo, 51st edition, 2006

Gall, Norman, *Lula and Mephistopheles*, Fernand Braudel Institute of World Economics, São Paulo, 2005

——, *School Reform in New York and São Paulo*, Fernand Braudel Institute of World Economics, São Paulo, 2007

——, *Oil in Deep Waters*, Fernand Braudel Institute of World Economics, São Paulo, 2011

——, Bruno Paes Mano de Maryluci Araújo Faria, *Diadema*, Fernand Braudel Institute of World Economics, São Paulo, 2005.

Gaspari, Elio, *A Ditadura envergonhada*, Comphania das Letras, São Paulo, 2002

Giambiagi, Fabio and Claudio Porto (eds), *2022: Propostas para um Brasil melhor no ano do bicentenário*, Elsevier Editora, Rio de Janeiro, 2011

Giannetti, Eduardo, *O Valor do amanhã*, Companhia das Letras, São Paulo, 2005

——, 'Brazilian Culture in the 21st Century', *Bulletin du Bibliophile*, forthcoming

Gonçalves, Marcos Augusto, *1922: A semana que não terminou*, Companhia das Letras, São Paulo, 2012

Gordon, Lincoln, *Supplement to Brazil's Second Chance: En Route Toward the First World*, Brookings Institution, Washington, DC, 2003

Gotlib, Nádia Battella, *Tarsila do Amaral: A modernista*, Editora Senac, São Paulo, 1997.

Graham, Richard, 'Brazil from the Middle of the 19th Century to the Paraguayan War', in Leslie, Bethell (ed.), *Cambridge History of Latin America*, Vol. 3 Cambridge University Press, 1985

Haber, Stephen (ed.), *How Latin America Fell Behind: Essays on the Economic Histories of Brazil and Mexico, 1800–1914*, Stanford University Press, 1997

Hemming, John, *Red Gold: The Conquest of the Brazilian Indians*, Papermac, 1978

——, *Tree of Rivers: The Story of the Amazon*, Thames & Hudson, 2009.

Hunter, Wendy, *The Transformation of the Workers' Party in Brazil, 1989–2009*, Cambridge, 2010

Hunter, Wendy and Timothy Power, 'Rewarding Lula: Executive Power, Social Policy and the Brazilian Elections of 2006', *Latin American Politics & Society*, Vol. 49, No. 1, Spring 2007

Instituto de Pesquisa Econômica Aplicada (IPEA), *Boletim de Politicas Socias*, No. 16, 2008

——, 'A Década inclusiva (2001–2011): Desigualdade, pobreza e políticas de renda', *Comunicado*, No. 155, 25 Setember 2012

Inter-American Development Bank, *The Politics of Policies*, David Rockefeller Center for Latin American Studies, Harvard University Press, 2006

Joyce, Helen, 'Grounded: A Special Report on Brazil', *The Economist*, 28 September 2013

Keck, Margaret, *The Workers' Party and Democratization in Brazil*, Yale University Press, 1992

Kingstone, Peter R. and Timothy J. Power, *Democratic Brazil Revisited*, University of Pittsburgh Press, 2008

Klein, Herbert S., *The Atlantic Slave Trade*, Cambridge University Press, 2010

Lagos, Ricardo, *The Southern Tiger: Chile's Fight for a Democratic and Prosperous Future*, Palgrave Macmillan, London, 2012

Lamounier, Bolívar, *Da Independência a Lula: Dois séculos de política brasileira*, Augurium Editora, São Paulo, 2005

Lehmann, David, *Struggle for the Spirit: Religious Transformation and Popular Culture in Brazil and Latin America*, Polity Press, Cambridge, 1996

Leitão, Miriam, *Saga Brasileira: A Longa Luta de um Povo por sua Moeda*, Editora Record, Rio de Janeiro, 2011

Léry, Jean de, *History of a Voyage to the Land of Brazil*, University of California Press, Berkley, 1992

Levine, Robert M., *Vale of Tears: Revisiting the Canudos Massacre in Northeastern Brazil, 1893–1897*, University of California Press, Berkley, 1995

—— and John J. Crocitti (eds), *The Brazil Reader: History, Culture, Politics*, Duke University Press, Durham, North Carolina, 1999

Lévi-Strauss, Claude, *Tristes tropiques*, Penguin, 1992

——, *Saudades de São Paulo*, Companhia das Letras, São Paulo, 1998

Lewis, Colin M., 'Public Policy and Private Initiative: Railway Building in São Paulo 1860–1889', *Institute of Latin American Studies Research Papers* No. 26, University of London, 1991

Lisboa, Marcos de Barros, *A Agenda perdida*, Rio de Janeiro, September 2002

Luna, Francisco Vidal and Herbert S. Klein, *Brazil Since 1980*, Cambridge University Press, 2006

Macdonald, N. P., *The Making of Brazil: Portuguese Roots 1500–1822*, The Book Guild, Lewes, Sussex, 1996

Macedo, Roberto, 'Distribution of Assets and Income in Brazil: New Evidence', in John Nellis and Nancy Birdsall, *Reality Check: The Distributional Impact of Privatization in Developing Countries*, Center For Global Development, Washington DC, 2005

Machado de Assis, *Papéis Avulsos*, Martins Fontes, São Paulo, 2005

——, *A Chapter of Hats and Other Stories*, Bloomsbury, 2009

McKinsey & Company, *Estudo do setor de transporte aéreo do Brasil: Relatório consolidado*, Rio de Janeiro, 2010

Maddison, Angus and Associates, *Brazil and Mexico: The Political Economy of Poverty, Equity and Growth*, World Bank Oxford, and Oxford University Press, 1992

Mainwaring, Scott P., *Rethinking Party Systems in the Third Wave of Democratization: The Case of Brazil*, Stanford University Press, 1999

Maxwell, Kenneth, *Naked Tropics: Essays on Empire and Other Rogues*, Routledge, 2003

Meirelles, Domingos, *As Noites das Grandes Fogueiras: Uma História da Columna Prestes*, Editora Record, Rio de Janeiro, 1995

Melo, Carlos, *Collor: O Ator e Suas Circunstâncias*, Editora Novo Conceito, São Paulo, 2007

Ministry of Finance, *The Brazilian Economy: The Challenge of Stability and Sustained Growth*, Brasília, 1996

Moog, Vianna, *Bandeirantes and Pioneers*, George Braziller, New York, 1964.

Nabuco, Joaquim, *Essencial*, Penguin/Companhia das Letras, São Paulo, 2010

Neri, Marcelo (ed.), *Microcrédito: O Mistério Nordestino e O Grameen Brasileiro*, Fundação Getúlio Vargas, Rio de Janeiro, 2008.

Nobre, Marcos, *Imobilismo em movimento: Da abertura democrática ao governo Dilma*, Companhia das Letras, São Paulo, 2013.

Nóbrega, Maílson da, *Além do Feijão com Arroz: Autobiografia*, Civilizacão Brasileira, Rio de Janeiro, 2010

—— and Gustavo Loyola, 'The Long and Simultaneous Construction of Fiscal and Monetary Institutions', in Lourdes Sola and Laurence Whitehead (eds), *Statecrafting Monetary Authority: Democracy and Financial order in Brazil*, Centre for Brazilian Studies, Oxford, 2006

Nye, Joseph S., *Soft Power: The Means to Success in World Politics*, Public Affairs, New York, 2004

OECD, *Economic Surveys: Brazil*, Paris, October 2013

Oliven, Ruben, *Tradition Matters: Modern Gaúcho Identity in Brazil*, Columbia University Press, New York, 1996

Organization of American States, *Report on Citizen Security in the Americas*, Washington DC, 2012

Page, Joseph A., *The Brazilians*, Addison-Wesley, Reading, Massachusetts, 1995

Paraná, Denise, *Lula, o filho do Brasil*, Fundação Perseu Abramo, São Paulo, 2002

Pearlman, Janice, *Favela: Four Decades of Living on the Edge in Rio de Janeiro*, Oxford University Press, 2010

Pinheiro, Daniela, 'Lindinhos e privates', *Revista Piauí*, No. 20, May 2008

——, 'Na Boca do Povo', *Revista Piauí*, No. 85, October 2013

Reid, Michael, 'The Disorders of Progress: A Survey of Brazil', *The Economist*, 27 March 1999

——, *Forgotten Continent: The Battle for Latin America's Soul*, Yale University Press, 2007.

Resende, Beatriz, 'Brazilian Modernism: The Canonised Revolution', in Vivian Schelling, *Through the Kaleidoscope: The Experience of Modernity in Latin America*, Verso, 2000

Ribeiro, Darcy, *O Povo Brasileiro*, Companhia das Letras, São Paulo, 1995

Ricupero, Rubens, 'O Brasil e o mundo: A política exterior após Lula', *Braudel Papers*, Instituto Fernand Braudel, São Paulo, 2010

Risério, Antonio, *A Utopia brasileira e os movimentos negros*, Editora 34, São Paulo, 2007

Robb, Peter, *A Death in Brazil*, Bloomsbury, 2004

Rock, David, 'Society and Politics in Argentina 1880–1916', in Leslie Bethell (ed.), *Argentina since Independence*, Cambridge University Press, 1993

Rodrigues, José Roberto, Julia Moraies Soares Afonso and Kleber Pacheco de Castro, 'Avaliaçao da estrutura e do desempenho do sistema tributário brasileiro', Documento para Discussão, Banco Interamericano de Desenvolvimento, January 2013

Roett, Riordan, *The New Brazil*, Brookings Institution Press, Washington DC, 2010

Rohter, Larry, *Brazil on the Rise: The Story of a Country Transformed*, Palgrave Macmillan, New York, 2010

Rosas Moscoso, Fernando, *Del Rio de la Plata al Amazonas: El Perú y el Brasil en la época de la dominació ibérica*, Editorial Universitaria, Universidad Ricardo Palma, Lima, 2008

Rouquié, Alain, *The Military and the State in Latin America*, University of California Press, Berkley, 1987

Sadlier, Darlene J., *Brazil Imagined: 1500 to the Present*, University of Texas Press, Austin, 2008

São Paulo Justice and Peace Commision, *São Paulo: Growth and Poverty*, The Catholic Institute of International Relations and the Bowerdean Press, 1978.

Scheper-Hughes, Nancy, *Death Without Weeping: The Violence of Everyday Life in Brazil*, University of California Press, Berkley, 1992

Schneider, Ronald M., *Brazil: Culture and Politics in a New Industrial Powerhouse*, Westview Press, Boulder, Colorado, 1996

Secco, Lincoln, *História do PT*, Ateliê Editorial, São Paulo, 2011

Selee, Andrew and Enrique Peruzotti, *Participatory Innovation and Representative Democracy in Latin America*, Woodrow Wilson Center Press and Johns Hopkins University Press, Washington DC and Baltimore, 2009

Singer, André, *Os Sentidos do Lulismo: Reforma gradual e pacto conservador*, Companhia das Letras, São Paulo, 2012

Skidmore, Thomas, *Politics in Brazil 1930–1964: An Experiment in Democracy*, Oxford University Press, 1967

——, *The Politics of Military Rule in Brazil 1964–85*, Oxford University Press, 1988

——, *Brazil: Five Centuries of Change*, Oxford University Press, 1999

Souza, Amaury de and Bolívar Lamounier, *A Classe média brasileira: Ambições, valores e projetos de sociedade*, Elsevier Editora, Rio de Janeiro, 2010

Spektor, Matias, *Kissinger e o Brasil*, Editora Zahar, Rio de Janeiro, 2009.

Sullivan, Edward J. (ed.), *Latin American Art in the Twentieth Century*, Phaidon, 1996.

Tendler, Judith, *Good Government in the Tropics*, Johns Hopkins University Press, Baltimore and London, 1997

Toledo, Roberto Pompeu de, *O Presidente segundo o sociólogo: Entrevista de Fernando Henrique Cardoso*, Companhia das Letras, Sâo Paolo, 1998

Topik, Stephen, 'The Hollow State: The Effect of the World Market on State-Building in Brazil in the Nineteenth Century', in James Dunkerley (ed.), *Studies in the Formation of the Nation State in Latin America*, Institute of Latin American Studies, 2002

Unger, Brooke, 'Dreaming of Glory: A Special Report on Brazil', *The Economist*, 14 April 2007

Vainfas, Ronaldo, *Antônio Vieira*, Companhia das Letras, São Paulo, 2011

Veloso, Caetano, *Verdade tropical*, Companhia das Letras, São Paulo, 1997

Velloso, Raul, César Mattos, Marcos Mendes and Paulo Springer de Freitas, *Infraestructura: Os caminhos para sair do buraco*, Instituto Nacional de Altos Estudos, Rio de Janeiro, 2012

Villa, Marco Antonio, *A História das constituições brasileiras*, Leya, São Paulo, 2011

Viotti da Costa, Emilia, 'Brazil: The Age of Reform 1870–1889', in Leslie Bethell (ed.), *The Cambridge History of Latin America*, Vol. V, Cambridge University Press, 1986

Wiarda, Howard, *The Soul of Latin America: The Cultural and Political Tradition*, Yale University Press, New Haven and London, 2001

Wilcken, Patrick, *Empire Adrift: The Portuguese Court in Rio de Janeiro 1808–21*, Bloomsbury, 2004

Williams, Richard, *The Death of Ayrton Senna*, Penguin, 1995

World Bank, *From Inside Brazil: Development in a Land of Contrasts*, by Vinod Thomas, Washington DC, 2006

——, *Growing Old in an Older Brazil*, by Michele Gragnolati *et al.*, Washington DC, 2011

——, *Economic Mobility and the Rise of the Latin American Middle Class*, by Francisco G. Ferreira *et al.*, Washington DC, 2012.

Zweig, Stefan, *Brazil: A Land of the Future*, Ariadne Press, Riverside, California, 2000

Index